THE HIDDEN LINCOLN

from the

Letters and Papers of William H. Herndon

THE HIDDEN
LINCOLN

FROM THE LETTERS AND PAPERS OF
William H. Herndon

EMANUEL HERTZ

NEW YORK : THE VIKING PRESS
1938

PUBLISHED IN FEBRUARY 1938

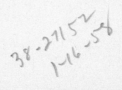

TO THE MEMORY

OF

WILLIAM H. HERNDON

lawyer, abolitionist, and patriot, whose one object in life was to reveal Lincoln to the American people as he knew him, from the slave market in New Orleans to Gettysburg and from Clarey Grove to the second inaugural.

"THE STRUGGLES OF THIS AGE AND SUCCEEDING AGES FOR GOD AND MAN—RELIGION, HUMANITY, AND LIBERTY, WITH THEIR COMPLEX AND GRAND RELATIONS—MAY THEY TRIUMPH AND CONQUER FOREVER IS MY ARDENT WISH AND MOST FERVENT SOUL-PRAYER.—FEB. 23, 1858."

(From the inscription on Herndon's tombstone)

Contents

Illustrations

Foreword

To say that our people owe a great debt to Mr. Hertz for his patient and untiring study of everything which relates to the life and work of Abraham Lincoln is only to state the obvious. The material here produced from the Herndon letters is rich indeed. These records are intimate, informal, and most revealing.

The curious combination of simplicity and richness which constituted Abraham Lincoln's character gets new evidence for its fuller understanding from what is here written. One would think that to say anything new about Lincoln had long since become impossible, but it certainly is practicable, as Mr. Hertz has shown, to discover and to interpret new material concerning one of the best-known personalities in modern public life.

NICHOLAS MURRAY BUTLER

Christmas Day, 1937.

THE HIDDEN LINCOLN

The Original Herndon Letters

FOR a thousand years and more it was customary in the city of Rome for builders of important structures to take their building materials from the Colosseum without any interference on the part of the city authorities. Until the Colosseum was finally made safe by law from further destruction, practically every important new building in Rome contained part of it. Similarly the Lincoln documents gathered and prepared by William H. Herndon in the sixties of the last century have been used for seventy years as the foundation stones of later biographies. Every biographer from that day to this has either consulted Herndon in person or relied on letters or writings left by him.

The first biographers all saw or consulted Herndon before they did any of Lincoln's other associates. William Dean Howells, for his campaign biography of 1860 and 1864, referred to Herndon for facts on Lincoln's life in Springfield. Holland rushed to consult Herndon after the President's assassination in order to prepare the first Life of Lincoln. Arnold in order to write his book haggled with Herndon over the purchase of the latter's papers, though in that book he does not mention Herndon in his preface or otherwise acknowledge his indebtedness. Lamon purchased copies of Herndon's papers and turned them over to Chauncey F. Black, who was thus enabled to write "their" book; while he was writing the book, Black wrote as many as seventy-five letters to Herndon, and Herndon always helped. Nicolay and Hay both borrowed from Herndon, but made no mention of him, perhaps because they feared the displeasure of Robert T. Lincoln, whose private papers were the most important source of material for their voluminous work. Ida M. Tarbell quoted Herndon's conclusions —she could not help doing so, honest and painstaking biographer that she is. As for Jesse W. Weik, all he ever did was to quote Herndon; the voice was the voice of Weik, but the facts were the facts of Herndon. When Weik finally wrote his own book, it was based on what he had found in the Herndon treasure trove, which he had purchased

3

or rather inherited from the feeble and moribund Herndon. Beveridge was completely controlled by the notes gathered by Herndon and owned by Weik, and the first volume of his book (in which there are 752 references to Herndon documents) is based almost entirely on what he found in these manuscripts. Sandburg in his two-volume biography refers to Herndon ninety-four times. Charnwood, while he did not consult Herndon, used a digest of all the consultations of others.

Raymond, Barrett, Leland, Rothschild, Stoddard, Hapgood, all knew and quoted Herndon. Barton pleaded with Weik to be permitted to see Herndon's original papers, but failed to get them. The good-natured and accommodating Herndon was dead—and Weik was not so accommodating. Charles H. Hart wrote to Herndon, and gathered a fine series of letters covering a great many phases of Lincoln's life, but he never published them. Many of Herndon's letters appeared in newspapers in response to the requests for information by various persons. For twenty-five years, to the very last day of his life, Herndon unselfishly gave himself, his strength, his limited substance, and practically all his time, first to the writing out of all he knew and all he remembered of his famous partner, and then to the gathering of the material which was to be the foundation of every biography of Abraham Lincoln thereafter.

Immediately after the assassination of Lincoln, the great effusion of sorrow at his untimely and tragic death, the belated realization of the martyred President's supreme service to the nation, provided an atmosphere in which all the enormous quantity of living material on his life and character then available could easily have been brought together. Yet nothing was done, either by Congress or by Lincoln's influential and literary friends, to gather such valuable but perishable biographical contributions. As a result, a definitive Life of Lincoln is still a dream unfulfilled, and a natural hesitation in revealing certain aspects of Lincoln's life has hardened into a policy of secrecy. Aside from a few superficial books written for special purposes, nothing of biographical importance took place until thirty years had passed, when Nicolay and Hay prepared their series of articles for the *Century Magazine*. And in that time it had become all but impossible to permit the discussion of some of the information supplied by Lincoln's contemporaries.

There was one man in Springfield, however, who, when he returned from Lincoln's funeral, determined to dedicate the rest of his life to the task of gathering all the material that would be necessary for the definitive biography of his lifelong friend, law partner, and political leader. William H. Herndon knew that with the passage of time the recollections of persons who had known Lincoln would acquire a superlative value. He began by setting down everything he himself knew about Lincoln from a daily contact of twenty years; then he talked to others in Springfield who had known Lincoln, thus supplementing and verifying his own recollections of Lincoln the husband, the father, the lawyer traveling over the Eighth Circuit and pleading in the higher courts, the spinner of yarns, the member of the State Legislature and of Congress, the political rival of Douglas, the candidate for the Presidency of the United States—of Lincoln up to February 12, 1861, when he left Springfield for the last time. Referring to the sign "Lincoln and Herndon," Lincoln had then said, with a significant lowering of his voice: "Let it hang there undisturbed. Give our clients to understand that the election of a President makes no difference in the firm. If I live, I'm coming back some time, and then we'll go right on practicing as if nothing had happened." He lingered for a moment and then passed into the narrow hallway—never to return.

Herndon prepared a list of names of people outside Springfield who might from personal acquaintance have known any facts about Lincoln's life from the day of his birth until the day of his death that might have escaped his own memory and researches. He visited Lincoln's relatives in Kentucky, Indiana, and Illinois and obtained from them statements which he reduced to writing. He did the same with Lincoln's early neighbors, the tradespeople with whom he had dealt, the women he had met, and the girls he had courted. In pursuit of his clues Herndon corresponded with men and women all over the Union, tracking some of them down to the most distant points, and eliciting from former associates and friends testimony of so intimate a quality that the real Lincoln is made to live in their letters. Herndon sent them a series of precise questions, and persisted with additional letters until all his questions had been answered.

Turning next to Lincoln's professional life Herndon proceeded to interview, and to prepare the records and recollections of, the judges before whom Lincoln had practiced. These recollections were either written by the judges themselves or by Herndon at their dictation. He then hunted up the lawyers with whom Lincoln had practiced at the bar—scores of them—and subjected them to the same procedure. There are reminiscences of lawyers who rode the circuit with Lincoln, who heard from his own lips the story of his life and listened to his tales before the fires of wayside taverns. Herndon looked up the leading politicians with whom Lincoln had worked and whom he had met, and no other public man had known so many politicians, North and South, as had Lincoln. He consulted the Long Nine and the other members of the Legislature with whom Lincoln had served during his five terms. He gathered also the statements of Lincoln's political opponents. He was not looking for eulogy—he was looking for facts.

Until 1888 Herndon gave practically all his time to this work of assiduous research; that year he finally made up his mind that a Life of Lincoln must be written then if he was ever to write one at all. His critics have been quick to emphasize the fact that he began to write his biography nearly twenty-three years after Lincoln's death. That he lectured on Lincoln in the years 1866–1870, composed newspaper articles, and wrote hundreds of letters in answer to the inquiries of all the other biographers should certainly annul whatever impugning of Herndon's motives is intended by this charge of undue delay. That Herndon's letters to interested persons are all consistent with each other, and tell the same facts, over a period of twenty-three years, should certainly remove the doubt that this lapse of time casts upon the reliability of his memoirs. Nicolay and Hay took longer to write their book, and they were affluent, and did not face the struggle for existence or make the sacrifices Herndon made; but to them it was accounted a virtue that they did not rush immediately into print but waited long enough to gain the proper perspective, part of which indeed they gained from Herndon's lectures and letters and from the facts Herndon had supplied for Ward Lamon's book. Herndon's conclusions were based upon a vast amount of evidence painstakingly collected and carefully studied for a score of years; he had the right to feel that he was now fitted to write the biography of his friend.

On the period of Lincoln's life before he left for Washington in 1861 Herndon stands alone as a biographical authority. It is conceded by almost all, no matter how grudgingly by some, that without Herndon's records no complete life of Lincoln is possible. Yet there has been a curious unwillingness to allow to Herndon the credit for what he has done, almost a conspiracy to keep from historians such of Herndon's researches as would seem to be necessary for a truthful and complete history of Abraham Lincoln. Herndon himself cared for no acknowledgment; he freely gave of himself, his time, and his substance to whoever expressed an interest in Lincoln's real life; and the sole purpose of his own life was to tell the true story of Lincoln's.

If we examine every Lincoln biography of importance down to Beveridge's incomplete effort, we find no proper credit given to Herndon for what he did. Even Beveridge, while he praises Herndon's zeal and outstanding achievement in unmeasured terms, does not trouble to quote Herndon's conclusions; he simply cites such excerpts from Herndon's statements as suit his purposes.

In the early seventies Ward H. Lamon decided to write a Life of his friend and chief. Aside from Herndon, Lincoln had no closer or more loyal friend and admirer than Lamon, his constant confidant, first as a partner on the circuit and then during Lincoln's entire stay in Washington. Lamon gathered the facts, wrote to many people who had known Lincoln in Washington, obtained their opinions in the form of letters, and then turned all these over to Chauncey F. Black, his literary collaborator. Black was a more congenial associate to Lamon than Weik was to be to Herndon, and he sought to save as much of Herndon's data as possible. Lamon therefore persuaded Herndon to sell him some of his collected materials.

"Early in 1869," says Lamon, "Mr. Herndon placed at my disposal his remarkable collection of materials—the richest, rarest, and fullest collection it was possible to conceive. Along with them came an offer of hearty co-operation, of which I have availed myself extensively, that no art of mine would serve to conceal it. Added to my collections, these acquisitions have enabled me to do what could not have been done before—prepare an authentic biography of Mr. Lincoln.

"Mr. Herndon had been the partner in business and the intimate personal associate of Mr. Lincoln for something like a quarter of a century; and Mr. Lincoln had lived familiarly with several members of his family long before their individual acquaintance began. New Salem, Springfield, the old judicial circuit, the habits and friends of Mr. Lincoln, were as well known to Mr. Herndon as to himself. With these advantages, and from the numberless facts and hints which had dropped from Mr. Lincoln during the confidential intercourse of an ordinary lifetime, Mr. Herndon was able to institute a thorough system of inquiry for every noteworthy circumstance and every incident of value in Mr. Lincoln's career.

"The fruits of Mr. Herndon's labors . . . comprise the recollections of Mr. Lincoln's nearest friends; of the surviving members of his family and his family-connections; of the men still living who knew him and his parents in Kentucky; of his school fellows, the whole population of New Salem; of his associates and relatives at Springfield; and of lawyers, judges, politicians, and statesmen everywhere, who had anything of interest or moment to relate. . . . They were collected at vast expense of time, labor, involving the employment of many agents, long journeys, tedious examinations, and voluminous correspondence."

But the Life that Black wrote for Lamon was not what was finally printed as Lamon's Life of Lincoln. Judge David Davis and Leonard Swett prevailed upon Lamon to bring his manuscript to Chicago, and there took place an incident which it is fortunate that we have Horace White to confirm:

"The book was nearly ready for publication and Lamon had submitted the page proofs to Swett and Davis for their criticism. They found in it a chapter showing or arguing that Lincoln was not the son of Thomas Lincoln, his reputed father, but of some other man. In short that, although born in wedlock, he was really illegitimate. They (S. and D.) were horrified. They got Lamon into a room, locked the door, and kept him there nearly a whole afternoon, trying to force him to take that chapter out of the book, and they succeeded after great difficulty. Swett did not tell me what proofs Lamon advanced to support his statement but he said that they were *prima facie* strong."

Again according to Horace White, "Swett said that he and Davis got Lamon into a private room and labored with him half a day to get the matter stricken out; that Lamon was very obstinate, contended that it was no discredit to Lincoln but rather creditable than otherwise, since he had risen so high from such a lowly origin, etc., etc.; but finally they did succeed in getting the worst part of the matter stricken out. My recollection is that Swett told me this on the very day that he and Davis had the interview with Lamon. At all events it was at very nearly the same time."

When Herndon finally decided to publish his own book, he retained the services of young Jesse W. Weik as a collaborator in the actual writing. Herndon, in Springfield, sent Weik, in Greencastle, Indiana, a rough draft of each chapter, to be given more elegant literary form. Some of these drafts were complete monographs; some were merely contained in series of letters written to Weik from day to day. Most of the substance in these letters Herndon had previously already communicated to others. Yet even Weik, whom he had especially picked for this work, did not make full use of his letters, compositions, findings, and conclusions. Weik, too, reinterpreted Herndon's statements and used only such portions of them as he approved of. Aside from the short preface written by Herndon, nothing was printed as Herndon intended. The preface, short as it is, tells of Herndon's purposes—many of which were in fact frustrated by the recipients of his letters and by his co-worker, Weik. And as if Weik's distortions were not sufficient, the editor in the office of Belford, Clarke & Company—the publishers, soon to be bankrupt, of this unfortunate venture—again revised Weik's version of what Herndon wrote.

Herndon complained bitterly of the treatment of his manuscript, but his protests were of no avail. Weik never specifically replied to Herndon's complaints; he simply ignored them. The two men met but rarely, and Herndon, old, weak, and disappointed, gave up the fight. He had received less than $300 from Weik, not only for his work in the writing of the book, but also for his entire collection, the amassing of which had consumed most of his mature years. After the failure of Belford, Clarke & Company, and the financial disappointment of both Weik and Herndon, the whole collection of facts was again buried until 1922, when Weik, in his old age, resurrected portions of it in a book entitled *The Real Lincoln, A Portrait*. Jesse W. Weik is here at last generous to his friend Herndon; he pays him a much-deserved tribute in his opening pages by quoting the estimate of Herndon's work by one of Lincoln's closest friends, Henry C. Whitney, of Urbana, Illinois, who says in a letter to Herndon:

"You saw Lincoln as he was and know him far better than all other living men combined. Armed with such knowledge it follows that you know better than others how to delineate him. You have the acuteness of vision that we attribute to Lincoln; you acquired much of his analytical power by attrition and you thought deeply as he did. He had unbounded confidence in your intuitions and your adhesion to him. I shall never forget the day—January 6, 1859—when a Legislature of Illinois met in joint session and elected Stephen A. Douglas, instead of himself, to the United States Senate. I went to your office and found Lincoln there alone. He appeared to be somewhat dejected —in fact I never saw a man so depressed. I tried to rally his drooping spirits and thus extract all the comfort possible from the situation, but with ill success. He was simply steeped in gloom. For a time he was silent; finally he straightened up and thanked me, but presently slid back into his chair again, blurting out as he sank down: 'Well, whatever happens I expect everyone to desert me now, but Billy Herndon.' "

In his introduction to John Fort Newton's excellent book, *Lincoln and Herndon*, F. B. Sanborn says:

"Among those originals I found the whole of the five years' correspondence between Parker and Herndon, the law partner of Abraham Lincoln for more than twenty years. I saw the historical and political value of this peculiar interchange of opinion and fact, by which Parker was brought near the mind of one of his latest friends, who was to complete the work of slave-emancipation—in which Parker had been active for nearly twenty years before his death—and was to die as the second great martyr in the cause of American emancipation. But it was not convenient for me to edit these letters; nor was the time ripe for this, thirty years ago. This Mr. Newton has now done with research and discretion, collating, correcting, and combining the mass of material accumulated since Lincoln's death, and contributing his own verdict on the characters and events of the crisis. He has added new material, bearing on the relations between Lincoln and Herndon, to whom earlier writers have by no means done justice; but who in this book stands revealed in his actual character, as the most important witness and chronicler of his partner's career. He writes from his own point of view, and with the advantage that lapse of time gives to the seeker after that most elusive chameleon, historical truth. It is a work well done, and will stand the test of after years, which unsparingly judge the mere eulogy or invective that would pass for biography.

"In the volume now completed, my early and beloved friend, Theodore Parker, becomes almost a shadowy figure in the vast drama of national regeneration; since he died, like Moses, within sight of the Promised Land that he was never to enter. But his work has been so well done, and was so heartily recognized by Herndon, in these enthusiastic and picturesque letters, that this shadow stands for something substantial, which the many volumes of Parker's discourses will certify and make good. He appears here as in some sort the inspirer of Herndon, and through him of Lincoln—the grandest personage of our long unfolding drama, and one of the most tragic."

William H. Herndon, the son of Rebecca (Day) Johnson and Archer G. Herndon, was born on December 25, 1818, in Greensburg, Kentucky. The family moved to Illinois in 1820 and to Springfield in 1825. He was educated in the Preparatory Department of Illinois College, where he absorbed its anti-slavery atmosphere. It was there that the first seeds were sown which made him an abolitionist. An impassioned public utterance on the lynching of the anti-slavery editor Elijah Lovejoy caused his father to recall the "abolitionist pup," and a breach occurred between father and son which remained unhealed. After taking some odd jobs, Herndon began to study law and soon after his admission to the bar became Lincoln's partner. The partnership was dissolved by Lincoln's death. Herndon occupied the same office for the rest of his life, first in partnership with Charles Zane, one of Lincoln's office boys, who later became judge of the United States District Court for the Southern District of Illinois. Herndon's last partner was Alfred Orendorff.

On March 26, 1840, Herndon married Mary J. Maxey, by whom he had six children; after her death he married on July 31, 1861, Annie Miles, who bore him two children. The second marriage was in part a result of his making good on a political promise to the young bride's brother, for whom he procured an appointment from Lincoln.

Herndon did not have the makings of a politician, although he did serve one term as Mayor of Springfield and was State Bank Examiner, which position came to him through the influence of Lincoln and to which he was reappointed by Governor Yates at the request of Lincoln just about the time that Lincoln left for Washington. He was also candidate for presidential elector in 1856. Before Lincoln's departure to Washington, Herndon acted not only as his partner, but as his spokesman and his adviser. After 1861, when his partner had achieved national fame, he began the gathering of all the important material about Lincoln's life which was to become, after Lincoln's assassination, the main occupation of his own life.

As has been truthfully said, it was unwavering and inflexible devotion to the truth that formed the predominating trait in the character of William H. Herndon. In this respect he resembled his illustrious law partner. Both men up to a certain point were very much alike, but there was this difference: Lincoln, deeply cautious and restrained, was prone to abstract and thoughtful calculation. Herndon, by nature forceful and alert, was quick, impulsive, and often precipitate. If he detected wrong he proclaimed the fact instantly and everywhere, and fought at the drop of the hat, and fought incessantly, pushing blindly through the smoke of battle until he was either hopelessly overcome or stood exultant on the hilltop of victory. Younger than Lincoln, he was more venturesome, and magnificently oblivious of consequences.

Conscious of his limitations, Herndon knew that he was too radical and bold to achieve success in politics, and he therefore sank himself in the fortunes of his more happily poised partner. In the end posterity will accept the verdict of Herndon's friends that, despite his faults, he was a noble, broad-minded man, incapable of a mean or selfish act, brave and big-hearted, tolerant, forgiving, just, and as true to Lincoln as the "needle to the pole."

Beveridge encouraged and urged Weik to write his later book as a vindication of Herndon: "You are quite right about Herndon. In all my investigation, his character shines out clear and stainless. As I said of him in my review of your book, he was almost a fanatic in his devotion to truth. Wherever he states a fact as such, I accept it, unless other indisputable and documentary proof shows that his memory was a little bit defective."

Senator Beveridge himself, after writing the Life of Chief Justice John Marshall, decided to write a companion book on Abraham Lincoln. Beveridge not only became acquainted with all the Lincoln students and collectors of Illinois, Indiana, and Kentucky, who all assisted him and gave him access to their collections, but he also had the close co-operation and friendship of Weik, who generously turned over to him everything that Herndon had collected and written (throughout his book Beveridge refers to this as the Weik Collection);

but Beveridge did not possess the attributes that a devoted biographer of Abraham Lincoln ought to have. A true Boswell has one hero only, to whom he dedicates his entire life. Beveridge used only so much of the Herndon material as he saw fit—a shocking liberty to a genuine Boswell, such as Beveridge admitted Herndon to be:

"I do not, at the moment, recall another case in history where immediately after the death of a great personage, the facts of his personal life were collected so carefully, thoroughly, and impartially by a lifelong friend and intimate professional associate, as the facts about Lincoln were gathered by William H. Herndon. Almost from boyhood Herndon had been an idolater of Lincoln; and for seventeen years the two men were partners in the practice of law. So Herndon saw more of Lincoln and heard more from Lincoln's lips than any other human being, excepting only Lincoln's wife.

"Almost at once after the assassination, Herndon began to collect material relating to his hero. He wrote to everybody who ever knew Lincoln or his parents—everything about Lincoln is covered, up to 1861; Herndon's industry and persistence in this are astonishing. . . . In his letters he asked questions upon every conceivable point. . . . Some questions were not answered clearly, and Herndon wrote again and again, until the smallest detail was made plain. Often, as in the case of Sarah Rickard, he would have to write several times before he got any answer at all. But he stuck to it. Most of those who had known Lincoln as boy and young man had scattered far and wide over the United States; no matter, Herndon traced them. Those whom he could reach personally, he interviewed, and immediately wrote out notes of what they said. I have read in the original manuscript these transcripts; they show on their faces that they were written by a trained lawyer, skilled in the taking of depositions and the making of notes of statements by witnesses. I have read, too, the original letters to Herndon in answer to his inquiries, and also Herndon's own letters about Lincoln, as well as his entire manuscript on the subject. Everywhere it is obvious that Herndon is intent on telling the truth himself and on getting the truth from those who could give personal, first-hand information. . . .

"Herndon had gone with Lincoln in his circuit riding; and he knew intimately the lawyers and judges with whom Lincoln spent all his professional life outside the office of Lincoln and Herndon, where, of course, the junior partner was in closer contact with his senior than anybody else possibly could have been.

"Herndon was forty-seven years of age when Lincoln was murdered. For fourteen years after that event, he kept up his Lincoln researches, delivering several lectures on phases of Lincoln's life, practicing law, and keeping up a large general correspondence.

"Perhaps it is not unworthy of note that it was to Herndon, and not to Lincoln, that, for years before his nomination for the Presidency, such men as Parker, Sumner, Seward, Phillips, Greeley, and Garrison wrote. To be sure, the youthful and ardent Herndon always began the correspondence; yet, even so, it was to him and not to his partner that these brilliant men, molders of the public opinion of the time, looked for reports of conditions in Illinois. It is extremely curious that, judging from their letters to Herndon, these leaders seemed not to have realized that Lincoln amounted to anything during that period."

After Herndon's death, almost every biographer of Lincoln who wanted to do justice to his subject communicated with Weik and begged him for a glimpse of the Herndon material. No one knew of the similar letters Herndon had written to Hart, Arnold, Lamon, Bartlett, and Whitney. Consider the importunate letters of Dr. Barton; he wrote about a hundred of them, and finally became so insistent that Weik submitted the question to Beveridge, and the decision given by the Senator was in the negative: "After giving prolonged and careful thought to the matter of letting Barton have any of your material, and, in view of your broad-minded and generous letter and the confidence you repose in me, I consulted about it, *in absolute confidence,* with Worthington Chauncey Ford, Ellery Sedgwick, and Greenslet, all of whom firmly believe that, under the circumstances, I should not part with any of this material. . . . In view of the combined judgment of all four of us . . . my advice is . . . to tell him frankly that you cannot part with any further material and thus end the correspondence."

Thus did Beveridge, after himself lifting no more than a corner of the veil over Herndon's researches, prevent their being revealed to others. From 1889 no one was allowed to have access to this mine of information until in 1922 most of it had passed into other hands and a good deal of it into the Henry E. Huntington Library along with the Lamon and Hart Collections.

But long before this a series of articles began to appear in *Century* which were ultimately to become Nicolay and Hay's great ten-volume work on Lincoln—certainly intended to be, and widely greeted as, the definitive biography of the Civil War President. Herndon read the articles as they appeared, and his criticism, scattered through his letters to Weik and others, was deadly. "They are aiming," he says, "first, to do a superb piece of literary work; second, to make the story with the classes as against the masses. It will result in delineating the real Lincoln about as well as does a wax figure in the museum. . . . Nicolay and Hay have suppressed many facts—material facts of Lincoln's life, and among them are Lincoln's genealogy, paternity, the description of Nancy Hanks, old Thomas Lincoln, the Ann Rutledge story, Lincoln's religion, Lincoln's spells of morbidity, the facts of Lincoln's misery with Mary Todd, Lincoln's backdown on the night that he and Mary Todd were to be married, etc., etc. I do not say that they did not mention some of these things in a roundabout way, but I do say that the kernel, 'nib,' or point of things has been purposely suppressed. Nicolay and Hay do know the facts fully, as I am informed on good authority. . . . Nicolay and Hay handle things with silken gloves and a camel-hair pencil. They do not write with an iron pen. . . . Some of the finest episodes in Lincoln's young life are omitted or evaded or swallowed up in words. . . . They are writing the Life of Lincoln under the surveillance of Bob Lincoln. Nicolay and Hay, in my opinion, are afraid of Bob. He gives them materials and they in turn play hush. This is my opinion, and is worth no more than an honest opinion."

It is curious that John Hay himself admitted the justice of this sort of criticism in a letter to Herndon, which incidentally contains what is perhaps one of the finest estimates of Lincoln's character: "No great man was ever modest. It was his intellectual arrogance and unconscious assumption of superiority that men like Chase and Sumner never could forgive. I believe Lincoln is well understood by the people. Miss Nancy Bancroft and the rest of that patent-leather kid-glove set know no more of him than an owl does of a comet blazing into its blinking eyes. Bancroft's address was a disgraceful exhibition of ignorance and prejudice. His effeminate nature shrinks instinctively from the contact of a great reality like Lincoln's character. I consider Lincoln Republicanism incarnate, with all its faults and all its virtues. As, in spite of some rudeness, Republicanism is the sole hope of a sick world, so Lincoln, with all his foibles, is the greatest character since Christ."

Hay idolized Lincoln, but he also loved Robert, his boyhood friend. He did want to please his friend, even to the extent of omitting from his biography anything Robert desired left unsaid. Both Hay and Nicolay, Lincoln's other secretary and hero-worshiper, admit to writing to please Robert. In Hay's letter [1] to Robert T. Lincoln (January 27, 1884), requesting Robert to look over the chapters embracing the first forty years of his father's life, he says:

"I need not tell you that every line has been written in a spirit of reverence and regard. Still, you may find here and there words and sentences which do not suit. I write now to request that you will read with pencil in your hand and strike out everything to which you object. I will adopt your view in all cases, whether I agree with you or not." Robert Lincoln must have taken this injunction very seriously, since the first forty years of Lincoln's life are summarized in only 282 pages out of the 4709 pages of the completed book.

In his letter to Robert Lincoln on January 6, 1886, Hay writes: "I was very sorry to see by a letter you wrote to Nicolay that you were still not satisfied with my assurance that I would make these first chapters all right. Even before you read them I had struck out of my own copy here nearly everything that you objected to and had written Nicolay to make the changes in his . . . since then I have gone over the whole thing and will again, reading every line so far as possible from your point of view, and I don't think there is a word left in that would displease you. But, of course, before final publication I shall give you another hack at it with plenary blue pencil powers."

In his letter of March 5, 1888, Hay says: "I thank you for the corrections, all of which I have of course adopted."

To Henry Adams, Hay writes, August 4, 1889: "I only wonder at the merciful Providence which keeps my critics away from the weak joints in my armor. Laws-a-mercy; if I had the criticizing of that

---

[1] This and the letters referred to below appeared after Hay's death—in his diary, "printed but not published," and distributed only among friends of the Hay family.

book, what a skinning I could give it! I can't amend it, but could *éreinter* it—I would break its back *de la belle manière*."

Not satisfied, it would seem, with his part in emasculating certain portions of Nicolay and Hay's great work, Robert Lincoln went on to an action which has not even yet been fully disclosed. Senator Beveridge requested of Robert Lincoln permission to examine all the papers which formed the basis of Nicolay and Hay's work in order to check on its correctness. Robert Lincoln informed Senator Beveridge that he thought Beveridge's work superfluous, if not useless, as he considered Nicolay and Hay's volumes the last word, the encyclopedia, of Lincoln information, the fairest and most complete compendium of the events of Lincoln's life, as well as the only impartial commentary on that life; and he said so repeatedly, not only in conversation but also over signature. He had been of that opinion for more than a quarter of a century before Beveridge made his request. Robert Lincoln therefore refused Beveridge's request to check the papers which had been given to Lincoln's former secretaries and which they had freely used and in many cases—too many—edited (they had even edited Lincoln's farewell address at Springfield, omitting a human sentiment or two that did not please them).

Beveridge made further futile efforts through friends of Robert Lincoln, but Lincoln became adamant on the subject. In order to make it impossible for Beveridge ever to see the documents, Lincoln made a deed of gift presenting them all to the Library of Congress, on condition that they were not to be opened or seen by anyone without his consent or the consent of his wife, in writing, until twenty-one years after his death. These documents are now classified in folders and lodged in bookcases bearing the legend: "Not to be consulted," and there they will remain until 1947. But before presenting them to the Library of Congress, Lincoln subjected the papers to a purge. A friend of the late Horace G. Young, President of the Delaware & Hudson Railroad, tells the following story:

"Horace G. Young was an intimate friend of Robert T. Lincoln, and he and Mr. Lincoln were accustomed to spend part of each summer together. A few years before Mr. Lincoln's death, Mr. Young went as usual to visit him at Mr. Lincoln's home in Manchester, Vermont. On arriving at the house he found Mr. Lincoln in a room surrounded by a number of large boxes and with many papers scattered about the floor, and with the ashes of many burnt papers visible in the fireplace. Mr. Young asked Mr. Lincoln what he was doing, and Mr. Lincoln replied that he was destroying some of the private papers and letters of his father, Abraham Lincoln. Mr. Young at once remonstrated with Mr. Lincoln and said that no one had any right to destroy such papers, Mr. Lincoln least of all. Mr. Lincoln replied that he did not intend to continue his destruction—since the papers he was destroying contained the documentary evidence of the treason of a member of Lincoln's Cabinet, and that he thought it was best for all that such evidence be destroyed. Mr. Young immediately visited Dr. [Nicholas Murray] Butler, who was in town, and told him what Robert T. Lincoln was doing. Dr. Butler promptly called on Robert T. Lincoln and argued and pleaded with him and finally prevailed upon him to desist—and place the papers where they would be safe in order that they might be preserved for posterity."

Dr. Butler's own account [1] of the incident is as follows: "It was Mr. Horace G. Young, then at Manchester, Vermont, who brought to my attention within a few hours after I arrived from Europe the fact that Robert Lincoln was about to burn a collection of his father's papers, and that he, Mr. Young, had been unable to persuade him not to do so. I went immediately to his house and had a most earnest discussion of the whole subject with Mr. Lincoln in his library. I went so far as to insist that the papers did not belong to him, since his father had belonged to the country for half a century and the papers therefore belonged to the country also. Robert Lincoln finally acceded to my urgent and insistent request for the preservation of the papers and sent them under seal to the Library of Congress, there to remain unopened for fifty years.

"Subsequently, Senator Beveridge, then engaged on his Life of Lincoln, having heard of the incident, asked me to procure for him opportunity to examine these papers. I have the correspondence with Robert Lincoln in which he declined flatly to grant Beveridge's request."

The diary of Orville H. Browning, United States Senator from Illinois, did not fare any better. Here was a calm, dispassionate historian and observer, certainly a friend of Lincoln and a colleague at the bar of Illinois, who wrote his diary and made entries from day to

---

[1] In a letter to the writer, dated November 5, 1937.

day. That diary remained secreted until a few years ago, when it was turned over to the University of Illinois and was then permitted by the owner to be edited and printed only on condition that certain sections and entries be omitted. They were omitted.

So it went. McClure's papers on Lincoln were destroyed by General McCausland; Robert Levi Todd, one of Lincoln's intimate associates, left his papers to Todd Gentry, who destroyed them. Lincoln's enemies in the South destroyed many documents, as did collectors who were interested in saving only Lincoln's signature. Even the elements joined in the destruction, the Chicago fire having been responsible for the loss of much significant material.

For these reasons alone, the work of Herndon, a man who put the passion for truth before any "kid-glove" considerations, would become of paramount historical importance. Unfortunately Herndon's book too succumbed to the forces that were responsible for the policy of hush. Even so, as finally published by Belford, Clarke & Company, in its mutilated form, poorly printed, on poor paper, in three ridiculous little volumes, Herndon's Life still raised a storm of criticism for some of the things it contained; for this censored book [1] has been the chief source of practically all we know of Lincoln up to the day he left Springfield. Herndon simply wanted Lincoln to become as familiar to all Americans as the air we breathe, and for this reason he wanted each detail of Lincoln's life spread fairly on the record. He was not allowed to do this in his own book, and he died penniless and slandered.

This, then, until recently seemed to be the whole pathetic story of William H. Herndon, who strove to lay down the foundations of the true history of the great man to whom he had given his whole heart; whose secretary, adviser, and partner he had been; to whom he had been purveyor of every book, newspaper, magazine, or pamphlet Lincoln needed; whose ambassador-at-large and confidential agent to such men as Theodore Parker, Horace Greeley, and the leaders of the Republican party in the East he was. But for some years many of the documents have been reposing in the Henry E. Huntington Library in San Marino, California, including the originals not only of Herndon's draft chapters for Lamon's book and of his letters to Weik, but also the complete series of letters he wrote to Charles H. Hart, Ward

---

[1] It was republished in two volumes under the editorship of Horace White in 1895, and finally appeared in 1935 in one handy volume as edited by Paul M. Angle.

H. Lamon, I. N. Arnold, and others, all of them containing and repeating those results of Herndon's researches which he was never able
to make public.

When, in November 1933, the Herndon documents given to Weik
were made available for my inspection, I kept reading for six months
thereafter—all of it. As these invaluable papers unfolded before me,
I felt like Balboa standing on a peak in Darien viewing the Pacific
Ocean for the first time. In 1931 I had published 1250 Lincoln documents hitherto unknown, and they have played a part in the reap-
praisal of Lincoln, but this find was fundamental and massive and
called for independent publication. I went to the Huntington Library
to examine for myself the greatest collection of unused Herndon material in existence.

"Here is the most important item in this entire collection," Herndon
had said, as he pointed to a small leather-covered notebook about six
by four inches in size, the two covers being fastened together with a
brass clasp. "In its pages you will find . . . all the ammunition Mr.
Lincoln saw fit to gather in preparation for his battle with Stephen
A. Douglas." He then explained that, as the contest of 1858 was approaching, Mr. Lincoln took this book, originally a blank book which
had been used by himself and his partner to keep track of citations of
cases, and proceeded to paste in its pages newspaper clippings, tables
of statistics, and other data bearing on the great and absorbing questions of the day, with a few sentences scribbled in here and there.
"When this little storehouse of political information was filled," observed Herndon, "Mr. Lincoln fastened the clasp, placed the book in
his coat pocket, there to repose during the campaign and to be drawn
upon whenever the exigencies of debate required it." Only two pages
of this book ever came to light. Now the whole book is available.

The book contains about one hundred and eighty-five clippings; the
first item in the book is the second paragraph of the Declaration of
Independence. Lower down on the same page we find a paragraph from
a speech by Henry Clay: "I repeat it, sir, I never can and never will
and no earthly power will make me look directly or indirectly to spread
slavery over territory where it does not exist. Never while reason holds
her seat in my brain—never while my heart sends the vital fluid
through my veins—NEVER." Next, Lincoln inserted a portion of the

opening of his speech before the Republican State Convention, wherein he gave utterance to the doctrine that "a house divided against itself cannot stand."

It is strange that no mention seems to be made by Herndon of a second notebook compiled by Lincoln, equally if not more important, and more scientifically prepared, than the Douglas debate notebook. This second little notebook Lincoln prepared on the subject of slavery. It contains about the same number of newspaper clippings and excerpts as does the Douglas book, but this is indexed, so that Lincoln was instantly able to find and quote the proper passage on almost any phase of the slavery problem without fear of challenge. No wonder Douglas repeatedly stated that he would rather face the whole United States Senate than Lincoln alone.

Herndon's six series of letters were written in 1866, 1868, 1870, 1886, 1889, and 1891—and their very repetitiousness is of significance in disproving the charge that Herndon's memory played him false. Hence I have retained many letters for reproduction for that reason alone. Other letters have been included because of the light they throw upon Herndon's character and credibility. Otherwise a great deal has been omitted from the collection by reason of its irrelevance to the Lincoln question. Herndon's letters are here reprinted in strictly chronological order, but some approximation to a division according to recipients has been arrived at by marking off the total series of letters in Part One of this volume into five sections: the first of letters mainly to Hart, the second to Lamon, the third to Weik, the fourth to Whitney and Bartlett, and the fifth to Bartlett and Weik.

To these has been added Part Two, consisting, first, of the evidences on which Herndon based his conclusions—letters written to Herndon in response to his requests for information and statements and affidavits gathered by Herndon—and, secondly, of those conclusions themselves as expressed by Herndon in his monographs and draft chapters. In this Part the distinction between Herndon's own writings and the statements of others has been made apparent to the eye by the typographical device of having the latter set in smaller type. Spelling and punctuation, but not grammar or other peculiarities of style, have been normalized.

Here at last is Herndon's work in Herndon's own language and in the language of the people he interviewed—David Davis, the Justice of the Supreme Court of the United States, who rarely wrote or spoke of what he knew of Lincoln; Joseph Gillespie; James H. Matheny; Sarah Bush Lincoln, Abraham's devoted stepmother; Grigsby; Dennis and John Hanks; E. B. Washburne, Congressman and Cabinet officer and minister to France; Norman B. Judd, great lawyer and political leader; John Wentworth, Congressman and Mayor of Chicago; Jesse K. Dubois, lawyer and banking commissioner; Governors William H. Bissell, Richard Yates, and R. J. Oglesby of Illinois; John L. Scripps, editor of the Chicago *Tribune;* John B. Helm; Joshua F. Speed, admittedly Lincoln's closest friend and adviser; John T. Stuart, Lincoln's first partner, a lawyer of ability; Hannah Armstrong, who helped Lincoln, who in turn defended her son charged with murder and won his acquittal after a remarkable struggle; John McNamar, Ann Rutledge's first affianced; Henry C. Whitney, one of the younger men in whom Lincoln had confidence; Leonard Swett, lawyer who practiced in the Eighth Illinois Circuit and was a friend of Lincoln; Ninian W. Edwards and his wife, the sister of Lincoln's wife; John H. Littlefield, one of Lincoln's faithful law clerks; Jesse W. Fell; Lawrence Weldon, a lawyer who traveled the circuit with Lincoln and was later one of his appointees; F. B. Carpenter, painter who lived at the White House for six months; Orlando B. Ficklin, lawyer and intimate friend of Lincoln; Charles S. Zane, law clerk and Justice of the United States District Court; Stephen T. Logan, great lawyer and Lincoln's partner; Pascal B. Enos, engineer and surveyor; Joseph Medill, editor and owner of the Chicago *Tribune;* Lyman Trumbull, Senator and political leader; Mentor Graham; Rebecca Herndon, Archer G. Herndon, Elliott B. Herndon, J. Rowan Herndon, and James A. Herndon —all related to William H. Herndon; Horace White, editor of the Chicago *Tribune* who accompanied Lincoln during the debates with Douglas, editor of the New York *Evening Post,* and one of the most reliable of Lincoln students and biographers; Joseph G. Cannon, lawyer, Congressman, and Speaker of the House of Representatives, who saved Lincoln's stepmother from prosecution for larceny while her son was in the White House; Daniel E. Voorhees, long a Senator, who heard Lincoln on the circuit and talked and wrote about Lincoln; Adlai E. Stevenson and Henry Wilson, both Vice-Presidents of the

United States; Charles A. Dana, editor of the New York *Tribune*, Assistant Secretary of War, and finally editor of the *Sun;* and Henry Ward Beecher, clergyman, orator, publicist.

After reading this entire collection, situated in Huntington, in the Library of Congress, and in the Herndon collections, consisting of more than ten thousand pages of original material, I came to the conclusion that both Herndon and Lincoln had been defrauded of the appreciation due them by the neglect of these documents. "You owe a tremendous debt of gratitude to dear old Herndon," Beveridge writes to Weik, "and what is more important, you owe it to the world to rescue that splendid old gentleman from the morass of misrepresentation and even slander into which interested and prejudiced persons threw him."

Slandered Herndon certainly has been: "Herdon was a liar," "Herndon was a drunkard," "Herndon was a drug addict," "Herndon was jealous," "Herndon was ungrateful," "Herndon was enraged that Lincoln did not take him along and make him a part of his administration." Herndon's controversy with the Reverend James A. Reed over Lincoln's religion, as quoted in Lamon's Life of Lincoln, was the cause for the appearance in the press of items charging Herndon with being a lunatic, a pauper, a drunkard, an infidel, a liar, a knave. These libels Herndon answered from time to time as best he could.

In September 1882, the Cherryvale, Kansas, *Globe-News* published the following article:

"Lincoln's Old Law Partner a Pauper"

"Bill Herndon is a pauper in Springfield, Ill. He was once worth considerable property. His mind was the most argumentative of any of the old lawyers in the State, and his memory was extraordinary. . . . Herndon, with all his attainments, was a man who now and then went on a spree, and it was no uncommon thing for him to leave an important lawsuit and spend several days in drinking and carousing. This habit became worse after Lincoln's death, and like poor Dick Yates, Herndon went down step by step till his old friends and associates point to him as a common drunkard."

On November 9, 1882, Herndon issued a broadside which he entitled "A Card and a Correction." After implying that Reed and others who

held opinions concerning Lincoln's religion opposite to his own were
in no small measure responsible for this and similar allegations, he
made his defense in the following words:

"There are three distinct charges in the above article. First, that I
am a pauper; second, that I am a common drunkard; and, third, that
I was a traitor, or false to my clients. Let me answer these charges in
their order. First, I am not a pauper, never have been, and never expect
to be. I am working on my own farm making my own living with my
own muscle and brain, a place and a calling that even Christianity with
its persecution and malignity can never reach me to do me much harm.
I had, it is true, once a considerable property, but lost much of it in the
crash and consequent crisis of 1873, caused in part by the contraction
of the currency, the decline in the demand for agricultural products,
which I raised for sale, in part by the inability of the people to buy,
etc., etc., and for no other reasons.

"Second, I never was a common drunkard, as I look at it, and am
not now. I am and have been for years an ardent and enthusiastic temperance man, though opposed to prohibition by law, by any force or
other choker. The time has not come for this. It is a fact that I once,
years ago, went on a spree; and this I now deeply regret. It, however,
is in the past, and let a good life in the future bury the past. I have not
fallen, I have risen; and all good men and women will applaud the deed,
always excepting a small, little, bitter Christian like the Right Rev.
pastor and liar of this city, to whom I can trace some of the above
charges. In my case this minister was an eager, itching libeler, and
what he said of me is false—nay, a willful lie.

"Third, I never was a traitor or untrue to my clients or their interests. I never left them during the progress of a trial or at other times
for the cause alleged, drunkenness. I may have crept, slid, out of a
case during the trial because I had no faith in it, leaving Mr. Lincoln,
who had faith in it, to run it through. My want of faith in the case
would have been discovered by the jury and that discovery would have
damaged my client, and to save my client I dodged. This is all there is
in it and let men make the most of it."

Another charge repeatedly made against Herndon by persons who
considered defamatory his lectures on, and investigations into, Lincoln's life was that Herndon hated Lincoln for not considering him
for some prominent office in his administration. Herndon long ago

acquitted Lincoln of ingratitude. He tells that the appointment of himself, Herndon, to office was the very first thing Lincoln thought of after his election. It was Herndon who refused to become a member of the administration. He told Lincoln that he was content with the office of State Banking Commissioner, which he then held, and Lincoln immediately proceeded to Governor Yates to make sure of Herndon's reappointment to that post.

If these papers serve to rehabilitate Herndon, they will not, as many have feared, do harm to Lincoln's name and fame. They contain the best yet said as well as the worst of the man Lincoln; and they may clear up many a problem which has not been heretofore understood, and which, because it had hitherto to express itself in guarded hints and rumors, created an atmosphere of slander. An unbiased and accurate Life of Lincoln is now much more nearly possible, and the American people who produced out of themselves so great a man deserve no less.

No one seriously questions the accuracy of the statements Herndon made in his letters to Theodore Parker; perhaps it has not as yet occurred to anyone to do so. In Dr. Newton's *Lincoln and Herndon* are fifty-two letters which show the great friendship between Parker and Herndon. Nor is there any general criticism of the accuracy of the main facts stated in Herndon's lectures or in his book, for most biographers have themselves appropriated these facts. Indeed a Life of Lincoln without quotations from Herndon cannot be written. The criticism of Herndon has usually been on the score, first, of his conclusions and, secondly, of the specific proportion between truth and error.

Now as to both these approaches, the argument has after all hitherto been conducted on the basis of insufficient evidence. Those who accuse Herndon of unreliability in fact and hastiness in conclusions have never had before them all of Herndon's evidence or a complete statement of his case. They have not known the remarkable extent to which Lincoln's friends and associates bore out Herndon's researches and opinions. None delved so deeply into the intimate details of Lincoln's life as did Herndon. How then can such persons decide as to the proportion of fact and fancy in Herndon's public statements?

Here at last is Herndon's complete evidence, the full record of the steps by which he reached his conclusions, the supporting testimony of his and Lincoln's contemporaries. The principals of the story are no longer alive, and no excuse remains for silence. These seventy years have made meaningless the passions which were responsible for the misunderstanding of Herndon and his motives. Now we who love the memory of Lincoln may properly thank the fate which gave us William Herndon's unflagging passion for completeness. "Men collect gold," says Chrysostom, "not only in lumps but also in the minutest fragments." All may now subscribe to the appraisal of Herndon's work by a man who knew Lincoln intimately, second perhaps only to Herndon and Lamon, the great journalist Horace White:

"What Mr. Lincoln was after he became President can best be understood by knowing what he was before. The world owes more to William H. Herndon for this particular knowledge than to all other persons taken together. It is no exaggeration to say that his death . . . removed from earth the person who, of all others, had most thoroughly searched the sources of Mr. Lincoln's biography, and had most attentively, intelligently, and also lovingly studied his character. He was generous in imparting his information to others. Almost every Life of Lincoln since the tragedy at Ford's Theater has been enriched by his labors."

—EMANUEL HERTZ

January 1938

Part One

LETTERS

FROM HERNDON

Springfield, Ill., January 8, 1866.

Mr. Hart.

My dear Sir:

I have not published my two lectures. My friends got up condensed things—reports of them. I am an extremely lazy man and have to be kicked to act. It took three hours to read them—and hence you have only seen mere extracts. Many things were left out, and not noticed, because time and space, especially space, in the papers forbade a longer notice of them. I was just and truthful in the lectures—made no humbug statements and fussy flourishes. I dearly loved—and now reverence the memory of my dear friend. I wrote the lectures *solely* for the purpose of putting him where he in fact and truth and question belongs. I have not any autograph letters of Mr. Lincoln now—gave all away—am sorry I cannot accommodate you.

Yours truly,

W. H. HERNDON.

Springfield, Ill., January 13, 1866.

Mr. Hart.

My dear Sir:

Some few days since I addressed you a hurried note, stating that I had no "autographic letters." This is a condensed expression, meaning—I had no letters with the signature of Mr. Lincoln attached to them, but that I probably had other papers with his signature attached thereto. The expression saves me much time—wind and ink. You will excuse me, will you not?—write dozens of letters weekly on the same subject, etc.

Enclosed you will find a bond for costs, signed by Mr. Lincoln, which I will give to you. It is now the best thing I can do—probably the best thing you will get of anyone at any time. I would not spare this to everyone, let me assure you. I could have given it away a thousand times. The signature is Mr. Lincoln's as well as the body of the bond.

I have been written to from the East notifying me that my queer lectures—even in a condensed form, and as poor as they are—will be published. If they are and copies are sent to me, I will send one to you. I ask you to excuse what is odd in me and my language. We are rough and ready out here rather than educated and polished.

Yours truly,

W. H. HERNDON.

Springfield, Ill., February 12, 1866.

Mr. Hart.

My dear Sir:

Your kind letter of the 7th *inst.* is this moment handed me. The papers—the *Bulletin* and *Press*—are likewise received, and for all which I thank you. I wrote to you a good-natured letter a few days since withdrawing my requests and now let me explain. I sent you a kind of memento of Lincoln—namely his handwriting—etc. This fact, I have no doubt—*none at all*—placed you in feeling kindly toward me. One day I got a notion in my head that I would get a notice published after about nine months' toil in that line. *Foolishly,* as I now think, I asked you to do what you did. I think I was hasty and honestly repented of what I did—you should not have been asked. This is my sole reason for doing as I did in my last letter. But the deed is done and let me again say—I thank you. You must believe me when I state the reason so frankly. . . .

I would be a thousand times obliged to you if you would send me the facts—information you write about—namely the conversation between Lincoln and your father. If you have any suggestions to make—questions to ask about Mr. Lincoln—any peculiarity or specialty of him you wish drawn out, please write to me and accommodate *mankind,* myself included, as a matter of course.

Your friend,

W. H. HERNDON.

No sermons or eulogies here—curious!

Springfield, Ill., March 9, 1866.

Mr. Hart.

My dear Sir:

Your kind and excellent letter, dated the 3d *inst.*, has been duly received. I thank you for it ; and now why should I not like it? It contains valuable information in several ways—first, it shows the kind and quality of Mr. Lincoln's virtues; secondly, it shows his unrest, etc.; thirdly, it shows his feelings as Executive; fourthly, it shows discrimination of men; and, fifthly, wit, etc. I shall use the contents with great pleasure. The example of the wit you send me, I think excellent. It is new to us.

I have not yet spoken to anyone about publishing my book. I have been written to by some but no arrangements have been made with anyone. Have you any suggestions to make? The idea which you suggest about publishing a list of sermons, eulogies, etc., is a good one, and should be done; and should you ever get time to complete one I should like it very much. I cannot tell when I shall be ready to go to press. Hence you have "time on time." I thought I should publish, as addendum, the Program of Funeral Ceremonies here. Your idea fits in exactly with my own.

You owe me no apologies—as your letter is in on time. By the by— did you get a letter of mine, explaining why I attempted to withdraw my request made of you? The letter was intended to show that *I did wrong* in making the request and *for no other reason did* I attempt to withdraw it. I hope you get the letter.

We have had a kind of wild excitement here over the President's veto and his speech. We are a wild set of boys out here and must be excused.

Your friend,
W. H. HERNDON.

Springfield, Ill., April 13, 1866.

Mr. Hart.

My dear Sir:

Your kind letter, dated the 5th *inst.*, is this moment handed me and for which I am much obliged. I was absent on the "circuit"—doing law duties, etc., or should have answered sooner. What I say to you is always sincere and as candid as I know how to talk. I love to ask others —love to get hints and criticisms and suggestions from others. Hence my requests of you. I shall be glad to get your "Bibliography" when completed. Take your own time, friend. I shall avail myself of your kind suggestions in reference to the publication of my poor little book —think your ideas are correct—know so. Friend—I thank you for

that too exalted notice of me. I do not know who wrote it—only guess
—I thank you for your kind favors—and will try and repay some
time.

My dear friend, I never had my face photographed—expect I'll
have to do so to please my wife, and friends. If I ever do, I shall send
you one—on one condition—namely—you must not get scared at it.

I have been out on law business—doing Circuit Court duty—heavy,
laborious work, and am wearied. I am going to Kentucky soon to
search for, hound down, some facts, and when I return I shall once
more sit down to biographical dates. Oh, what an admirable sweet
good boyish record "Abe" has left behind, i.e., his childhood's life for
the world to love and to imitate. I sincerely wish I were a competent,
a great man to write my friend's life—but I *can* gather *facts* and give
truth to mankind.

Your friend,
W. H. HERNDON.

Springfield, Ill., June 29, 1866.

Mr. Hart.
My dear Sir:
Your letter, dated the 26th *inst.*, is this moment handed to me. You
owe me no apologies, but as you offer them, let me say—all right. I
am glad you have done your work—or nearly so—i.e., the finishing of
your "Bibliography." The list is quite perfect. However, let me suggest
one lecture. The title reads thus—"The Life and Character of Abraham Lincoln—A Lecture by Hon. Mark W. Delahay, of Leavenworth,
Kansas." Mr. Delahay is Judge of the District Court of Kansas—a
U.S. court. I hold the lecture in my hand and copy the title, etc.—word
for word. I have not critically read the lecture. My lectures were never
published in any way, except by shorthand, and then only portions of
the lectures were published. The language and ideas are correct so far
as they go. They never were published in pamphlet form. I intend to
have my biography published in Philadelphia or New York.

I hope to write a correct biography when it can be done. I shall make
it truthful or not at all, and men shall intuitively feel that the biography is true—correct and fair. The trouble is very, very great, I
assure you. Thousands of floating rumors—assertions and theories,

etc., etc., have to be hunted down—dug out—inspected—criticized, etc., etc., before I can write. I can't scribble on a sentence without knowing what I am doing. Between you and I, I am as busily engaged today in collecting materials—times—places, etc., etc., etc., as ever— —am going to Kentucky in July—in search of new and important facts.

By the by—in looking over some old papers the other day I found several *"representative"* letters addressed to me by Mr. L. when in Congress. I will send you a good one when I am done—one that contains ideas, views, principles, etc., etc.—good letter. Don't let me forget my promise.

Your friend,
W. H. Herndon.

(Hope you will have a good time in Pennsylvania at Miller.)

Springfield, Ill., July 22, 1866.

Mr. Hart.

My dear Sir:

I received your kind note, dated the 9th *inst.*, enclosing to me a copy of your remarks and resolutions on the death of the Hon. Lewis Cass. They seem to me as just and in the proper spirit.

The lecture of Mr. Delahay is a broadside—your titles are full and complete, and hence are entirely satisfactory to the mind. I shall get you a copy of Mr. Delahay's lecture, if possible, and send to you. Many orations, sermons, etc., were delivered in Illinois on the death of Mr. Lincoln, but do not think that many of them were ever published. I have written to Chicago to get any and all printed lectures, orations, sermons, etc., etc., and if I get any I will send to you. Speaker Colfax delivered one in Chicago—soon after the death of Mr. L. It was published in the newspapers of Chicago. Others were delivered but can say no more.

You can finish your "B[ibliography]" when you wish. A year will do me. So take your own time. My professional business disturbs me— takes me off—divides my mind and I "can't go fast." I have many old relics of Mr. L. which I wish you could see, and among them is a love letter which he wrote to his sweetheart at the age of twenty-three.

Honor "sticks out" in it as in all his after life. I have a leaf of Mr. L.'s old copybook made in 1824—when fifteen years of age. I wish you could see it; it is neat—clean and exact in what is done—one of his characteristics. Mr. L.'s life is a sweet, clear, clean, manly made life. The more I study it the more I like it. I sometimes thought that some of his peculiarities were things drawn on for effect, but letters to friends—his gentle boyhood, manhood, through all situations, positions, and conditions—are identical—one and the same—ever honest and simple and sincere. His is a primitive type of character that the young must admire and over whom it must exercise in all coming time a vast influence. You once said to me that you thought I somewhat exaggerated. In some particulars I may have done so. Will you please tell me where—in what—I see above the truth in your opinion? I shall be obliged to you. I want to be exactly correct in my estimate of Mr. L. Please say to me what you think and I promise you to mend my mistake. Come—be candid. I'll admire you the more for it.

Won't you excuse this long letter?

Your friend,
W. H. HERNDON.

Springfield, Ill., September 1, 1866.

Mr. Hart.
My dear Sir:

I want to ask a favor of you, and it is this—I want you to clip and to send to me from the leading Philadelphia papers the account of Mr. L.'s arrival and doings in your city—from his entrance to his final departure. Please do this for me and mark which paper from, so that I may know which is which. You will please give me the same in reference to Harrisburg, if you can. I know no one in Harrisburg and hence must *bore* you. I must bother and bore friends, which I regret—deeply so.

I hope and pray that the good Union men now gathering in your city may have a good time and finally meet with entire success.

Your friend,
W. H. HERNDON.

Springfield, Ill., September 12, 1866.

Friend Hart:

Your letter, dated the 8th *inst.*, is this moment handed to me. I was hurried when I wrote you and was not plain or explicit, I am afraid. I wished some newspaper account of Mr. Lincoln's visit to Philadelphia, and the conspiracy of Baltimore in February 1861. As Mr. Lincoln passed through Philadelphia in 1861 to Washington he made you a speech at Independence Hall. I wanted an account of his reception, etc., and the conspiracy at Baltimore, given as editorials by correspondents of your papers. I would not trouble my friends could I avoid it. You really must excuse me.

Your friend,
W. H. HERNDON.

None of Lincoln's friends—no Republican—went to see Johnson— cold and withering reception.

H.

Springfield, Ill., November 1, 1866.

Friend Hart:

Your kind letter dated the 29th *ult.* is handed to me at my desk. I thank you for those two papers you sent me—had never seen the notice before. . . .

I am in court—am busy indeed—yet am preparing a lecture substantially thus—"Lincoln, Miss Rutledge, New Salem, Pioneers, and *the Poem*"—after two years' labor I've found out the history of the poem called "Immortality," in short here as: "Oh! Why should the spirit of mortal be proud?" The story is a fine one and as soon as delivered will send you a copy—in full. I want no more short report of my printed lectures. The facts which I shall reveal, for the first time in the world, throw a footlight on Mr. Lincoln's sad life, etc., etc. Can't say more—excuse me, won't you? I have read notes to a lady, Miss —— of Boston, and hope she won't reveal till I get ready; but you know the world. Again excuse me.

Your friend,
W. H. HERNDON.

Springfield, Ill., November 16, 1866.

Friend Hart:

I sent you on yesterday evening a lecture on Mr. Lincoln, as promised. It was, my dear friend, written while I was at court—part in one copy and part in another. I claim no literary power, taste, etc., but I do claim to possess *the wish* to tell the truth. I think the *matter* good. Please read it, form your opinion, and write me candidly what you think of it in the light herein spoken. If you see any comments on it in the papers, please clip out and send to me. I wish to have them as a guide—how far to go—what to say, etc., hereafter.

I hope I said nothing in any of my hurried notes to you, throwing cold water upon your highly important undertaking.

I am your friend,

W. H. HERNDON.

Springfield, Ill., November 20, 1866.

Friend Arnold:

I wrote you a hasty note on Saturday, and now propose to finish my defense. You ask me if Mr. Lincoln was ever crazy in Menard County—was insane in 1835; and in answer to which I say—he was, as the people in that region understand craziness or insanity, and I *fear* much worse than I painted it, though I told the story as my reason and evidences make it—show it, and see it. You ask me if Mr. Lincoln *in fact* made the identical speech which I put in his mouth. He did not make that speech in words, though he did in substance and spirit—just as I have told them.

Again—did you know that Mr. Lincoln wrote a work—a book on *Infidelity*—and that his friends say they burnt it up? Beware that some leaf is not slumbering—to be sprung on you, when we are dead and gone, and no defense being made—he, L., will go down all time as a writer on infidelity, atheism, etc. How are you going to meet this? Don't scold and suspicion even by shadowy vision indirectly your true friend, your co-laborer, till you know all—know it as I do, and as time *will have it* and make it irrespective of you and myself. My own present opinion is that that book was written in 1835 and 6, written through the spirit of his misery, through the thought and idea that God had forsaken him, and through the echoes of Lincoln's mental condition, suffering, a burden of wild despair. The dates as I have them make *the book* before the crazy spell but every knowledge of Lincoln and my reason tell me that the book was written in 1836. I am now in search of *the facts*—the true and exact facts as to time, place, and persons. Men place the book before the spell, *and I after it*. I will write you my final conclusions about the facts. Let me alone (smiling and good humoredly), I have my own work and mission. I may here say, as I have said before *to you*, that I worship, reverence Lincoln, his memory and fame. I loved him while living and reverence him now that he is dead and gone; he was the best friend I ever had excepting my own wife and my mother; he was the best friend I ever expect to have, save mother and wife; and I repeat *to you* that I think Mr. Lincoln was the best man, the kindest, tenderest, noblest, loveliest, *since Christ*. He was better and purer than Washington; and in mind he stands incomparable, grandly looming up. He is now the great central figure of American History. God bless Abraham Lincoln!

Again—did you know that Mr. Lincoln was *"as crazy as a loon"* in *this city in 1841;* that he did not sit, did not attend to the Legislature, but in part, if any (special session of 1841); that he was then deranged? Did you know that he was forcibly arrested by his special friends here at that time; that they had to remove all razors, knives, pistols, etc., from his room and presence, that he might not commit suicide? Did you know that his crazy bout was partly caused by *that old original love* coming in conflict with *new relations about to be assumed?* His fidelity to it *was sublime*. Did you know that all Lincoln's struggles, difficulties, etc., between himself and wife were partly, if not wholly, caused by Mrs. L.'s cognition that Lincoln did not love her, and *did love another?* Lincoln told his wife that he did not love her, did so before he was married to her; she was cognizant of the fact that Lincoln loved another. Did you know that the *Hell* through which Lincoln passed was caused by these things? Mrs. Lincoln's knowledge that Lincoln did not love her and did love another caused much trouble between them. I say, Lincoln told her *he did not love her.* The world does not know her, Mrs. L.'s, sufferings, her trials, and the causes of things. Sympathize with her. I shall never rob Mrs. Lincoln of her justice—justice due her. Poor woman! She will yet have her rewards. All these facts are not to go into my biography *now*, and yet the world will know all in spite of your wish or my desire, or any man's will. Do you not know—you ought to know—that the Chicago *Times* and some mean men have these facts stowed away in their malicious brains and desks, and I propose and will meet the facts face to face and modify where I cannot truthfully deny? Justice to the dead and to all mankind demands it now when it can be done. Poor man! the world knows thee not, and who shall defend thee and set thee right before the world, *and chain and rivet* the deep, eternal, and forever abiding sympathy of mankind to thee? My dear sir, what makes Europe and America love Christ? It is our sympathy that is at the root; and *shall I* strip Abraham of his crown and cross? It is criminal to do so. Did you know that Mr. Lincoln was informed of *some facts* that took place in Kentucky *about the time he was born* (was told so in his youth), that eat into his nature, and as it were crushed him, and yet clung to him, like his shadow, like a fiery shirt around his noble spirit? Lincoln for more than fifty long years walked through *his* furnace, had his cross and crown. Friend, what's the cause of his sadness, his gloom, his *sometimes* terrible nature? What made him so tender, so good, so honest, so just, so noble, so pure, so exalted, so liberal, so tolerant, so divine, as it were? It was the fiery furnace through which God rolled him, and yet the world must not know it, eh! Good heavens! shut out all light, freeze up all human sympathy from *this sacred man!* Never, no, never. All that I know of Mr. Lincoln only exalts him, brightens and sublimes him, and will endlessly draw the sympathies of all mankind to him. Kind man, good man, noble man, who knows thy sufferings but one man, and God? God bless thee, thou incomparable man!

Would you have Mr. Lincoln a sham, a reality or what, a symbol of an unreality? Would you cheat mankind into a belief of a falsehood by defrauding their judgments? Mr. Lincoln must stand on truth or not stand at all. This age is remorseless in its pitiless pursuit of facts, and do you suppose you and I can escape the honest judgments of mankind? Mr. Lincoln always admitted facts, and avoided them if he could. He never told a lie by suggestion or suppression; he thought it criminal; and shall I by suggestion or suppression lie? The man that dares *now* tell the truth, all and every necessary truth in reference to Lincoln, mankind will bless, and curse him that lies. *Mark my words, friend.* All truths are necessary that show, explain, or throw light on

Mr. Lincoln's mind, nature, quality, characteristics, thoughts, acts, and deeds, because he guided the Rebellion—rather suppressed it— and guided the grandest of Revolutions through its grand consummation.

We have had a great Rebellion—ending in a magnificent Revolution. Mr. Lincoln guided it. Mankind will know the causes, facts, and the relations of things, if the truth is told, and they will not if a lie is told. Cheat and delude mankind into a false philosophy ending in ruin! My duty is to the ever living man—and to God—not forgetting my own poor self—before the memory of the dead that hears not and cares, it may be, not. Truth is due mankind, and would you prefer a false ideal character that you make by suggestion or suppression through pen and paint above the real that God has made? The age of blind hero worship, thank God, has gone, and the worship of the truth is coming. My duty is to truth, man, and God. My mind is made up, and nothing but facts, experiences run and purified through reason, shall ever change my course.

My dear friend, all that is said is kindly said, but firmly said.

Your friend,

W. H. HERNDON.

P.S. Since I began to gather *facts* nearly two years, I have undergone various shades of opinion and belief, and after two years' reflection on the facts, beliefs, and opinions of others, you now have my own opinion of the man and the spirit of my book. You may show this to as many men as you choose—the more the better opinion, idea, i.e., you will have.

Springfield, Ill., November 26, 1866.

Friend Hart.

My dear Sir:

I have just returned from Chicago, and now wish to say a word or two to you. Enclosed is a copy of a letter which I wrote to the Hon. I. N. Arnold of Chicago,[1] who is writing a life of Mr. Lincoln. He is a good man, but I don't think he is a man of much nerve; he is an honest

---

1 See p. 36.

man, yet I think he is a timid man. Now, first as to the program or place of things. My first two lectures, as you are aware, were attempts to analyze Mr. Lincoln's mind. My third lecture was to show his Patriotism and Statesmanship. My second and third lectures were attempts to show the *practical application* of that mind to things, etc., while I analyze it, etc. My fourth lecture is an attempt to show external influences on it—material and mental—matter and mind on mind. My fifth lecture *is to be* on his infant and boyhood education—the means, methods, and struggles of it, his mind, to know and to develop itself. When these things shall be done, corrected, annotated, etc., I think I shall have rendered mankind some five cents' worth of service. Possibly they will so hold. When these things are done, mankind could spare me well, I giving them the record which I have made of the man *worth one million of dollars* to the race.

So much for an introduction. After having read Arnold's letter, my letter to him, you will prick up your ears. However—you will now begin to detect a purpose in my fourth late lecture, not guessed at before; and it is this. Mrs. Lincoln must be put properly before the world. She hates me, yet *I can* and *will do* her justice; she hates me on the same grounds that a thief hates a policeman who knows a dangerous secret about him. *Mrs. Lincoln's domestic quarrels in my opinion sprang from a woman's revenge which she was not strong enough to resist.* Poor woman! The world has no charity for her and yet justice must be done her, being careful not to *injure* her husband. All that I know ennobles both, and their difficulties sprang from human nature—a philosophy, if you please. You must have faith in me. I am willing to live by and to die by my letter to Arnold. The composition I care nothing about, in its artistic beauty, but the substance and spirit I do care for.

Mr. Arnold is *afraid*—that is the word—that I shall drop some *necessary* truth that Lincoln's enemies will use to unholy purposes. I am not responsible for the misapplication, misappropriation, or other wrong use of a *great necessary truth in Mr. Lincoln's life.* I have a sublime faith in the triumph and eternity of truth, of humanity, man and God; they will put Arnold, you, and myself just where we belong. Is any man so *insane* as to suppose that any truth concerning Lincoln, or in relation to his thoughts, acts, and deeds, will be hid and buried out of human view? Pshaw! Folly! The best way is to tell the whole truth, and let it by its very presence and eternity crush and burn up all lies. Let it "burn to ashes what it lights to death."

I propose as one of Mr. Lincoln's friends to meet the slumbering facts, deny them where I can, and modify where I cannot absolutely deny them. My judgment, and I appeal to mankind in the future, is that if the matter is talked over *now* the subject will be dropped in a hundred years or *less* from today. My judgment is—poor as it may be—that if these facts are concealed from mankind by his, L.'s, biographers now, they will grow and develop into a huge ever discussed lie, bothering and fretting mankind forever. I know human nature; hide a mouse in a crack, and shade it, it will in the minds of men grow and expand into an elephant. So curious is the human mind. Glut its desires and turn away a perpetual howl. This is my judgment; and I'll risk it during all coming time. I think I know what I am doing. The friends of Mr. Lincoln had better *sift* the questions *now and here* while there are living witnesses on the globe and living friends ready and willing to see and to have fair play.

Mr. Lincoln can stand unstaggeringly up beneath all *necessary* or other truths. Timid men would rob Mr. Lincoln of his crown and cross, and steal the opinions, the philosophy, the reasons of mankind by the robbery of their judgment and logical faculty through a suggestion of falsehood or the suppression of the *necessary* facts of a great man's history.

Please keep these letters safe till I go hence.

Your friend,

W. H. HERNDON.

P.S.   If you will change the program a little of the publication of my lectures, you will see, first, the education of the infant mind and its development; second, external influences—mind and matter in it; third, the analysis of the man's mind; and, fourth, the practical workings of that mind.

HERNDON.

You may show these letters to as many men as you please. The word suspicion does Mr. Arnold injustice. The word is *fear*. Don't publish; anyone may copy, though not to be published.

HERNDON.

Springfield, Ill., November 28, 1866.

Friend Hart.

My dear Sir:

. . . The reason I chose, made, the program of publication that I did was because the analysis of Mr. Lincoln's pure abstract mind *was an absolute necessity.* The second lecture of like, but of inferior necessity—less value, etc., and so in the order of publication. I don't care whether men like this or not, nor whether they like my lectures or not. My day is tomorrow, not today, and to tomorrow I appeal. Men have not my Lincoln record to read, to know, and to study. Hence they do not know what is wise, what is policy, etc., etc., in the necessity included. I rest easy, calm, and cool. It is hard to beat a man when the game stands three and three, if that man has high-low-jack, and the game in his own hands. So I laugh and grow fat when I see men fretting themselves over what I say.

Now you are informed fully of my present plan, as to the five lectures.

Your friend,

W. H. HERNDON.

Springfield, Ill., December 3, 1866.

Mr. Cronyer.

My dear Sir:

Some few days since I wrote you a short note on the question of Mr. Lincoln's religion. I did this at your request, and as so short a letter as that is calculated to convey any idea, or no idea, I propose at your request to state especially what I know of Mr. L.'s religion. I sent you a lecture of mine delivered a week or so since, which I wish you to consider while reading this. You will perceive by that lecture that Mr. Lincoln's mind was shocked, shattered, by Miss Ann Rutledge's death. I told you in my letter that Mr. Lincoln once wrote a work on Infidelity so-called. This was and is true. Mr. Lincoln was told when a boy some *asserted* facts—facts that somewhat disgraced some of his dear relatives. This story clung to him during all his life, a fire shirt, scorching him; he suffered that one suffering till 1835, when his love's death duplicated his suffering. The facts, as I can get them, are that he wrote the book on Infidelity before 1835. But from what I know of Mr. Lincoln, and his double cross, I aver that that book was a burst of despair. The book was a lofty criticism, a high spiritual rationalistic criticism, like, as I understand the various evidences, my own knowledge of Mr. Lincoln included, Bishop Colenso's conclusions. There was no sneer, scoff, or ridicule of the Bible but a noble looking into it, and a charitable telling of his conclusions of its fallibility and plenary inspiration. Lincoln wrote under the idea that God had cursed and crushed him especially. It is possible that he was severer on the Bible than I state. I give you my opinion, and that is mine from what I know of Mr. Lincoln's own ideas [rather] than from what others state. Some men do think that Mr. Lincoln did scoff and sneer at the Bible. This is not so; he had no scoff, nor sneer, for even a sacred error; he had charity for all and everything. God rolled Mr. Lincoln through His fiery furnace *specially*—that he might be His instrument *in the future*. This purifying process gave Mr. Lincoln charity, liberality, kindness, tenderness, toleration, a sublime faith, if you please, in the purposes and ends of his Maker.

Mr. Lincoln, as he has often told the world, had faith in the People and God; he has told you, the People, that Providence rules the universe of matter and substance, mind and spirit. That a law enwraps the universe, and that all things, beings, minds, were moving to their appointed end. Hence Mr. Lincoln could not believe, as a rational man, a logical-minded one too, a very logical-minded one, that the Bible was the *peculiar*, only, and *special* revelation of God, as the theologic Christian world understands it; i.e., as they preach it. He did not believe that a few chosen men were *particularly, specially*, excluding all other men, *inspired*, as the theologic Christian world understands it; i.e., as they preach it. It was *impossible* his mind was so organized for him to see or believe in such doctrines. Mr. Lincoln did not believe in the Miraculous Conception of Jesus, as the theologic Christian world understands that question, subject. I say to you he believed in a universal and an unvarying eternal law of things. He holds this up to you, and flares it always and everywhere in the faces of the people. I say to you that Mr. Lincoln was liberal, tolerant, having charity for all. Mr. Lincoln had no conception of forms, rules, formulas, and technical dogmas in science, law, or religion. He really was deficient in this particular, as I think. Mr. Lincoln could not endure a discussion of such things; he could not read them; he never visited wrangles of this kind.

While all this is true, yet he had a high respect for any man's sacred, liberal, or other opinion; he believed in the absolute necessity of some form of Christianity, and never did, after reflection, attempt to disturb any man's opinion, obtrusively so at least; he loved the *broad* Christian philosophy, maxims, sayings, and moral of Christianity, not because any particular man said them, but because they were and are great, grand leading truths of human consciousness, the highest and loftiest inductions, deductions, if you please, of human reason or intuitions of the human soul.

Mr. Lincoln's mind was severely logical; he did in some moods, I think, doubt immortality; the evidence before me is plain, and to that effect, and yet he generally believed in immortality; his doubts on this question were as follows: he doubted his precise identity, individuality, and earthly consciousness, with all his memories; he has said to me: "That would be a terrible thing." I mean to say he said this substantially, and yet I say he believed, had faith in immortality. This I know is denied by some men here; i.e., some men *think* that Mr. Lincoln thought the soul a mere *spirit* force, a mere *animo-spirit*. I mean by that word a vital force. This is not true, for he himself says to a brother about his dying father, this: "I sincerely hope father may yet recover his health; but at all events tell him to remember to call upon and confide in *one* [1] *great, one good* and merciful Maker, Who will not turn away from him in any extremity. He *notes* the *fall* of a *sparrow*, and *numbers* the hairs of our heads, and He will not forget the dying man, who puts his trust in Him. Say to him that if we could meet now it is doubtful whether it would not be more painful than pleasant, but that if it be his lot to go now he will soon have a *joyous meeting with many loved ones gone before and where the rest of us*, through the help of God, hope ere long to join them. Affectionately,   A. Lincoln."

This letter, the original one written by Mr. L. to his stepbrother John D. Johnston, dated the twelfth, 1851, *is now in my hands*. I copied

---

[1] "The word 'one' should be 'our,' corrected by letter to Mr. Cronyer by letter December 17 or 18—telling him to notify, etc. W. H. H." See reference to this in Herndon's letter to Lamon, February 24, 1869, on p. 59.

the above sentence, all there is on that subject, from the letter, my wife and I comparing.

This letter of Mr. Lincoln's literally read and interpreted proves all I say or nearly so. The *underscored* words are not so italicized in the original. I must be fair. From what I have said, from what Mr. Lincoln has said at various times and places and on various occasions, you *must* not believe all you hear. Mr. Lincoln, in justice to him, never said, while speaking to the loyal colored people of Baltimore, of the Bible or New Testament, this: "But for *that Book* we could *not* know right from wrong."

Mr. Lincoln, in my opinion, according to my recollection, thought all evil *apparent* evil in the end, not absolute evil; he thought pain in this world educative, and he positively denied all punishments as punishment in the future world; if he did not totally and entirely positively deny all such punishment for any purposes or ends. You now have my opinion and best remembrance of Mr. Lincoln's *religion*. I am not afraid that this letter will ever be contradicted. Mr. Lincoln belonged to no church and believed in none. Mr. Lincoln was an intensely sincere and honest man, and as Judge Davis said of him: "When he was convinced on any question, when he believed he was right, he acted, and the terrors of mob opinion had no terrors for him." I quote Judge Davis substantially. I agree to this opinion of Judge Davis, and now do you for an instant suppose, my dear sir, that if Mr. Lincoln was really a converted man to the faith of three Gods, Revelation, Inspiration, Miraculous Conception, and their necessity, etc., as some of the Christian world pretend to believe of Mr. Lincoln, *that he would not have boldly said so and so acted like a deeply sincere man and an honest one fearlessly of that mob furor?* I know what I am saying, I think. I have evidences to support me. This letter is written with some little thought and care, I confess, and it is at your service. Do with it as you please, except its present publication. Read it to as many as you please and allow anyone to take copies or send copies to whom you please.

Truly yours,
W. H. Herndon.

P.S. Mr. Lincoln never to my knowledge repudiated his original little book; he never said he was a universalist, unitarian, rationalist, theist, or what not, and I dare not say what he was technically. I will write you again on Holland, Bateman, and such like men, sayings, and things, will give you a history of Holland's and Bateman's statement, etc., while things are fresh and I am living. Such speeches [as] are recorded in Mr. Carpenter's book, page 199, I deem a farce. Mr. Lincoln was a hypocrite or such things are false.

W. H. HERNDON.

Springfield, Ill., December 11, 1866.

Mr. Carpenter.

My dear Sir:

I duly received your kind, pointed, and excellent letter, dated the 4th *inst.*, and for which please accept my thanks. You interpret me correctly. I am a pre-Raphaelite, i.e., a lover and worshiper of exact truth and nature, and religiously believe they should be followed, the former more than the latter. I think it eminently proper in artists when they are about to embody their thoughts into form, enwrapped in matter, to idealize the *idea*, the *abstract idea*, and so far you and I agree. But when you wish to paint a *thing*, a *scene*, a *man*, then follow nature. Here you and I differ. The difference lies in the *Idea* and the *Thing*. Your letter is manly and honest; and in my estimation you are lifted higher than before it was written. I admire your style of a man; and now let me say a few words in self-defense. I know, did know, Mr. Lincoln well, knew his sorrows and aspirations, his thoughts and history. I know, I feel, that for, say, fifty years God rolled Abraham Lincoln through His fiery furnace. He did it to try Abraham and to purify the man for His purposes. One of the things, the agonies, I shall not name and the other is the death of Ann Rutledge. This purifying process, this fiery birth, made Mr. Lincoln *humble, tender, forbearing, liberal, sympathetic to suffering, kind, sensitive, tolerant; broadening, deepening, and widening his whole nature; making him noble and lovely,* THE NOBLEST AND LOVELIEST CHARACTER SINCE CHRIST. I can and have trailed the child, boy, and man day by day since February 12, 1809. And now shall the world be shut out of this temple of intelligence, prohibited from seeing and knowing what I see and know?

We, America, the people of America, have just passed through the greatest rebellion the world ever saw, *ending in a sublime Revolution.*

The future should know the facts and law of it. They can only know them by being told truthfully what they are. Mr. Lincoln was President, guided the ship of state over the Rebellion that was planned and planted for thirty years to wreck it. His ideas, thoughts, methods, plans, means, and program formed a part of the means, methods, etc., of its suppression. His thoughts shot into acts are his administration. To know the man well by nature, as made by nature, and modified by accidents, surroundings, and conditions, including men, is to know his thoughts, and to a certain extent the causes of them and their motives. Philosophy is marching that way; history will soon follow—so will biography. The tendency, nay, it is a fact that the age moves to a higher and grander individuality, through a higher and grander development of the man. The tendency, nay, it is a visible fact that this individuality, through development, approximates, is ever approximating, to absolute truth. In proportion as this march is made, so dies blind bat-eyed hero worship. We are marching to the worship of Truth, absolute Truth, Right, and Justice.

Three things enter into my ideas: first, self-respect; secondly, respect for the dead; and, thirdly, *the People*. The whole truth will erect the true man's true idea. Shall I suppress or suggest falsehood in order to build up a false ideal that the reading world may worship? I have two plans in view: one is to burn up my Lincoln record—*the finest in the world or ever will be*—or to write the exact truth as I see it. The great, keen, shrewd, boring, patient, philosophic, critical, and remorselessly searching world will find out all things, and bring them to light, and the question is now: who shall do that—a man's friends or his enemies? Shall it be done *now* or left for the future world to wrangle over, and yet forever debate. "Close this door," experience cries. The very existence of Christ is denied because he had no good truthful biographers. You have done much for Mr. Lincoln's memory—and yet I see a blank I would gladly fill. I want, and intend, to have the generous broad and deep sympathies of the universal heart for good and noble Abraham. You see, it will all come right. Trust God and the People.

What I said about Mr. Lincoln is true, and we cannot dodge it. Experience says: "Meet it, and modify the idea that *will grow to be*." My philosophy is to sink a counter nail and blow up my enemies— Lincoln's future traducers—and I do it for him, and the People, who build their philosophy of human history out of human thoughts, acts, and deeds. Other philosophy now is, my friend, a crime. I acknowledge that what I said is calculated to create a twinge of nerve. I have weighed results, fully, fully, and I bide my time. However, what I said is no more than if I had said that Mr. Lincoln was momentarily made crazed by laughing gas taken from a physician, not a fit; and you will live to see the day you will say so.

Mr. Lincoln was the best friend I ever had or expect ever to have, except my wife and mother. I think he is the noblest and loveliest man since Christ—so you perceive that my *motives* are good whatever may be my judgments. I know I shall have to appeal to Time. I cannot argue with a sacred feeling; it is deaf, dumb, blind, and holy. It must argue with itself. Hence, I want time.

We exist in the midst of two civilizations—one in the North and one in the South. The one will try and make Mr. Lincoln a perfect being, a supernatural man, and the other will say he is a devil; and so he will travel down all time misapprehended, not understood—and, pray, whose fault will it be? Lincoln's friends'. The middle man is needed. Hence I have two things in view: first, *sympathy* for Lincoln, and, secondly, solidity for his memory. Appeals will be made to my record. My Lincoln's life is only a *record*. No man can now write an artistic life of Lincoln. Your life—sayings and doings of Lincoln—will outlast all the lives of Lincoln written during this age. *Mark that.*

I am happy to know your portrait of Mr. Lincoln by your friend Halpin is soon to be out. If you know me right well you will know that I speak the truth when I say: I hope you entire success, and I believe you will get it—*catch it.* I shall, my dear sir, let me say *friend,* be happy to see your "proof sheet," and will at your special request study it closely and long "till it does grow." I wish all men working in my line and path well, in fact the whole world well, but I must say especially all who wish to build up for Lincoln a fame, a name, a monument that time will itself consecrate. I will, after having studied your proof impression sufficiently long, give you my poor opinion. You know I am no artist, wish nature had made me so; it has given me a desire without the faculty of use.

I am under many obligations to you for your excellent book, your *Six Months in the White House.* By the by, I do envy you, did you know it? I must be honest. The selections are excellent and made with taste. I hope, I know, you do not *father* all that is said. I hope it "will come safe to hand." If I ever can come to New York I shall call and see you. This I promise you most sacredly. But won't I get lost? And if I do, will you, like a good friend, hunt me up? Come, promise me this as condition precedent.

One other word, you pay me a high compliment in mentioning my analytic lecture, the one you refer to in your book, and for which I thank you. My fourth lecture, as Douglas once said of same event, "set me back." My fourth lecture is a miscellaneous one, and of necessity is in the telling disjointed; its incoherence lies not in the idea but the matter, and so far your criticism is correct. When you come to read L.'s biography and see him more in and about New Salem, book under arm, pale from excess of study, or see him running his compass for points, courses, distances, with an eye ever on bread, you will, I think, lift your criticism from the incoherency to the idea of unity that under-floats the lecture. Have faith and I'll move forward a little again in my fifth lecture, which I shall send you, if I get time to write it out and print it. So, good-by. I hope this will reach you Saturday night in order that you may rise early Sunday morning and finish it by "tea." Will you, my dear friend, excuse me? If you have a wife and little one keep them for me, and I'll do ditto here for you.

Your friend,
W. H. HERNDON.

Springfield, Ill., December 12, 1866.

Mr. Hart.
My dear Sir:

Your kind and charming note, 'mid the incongruous notes of many curses, etc., dated the 10th *inst.* is this instant handed to me, and for which I thank you. I am censured by some who do not and cannot know what I am at. It takes a cool philosophy to bear to be misrepresented and to be misunderstood when one has in his own hands evidence, proofs that would instantly allay all; and from that same censuring throng would come: "God bless you, you are right, go on." I think I can bear it coolly, calmly. Would to God the world knew what I do, and save me the necessity of being the man to open and explain all clear as the noonday sun! Mrs. Lincoln will scold me, poor woman, without knowing I am her friend, determined to put her right before the world for all time. She too has borne her cross, and she shall have justice if I live. Would that I could but talk to you one hour. Mr. and Mrs. Lincoln's marriage was an unfortunate one, and I say to you that what I know and shall tell only ennobles both—that is to say, it will show that Mrs. L. has had cause to suffer, and be almost crazed, while Lincoln self-sacrificed himself rather than to be charged with dishonor. Such a man the world never saw—and never will see again. God bless him— so pure, so tender, so good, so honorable, so noble, so lovely, the very noblest and loveliest man since this orb began to spin. Mrs. Lincoln was shoved through her furnace, but, poor woman, she rebelled! Lincoln suffered as it were by crucifixion for forty-five or fifty years; and that process caused his glory, and yet the world doesn't, it seems, want to know it. You have perceived that I am not a very orthodox Christian and yet I believe that Lincoln was God's chosen one.

As to my lectures, I am to publish the five themselves, as analysis of Mr. L. The remainder of the life will be a record of the facts of L.— his thoughts, acts, etc., etc. This was my first idea, and it remains unchanged. I may, however, modify my plan, scheme, or what not. Can't now tell. Probably I shall publish the analysis this winter, spring, or summer coming. I do love Lincoln and do respect Mrs. Lincoln, and yet I suppose there are men in the world who think, and probably say, that I am actuated by malice, revenge, etc. Let me say to you that Mr. Lincoln did tender me an office, a rich one; but I refused it, because I did not want it. The last letter he ever wrote to me contains this expression: "God bless you, says your friend—A. Lincoln." And I echo back the same to him. Now you have another idea and yet all this must not make me a coward, and a liar.

If you will promise me as a friend and gentleman that you will never reveal to mortal man or woman what I shall write you in reference to a hint in the Arnold letter, and in yours of the 10th *inst.* now before me, and being answered, I'll tell you—conditioned on another fact, that you will burn up the letter. I have told but one other man in the world and made him do as I require of you. I hope you will not take this offensively, for nothing is intended other than what I say.

I fear, suspicion, that I have wounded beyond heal, beyond cure, my good friend Chas. G. Leland. The lecture did it, I suppose, for I have been as kind to him as I know how to be to any man. I appreciate his genius and his character, but if such things must be, so be it. I cannot be a liar, I must be brave, and keep my own self-respect, or sink. I don't propose to do that yet.

By the by, I have had my record of Mr. Lincoln taken to the book bindery. It is bound in excellent heavy leather, spring back, strongly done, etc. The record makes three volumes, each the size of Webster's dictionary on legal cap. It has cost me two years' hard labor with all my advantages, and they were not small. The record costs in money actually paid out $153. The original is at my house, and a copy of the same is bound, and in bank vaults beyond fire. If I should die, the record is safe. It explains all fully, each assertion backed by written vouchers, evidences of good men and women in Kentucky, Indiana, Illinois, and other places, men and women whom I know. I have, say, two hundred or more of L.'s letters, in the record, etc. Pardon me.

Your friend,
W. H. HERNDON.

Springfield, Ill., December 28, 1866.

Friend Hart:

Your kind and encouraging letter, dated the 24th *inst.*, is received, and for which please accept my most sincere thanks. I have not determined absolutely in publishing my five lectures by themselves, am doubtful of the propriety of such a course myself. I will walk cautiously, talk to friends, etc. I am really happy to hear that friend Leland is as ever. Say to him for me: "Leland, success to your new undertaking." I shall be very glad to hear F. W. Smith's statement about the case of Smith & Bros. In reference to collecting Lincoln's letters, speeches, state papers, etc., etc., I have really thought about it and suggested it to Judge Davis, who said: "I'll think about the matter and tell you what to do."

Mr. Lincoln is hard to get at—i.e., it will take so much talk, explanation, etc., to get him properly before the world, that I almost despair. He's a good, great, noble man, the great *unknown* just now. He is the finest character made since the world began to spin—at least one of the very finest. Don't think me crazy.

Now as to what you desire. Mr. Lincoln is a sad, sad, melancholy man. This is so organically, or functionally, caused by conditions, etc. It is partly organic and partly functional caused by conditions. In the first place his grandmother was a halfway prostitute—not a common one, as I understand the facts. I say this is truth, for Mr. Lincoln told me so. Mr. Lincoln's mother was an illegitimate. This is truth, for Mr. L. told me so. As a matter of course Mr. L. knew this. It saddened his own mother, and it saddened Lincoln—sadness more or less has been stamped on him. Again—and what is worse—Mrs. Lincoln, A. Lincoln's mother, *fell*—*fell* in Kentucky about 1805—*fell* when unmarried—*fell* afterward. Thomas Lincoln left Kentucky on that *account;* and for no other as I understand the story. There can be not much doubt of this as I now think, and *yet there is room for mistake.* I am going to Kentucky to search this whole matter to the bottom, and if false I shall scare some wicked men, I assure you. I must get *absolutely* right myself before I dare open. Mr. Lincoln was informed of all this; probably it was thrown up to him in Indiana and—don't know it —have heard so. As a matter of course in so sensitive a soul as Lincoln's it burned its way and left him a withered melancholy man. Good heavens, what a world! Poor, patient, suffering, cross-bearing, sublime Lincoln! Did not God roll him through His furnace? Take all this, and the Ann Rutledge scrape, condition; and you will perceive that Lincoln's work on infidelity—burnt up by friends—was a blast, Job-like, of despair. Now does not melancholy drip from the poor man? Mrs. Lincoln, Lincoln's wife, I think, knew much of this—think Lincoln revealed it to her, and hence in part—*Hell, Hell.* Good Lord, will the world have a wide, a sublime, charity for all! Do you not see Lincoln's Christ-like charity, liberality, toleration, loom up and blossom above all? Who could have survived but Lincoln—the great, good, strong, noble, *God-loved man?* This is no disgrace to Lincoln. He is the creator of the House of Lincoln—the architect of the Lincoln fame, world-wide and eternal. What an honor! Democratic institutions—what a Justice, what a Right, what a Power and Glory they are! Now open your eloquence on the power of the individual man to rise above conditions and of democratic institutions as guardian of fair play in the Eternal Right. I wish I were an inspired man, even an eloquent man, but I am dumb in presence of the sublimity of Right.

Please hide this away or burn it, keep it a dead secret, I think the editors and devils of the Chicago *Times* have the bad side of these facts and intend to flash them on mankind when we are dead and gone. That paper said about eight months since: "Beware, you Lincoln men! I'll

LAW OFFICE
OF
HERNDON & ORENDORFF,

W. H. HERNDON,
A. ORENDORFF.

Springfield, Ill., Mch 17 1869.

Friend Lamon

My Dear Sir:

After consulting with friends in New York — Philad, & at home I have come to the conclusion to make you an offer: it is this — I will take four thousand dolls for my facts — memoranda — manuscripts &c — that is to say their use till you finish your biography. Give me two thousand dolls down & leave the other two thousand dolls in one & two years, drawing 10 per ct per annum from date till paid. I worked three years — did hard work at that — lost time in going to Indiana & other places — Spent about $1800; and lost my office business during the lost time &c — hired a copyist to record what I gathered — hired book binders to bind the volumes &c.

FACSIMILE OF A LETTER TO LAMON

In 1860

*Courtesy of the Henry E.
Huntington Library*

WILLIAM H.
HERNDON

In 1888

*Collection of
Frederick H. Meserve*

spoil your hero." You have now the philosophy of my drifting, my counter minds, etc., etc. When you hear men scolding me, please say to them: "Do you know what you are talking about? Have faith in the only man who knows what to do to hedge, dodge, explain, modify, or deny, etc." Excuse this.

Your friend,
W. H. HERNDON.

Springfield, Ill., January 12, 1867.

Friend Hart.

My dear Sir:

Your kind letter, dated the 7th *inst.*, is just handed to me. I regret to hear of your sickness, but glad you are recovering. Quit handlicks[?], go to play, and cease your wear and tear of soul. No man knows how to reply to what I told you—except this: "It's all a lie"—saving what Lincoln told me. I am going to Kentucky myself and look into the eyes of men and women, watch their features, investigate their motives, inquire into their characters, opportunities, veracity, etc., etc., thoroughly, well, to the bottom and below the bottom, if I can go below. There is some mistake as to identity, or something, and I'll find it out and expose those engaged in it. I am decided on this, cost what it may— even life. I feel that there is a wrong somewhere, but can't tell you now. The Chicago *Times* has got what I tell you and has said: "Beware how you Lincoln worshipers blow your man. We'll sink him." This is true. I never tell you anything that is not ditto. I hated to say what I did of Holland, but he treated me so shabbily that I couldn't help it. I am "cussed" a good deal by men, little things, that can't understand me, and prefer *that* to opening to the world just now my plans. I am the only man in the world who knows how to defend Lincoln and yet I am "cussed" by those who are his friends. I can bear it all and look to *time.* So far as I am concerned I don't care how Lincoln came into the world; the lower he was created, the higher and grander—looking at all things—to me he is. I am a broad, liberal, tolerant man. God bless Abraham anyhow.

When I spoke of making these revelations to the world I did not intend to tell what I write you, only a part of it in very indirect language, by hints, saying that some of the near and dear relatives of L. so acted as to crush the soul of Abraham. This was all. I intended boldly to deny all insinuations not told me by Lincoln, not saying or hinting where I got the information. I will get it all right, so that I can swear to it and then expose all concerned. Have faith. . . .

Your friend,
W. H. HERNDON.

Mrs. Catherine H. Dale is the author of the letter you speak about. I did not see it till published—should rather she had said nothing, letting time make my defense. However, it is all substantially true and correct.

Springfield, Ill., March 2, 1867.

Mr. Hart.

My dear Sir:

. . . You state that many papers are speaking hard of me. So be it. What they do say, good or evil, does not move me in the least. They do not know me, my plans, my motives, etc., and hence all they do say is foolish, or shrewd guesses. If I had all such men in a pen, I could point out to you certain brand marks such as "hero worshiper," "orthodox Christian," "grumblers," "jealousy," etc. What have I done but tell the truth? Why speak hard words of him who loves and tells the truth fearlessly? If truth disturbs our conception of things, falsehood is preferable when it confirms the conception. Do such whiners and complainers expect to stop the genius of investigation in the race of man? Folly! Every important fact of Mr. L. shall be known, come what will. I, my friend, can afford to be misunderstood and abused, have expected it, and do now expect it. No true man ever lived that was not abused. Why should I hope to escape? Hope is folly to me in this matter. I feel this way I tell the truth, love all men, have in my own hands unimpeached and overwhelming evidence of all I shall say or utter. I shall do no man any harm, all men justice, the living and the dead. I shall have truth on my side, justice, and a good conscience. So *"let 'em rant."* My records of Mr. Lincoln shall go down the files of time, if I have to send them to England, Russia, unless confiscated by false men and burned before landing, etc. If the people are misled it shall not come from me, nor my side of the house. I did address someone in Philadelphia a hasty private note, etc., on the Lincoln and Douglas debates, did speak the truth, as I know it to exist.

The letter from this city to the New York *Tribune* some time since was written by a Mr. Townsend of the *Tribune* office, as I understand. The gentleman lectured here, and suppose he wrote the letter—don't know it. People must be hard run "to run up against" an anonymous letter! The letter contains a sentence which surprises you. Mr. Lincoln's own mother was a woman of very strong mind; it was not only strong but it was quick. She was a child of some *high blood rake* in Virginia, not from a common man. When Lincoln spoke to me as he did, he had reference to his mother's *mind*, nothing else, and it was thus I told it. Letter-writers are not particular, catch an idea by halves and then open. It is a fact that Nancy Hanks, Lincoln's mother, was a superior woman in *mind*. There is no doubt of this, and it was of that phase of Mrs. Lincoln that her son spoke to me; and the evidence before me is overwhelming on that special phase. As to morals, that is another question.

Arnold's book is out; have not read it, and therefore can't give you an opinion of it; wish it was good, wish it well, etc. I wish there were a hundred lives of Mr. Lincoln, each excellent, and looking out of different eyes, etc.

Hope you are well before this running, rambling and tedious, as well as uninteresting letter reaches you.

Your friend,
W. H. HERNDON.

Springfield, Ill., December 18, 1867.

Friend Lamon:

Today I send you my three lectures. None was ever published, only stenographed *in part* by friends. The one on Lincoln's patriotism, etc., was never *in any part* published or stenographed, so is new to you. I send other things as promised, more too than promised. Today I send two letters of Lincoln which I forgot to send in the other bundle. Publish them in your biography. The "*Lincoln Shields duel*" will now—after reading what I send you—be plain and clear. Give it fully. Monday I will send you some briefs of Mr. Lincoln on some important suits in the Supreme Court and Sangamon Circuit Court. They are good. No legal speeches ever made by Mr. Lincoln were ever published that I now recollect of; will send if I find out any in my scribbles through old musty papers, speeches, and records; will send you everything I think worthy, etc. With the papers sent today are two little memorandum books. Hold them secret and, secondly, private except to you and "corps" of literary friends. The same with much of the records. Be careful and judicious in all things. I hold myself responsible to you for the truthfulness of my record to the extent that the copies are true, faithful and genuine, made out from the originals. You judge among the conflict of things who tells the truth; I do not guarantee, nor say, nor insist, that every man or woman in that record tells the truth. Reconcile all if you can. Follow your own good judgments.

Your friend,

W. H. HERNDON.

Springfield, Ill., November 27, 1868.

Friend Hart:

I wish to ask of you a favor, and it is this: I want to borrow, say, $8000 on five years' time, interest payable annually, or semi-annually if it *must* be so. I will secure the money by mortgage on three hundred acres of land, free from all incumbrances, land worth per acre $50 or $75, lies five miles from this city and within two miles of the Chicago Alton etc. R.R. I can get money here in *short* time but it don't do me any good. See for me some of your monied men, institutions, trustees, guardians, etc., and ascertain if the money can be had. I am worth $50,000, am farming, raising stock, planting orchards, etc., etc. Please assist me.

Your friend,

W. H. HERNDON.

Ward H. Lamon.

My dear Sir:

When you spoke to me about my records—facts and manuscripts of Mr. Lincoln—I was not prepared to speak. In fact was taken aback. However, I am glad that I could not then speak, because I do not think you know the amount, value, and importance of the records, facts, etc., of Mr. Lincoln's life, got, collected, and transcribed by me. I have been about three years in collecting, comparing, and analyzing the facts of Mr. L.'s life. I have paid for the facts on visits, trips, etc., in Illinois and Indiana and in various counties of both States more than a thousand dollars. The facts and opinions, statements, etc., in reference to Mr. Lincoln have been got from gentlemen and ladies of indubitable veracity in Kentucky, Indiana, and Illinois, not omitting Virginia. My records, facts, etc., are broad, sweeping, and critical, looking at good sides—and bad ones—perfect sides and imperfect ones. I took facts, not fancies. Took truth as my guide, not falsehoods as suggested by hero worshipers or hero haters. I have got the undoubted facts of his boyhood—his infancy included—have got his manhood history as it was acted by Mr. Lincoln. I had advantages over all other men in knowing the facts of Mr. L.'s life—knew where to go, whom to see, what to get out of each woman and man, and what strings to pull. I have got Mr. Lincoln's love letters written to a lady now living in Missouri, written soon after the death of the loved Ann Rutledge. I think, in fact I know, that my records, facts, manuscripts, etc., of Mr. Lincoln are the most perfect on record. He who writes a biography of Mr. Lincoln from my facts writes the only true life of the good and great man that can by any possibility be written now or in the future. There is a fortune in the records, etc., when put in the shape of a biography. I keep the originals at my own *private house* under lock and key. I keep copies put up in bound volumes in the First National Bank for safety. I have three large bound volumes, besides other matter, probably enough to make another smaller volume, say one-half or one-third the size of the larger ones. I have written some four lectures on Mr. Lincoln; some went to Europe, etc., though never fully published, simply stenographed in part; have various notes, memoranda, etc., including some pictures of the customs, habits, etc., of the West, i.e., pen sketches of our people and customs, habits, etc. All these are at your disposal, use, etc., if you and I can come to some conclusions as to terms, etc. I will sell out to you, agreeing to write nothing about Mr. Lincoln for ten years, probably reserving a right to deliver a lecture or two on Mr. Lincoln to our own people here, not elsewhere. Ward, there is fame in this, there is money too, my good friend.

Though this letter is private, you may *show* it to whom you please, nothing further, remember. I shall write to you again, am now busy in court.

Your friend,
W. H. HERNDON.

Springfield, Ill., February 24, 1869.

Mr. Hart.
My dear Friend:

Your very kind letter, dated the 18th *inst.*, is at hand, and for which please accept my thanks. . . . Some few days since a gentleman from Washington came into my office and wished to purchase my manuscripts, notes, memoranda, and facts in relation to Lincoln's life, the contemplated one. I have been gathering facts, etc., for three years; have spent about $1800 in traveling to Indiana, parts of Illinois, etc., gathering up the facts; and I think I may say to you that no man can write a lasting life, a good standard biography of President Lincoln without my memoranda, etc. As you are aware, I had, fortunately, superior advantages over most men in knowing facts and where to go, and to whom to go, etc. Now what I wish is this—give me your opinion, after consulting friends, bookmakers, and sellers among others, as to the value of the memoranda; what a man ought to pay for them or the use of them. Fame and money are the rewards of him who writes a standard biography of President Lincoln.

I may not sell, may finish the life myself, can't tell.

As to a letter from President Lincoln to me or to others, I fear [it] is out of my power to give. I have something which is more sacred. It is his boyhood copybook, arithmetical sum book, etc., the leaves of which I will distribute to my—rather Mr. Lincoln's—friends as soon as I get through with the book. Will never forget you. Excuse.

Your friend,

W. H. HERNDON.

Springfield, Ill., February 24, 1869.

Friend Lamon:

Judge Logan has just handed to me your letter in which you make certain requests, etc. I shall answer it in full as soon as I get time. You may use such parts of my lectures in your book as you please, giving me credit, etc., if you wish. I think I said so to you verbally, and I stick to what I say. I have no confidence in Dennis Hanks, Bill Green, and some others. They may be correct or may not. The other Hanks—John—I believe in, think him a good man and a truthful one, *but does not always know.* He is interested in covering up the general *lechery* of the Hanks and Lincoln family. Mr. Lincoln told me himself that his mother was a bastard, a child of a Virginia nabob. Mr. Lincoln's mother was a Hanks. . . .

I have no promises to anyone but to Miss Owens—you can give her maiden name, though not the married name. As to Bateman, he says I must not publish anything he said. I will send you a letter on Lincoln's religion in a day or so. . . .

Your publisher is—well—well—very anxious for something that will do him, nor you, any good. I have in my opinion sent you all that can do you any good and more than I thought I ever should; *still*, I will send you all the original papers and you can pick out and scan them for yourself.

I withdrew a letter from the Reverend Mr. Conger because there was a mistake in it. Lincoln's letter reads *"our"* and I put it *"one God"* by mistake and hence withdrew the letter.

Your friend,

W. H. HERNDON.

Green is not a liar, but a *blow*, a "hifalutin" exaggerator, etc.,—good clever fellow for all that.

Springfield, Ill., February 26, 1869.

Friend Lamon.

My dear Sir:

Your letter, dated the 23d *inst.*, is this moment handed to me. There is one expression in your letter which I wish to correct, and it is this: I have no biography as yet of Mr. Lincoln, only sketches, manuscripts, lectures, facts, opinions, etc. I wish to correct your idea at the start that I have a biography. I have written some few things for my own pleasure, and the pleasure of my friends, no connected history. My record, manuscripts, facts, etc., come in in their proper place, order, and time. For instance the Virginia facts come first in the record, then the Kentucky facts, then the Indiana facts, then the New Salem facts, and then the Springfield facts—the Illinois facts generally. As I had the facts gathered, I had a clerk to transcribe them in order in a bound volume written on our clerk's paper—say the record is between three and four reams of paper, large size. The biographer has all the facts before him in order in the record before him. All he has to do is to take my records and open them and read, know, analyze, and recombine the facts, etc., etc., and write. That is all he has to do. I think there is perfect order and arrangement. Possibly, *probably*, I had better say that some few facts, papers, are out of order; few, very few if any is out of order, I may say. I'll make the world pay for these records some time. They are the most perfect of any living or any dead man—probably Johnson's biography by Boswell excepted. Since you have mentioned this subject to me I ought to say to you as a friend that I had a proposition once to buy my records, have the same proposition now before me. This much I thought due you and I so state it. If you do not buy, I probably shall finish my biography in a year or so, can do it, wish to do it. Lamon, strange as it may appear to you, let me say: I do not covet fame or wealth! Hence I am in no hurry to complete the biography. I need kicking, scolding, "cussing," etc., in order to make me trot along briskly with head up and tail up, gaily snorting along the great road of life. I should like to see your biography when finished, like to read 'em very much. I guess your facts of Mr. Lincoln since 1860 are full and complete. My facts of Mr. Lincoln from the womb to landing at Washington, "as the gal says," is more so. Lamon, I should prefer to sell out horse, foot, etc., than to do otherwise. I want money, money; still, if you have no money, you can have without money on time making me safe, etc., etc., and paying down some few dimes, so that I can pay my debts. Am in court writing under calls from clients, amidst Edwards's speech before the jury, on a criminal case. How he howls morals and religion—bah!

Your friend,
W. H. Herndon.

Springfield, Ill., March 17, 1869.

Friend Lamon.

My dear Sir:

After consulting with friends in New York, Philadelphia, and at home, I have come to the conclusion to make you an offer; it is this: I will take $4000 for my facts, memoranda, manuscripts, etc., that is to say, *their use* till you finish your biography. Give me $2000 down and secure the other $2000 in one and two years, drawing 10% per annum from date till period. I worked three years—and hard work at that—lost time in going to Indiana and other places, spent about $1800, and lost my office business during the lost time, etc., hired a copyist to record what I gathered, paid bookbinders to bind the volumes, etc. I may say to you that *the records* will be worth $10,000 to you or any man who writes Mr. Lincoln's biography. If you conclude to take them, you may *publish to the world* that you have purchased the use of my records of the great President. This will give you force, give your biography value, etc., etc. Again, I want it understood that no word is to be erased, changed, no leaf torn, no mutilations, no alterations, interlineations, etc., of the records—want them returned to me when you are done with them in the exact order and condition you received them, wear and tear in their careful use only excepted. They shall stand as your witness to the end of time. May I say to you that, since I have been talking, etc., advising, etc., about this business, others will take the records if you do not want them?

Your friend,
W. H. Herndon.

Springfield, Ill., September 17, 1869.

I have this day sold to W. H. Lamon of Washington, D.C., my Lincoln records in three volumes for the consideration of four thousand dollars cash in hand paid. He is now the sole owner and possessor of said records and is empowered and authorized by me to sell, publish, use, or dispose of said records as he wishes or will. Lamon promises to use discretion and good judgment as to what shall be published, sold, or made public at the present time.

W. H. HERNDON.

Springfield, Ill., February 12, 1870.

Friend Hart:

Your note, dated the 8th *inst.*, is this instant handed to me, and in answer to your questions let me say: Mr. J. T. Stuart was Mr. Lincoln's *first* partner—"Stuart & Lincoln." This partnership began in the summer of 1837 and lasted about two years. The next firm of which Mr. Lincoln was a partner was "Logan & Lincoln." Hon. S. T. Logan was Mr. Lincoln's *second* partner. This partnership began about 1840 and ended about 1843. The third firm of which Mr. Lincoln was one was "Lincoln & Herndon." This firm began in 1844 and ended the day Mr. Lincoln died. I am Mr. Lincoln's *third* partner. Mr. Lincoln had no other partners than the above to my knowledge.

Your friend,
W. H. HERNDON.

Springfield, Ill., February 25, 1870.

Friend Lamon:

I have always been averse to the use of my evidence in the world of matter or of man, hate to see my name stuck up . . . in any way, instinctively shrink from publicity, notice, or flattery. But as you demand my information, I shall give you from time to time some facts, some information. I sent you some days since more at the request of Mrs. Armstrong than of myself a short account of what I had to say on Lincoln's "house divided against itself" speech, should not have sent it for the same reason that I have refused, failed to say more, write more to you, namely, I do not wish to be considered a blow, boast, or fool who wishes to be noticed, etc., etc. In answer to your various queries, let me say: First, you say some of my notes are interpolated, etc. Sometimes I did this for various reasons. I had some of the papers with me in Indiana and thought I might lose them, and hence I stated things to avoid the consequence of the loss, that is, I didn't want people to know everything, *nor the exact truth at all times*. Secondly, sometimes, as it is with all men, I believed one way and, when I heard further *evidence, believed another way*. In the matter of Lincoln's legitimacy, at one time I thought the world lied in him when it stated that he was a bastard. On further investigation, I now and have for years believed him the son of Enloe. My opinions are formed from the evidence *before you*, and *in a thousand other things*, some of which I heard from Lincoln, others are inferences springing from his acts, from what he said, and from what *he didn't* say. In the first place, Lincoln himself told me that his mother was a bastard, that she was an intellectual woman, a heroic woman, that his mind he got from his mother, etc. This was told me about 1852, three miles west of this city on our way to court in Petersburg, Menard County, and State of Illinois; he told me about Dennis Hanks's bastardy. He told me that his relations were *lascivious, lecherous*, not to be trusted. Again, it is a fact that Thomas Lincoln had children when in Kentucky, and when he went to Indiana he had none, ceased to have any. If you remember, Mr. Thomas Lincoln courted his *second wife* when a girl, that she rejected him, that she subsequently married another man, that Thomas Lincoln married—both Lincoln's mother and Lincoln's step mother by their husbands had children—that Lincoln's second *wife was prolific* when her husband lived, that in the prime of life she married Thomas Lincoln and ceased suddenly to be prolific when she was so with her first husband. *It is true* that Thomas Lincoln had a fight with Enloe, as said, because he caught Enloe with his wife. *It is true* that Lincoln left Kentucky and why, I was informed, to take her away from Enloe and general surrounding bad influences. I may not have recorded this, but I have been told so and it looks to me to be proven forever true. *It is true* that Lincoln was incapable of getting a child; *because he had the mumps, etc.* Lincoln was in Indiana in 1844, I think—your records will tell you when—and that he put up no tombstone to his mother's grave; and I forget whether he ever went to see her grave. *Your records will state the truth exactly.* For these reasons and for others floating in my mind I am convinced that the weight of evidence is that Mr. Lincoln was an illegitimate. *The evidence is not conclusive,* but men have been hung on less evidence. From what Lincoln has casually and indirectly said, I was convinced that his illegitimacy was thrown up to him when a boy. I *think* he was told of the fight between his father and Enloe, *and the cause of it.* I got this as I remember it in casual conversations in Indiana. I did not reduce everything to writing, not at that time deeming it of importance. Now I know better. I left out nothing important to the understanding of Lincoln, *standing by himself.* That is all right. As to Mr. Lincoln's melancholy, it is partly organic and partly historic. Mr. Lincoln was of a low physical organization, good digestion, slow circulation, slow functions, blood not hot, not impulsive, cold flesh, liver had no action, bowels slow, sometimes feverish, sometimes cold, *had not a strong life but a tenacious one,* would have lived a hundred years, had no haste, no impulses, had no wear and tear of cellular tissue, muscle, or nerve. He took life easy, had no haste, no spontaneous emotion, no impulse, *was sympathetic and emotional in presence of the object.* I know Lincoln better than I know myself. He was so good and so odd a man, how in the hell could I help study him! Mr. Lincoln's poverty, a curse of his origin, the origin and chastity of his near and dear relations, his father's cold and inhuman treatment of him sometimes, the death of Ann Rutledge, his intense ambition, and society not energetically recognizing his greatness, etc., etc., intensified his organic melancholy.

One word here about his intense popularity in Menard County in 1834. He was popular in that county, because for a local reason. He advocated a canal from the Sangamon River some few miles below Petersburg down the bluffs—being lower there than near the Illinois River, to Beardstown—thus putting New Salem and Beardstown in nearer contact. See his letter copied in your records. This gave Lincoln a popularity not otherwise got. I have no time to be more particular, can't write a history. When I am wrong, your records will correct me. I appeal to them, putting my own remembrance of things alongside.

As to Mr. Lincoln's religious views, *he was in short an infidel,* was a universalist, was a unitarian, a theist. He did not believe that Jesus was God nor the son of God, etc., was a fatalist, denied the freedom of the will, wrote a book in 1834 or 5—*just after the death of Ann Rutledge,* as I remember the facts *as to time.* He then became more melancholy, a little crazed, etc.; [he] was always skeptical, read Volney in New Salem and other books. Samuel Hill of Menard was the man who burned up Lincoln's little infidel book. Lincoln told me a thousand times that he did not believe that the Bible, etc., were revelations of God, as the Christian world contends, etc. Will send you a printed letter soon on this subject. You have Mr. Hill's statement as well as Bale's, which see. See A. Y. Ellis and J. H. Matheny's testimony in your possession. The points that Mr. Lincoln tried to demonstrate are, first, that the Bible was not God's revelations ; and, secondly, that Jesus was not the son of God. I assert this on my own knowledge and on my own veracity, honor, or what not. Your own father-in-law, Mr. J. T. Stuart, James H. Matheny, etc., etc., will tell you the truth. I say they will confirm what I say, with this exception : they will all make it blacker than I remember it. Joshua F. Speed of Louisville, I think, will tell you the same thing. I think the book of Lincoln was written in *1834 or 5, just after the death of Ann Rutledge—I know it was after that sad event.*

I never completed my fifth lecture, was and am too lazy ; the notes of it, etc., now lie in my drawer. If you discover any grammatical errors, etc., in my lectures which you wish to quote, correct them, as I paid no close attention *to the papers* when I delivered them, was hurried when I penned them. A lawyer can't scarcely snatch time to eat, as you well know. The wonder is that I could get time to think about anything except—*whisky.* You can have my draft, etc., etc., of the fifth Lincoln lecture. You will find much loose evidence in the records as to Mr. Lincoln's boyhood and life. You must weigh the evidence as a lawyer does. It has been weighed by me and you can have the benefit of it if you will ask me for it, putting your questions sharp and close, and clean.

I cannot frame a genealogical tree of the Lincoln family for three generations, other than you find in your records.

What I stated to Arnold was and is true. Mr. Lincoln loved Ann Rutledge to his death, no mistake. He next courted Miss Owens, and next Mary Todd, and while so doing he lit on Miss Edwards's face. Lincoln never loved, i.e., dearly loved, his "Mary"—he was engaged to her when Miss Edwards ran across his path. His vow to Ann Rutledge's love and death, his promise to his Mary and their engagement, and Miss Edwards flitting across the path, etc., made Lincoln crazy the *second time*—see Judge Logan's (in a little book I last sent you), see Stuart's, Miss Edwards's, and other testimony in your records. *You must read over and over again the records.* If anything is proved, what I say to Arnold is proved. I know many if not all the facts myself. Lincoln, Speed, and I slept together for two or three years, i.e., slept in the same home, I being Speed's clerk; and Lincoln sleeping with Speed. I have heard Lincoln talk about the matter, and from what I know and from what I have been told by others in whom I have implicit confidence and trust, I say, if what I told Arnold is not proved, *nothing can be proved.* You may reduce the elements of causation this way: say that Lincoln's honor was pledged to Miss Todd, that he saw and loved another woman, Miss Edwards, and that he desired to break away from Miss Todd and to join Miss Edwards, and that the struggle caused the second crazed spells, and yet—I know that the Ann Rutledge element entered as strong as any element. His vow to her or her memory, etc., was as strong as his honor at any other time. Do you see? Read over your records again and again. It will save you much trouble and me too. The two suppositions of which you speak are not [undeciphered]. Co-existing, do co-exist nevertheless. The second insanity springs from his old love of Ann Rutledge. His engagements with his "sweet Mary," and his determination to break that engagement off, and to marry Miss Edwards if he could, I repeat, was the cause of his second insanity. These facts do co-exist and were the sole cause of his second insanity. I hate to differ from you, but I can't avoid it, nor see the difficulty you do. Excuse me. Read your records closely again and again.

The stars in Judge Davis's evidence were put there by my clerk, who could not read my handwriting, and so was left to fill up, which I forgot to do. That is all of that and no more nor no less.

In the matter of the genealogy, etc., character, etc., chastity, etc., of the Hanks-Lincoln-Sparrow family, I am satisfied that John Hanks, nor Dennis Hanks, know much about it——upon the same principle that I don't know anything of my relations' chastity, etc., because it is kept a secret from me. I am the last man in the world that knows the bad phases of my relations. They may play with their hats, and I am the last man in the world to know it. Again, John and Dennis Hanks were very young when they left Kentucky and Indiana especially. John Hanks would state the exact truth—*if he knew it.* Dennis Hanks would go a mile out of his way to lie. Bill Green is a good man but a *blow*— an *exaggerator.* In his dealings, etc., he is called "*Slippery Bill.*" All this is true and yet I like the man. I do not now remember anyone whom I would necessarily suspect, and yet I did watch all, criticized all, weighed all, which I want you to do toward me. Simply give me a fair chance to put myself right on the record.

The Sparrows and Hankses did immigrate into Kentucky together from Virginia, but the Sparrows did not come to Indiana, except on a visit, if that much—Dennis Hanks to the contrary notwithstanding. I think he says that the Sparrows came to Indiana. The Sparrows may have come from England, but God knows wherefrom—not John nor Dennis Hanks. *I doubt the whole biographical genealogy of the Lincoln family, etc.* The Sparrows did come from Virginia to Kentucky.

I have no fuller copy of the Book of Chronicles than you have got in your record. It is not complete, but I did the best I could to get it full.

As to the Lincoln poem on suicide I found out from Speed that it was written 1838, and I hunted up the *Journal* and found where the poem was, what day published, etc., etc., but someone had cut it out—supposed to be Lincoln. I could never find another copy, and so there is an end of that.

The *Trailor* case is: a man was supposed to be murdered here; two men, the Trailors, swore they saw the man killed—were parties to it, implicated Archibald Trailor, their brother, gave their evidences in open court, told when it was done, when and how, where body carried and thrown in a mill pond, went there, found buggy tracks, found hair. The two Trailors were found with the murdered man's money, some of it. To be short, the murdered man came to light, was living, had a crazy fit, ran off, was heard from, brought to this city, saved Arch Trailor's neck. There were strong corroborating circumstances that the man was murdered, etc. Lincoln worked out the facts, testimony, etc., etc., and sent it to Quincy in 1856, I think, to a man by the name of Jonas, a lawyer in Quincy who said he wanted it to publish, etc., which, as I remember, was done. Sent several times to Quincy to get it but could never get it. If I ever go to Quincy, I'll get if I can.

I guess no one remembers the exact language of the Thomas castigation. Logan can give you the substance. Write to him, and he'll send to you.

I do not remember the Dunlap temperance story just now as you put it. Copy it and send it to me and I'll answer. Don't remember any particular thing about the Wright trial spoken of by Grigsby as you put it. I remember the Webber story, remember the Wright trial; copy and send to me and let me see what you mean. I'll answer. I'll get Bill Jayne's statement in full and send to you. As to Lincoln's honesty, I doubt whether anyone knows anything against it. I guess it was a misunderstanding. I know Lincoln was intensely honest, have seen him tried so often and always true, that *I would rather doubt any man's . . . than to doubt Lincoln's honesty.* This is my own opinion.

As to Bateman's sayings about Lincoln's religion, it is all bosh. I'll send you a printed letter soon on that subject. Holland's account of Lincoln's religion was partly taken from Bateman. I don't think that Bateman told all that Holland says that Bateman says, etc. Wait patiently, and I'll send, etc.

Lincoln told me whom he had written to on the subject of his Cabinet, but forget the names. As I remembered, two lived in the North and two in the South. Don't remember the others, etc. I'll think this over and send you what I recollect—bad memory on names. . . .

From the facts before me Mr. Lincoln as early as 1830 began to dream of a destiny. I think it grew and developed and bloomed into beauty, etc., in the year *1840 exactly.* Mr. Lincoln in that year was appointed general elector for this State. Mr. Lincoln told me that his ideas of something burst in him in 1840. He was flattered in 1833, 4, and 5 by Offutt and others in New Salem—see your records—and made to believe that he would be a great man and *he dreamed of it* then, as he told me—always delicately and indirectly. My remembrance is that it was the year 1840 when he commenced to have a State reputation. This was the exact time that his convictions developed into a religious fervor. He always had a conviction more or less of ruin. This sprang from his physical organization, as I think, and yet it grew in him all his life—so he told me, often spoke of it to me in my office and on the circuit when we traveled together.

I am not limited in my information further than Miss Owens and Bateman, who put me on honor and under privacy. Bateman lied to Holland as Holland lies in his biography of Lincoln. You know this as well as I do. If Lincoln were living he would think that Bateman did him more injustice than the living and the dead combined. He scorned the idea that God scorned, even by a shadow, a lovely daughter of His own.

You are at perfect liberty to use any and all parts of my lectures or

Isaac N. Arnold
Collection of
Harry MacNeill Bland

HERNDON'S
CORRESPONDENTS

Charles H. Hart
Collection of
Harry MacNeill Bland

ABRAHAM LINCOLN
From a Photograph by W. J. Thompson (1858)

letters in your biography of Lincoln that suit you—only excepting some of my private notes to you. Try and not hurt the feelings of anyone, if you please, and in using my lectures and letters give me credit, if you wish; and otherwise if you wish. Suit yourself on that question.

I have now answered in a running and rambling way all your questions, and as I am tired out I'll say no more. Will write you again. Do you think you and Black and friends can *translate* this? I have not corrected it and wouldn't for ten dollars and wouldn't write it for $50. You know I am spontaneous, quick, off-handed, right and ready, and hate a quill—hate the mechanics of "the pen, like hell—so I do." Correct errors. Give Reverend Black my best respects, etc.

Your friend,
W. H. HERNDON.

Had you better come out to Illinois, bringing your records and making notes, questions, etc., in writing before starting? I hate to write so terrible. Possibly I might come to Washington in May. Keep all my letters, etc.

W. H. HERNDON.

. . . See Holland's life of Lincoln, pages 236–40—all false.

Springfield, Ill., March 6, 1870.

Friend Lamon:

I have sent you several things, letters, etc., which may be of more or less value to you. I hope they may assist you some in your biography of Lincoln. As to Lincoln's legitimacy, I do not wish you to understand that I assert that he was illegitimate. What I mean to say is this: It is my opinion that the weight of the evidence tends, strongly tends, to prove that he was an illegitimate. That preponderance of evidence, as I think, has led my mind to the affirmative. It appears from your records that one *Haycraft*, clerk of the circuit court of Hardin County (in Elizabeth), Kentucky, wrote to Mr. Lincoln about his mother, evidently to find out some facts. Mr. Lincoln, I say, as appears from your records, answered the letter, saying in substance that *"you are mistaken in my mother."* Mr. Lincoln does not state wherein the man was mistaken, gives no light. I regret that Lincoln did not state wherein the man was mistaken. Prentice got up some evidence on this question in 1860, and the rumor thereof reached here, and I was told all the particulars as early as 1861 or 1862 as I now recollect. Human memory is uncertain and it is possible that somewhat of my ideas and opinions is made up of rumor and rumor alone. I state this to you to put you on your guard as to what I say, and what all men say. Much of the matter is ten years old, and watch all men, weigh well what is said, search for opportunities, casts of mind, education, and veracities. Follow no man simply because he says *so and so.* Follow your records, sharply criticizing as you go. When I was around taking evidence soon after and long after Mr. Lincoln's death, *much, much* was told me which I did not reduce to writing, but which, *much of which,* floats about in my memory. Time may have modified, altered, or changed what was told me. I rejected much which was told me, because what was told me was contrary to what I knew, contrary to my records, and contrary to nature; still, I now wish I had written it out to show the follies, prejudices, errors, and falsehoods, the foundations of all human history.

I used to believe in the substantial history of the world, to believe in the truthfulness of biography, but since I knew Lincoln and read and hear the multitudinous follies, prejudices, errors, falsehoods, I doubt all, nay, reject all. I am sorry for this, but I can't help it. When I was a student of history, as well as of biography, I only doubted—*slightly doubted.* I then made a resolve that I would, if ever opportunity offered, write out a truthful history or biography of the man, mental, moral, religious, etc., analytically, as well as otherwise, so that the reader would have a full view of the whole subject, thus enabling the student and reader to judge more correctly than if he only saw a part of the subject. This idea grew on me as I got older and doubted more the older I grew. To fulfill this original idea fully and completely, as I had now a good man, a good subject with fair opportunities, *I determined* to get up a complete record of Lincoln, so far as it was in my power to do. I threw off, so far as I could, all preconceived opinions and prejudices, all friendships or enmities, everything that clouded my vision. I was determined, at one time, to write out Mr. Lincoln's history—biography rather—cost me what it would: loss of money, loss of friendship, or loss of everything but honor. Pecuniary circumstances over which I had no control compelled me to sell my records to you. When I was getting up the records, people tried to induce me *to state only what Mr. Lincoln was* and not what *he was not.* I kept on in pursuit of my original idea, determined to give the world light, if I could. I think that to state only what a man *was* only presents half the man, and to get the whole it was necessary to state what *he was not*. The first part of this proposition showing what he did and why he did it, and the second showing what he *did not* and the reasons why. I thought that all the man, his positive side and his negative side, should be known. Hence the records which you have are as they are—both sides fully represented, as I think. I am satisfied that I was correct, and yet correct, still correct, in other words.

Mr. Lincoln was my good friend, well tried and true. I was and am his friend. While this is true, I was under an obligation to be true to the world of readers—living and to live during all coming time—as long as Lincoln's memory lived in this world. Lincoln rose over so many disadvantages that he seems to me a hero, having lived a grand good life. Such a life shoots faith and hope deep into the souls of the young aspiring men of this land. Seeing Lincoln, as I see him, he is a grand character. I see him in my mind from his cradle to his grave, and I say Lincoln's life seems a grand march over the forces and resistances of nature and man. Do not think me a hero worshiper. I know so much of Lincoln's trials and troubles and difficulties that I see and feel them all as my own—so closely do they touch me and my good dead friend.

Now in writing your biography, I wish to say one word more, and it is this: You state in one of your letters to me that you suppose that I am under obligations of secrecy to many persons. To a certain extent I am, as I suppose. I wrote you and gave you the names of such persons as I had pledged a secrecy. I do not remember others just now. Possibly Leonard Swett says something in his evidence about this secrecy. Probably it was in his letter coming with his evidence. Probably I am under obligations to others. Do I understand you as saying that in your biography of Lincoln you intended to use the names of all persons giving this or that particular or general information? For instance, Mrs. Lincoln, Miss Edwards, and others gave me information. Do you intend to give up their names as authorities of this or that assertion? If this is your plan, I think it is wrong. Assert it somewhat this way: From the evidence before me, this seems to be true. Or: it is true by my records, Herndon's records, or in any way so as to avoid giving the names of men and women for every assertion. You are at perfect liberty to give up my name and quote me as often as you see proper. I think I state nothing but what is true, at least, nothing that I do not believe to be true. If I err it is in favor of Lincoln as I verily believe, because I am prejudiced a little in his favor. In fact I was accused of being partial toward Mr. Lincoln when I promised in my lectures or publicly that I would strip myself of all prejudice. I was likewise said by Mr. Lincoln's friends—mere blind hero worshipers—to be prejudiced against him. I felt then that I was correct, quite correct; and feel so yet. Would it not be better, friend Lamon, not to refer to any name except such as you get the absolute consent of? Write, say, to Stuart, Swett, Speed, and all other men and women, and ask them if their names may not be used as authority.

Again, would it not do to say in your Preface or Introduction or what not, to state that you have records, etc., and if any men doubt, if any women doubt, let them come to you and convince themselves of the fact and truthfulness of what you say? I am afraid that the giving up names will blow this social American world wide open. What say you? What think you? Be cautious, be wisely discreet, be prudent and shrewd. Let us create no ill feeling or severe criticism from a morbid press eager to say something.

If you will send me the proof sheets of your Biography early and long before you are ready to issue it, I will give you all the assistance I can in the world of *fact* and the world of *opinion* and in the world of *prudence*. As to other things you are better judges, you and friends, than I am. You had better be in no very great hurry in finally issuing your book. Hard times will cut a material figure in its sale, as I see it. You are the better judge, however, of this than I am. . . .

> Your friend,
> W. H. HERNDON.

Springfield, Ill., March 6, 1870.

Friend Lamon:

Once Lincoln got kicked at a mill and knocked crazy. Mr. Lincoln told me this: that he had to shell the corn with his hands and take it to mill on horseback, corn in one end and rocks in the other; that he went to mill on his father's old mare; that he "*had to wait his turn to grind*"; that it was getting late in the evening, he then being some two (2) miles from home, not fifty, as stated by Holland; that he hitched in his old mare to the sweep-pole or lever that turned the wheel, and Lincoln, being in a great hurry to get through with his grist, urged up the old mare to her full speed, round and round, round and round and faster and faster; that he thought she ought to go faster and that he struck her, with a stick, saying at the same time, or *intended rather to say:* "Get up—you lazy old devil," and just as he struck her and got to the words which *were uttered:* "Get up—" the old mare protested with her heels on Lincoln's head against such treatment. Lincoln just as he had uttered: "Get up," was kicked, knocked crazy, was picked up, carried home, came *to* that night, say about twelve o'clock, and that, upon coming to consciousness, Lincoln finished the sentence: "you lazy old devil." He finished the sentence just as he intended to speak it, commencing where he left off. Lincoln told me this; and he and I used to speculate on it. The first question was: why was not the whole expression uttered; and the second one: why finish at all? We came to the conclusion—I being somewhat of a psychologist as well as physiologist—he aiding me and I him, that the mental energy, force, had been flashed by the will on the nerves and thence on the muscles and that that energy, force, or power had *fixed* the muscles in the exact shape, or form, or attitude, or position, to utter those words; that the kick *shocked* him, *checked* momentarily the action of the muscles; and that so soon as that check was removed or counteracted by a returning flow of life and energy, force, and power in their proper channels, that the muscles fired off, as it were functioned as the nervous energy flashed there by the will through the nerves—acted automatically under a power in repose. This seemed to us to be the legitimate conclusion of things.

Let me say a word or two about Lincoln's mother and Lincoln's opinion of her. As I told you before, Mr. Lincoln openly and candidly and sincerely told me that his mother *was a bastard.* The exact idea that suggested the thought to tell what was told me by Lincoln was this: Lincoln and I had a case in the Menard circuit court *which required a discussion on hereditary qualities of mind, natures, etc.* Lincoln's mind was dwelling on his case, mine on something else. Lincoln all at once said: "Billy, I'll tell you something, but keep it a secret while I live. My mother was a bastard, was the daughter of a nobleman so called of Virginia. My mother's mother was poor and credulous, etc., and she was shamefully taken advantage of by the man. My mother inherited his qualities and I hers. All that I am or hope ever to be I get from my mother, God bless her. Did you never notice that bastards are generally smarter, shrewder, and more intellectual than others? Is it because it is stolen?" This is a substantial statement made to me by Lincoln just on a hot overlapping spring creek on the road to Petersburg two and a half miles west of this city about 1851 and about which there is nor can be any material mistake and in these last expressions I have sometimes thought that Lincoln intended to include himself. I do not assert this to be so: it only *seems so*, by a loose intendment made by me, a loose impression made by me. The manner of Lincoln I never shall forget—nor what was said, nor the place, whatever may become of time.

There is much in Holland's life of Lincoln which is true, as I gave him much, though he did not record what I said correctly. . . . I doubt the Parson Elkin story, that part which says that Lincoln wrote to the parson. Lincoln was about eight years old, lived in a wilderness, had no paper, as always, at hand, no ink, etc. Think the story came from Dennis Hanks. . . . Mrs. Lincoln died—as said by some with the milk sickness, some with a galloping quick consumption. Lincoln's readings are exaggerated in Holland. . . . Lincoln didn't read the Bible much if any, didn't read Henry Clay's life by Prentice in 1830, nor 28–9; because it was not then printed, as I remember. It came here about 1833, when Lincoln read it, if ever. Look up the matter. Lincoln borrowed of Mr. Crawford, Weems's *Washington* and not Ramsey's *Washington*. Is there such a life of Washington as Ramsey's life? I know that Ramsey wrote a history of the United States, but did he write Washington's life? Look into this. It is said that Lincoln read Plutarch's *Lives*. This is not so. The boat story as told by Holland is untrue. Lincoln never tried to build a boat for himself nor his father to carry off the extra products of the Lincoln farm. Pshaw, the idea is ridiculous! If the Lincoln family got enough to eat on a few acres of ground tilled by Thomas Lincoln and "Abe," they should have thanked God and taken courage. I doubt the dollar story therefore. . . . The dollars part may have happened or taken place at some other time and place and yet I doubt. Holland tells many things in the first, second, third, and fourth chapters which are true. I was told them by Lincoln and I told Holland; will read Holland and pick out what I know to be true as I learned them from Lincoln and others.

Be it remembered that I have walked over the Lincoln farm, saw everybody, etc., in Indiana, and know whereof I speak. . . .

Mr. Holland makes Mr. Lincoln dream of his destiny about 1837; mistake, it was in 1840. . . . Holland exaggerates Lincoln's popularity. . . . I gave you the true version in one of my letters to you. Holland tells a story about Lincoln's honesty as postmaster. . . . This is substantially so; think I was present at the time or heard it directly after it happened. Lincoln and I were going to Petersburg in 1850, I think. The political world was dead, the compromise of 1850 seemed to settle the Negroes' fate, etc. Things seemed to be stagnant and all hope for progress in the line of progress, etc., freedom, etc., seemed to be crushed out. Lincoln was speculating with me about the deadness and despair of things and deeply regretting that his human strength and power were limited by his nature to rouse and stir up the world. He said gloomily, despairing, sadly: "How hard, oh, how hard it is to die and leave one's country no better than if one had never lived for it! The world is dead to hope, deaf to its own death struggle made known by a universal cry. What is to be done? Is anything to be done? Who can do anything and how can it be done? Did you ever think of these things?" . . .

Holland has got a part of this. . . . The fight of Lincoln, his offer to defend Col. E. D. Baker, and what he said on that occasion is true to the letter. . . .

I think none of all these things are in your record and yet I know them to be true, as stated herein substantially. Your record will complete what is incomplete. I did not record many things that I knew to be true, because they were familiar to me, and I knew I could draw on my memory if I should attempt to write the biography of Lincoln. . . . What I meant to say about the Lincoln genealogical tree was that, so far as my investigation of witness in this matter, I failed to be satisfied through such investigation. Lincoln's biographies make it plain, and yet I could find myself no human testimony proving and clinching beyond doubt the truthfulness of the genealogy of Lincoln. . . .

Some few days, probably on the day he received an invitation to deliver his Cooper Institute speech, he came into the office and looked much pleased, not to say tickled. He said to me: "Billy, I am invited or solicited to deliver a lecture in New York. Should I go?" "By all means," I replied, "and it is a good opening too." "If you were in my fix, what subject would you choose?" said Lincoln. "Why, a political one, that's your forte," I said to Lincoln. Mr. Lincoln had some year or two before this delivered a lecture here, at Jacksonville and other places, and it was so poor that it was a failure, utter failure. I heard it. Mr. Lincoln had not the fire, taste, reading, eloquence, etc., which would make him a lecturer, had no imagination, no fancy, no taste, no emotion, and no readings in that peculiar line, and hence I advised him as I did. He would, in the absence of a friend's opinion, as soon take up the Beautiful as any other subject for a lecture when he had no sense of it. Lincoln had poor judgments of the fitness and appropriateness of things. He would wade into a ballroom and speak aloud to some friend: "How clean these women look!" Mr. Lincoln was a curious being; he had an idea that he was equal to, if not superior to, all things; thought he was fit and skilled in all things, master of all things, and graceful in all things. Lincoln had not good judgments; he had no sense of the fitness, appropriateness, harmony, of things. This nature forced itself on my observation and I could not avoid reflections and conclusions and the most of these I think you have in my lectures, etc., etc. Mr. Lincoln was a strong man, a good man, an honest man, a tender man, full of the integrity of human purposes, had a tenacity of purpose, a persistency and continuity of thought, the equal to which I never witnessed, and never expect to see.

But about the Cooper Institute lecture. I advised Mr. Lincoln to go by all means and to lecture on politics. I told Mr. Lincoln I thought it would help open the way to the Presidency, thought I could see the meaning of the move by the New York men, *thought* it was a move against Seward, thought Greeley had something to do with it, think so yet, *have no evidence*. The result you know. Mr. Lincoln's Cooper Institute speech was a profound one, as I think.

In one of my letters to you I said substantially that it did Mr. Lincoln's soul good to hear censure, condemnation, etc., and this is true when that censure, condemnation, etc., were directed to his *equal and rival*—the great who were struggling for the things, offices, etc., that Lincoln had his eyes on, his hopes on, and his soul. As to little men, or great men who did not "run counter" to Lincoln's ambition, he was pensive, indifferent, etc., saying by act: "Go it, husband—go it, bear."

Let what I say here modify what I said in my former letter. I write by snatches and *"ketches"* in court, during court hours, being disturbed by this man and that, etc., for this purpose and that, etc., etc.

Religion Again

James H. Matheny tells me that from about 1854 to 1860 Lincoln played a sharp game here on the religious world, that Lincoln knew that he was to be a great man, was a rising man, was looking to the Presidency, etc., and well knowing that the old infidel, if not atheistic, charge would be made and proved against him, and to avoid the disgrace, odium, and unpopularity of it, trampled on the Christian toes, saying: "Come and convert me." The elders, lower and higher members of the churches, including ministers, etc., flocked around him and that he appeared openly to the world as a seeker; that it was noised about that Lincoln was a seeker after salvation, etc., in the Lord; that letters were written more or less all over the land that Lincoln was soon to be a changed man, etc., and thus it was he used the Reverend James Smith of Scotland, old man Bergen, and others. I have often thought that there was something in this, but can't affirm it to be so. This is Matheny's honest opinion, and no man is superior to Matheny's judgments, etc., of human nature, actions, and motives, etc. He knew Lincoln as well as I did, I think. One thing is true: that the said Reverend Dr. Smith of Scotland presented Lincoln with a book written by said doctor; Lincoln brought it to the office, laid it down, never took it up again to my knowledge, never condescended to write his name in it, never spoke of it to me. Never let me know much about his religious aspirations from 1854 to 1860 in the above line, always appeared different, that scorning all Christian views. It is said by someone here that Lincoln told him that he was about converted, but that man—I do not know and can't find out—is said to be a blab, etc. I do not think that Mr. Lincoln was a hypocrite and yet I know he scarcely trusted any man with his more profound secrets. I had to read them in his facts, acts, hints, face, *as well as what he did not do nor say*, however absurd this last expression may appear to be. Mr. Lincoln was a secretive man, had great ambition, profound policies, deep prudences, etc., was retired, contemplative, abstract, as well as *abstracted*. Lincoln was about as shrewd a man as this world ever had and yet he was honest, fair, and manly, incapable of falsehood, of base deception, or of fraud, as I think. But you shall have all opinions and all sides and all facts and acts that I can find, and when you have all these you can judge for yourself.

I send you the Reverend Dr. Smith's letter from Scotland, giving me "*goss.*" I send the Chicago *Tribune's* article on the Ann Rutledge lecture. It says that the Ann Rutledge lecture is exploded, gone to the dogs, was imprudent, etc. When that Ann Rutledge lecture shall be exploded, the substantial facts of it, then Lincoln's name and memory will explode with it. You have the facts of it, the most of them in your record. You can see for yourself and you must judge for yourself. Smith's letter is simply folly, bombast, etc., and what he says of Lincoln's religion, the Bible, etc., means nothing. It is too general in its expression; he might say the same things of me speaking generally, and yet it wouldn't express my ideas at all, nor my philosophy, nor my religion. I believe that the Bible is the revelation of God, and that Jesus was the son of God, and so do I believe that the Declaration of Independence is the revelation of God and George Washington, a son of God. I can talk a week to technical Christians and they will assume that I mean so and so when I don't mean *so and so*. Glittering generalities won't do. I believe in miracles, think a man is a miracle and God's grandest miracle, believe in miraculous conception, think your conception was a miraculous one. Glittering generalities won't do. Read my letter to Smith and notice the questions closely. Then read Smith's letter to me and watch the answers closely and you will see that he answered no question. About miraculous conception, etc., he said no word. In fact he made no specific answer to anything. He knew I would prove him false if he should be precise, so he dealt in generalities. I could not answer Smith at the time of his letter, first, because I was engaged in more important things; and, second, I would have to drag Mrs. Lincoln into the field, because Smith took refuge under her, fought from behind her; and, third, because I should be compelled to say something of Smith's morals, temperance, integrity, and character generally; and, fourth, because I knew I had the facts and truths in my own hand, knew it would all come to light sometime, etc. Hence I bided my time. If Smith is correct, do him justice. Do Smith and all men exact and equal justice. Criticize all, thoroughly and well. If I make any broad mistakes with pen or otherwise in my rush and great hurry give me an opportunity to correct.

I send you Lincoln's letter to Wallace on protection. Don't know that it was ever copied in the records, think it was, but for fear it was not, I send it to you. Lincoln was a strong protection man. He and John Calhoun of Kansas, in this city in 1844, held a long discussion, say three or four nights, on protective tariffs. Both these men were strong men, strong on this question. Calhoun in 1844 was a strong, very strong, and clear-headed man, Lincoln's equal and the superior of Douglas, but whisky—whisky ruined him long, long before he went to Kansas. Calhoun was a noble man in his original nature—went to school to him—but *whisky*, poverty, etc., etc., did their work. He fell and yet in his fall he was a gentleman in every sense of the word. He loved Lincoln and as well as Lincoln could he returned it. I heard this discussion, "*toted books*," and "*hunted up authorities*" for Lincoln, as I did in law.

Your friend,
W. H. HERNDON.

Springfield, Ill., March 15, 1870.

Friend Lamon:

Your letter making certain inquiries is this moment handed to me. If I were you I should tell the truth as I saw it. I should suppress no truth and suggest no falsehood. If I thought Mr. Lincoln an illegitimate I should state it. I would draw a strong contrast between *what he was born and how he died*. He was born into the social world with a curse on him, a millstone tied to his neck, and yet by his own inherent force of a sacred purpose he on the tide floated to glory. *Show his origin and end* sharply contrasted. Contrast is a power; it makes things distinct. Sympathy is a power. State the facts of his origin so as to assure active sympathy and to bind it to him. Sympathy is a power. Give me the sympathy of the world and you may have its cold iron logic. Lincoln the unaided, uneducated, Lincoln the penniless barefoot boy, through [undeciphered] and persistency of an honest purpose, carved upon the world's history the character of *Honest Abe*. I should show his *low origin* and *high end* in bold contrast, running such parallels as history suggested, etc. I should then applaud this democracy, this government, and show that such a character under such lowly conditions would be an impossibility in Europe, etc., would show these things, holding them up to the young in this world for all coming time as stimulants, as living hopes urging them to a life of integrity, faith, and hope. This all seems grand to me ; and whether you know it or not, Lincoln's life to me was a grand life, knowing what I do of him. This is my idea, and I think the best course for you. You must do so, if you want your hero to shine. Without this whole truth business, I do not think it possible to make his life a grand struggle, making [incomplete] . . .

Springfield, Ill., March 23, 1870.

Friend Lamon :

I have been very busy in court for a month or more and had no time to finish anything or polish anything—wrote in a gallop, with a whoop. I wrote you a hasty letter yesterday, stating to you what you ought to do and what you ought not to do in relation to quoting authorities. I have another view of the case which I wish to present to your view and it is this : If you indiscriminately quote men and women on all questions, they will turn on me in this way : "When I gave you the information I trusted *you*, gave *you* the information, not expecting you would sell it to another. It was a personal trust in you."

On general questions not affecting Lincoln's mother, Lincoln's *birth* and parentage, Lincoln's *domestic* relations and his *religion*, I can see no objections to quoting names. To that extent I will trust your discretion. In all cases affecting the above things, including Lincoln's *courtship*, you must get the consent of those who gave me the information. Your records will show you where to write and to whom. I will see as many as I can and get their consent, will write to as many as I can and ask them for authority, but this must not release you from like efforts to all persons, for I may not get time, have got to go out on the circuit and plead for bread. I am satisfied that I gave promises to more persons than I have spoken about, have no doubt that I gave my word to Haycraft and to the clerk at Hodgenville, as well as to Speed and Helm. I do not say this simply because I can say it, but because it is probably true. It has been a long time since I got the in-

formation, and as I have passed through several hells since 1866 and
7, I may have forgotten my promises. To break this honor is to ruin
me and your book. We must walk discreet and have no attacks made on
us that we cannot well and truthfully defend. Where we are discreet
as well as true there we can stand and laugh, defying all charges of
little men and women. Your book must not go out with this danger
around it. Think well of these things.

Any question which will not raise a howl against us, me, yourself,
and your book, quote freely from men and, if you will and must, women.

If I can only stand on truth and honor, I do not care for the howls
of Christianity, of cringing timids, of policies, of fools and asses. I
expect to be attacked as no man has been attacked lately, but I do
not care for that *much*, when I know I have Truth, Honor, and Propriety on my side. I have long since determined to tell the truth and
the whole truth in reference to Mr. Lincoln's life, come weal or woe.
*The world wants one true life of one man to swear by and they will
get it, I hope, in your life of Lincoln.*

I have just seen John T. Stuart and he gives you this authority:
"Use my name on all things except where it would create unpleasant
feelings and on this question I give Lamon a broad discretion." If you
would only write to men and women, you could get their consent without any trouble, and how much better and safer for me, for you and
your book.

There is nothing in Indiana that you cannot use that I now remember of. There is nothing in the county of Menard, including Lincoln's religion, insanity, courtship, etc., that you cannot use—Green,
Cogsdale, Irwin, Hill, Bale, Spears, *Mrs.* Green, *Mrs.* Armstrong.
Probably I told Ann Rutledge's man, Lincoln's rival—forget his name
just now—that I would not use his name, left it blank on the Ann
Rutledge lecture as I suppose for that reason. You can learn his name
from your record; I think his name is McNeil or McNamar. . . .
It is only in cases that would create unpleasant feelings, cruel criticisms, etc., from which you [are] forbidden the use, so you see you have
a broad field, and if you wish to broaden it, widen it, deepen it, thunder-
cloud it, in order to flash and blaze, please write to the persons.

Suppose I know that I made no promise to any and all persons, do
you not know enough of human nature to know that timids, cowards,
policy men, squeamish women, gray hard youths, fools, and asses

would turn on me if they could make a dollar out of it or dodge a consequence of irritating circumstances, and how could I prove that I made no promise? You now have my ideas; would like to hear yours.

Your friend,

W. H. HERNDON.

Chinkapin, Sangamon County, January 15, 1874.

Dear Sir [1]:

You say you desire to know all possible things of the great and good dead. I have just now a few moments to spare, and I do not know how better to spare them than to tell you what Mr. Lincoln really was and what he was not. Mr. Lincoln was a kind, tender, and sympathetic man, feeling deeply in the presence of suffering, pain, wrong, or oppression in any shape; he was the very essence and substance of truth; was of unbounded veracity, had unlimited integrity, always telling the exact truth, and always doing the honest thing at all times and under all circumstances. He was just to men, he loved the right, the good, and true, with all his soul.

I was with Mr. Lincoln for about twenty-five years, and I can truthfully say I never knew him to do a wrong thing, never knew him to do a mean thing, never knew him to do any little dirty trick. He was always noble. In his nature he felt noble and acted nobly. I never knew so true a man, so good a one, so just a one, so incorrupted and incorruptible a one. He was a patriot and loved his country well, and died for it. Mr. Lincoln expressed his great feelings in his thoughts, and his great thoughts in his feelings; he lived in his thoughts, and thought in his feelings. By these his soul was elevated and purified for his work. His work was the highest and grandest religion, noble duty nobly done. Mr. Lincoln was cool and calm under the most trying circumstances; he had unbounded charity for all men.

In religion he was a theist, somewhat after the order of Theodore Parker. Mr. Lincoln was not a speculative-minded man; was, like Washington, severely practical; he never ran in advance of his age, and yet was always directing the ideas and feelings of men to purely

---

[1] An unknown correspondent, who published it in a newspaper probably of the same year. An undated clipping has been preserved in an old scrapbook. It is not known whether the original letter still exists.

practical ends, to something that would end in good. Mr. Lincoln never shaped his veracity, integrity, or virtue to circumstances; he fashioned and formed circumstances, so far as he could, to virtue, veracity, and to integrity. He scorned meanness everywhere and at all times, and was bold and manly in his denunciation of wrong, however and by whoever done; he was not a foxy, tricky man; he was a statesman high above all tricks. How such a man as Lincoln could walk up to the highest point of human grandeur, from such a low origin, God only knows. But he was so ordained from the beginning, and so it is.

Mr. Lincoln was a man of great fidelity to whatever he believed was right—was true to friends, never deserting them till they deserted virtue, veracity, and integrity. Mr. Lincoln could be, and was, trusted by the people with almost omnipotent power, and he never abused it nor shook the public's faith in him. He was true to his trust, true to his country, and true to the rights of man. What a noble man, and what a noble life he lived! Washington was America's creator; Lincoln was its savior. Mr. Lincoln now stands up against the deep blue sky the grandest figure of the age.

I have now stated to you Mr. Lincoln's leading characteristics, and if you like him better for them I am well satisfied with what I have told you. I have weighed every word and sentence, and can truly say they are true to Lincoln and Lincoln true to them. Lincoln was not a very social man. He was not spontaneous in his feelings; was, as some said, rather cold; he was rather reflective—not cold. However, take him all in all, he was as near a perfect man as God generally makes.

Yours truly,

W. H. HERNDON.

Section Three

Springfield, Ill., October 8, 1881.

Mr. Weik.

My dear Sir:

I promised, a few days since, to send you an autograph of Mr. Lincoln, if I could find one among my boxed papers, and that if I could not I would send you something more sacred, at least in my own eyes, than a mere autograph. I, as long ago as '75, promised to send you such writing or signature, if I could find one. When I received your note of July '81 I had not forgotten my promise nor you. This week I unboxed my papers and the result is as follows: I found two of Mr. Lincoln's autographs, only two as yet—one is a letter written by Logan & *Lincoln*—but signed or written by Mr. Lincoln *in person*—which letter is addressed to Messrs. Rowland Smith etc., of Louisville, Kentucky, and dated April 24, 1844. The other autograph is on a leaf of *Mr. Lincoln's* copybook and is sacred on two accounts: first, it is *Mr. Lincoln's* signature; and, second, it is a leaf of his arithmetical note or copybook, which as I now remember bears date 1824–26–28. Now for the *how* of finding the precious book. Soon after Mr. Lincoln's assassination I determined to gather up all the facts of his life— truly, honestly, and impartially, whatever it might cost in money or *infamy*—and to give the facts to the world as I understood them. I did so, and probably you know the result. I find that this age is not ready to meet its own great truths; it will meet and grasp old truths, great and noble ones that have cost tears and blood way in the morning of the race of man. In collecting and gathering up facts of Mr. Lincoln's young life I went in person to various places, towns, cities, counties, and States. In order to get at what I wished, I went and saw old Mrs. Lincoln, stepmother of the noble lad—a boy, a mere boy in 1824–26–28—in Coles County, Illinois. This was, say, in 1865. I examined her, interviewed her in person, and took notes of her conversation. She rose in mind high above her surroundings, she was a true woman. She told me then that Mr. Lincoln used, when a boy, to keep an arithmetical copybook in which he put down his worked out sums. She likewise then told me that the boy Abraham was in the like habit of putting down in another copybook—his literary one—all things that struck him, such as fine oratory, rhetoric, science, art, etc. He likewise put things, wrote sentences, on boards and other places and then read them, looked at them, over and over, analyzed them, thoroughly understanding them. He would translate them into his boyish language and *would* tell his schoolmates, friends, and mother what they meant, as he understood them; and tell his thoughts he *would;* and his schoolmates, friends, and mother *must* hear or he would "bust wide open."

The information thus given me by the good old lady, the kind and loving stepmother—God bless her—put me on nettles, as it were, and so we commenced the search, and found this, the arithmetical copybook, a leaf of which you now have. We could not find the other book; it is lost and lost forever, as our search was thorough. Mrs. Lincoln gave me the book with her own hands or by the hand of her grandson. On this leaf you will find some writing of young Abraham and is as follows, the want of caps included:

> Abraham Lincoln
> his hand and pen
> he will be good, but
> god knows when

On another leaf of the same book is this:

> Abraham Lincoln is my name
> and with my pen I write the same
> I will be a good boy, but God knows when

By this paper you can tell the extent of Mr. Lincoln's education in 1824–26–28. The letter is dated in 1844, at which time and *at this place* he was a great lawyer. In 1836 Mr. Lincoln was a tolerably good mathematician, as he was surveyor of Sangamon County. What he knew he knew plainly, clearly, thoroughly; he ran things down to the ultimate point, beyond which no man ever went. Study what you see on these papers and you will see the general extent of Mr. Lincoln's personally dug out education. Mr. Lincoln had unbounded and unlimited confidence in his own mental powers, he was himself and wholly self-reliant, asking no man anything; he searched for what he wanted, dug it out by the tap root, held it out before him till he knew it inside and outside. Someone has said: "Give me the amount of soap that a people uses and I can tell the height of its civilization." Apply this rule if rule it is to these papers and run out the rule. Many persons will say to scholars—young men struggling to climb high— "Imitate Mr. Lincoln in his methods." All of which is right, but remember that *it is the mind back of its manifestations* which is inimitable, not to be imitated; it is itself and nothing can be like it. A rat cannot be an eagle. I once said that Mr. Lincoln was a deeply and thoroughly religious man at all times and places and under all conditions and I now repeat it: his religion was of the noblest and grandest and the broadest kind. Lincoln was a noble man.

On looking at this leaf and knowing Mr. Lincoln as I do, what memories cluster amid my central being, while too writing this letter. Here is the name of *Lincoln* before me, and in my mind, and the newspapers overflowing with the sad intelligence of Garfield's death. The mind remembers Socrates and Jesus—*double* stars of the Old World—Lincoln and Garfield *twin* stars of the New. Oh, how each suffered in his own way and for the Eternal Right! The sublime thoughts, the noble deeds, the proud acts of these men will enter into all future time as moral forces and divine energies, lifting up to a higher level and a grander plain the whole race of man for all coming time. The hand of him who wrote these sums, this simple poetry, this letter, may molder into dust, but his name will outlast these eternal hills: *he dreamed dreams of glory, and glory is justly his.*

Your friend,
W. H. HERNDON.

P.S.   You will perceive that this letter is a hasty one. I have no time to tone it up nor to rewrite it.

HERNDON.

Springfield, Ill., November 24, 1882.

My dear Sir:

A few days since I received your kind note, for which accept my thanks. Enclosed you will find a letter from Abraham Lincoln to John D. Johnston—Lincoln's stepbrother—which I promised to give you; it is the only letter which I have left of Mr. Lincoln's; it is a genuine one written by the great man himself. I have kept the letter up to this day as an evidence that Mr. Lincoln was not an atheist; and, had he been one, that fact would not lessen him in my estimation, though not one myself. I had this letter once published, but before so doing I showed it to several of Mr. Lincoln's old and dear friends, who laughed at me for my credulity in believing that Mr. Lincoln believed in immortality and heaven, as stated in the letter; it was said to be merely a message of consolation from a dutiful son to his dying father. However, I had the letter published, and kept the letter as an evidence that Mr. Lincoln was not an atheist. I could have given the letter away many times, could have sold it for money, but I would not part with it. I think the question of his atheism is settled, and now I present it to you. I may say to you that the letter has the ring, it seems to me, of true metal, and yet I give no opinion. You have the letter and the facts of Mr. Lincoln's life before you, and you can judge as well as I can. I will soon in this letter give you a phase of Mr. Lincoln's life not generally known, and possibly it will not be believed by the worshiping world—I mean hero-worshiping world. I have no reference to the worship of the religious soul.

Mr. Lincoln for years supported or helped to support his aged father and mother; it is to the honor of [Lincoln] that he dearly loved his stepmother, and it is equally true that she idolized her stepson. Johnston, to whom the letter is addressed, was Lincoln's stepbrother, the son of Mrs. Lincoln by her first husband. Thomas Lincoln, the father of Abraham, courted his second wife in his youth; she refused to have him; he then courted Nancy Hanks and was married to her. A man by the name of Johnston courted Miss Sarah Bush—Thomas Lincoln's first flame—and married her. About the year 1819 both Mrs. Lincoln and Mr. Johnston died. Lincoln then in about one year again renewed his suit and it was accepted, and they were married. Each had two children by the first marriage and none by the second. John Johnston was an indolent and shiftless man, a man that was "born tired," and yet he was an exceedingly clever man, generous, and very hospitable. Lincoln deserves great credit for the care shown his father and mother—hard cash and warm heart-care. In the very letter which I give you this care is shown; he says in the letter: "You (Johnston) already know I desire that neither father nor mother shall be in want of any comfort, either in health or in sickness, while they live; and I feel sure that you have not failed to use my name, if necessary, to

procure a doctor or anything else for father in his present sickness."
Dutiful and affectionate son! Noble man! Mr. Lincoln was very poor
at the time this letter was written, not worth, in property, more than
three or four thousand dollars.

Mr. Lincoln purchased a piece of property in Coles County, this
State, as a home for his father and mother, and had it deeded in trust
for their use and benefit. The aged couple lived in Coles County at the
time. I do not now recollect all the particulars, and yet I once did. The
records in Coles County will show the facts, if anyone in the future
wishes to look the thing further up. Here is exhibited parental love
and duty, backed up by warm affection, care, good credit, land, home,
and money. This was true and genuine comfort and material aid. It
was not all gush, sympathy, and tears on paper; it was real, solid,
genuine comfort and support, such as we can live upon.

I now wish to give you a phase of Mr. Lincoln's life which is not
generally known, nor will it be believed readily by the multitude; and
yet it will be true to the letter and the spirit of his life. He was said to
be a very simple-minded man, devoid of the silences and ambitions in
life. I would advise you before you read this letter to read Holland's
Life of Lincoln, at pages 241–2, where you will find many diverse
[undeciphered] of Mr. Lincoln. Consider it inserted here. Mr. Lincoln was thought, as was before stated, to be a very simple-minded man.
He was simple in his dress, manners, simple in his approach and his
presence. Though this be true, he was a man of quite infinite silences
and was thoroughly and deeply secretive, uncommunicative, and close-
minded as to his plans, wishes, hopes, and fears. His ambition was
never satisfied; in him it was consuming fire which smothered his [un-
deciphered] feelings. Here he ran for every legislative office, from
the trusteeship of our then little village to the presidency, and during
all that time I venture to say that he never wholly opened himself to
mortal creature. He was skeptical, cautious, and terribly secretive,
confiding his plans and purposes, ambitions and ends, to no man. I have
known men in our office to listen to Mr. Lincoln's conversation for a
short while and then exclaim: "Oh, what a simple-minded man is Mr.
Lincoln! So plain! So unambitious! So confiding!" and the like, when
Mr. Lincoln's mind was not in our office but on a hot chase for the end
so devoutly to be wished. Of all Americans he was, most emphatically,
a man of the profoundest, widest, and deepest policies. He had his

burning and his consuming ambition, but he kept his secrets and opened not.

An interviewer, with the best of intentions in the world, once went to Mr. Lincoln's room in the White House while he was President, and said: "Mr. President, what do you think of the war and its end?" To which Mr. Lincoln politely and laughingly replied: "That question of yours puts me in mind of a story about something which happened down in Egypt, in the southern part of Illinois." The point of it was that a man badly burned his fingers in being in too much haste. Mr. Lincoln told the story admirably well, walking up and down the room and most heartily laughing all the while. The interviewer saw the point coming at him like the sting end of a hornet. As a matter of course he was cut to the quick, and quickly downstairs he rushed with an oath in mouth, saying he would "never interview that man again." He was as good as his word, and never tried to interview the President again. And thus it always was with Mr. Lincoln. . . .

While I say that Mr. Lincoln was ambitious, secretive, and somewhat selfish, do not infer from these words that he was a dishonest man, nor an insincere man, nor a hypocrite, nor a mean man, nor a base man. He was, on the contrary, full of honesty, integrity, sincerity; open, fair, and candid when speaking or acting. He was for Lincoln always, but with Lincoln's intense honesty. Mr. Lincoln was a wise man, a shrewd man, a long-headed man, full of his own policies. He was a marginal man, always leaving a blank on his paper, so that the future might write the future lessons thereon. Mr. Lincoln hated speculation, had no cranks, was not visionary and impracticable. He had relatively no imagination and no fancy, and was materially and purely practicable. He had one of the very best-balanced heads in America; and it was poised well on his shoulders. Henry Clay was his ideal statesman, a purely material and practical man. Mr. Lincoln's man was purely logical, and he followed his conclusions to the ultimate end, though the world perished. I never heard Mr. Lincoln harshly condemn any man, nor did I ever hear him praise but two men: one Thomas Jefferson, on paper; and the other, Henry Clay, in his speech and letters, and in his heart. Was this jealousy, or what? I think he cared for principles, and not much for men, especially if he did not want to use them for his own ends, which were generally high and noble. Mr. Lincoln had no low cunning, was not a trickster, a mere wire-puller.

He scorned and detested all such political arts. His mind required and lived on facts, figures, and principles. He was destitute of faith which comes and goes without evidence. His own reason and human experience were his authority, and these only with him were authority.

It is a fact that Mr. Lincoln was a peculiar man, a wonderful, marvelous, and mysterious man to the world generally. I was with him for about twenty-five years; and I think I knew him well. Mr. Lincoln never took the advice of any man or set of men, generally speaking. He never asked the opinion or advice of any man. He was self-reliant, self-poised, self-helping, and self-assertive, but not dogmatic by any means. He clung like gravity to his own opinions. He was the most continuous and severest thinker in America. He read but little and that for an end. Politics were his Heaven, and his Hades metaphysics. His tendency in philosophy was materialistic; he was an evolutionist; and yet, as the letter now presented to you shows, he believed in God, a Maker, immortality, and heaven. I am not now advocating any particular opinion or any object, nor denying one. I am simply stating facts, letting each man and woman draw his or her own conclusions. I give no decided opinion about the letter, except I know it is genuine, and now yours, which I hope you will keep to the end of your time, and then it may descend to the family as an heirloom, a great treasure indeed.

May I say again that Mr. Lincoln was a shrewd man, a long-headed man, a wise man, full of policies? Mr. Lincoln knew that Senator Douglas was in his way in the North, and so he, at Freeport, determined to kill him (politically). He put a question—and that, too, against his friends' advice and importunities—to Senator Douglas, which he knew the Senator must answer one way or the other, and he further knew that to answer the question either way was death to Douglas—death in the North if he answered one way, and death in the South if another. It was cold, well-calculated death any way. Douglas answered and of that answer he died. Again, after Douglas's death, in the North was only Seward to oppose him and Lincoln determined to kill or outstrip him. Hence his "house divided against itself" speech here in 1858, and his speeches, his "irrepressible conflict" speeches, in Ohio. Lincoln ridiculed when he could Seward's "higher law" idea, scared some of the Republicans with it, and got the confidence somewhat of the extreme Republicans; and in his great Cooper Institute speech in New York in 1860 he drove the nail in Seward's political coffin. All this was planned and coldly calculated by Lincoln. I know this to be true.

What! This a simple-minded man? This a politically "innocent dear" man? This a mere thing, without ideas and policies? Away with all such opinions! Look how he treated his Cabinet in the issuance of his great proclamation of emancipation. He consulted them simply about little and unimportant matters; and so said to them before he read it. He decreed to issue it. He simply wanted his Cabinet to hear it read, and that is all. This proclamation was issued as by doom, and what he did was not for the love of the slave or liberty, but to save the Union. It was to preserve his "oath registered [in] heaven." He kept his oath, saved the Union, and with a quick dash of the military pen he freed four millions of people.

In philosophy Mr. Lincoln was a realist as opposed to an idealist, was a sensationalist as opposed to an intuitionalist, a materialist as opposed to a spiritualist, and yet remember what he says in his letter. I said to you in a private letter that Mr. Lincoln was at all times and places and under all circumstances a deeply and a thoroughly religious man, sincerely, firmly, broadly, and grandly so. I do not say he was a Christian. I do not say that he was not. I give no opinion the one way or the other. I simply state facts and let each person judge for himself.

I say, in short, in terms of contradiction, if you please, that Mr. Lincoln was a perfect and an imperfect man, a strong man and a weak one; but take him all in all, he was one of the best, wisest, greatest, and noblest of men in all the ages.

Most respectfully yours,
WM. H. HERNDON.

Springfield, Ill., September 15, 1883.

Editor of the Indianapolis *Herald*:

In your issue of August 25, I see a letter written by a gentleman by the name of J. W. Gordon, which is dated August 20, 1883. In that letter, W. H. Lamon, author of the Life of Lincoln, and myself, are accused of laboring to cast reproach upon the parents of Abraham Lincoln. The aim and spirit of the letter are proper and most excellent.

The writer and I agree in sentiment and opinion. No one should cast reproach upon Nancy Hanks and Thomas Lincoln or Abraham Lincoln, or any of the family, big or little. I do not believe anyone can do so. The difference between Mr. Gordon and myself, as well as Lamon, is one of fact. The writer says that Lamon labored to cast reproach upon his benefactor, "by more than intimating that they (Nancy Hanks and Thomas Lincoln) were never legally married." I quote his words. Here is a charge, in substance, that Lamon says in his biography that Thomas Lincoln and Nancy Hanks were never married. The charge is in substance explicit. Now what are the facts? Lamon says in his biography of Lincoln, on page 10—I quote his words: "It is admitted by all the residents of the place (Elizabethtown, Kentucky) that they (Nancy Hanks and Thomas Lincoln) were honorably married." Mr. J. W. Gordon quotes his sentence from the same book that I do, and on the same page, and from the same paragraph; and why did he quote only a part and leave out the pith and marrow of the thing? Mr. Lamon admits that the couple were honorably married, though he failed to find the written record of the marriage in Hardin or the adjoining counties. Why does Mr. Gordon misquote and misrepresent Lamon? What was his motive for doing it? Was the thing an accident, an oversight? He quotes only a part of what Lamon says and leaves off the nib and sharp point of the main question. I shall make no charges against Mr. Gordon, because he may have acted honestly, and may have intended to be fair in his letter and the quotation therein, which is substantially correct as far as it goes. The gentleman now produces the record of the marriage of Thomas Lincoln and wife, and I am glad of it. Mr. Lamon did search for the records in Hardin and adjoining counties in Kentucky, and could not find them, and he so states the case in substance. He admits the marriage—that it was honestly done—and that it was followed by mutual acknowledgment, and by living and cohabiting together as man and wife. The records above spoken of were found in Washington County, and not in an adjoining county. What more could Lamon say as an honest biographer? No more. The record, as exhibited by Mr. Gordon, shows that Thomas Lincoln and Nancy Hanks were married on the 23d day of April 1806, and the Thomas Lincoln Bible, which I have seen, and now have a copy before me, says (it is in Abraham Lincoln's handwriting) that Sarah Lincoln was born on the 10th day of February

1807, less than five months from the marriage. Sarah Lincoln was their first child. She grew up and was married to a man by the name of Aaron Grigsby. Abraham Lincoln wrote out in his own hand a list of the marriages, births, and deaths of the family and put it in the Thomas Lincoln Bible. I suppose he forgot it. There may be mistakes in the above figures. I give Mrs. Lincoln and Thomas Lincoln the benefit of all doubts; it is easy to err in dates and figures. Looking at all the facts, did Lamon try to cast reproach on Thomas Lincoln and wife? Not a word of it. He simply stated the facts as they were before him. Mr. Gordon was a little too hasty in this matter. Lamon understands the facts of the case better than Mr. Gordon does.

Now as to myself. In the year 1873, I think, I delivered a lecture in this city to a large and intelligent audience in answer to similar charges and assertions as above by one Reed, James A. Reed, pastor of this city. Reed was too hasty in this controversy, just as Gordon was or is; he burned his fingers just as Gordon has scorched his. Mr. Gordon says in the published letter, this: "Mr. Herndon too has seemed equally willing to cast reproach upon the memory of the great martyr's parents." This I deny. No man cast reproach upon the parents of Mr. Lincoln. Mrs. Lincoln was a good woman—a noble woman and an intellectual one. Thomas Lincoln was a good man and an honest one. In my lecture spoken of here, and by Mr. Gordon, I said on looking over the whole evidence then known and before us of the marriage [that I knew] that Thomas Lincoln and Nancy Hanks were lawfully and honestly married. I simply asked the question, did they jump a broomstick as ceremony of marriage, etc? The question was simply a question and not a charge of any kind. I was debating the question on the proofs. Now the proofs of the marriage in proper form have been put in evidence, and they settle the question of the marriage and that is all they do settle. There is much behind them that is not necessary now and here to mention. I would advise Mr. Gordon not to jump into print, nor enter into this controversy till he understands all the facts. I am glad the records are all produced; they were produced before Mr. Gordon produced them as I am informed. I am satisfied of the lawful marriage of Nancy Hanks and Thomas Lincoln, and now bless their memories forever.

Most respectfully yours,
W. H. HERNDON.

Springfield, Ill., April 14, 1885.

Friend Weik:

I have just received your letter, dated the 12th *inst.*, and in answer to which, in part, let me say that I am still in court and busy, and don't know when I'll get out; but when I do I'll write to you. I am glad that you purpose writing some articles for the Cin[cinnati] *Com[mercial] Gaz[ette]*. . . . Do not say anything about my supposed theory of Lincoln's paternity, as it will be liable to misconstruction. I have the facts of Lincoln's paternity, etc., but have never given them to the world; will sometime, it may be. Some things are not clear to me, only have a kind of "theory" of the thing. I wish you were here and put your questions to me and let me answer orally. However, I'll answer if I can steal time from my business.

I prefer what Lincoln told me about his mother to what Dennis Hanks tells. You must watch Dennis, criticize what he says and how he says it, when and where "tight" or sober. Dennis loves to blow. Dennis came into the world at the back door out of a Miss Hanks; his father is Charles. Dennis has got things mixed up; he purposely conceals all things that degrade the Hankses. Dennis came out of one Hanks and Lincoln out of another; the girls were cousins as I now recollect it. Thomas Lincoln, Abraham's father, and Abraham Enloe had a severe fight over things. How goes this *fact* with Dennis's sixteen-year-old boy?

I saw the "great abolitionist," I think in 1858, just a little while before the race of Douglas and Lincoln *actually* began; went to see them at the implied request of Lincoln, as I understood his *hints;* did not let the "great abolitionist" know who sent me nor whom I *impliedly* represented; saw Trumbull, Sumner, Greeley, Parker, Phillips, Garrison, *et al.;* stated to them what I wanted, i.e., what the great West wanted. Told them that Douglas could not be trusted, that Lincoln could, gave them facts upon facts, and opinion upon opinion. All went well, except Greeley. I will write you sometime if I get time.[1]

Sorry to hear of your rheumatic ills.

Your friend,
W. H. HERNDON.

---

[1] See letter to Weik of December 23, 1885.

Springfield, Ill., October 21, 1885.

Friend Weik:

Mr. Lincoln's habits, methods of reading law, politics, poetry, etc., etc., were to come into the office, pick up book, newspaper, etc., and to sprawl himself out on the sofa, chairs, etc., and read aloud, much to my annoyance. I have asked him often why he did so and his invariable reply was: "I catch the idea by two senses, for when I read aloud I *hear* what is read and I see it; and hence two senses get it and I remember it better, if I do not understand it better." Sometimes in reading he would have his body on the sofa, one foot on one chair and one foot on the table. He spilt himself out easily over one-quarter of the room. I have had to quit the office frequently because of this reading aloud. In reading at his private house he would turn his chair down, upside down, lean it down, turn it over, and rest his head on the back of the chair, it forming an inclined plane, his back and body on the carpet, read aloud, stop, think, and repeat to himself what he read, and repeat it to you he would or faint. He was in no sense, except in politics, a general reader; he read specially for a special object and applied it. Mr. Lincoln was practical and thought things useless unless they could [be] of utility, use, practice, etc., etc.; he would read awhile, read till he got tired, and then he must tell a story, crack a joke, make a jest to ease himself; he hated study except for the practical to be applied right off as it were. In other words he had an end in view always. He was a long-headed strong man; he was reflective, not spontaneous; he was not a very generous man, had no avarice of the *get* but had the avarice of the *keep;* he was liberal and charitable in his views of mankind in all their relations. Mr. Lincoln was a man of thought. I have met him in the streets of this city possibly a thousand times and said to him: "Good morning, Mr. Lincoln," and he would spraddle, walk along as if I were not in existence, so abstracted was he. Can you read this? Am hurried, will write you again and again.

Your friend,
W. H. HERNDON.

Springfield, Ill., October 28, 1885.

Friend Weik:

By Mr. Lincoln's course in Congress in the Mexican War he politically killed himself here; he offered some resolutions in Congress calling for the "spot" where the first blood was shed by the Mexicans. This was in 1847–48, I think. Mr. Lincoln knew that he was politically dead and so he went most heartily to knowledge; he took Euclid around with him on the circuit and of nights and odd times he would learn Euclid's problems. Lincoln and I slept in the same bed; he read by tallow candlelight. The bedsteads in some cases were too short and so his feet hung over the footboard. He would study till twelve or one o'clock in the night. At this time he despaired of ever rising again in the political world; he was very sad and terribly gloomy, was unsocial and abstracted. The Kansas-Nebraska Bill was introduced into Congress in 1854 by Senator Douglas. Lincoln saw his opportunity and Douglas's downfall; he instantly on the introduction of that bill entered into the political field, and by force of his character, mind, eloquence, he became our abolition leader; he was too conservative for some of us, and I among them, and yet I stuck to Lincoln in the hopes of his sense of justice and the eternal right. I was the abolitionist and kept on my table such speeches as Theodore Parker's, Giddings's, Phillips's, Sumner's, Seward's, etc. Lincoln and I took from 1853 to 1861 such papers as the Chicago *Tribune,* New York *Tribune, The Anti-Slavery Standard,* Charleston *Mercury,* Richmond *Enquirer, National Era.* Garrison's paper was sent me by friends. I purchased all the anti-slavery histories, biographies, etc., and kept them on my table, and when I found a good thing, a practical thing, I would read it to Lincoln. I urged him along as fast as I could. I think I had May's history of the anti-slavery movements, had the decennial report of the anti-slavery conventions, etc., can't call them all over now. Lincoln now from 1854 to 1861 was in his glory, had hopes, bright hopes, to fill his aspirations. Will write.

> Your friend,
> W. H. Herndon.

Again and again you fix up in order of time, etc., etc.

The list of papers, etc., is important to know. Lincoln was well posted on both sides. I had a Southern work called *Sociology* by Fitzhugh, I think. It defended slavery in every way. This aroused the ire of Lincoln more than most pro-slavery books.

Springfield, Ill., October 29, 1885.

Friend Weik:

Mr. Lincoln was a good while preparing his "house divided against itself" speech; he was at it off and on about one month. If a good idea struck him, if a forcible one, he penciled down on a small slip of paper and put it in his hat, where he carried quite all his plunder, checkbook for the bank account, letters answered and unanswered, handkerchief, etc. After Mr. Lincoln had finished his speech by putting piece to piece and note to note he came into our office early one morning and said: "Billy, I want now to read my speech, and after I am done, I want your opinion of it in all directions"; and to which I replied: "Certainly, Mr. Lincoln, I'll listen attentively to it and give you my opinion of it in every direction." He and I forgot to lock the office door. When Lincoln had read the speech about half through, Uncle Jesse Dubois, auditor of [the] State, came into our office and said: "Lincoln, what are you doing?" and to which Mr. Lincoln said sharply, tartly: "It is none of your d——d business." Dubois left the office in a huff. When he had gone, Lincoln commenced reading the remainder of his speech, and when through he then asked me for my opinion of it. I said to Mr. Lincoln in reply this: "The speech is a good one, written with great power, and will bring you prominently before the American people. It is in advance of the age, but deliver it just as you have written it." He subsequently consulted some friends about it; some had one view of it and some another; some wanted this sentence struck out and some that, etc.; and then in the presence of the crowd he asked my opinion again and I emphatically said to him: "Lincoln, deliver and publish your speech just as you have written it; it will make you President of the United States." Lincoln did deliver it just as he had written it and read it to me in our office. Soon after the election was over and Lincoln was defeated, hundreds of friends flocked into the office and said to Lincoln: "I told you that that speech would kill you." This mortified Lincoln; he would say to them: "You don't fully comprehend its importance, but I suppose you all have or will desert me for that speech.

There is one man who will stick to me to the end; he understands it and its importance, and that man is Billy Herndon, my good old and long-tried friend."

Your friend,
W. H. HERNDON.

Lincoln had a million of curses from his foolish friends about this speech. He hated it and yet he was thoroughly convinced that it was the thing in the right time and he lived to see it.

Springfield, Ill., November 11, 1885.

Friend Weik:

Mr. Lincoln once had, in an early day, down in Coles County in this State, a heavy and a tight law suit. After the trial and before the jury had agreed, a question arose in the juryroom as to what was meant by the *preponderance* of evidence; the jury at last came into the courtroom and said: "We are hung on the question what is meant by the preponderance of evidence." The lawyers laughed at the ignorance of the jury, but said nothing. The Court put on its dignity and in writing, verbose and long, wordy and intricate, instructed the jury as to what was meant by the *preponderance* of evidence. The jury retired to the juryroom and, on counting *noses*, they found that "confusion was worse confounded." Soon they came into the courtroom again and said: "May it please the Court, we are hung again on the same question of the preponderance of evidence." The lawyer for the plaintiff, by the consent of the Court, tried his hand on an explanation of the word to the jury; he only added darkness to midnight with the stars and moon blown out of sight. Mr. Lincoln then asked the Court if he might try *his* hand on the question. The Court consented and said to Lincoln: "Do try your hand on this question, Lincoln." Lincoln arose and said: "Gentlemen of the jury, did you ever see a pair of steel yards or a pair of store scales? If you did I can explain, I think, to your satisfaction the meaning of the word. If the plaintiff has introduced any evidence, put that in the scales and have it weighed. Say it weighs sixteen ounces. If the defendant has introduced any evidence in the case, put that in the scales; and if that evidence weighs sixteen ounces, the scales are balanced and there is no preponderance of evidence on either side. There are four witnesses on each side of this case. If the plaintiff's evidence weighs one grain of wheat more than the defendant's, then the plaintiff has the preponderance of evidence—his side of the scales go down, is the heaviest. If this defendant's evidence weighs one grain of wheat more than the plaintiff's, then the defendant's side of the scales goes down, is the heaviest; and that movement of the scales tells what is the preponderance of evidence. Now apply this illustration to the state of your mind on weighing the evidence for the plaintiff and defendant." "We see the point, Abe," said the jury. This simple illustration of Lincoln gained his case. The defendant had the preponderance of evidence; rather, the plaintiff did not have it. This illustration shows most emphatically that Lincoln struggled to be plain to all minds—and especially to ignorant ones. This was one of his fortes.

Your friend,
W. H. HERNDON.

Springfield, Ill., November 12, 1885.

Friend Weik:

Mr. Lincoln was a peculiar man; he was intensely thoughtful, persistent, fearless, and tireless in thinking. When he got after a thought, fact, principle, question, he ran it down to the fibers of the tap root, dug it out, and held it up before him for an analysis, and when he thus formed an opinion, no man could overthrow it; he was in this particular without an equal. I have met Mr. Lincoln of a morning or evening and said to him: "Good morning, Mr. Lincoln." He would be so intensely, so deeply, in thought, working out his problem, his question, that he would not notice me, though his best friend; he would walk along, his hands behind his back, not knowing where he was going nor doing; his system was acting automatically. There was no thought in his actions, he only had *consciousness.* Some hours after he had thus passed me, he, on coming to the office, would say: "Billy, what did you say to me on the other side of the square this morning as we passed?" I would say: "I simply said good-morning to you, Mr. Lincoln." Sometimes this abstractedness would be the result of intense gloom or of thought on an important law or other question.

I once saw Mr. Lincoln look more than a man; he was inspired by the occasion. There was a man living here by the name of Erastus Wright;

he was, his business rather was, to obtain pensions for the soldiers of the Revolution's heirs, widows, etc., the soldiers of 1812's widows, heirs, etc. An old revolutionary soldier's widow applied to Wright, about 1849–50 to get her pension, which amounted to about $400. Wright made out the papers, got the pension, and charged the poor widow $200, half of what he got. The poor old woman came into our office quite blind, deaf, and on crutches, and stated to Mr. Lincoln her case. Lincoln at once sympathized with the woman and said: "Wright shall pay you back $100 or more." Lincoln went and saw Wright in person. Wright refused to refund. The old woman commenced suit, Lincoln giving security for costs. The case finally got before the jury with all the facts of the case fully told. Lincoln loomed up, rose up to be about nine feet high, grew warm, then eloquent with feelings, then blasting as with a thunderbolt the miscreant who had robbed one that helped the world to liberty, to *Wright's* inalienable rights. Lincoln was inspired if man was ever inspired. The jury became indignant and would have torn Wright up, mobbed in a minute, burst into tears at one moment and then into indignation the next. The judge and spectators did the same, according to the term that Lincoln gave his eloquence. The jury made Wright disgorge all except about $50.

HERNDON.

I write you nothing but what I know is true. Pick out what you like and throw the balance to the dogs, am in court and hurried, so excuse me.

HERNDON.

Springfield, Ill., November 13, 1885.

Friend Weik:

There were three noted story-tellers, jokers, jesters, in the central part of this State especially from 1840 to 1853: Lincoln of Sangamon County, William Engle of Menard, and James Murray of Logan. They were all men of mark, each in his own way; they were alike in the line of joking, story-telling, jesting. I knew the men for years. From 1840 to 1853 this section was not known for a very high standard of taste, the love for the beautiful or the good. We had not many newspapers; people in all of these counties would attend court at the respective county seats. Lincoln, Engle, and Murray would travel

around from county to county with the court, and those who loved fun
and sport, loved jokes, tales, stories, jests, would go with the court,
too, from county to county. People had not much to do at the time, and
the class of people that then lived here are gone, perished. It was a
curious state of affairs indeed. As compared with now it was rough,
semi-barbarous. In the evening, after the court business of the day
was over and book and pen had been laid [down] by the lawyers,
judges, jurymen, witnesses, etc., the people generally would meet at
some barroom, "gentlemen's parlor," and have a good time in story-
telling, joking, jesting, etc., etc. The barroom, windows, halls, and all
passageways would be filled to suffocation by the people, eager to see
the "big ones" and to hear their stories told by them. Lincoln would
tell his story in his very best style. The people, all present, including
Lincoln, would burst out in a loud laugh and a hurrah at the story. The
listeners, so soon as the laugh and the hurrah had passed and silence
had come in for its turn, would cry out: "Now, Uncle Billy (William
Engle), you must beat that or go home." Engle would clear his throat
and say: "Boys, the story just told by Lincoln puts me in mind of a
story that I heard when a boy." He would tell it and tell it well. The
people would clap their hands, stamp their feet, hurrah, yell, shout get
up, hold their aching sides. Things would soon calm down. There was
politeness and etiquette in it. Each must have his turn, by comity in
which to tell his story. The good people would, as soon as quiet reigned,
cry out: "Now is your time; come, Murray, do your level best or never
come here again to tell your stories." Murray would prepare himself
with his best. At first he would be a little nervous, but he would soon
gather confidence, rise up, walk about, telling his tale as he moved in
harmony with his story; he would tell it well, grandly, and the people
would sometimes before the story was ended catch the point and raise
such a laugh and a yell that the village rang with the yells, laughs, and
hurrahs, etc. Lincoln and Engle now were nervous and anxious for
their turns to come around. Lincoln would tell his story and then
followed Engle and then came Murray and thus this story-telling, joking, jesting, would be kept up till one or two o'clock in the night, and
thus night after night till the court adjourned for that term. In the
morning we would all be sore all through from excessive laughing—the
judge, the lawyers, jurymen, witnesses, and all. Our sides and back
would ache. This was a gay time and I'll never see it again. This is or

was the way we old Westerners passed away our time. We loved fun and sport—anything for amusement. We had no learning but had good common sense with a liberal broad view of things, were generous and as brave as Cæsar. When court had adjourned in Sangamon County, we went to Menard and then to Logan County. This story-telling was kept up faithfully from county to county and from term to term and from year to year. This custom or habit was our platform, show, Negro minstrel—was our all in the way of fun. The old knew it, the young can't conceive it. Each age has its own sport and so with each people. This may seem folly now, but it was real life to us then. All that we had to do, all that we could do, was to have joy and happiness in our own way. This old state of society was rude, but it had its virtues; *it was sincere and honest.* My old settler's speech which I sent you will help you to paint the scene. Draw on your imagination and fill up; it will please the people who read the story, people, state of society, etc., etc.

Pick out what you like and cast away the balance. I have no time to elaborate, amplify, etc., nor correct.

I forgot to say in my Wright story—the old revolutionary woman story—that Lincoln volunteered his services, charged nothing, and paid her hotel bill, etc. Correct the error.

Your friend,
W. H. HERNDON.

Springfield, Ill., November 14, 1885.

Friend Weik:

As early as 1860 Mr. Lincoln had reason to believe that he would be assassinated or that an attempt would be made to do it. On the day of the presidential election in November 1860 I went into Mr. Lincoln's office in the State house and said to Lincoln: "Lincoln, you ought to go and vote for the *State* ticket." He replied: "Do you really think I ought to vote?" and to which I said: "Most certainly you ought. One vote may gain or lose the Governor, Legislature, etc." He then remarked: "I guess I'll go, but wait till I cut off the presidential electors on the top of the ticket." He then cut off the head of the ticket. Col. Lamon and Col. Ellsworth and myself only were in the room. I winked to these gentlemen to go along with Lincoln and see him safely through the mass of men at the voting place. They understood me. Lamon went on the right side of Lincoln, Ellsworth on the left; and I at Lincoln's back just behind him. As we approached the voting place, the vast mass of men who had gathered to vote and to see Lincoln vote, as it was whispered that Herndon had got Lincoln to vote or agreed to do so, opened a wide gap for him to pass on to the voting place. The Republicans yelled and shouted as Lincoln approached; he was allowed to vote unmolested, and when he had voted and came out of the courtroom, the voting place, they again yelled and shouted. I must say that the Democrats on that day and place paid about as much respect to Lincoln as the Republicans did; they acted politely, civilly, and respectfully, raising their hats to him as he passed on through them to vote; they acted nobly on that day and at that place and time. Lincoln voted and was glad of it.

Directly after the Lincoln and Douglas campaign in 1858, soon after it was over, he, Lincoln, commenced receiving through the post office all manner of odd pictures cut out of newspapers, expressive of pain, starvation, sorrow, grief, etc., etc. Frequently threatening letters were received by him through the post office, all of which he burned at the time. The receipt of these showed the *animus* of the times to Mr. Lincoln. He said to me once: "I feel as if I should meet with some terrible end"; and so the great man felt through time and space instinctively his coming doom.

Your friend,
W. H. HERNDON.

Springfield, Ill., November 17, 1885.

Friend Weik:

In some particulars Mr. Lincoln was a peculiar man. For instance, he was very liberal and charitable to his fellow-man and yet he was not a generous man in his gifts or with his money; he had none of the avarice of the *get* but had the avarice of the *keep*. Mr. Lincoln was fully aware of the imperfections and faults of the race, and had great charity for man; I never heard him abuse anybody nor did I ever, except once or twice, hear him eulogize anyone; he attacked no one on the stump, because he was aware of his own lowly origin. His motto, in this particular, was: "Those who live in glass houses should not throw stones." Mr. Lincoln loved such books as Jack Downing, *Phœnixiana*, and Petroleum V. Nasby; he was a terribly gloomy man and yet he loved mirth, because it gave vent to his gloom and his melancholy. I have heard him say: "If it were not for these stories, jokes, jests, I should die; they give vent—are the vents—of my moods and gloom." If you were in your office and wished to read anything of interest, just beware how you talked. If you said much, *that much* would suggest to him a story that he heard on the circuit or down in Egypt, the lower part of this State. The thing once suggested, there would be an end of your reading. Close the book you must, you couldn't help it; he would tell one story and that would suggest another; and so the day would roll by pleasant or unpleasant to you; he had *no hold up* in this particular. Tell his stories he would, and read you could not—pleasant to you or not the mill would grind. Lincoln was not a social man, loved no man much, was more or less selfish, was rapt up in his own children, was childish in this, a tool or a slave to them, blind to their faults. Mr. Lincoln was Lawyer, Politician, Lecturer, and Inventor. He succeeded in the law and in politics, was an utter failure as lecturer and inventor.

Lincoln sometimes drank liquor, was a good chess-player, loved "fives," i.e., to play ball, knocking it up against a wall with the hand, two or three men on each side. This letter is purposely miscellaneous as you may wish to pitch, throw, such things in your piece. Probably I repeat some things, if so excuse me, as I do not keep notes of what I write.

Your friend,
W. H. HERNDON.

Springfield, Ill., November 19, 1885.

Friend Weik:

Mr. and Mrs. Lincoln never lived a harmonious life, and when she wanted to go to church or to some gathering, she would go at all events and leave Lincoln to take care of the babies. Mrs. Lincoln couldn't keep a hired girl because she was tyrannical to her and Lincoln perforce was compelled to look after the children. Of a Sunday, Lincoln might be seen, if in summer in his shirtsleeves, hauling his babies in a little wagon up and down the pavement north and south on Eighth Street. Sometimes Lincoln would become so abstracted that the young one would fall out and squall, Lincoln moving on the while. Someone would call Lincoln's attention to what was going on; he would turn back, pick up the child, soothe it, pacify it, etc., and then proceed up and down the pavement as before. So abstracted was he that he did not know what or how he was doing and I suppose cared less. If the little one fell out and Lincoln was told of it, he would say: "This puts me in mind of a story that I heard down in New Salem," and then Lincoln would tell his story and tell it well. The man and Lincoln would sit down on the curbstone of the pavement and finish the forenoon in stories, and when Mr. Lincoln saw Mrs. Lincoln coming from church—she screaming because Lincoln had the child out of doors in the fresh air—he ran into his room and gently took what followed—you know, a hell of scolding. Poor Abe, I can see him now running and crouching.

It happened that sometimes Lincoln would come down to our office of a Sunday with one or two of his little children, hauling them in the same little wagon, and in our office, then and there, write declarations, pleas, and other legal papers. The children—spoilt ones to be sure—would tear up the office, scatter the books, smash up pens, spill the ink, and p——s all over the floor. I have felt many and many a time that I wanted to wring their little necks, and yet out of respect for Lincoln I kept my mouth shut. Lincoln did not note what his children were doing or had done. When Lincoln finished his business, he would haul his children back home and meet the same old scolding or a new and intensified one. He bore all quite philosophically. Jesus, what a home Lincoln's was! What a wife!

One word about Lincoln's honesty and fairness. Many, many years ago one Charles Matheny sold a piece of land to a Mrs. (I forget her name) who was Lincoln's client. The number of the acres in the piece was guessed at or a great mistake was made. The lines of the survey ran east, west, north, and south, but from well-known objects to well-known objects, called monuments. The price of the land was so much per acre and the deed showed the terms of the sale. About the year 1858 Mr. Lincoln was written to by the lady to have her land surveyed, laid off into lots, etc. Lincoln got a compass, chains, etc., and surveyed the lands. In running off the land and calculating the number of the acres he found that Matheny had lost four or five acres of land in this city and that his client had gained it—say four or five acres more or less.

Old man Matheny in the meantime had died, leaving eight or nine children, some of whom had died, leaving heirs, children. Lincoln wrote to his client what he had done and what mistakes had been made and advised his client that she ought in morals and in law rectify the mistake, pay the Matheny heirs what was justly due them according to the acres at the original price agreed upon. The woman at first declined to rectify, but Lincoln wrote her a long letter again, stating what he thought was right and just between the parties. Some of the Matheny heirs were very poor and needy. Lincoln's last kind and noble letter brought the woman to her own sense of right, sent to Mr. Lincoln several hundred dollars. Lincoln was a friend to the Mathenys as well as to his client; he took the trouble of hunting up the scattered heirs and their descendants and paid them every cent that was due them and thus this man, noble man, was ever for justice and the eternal right. I hope you can make out what I write. Correct, etc., etc.—am this minute going to court. "Excuse haste and a bad pen," as this poor devil will say.

Your friend,
W. H. HERNDON.

Springfield, Ill., November 20, 1885.

Friend Weik:

You say that you want one more law case. I can give it to you. About 1859 there lived in a village about seventeen miles west of this place two young men of the first families. One of the young men was named Quinn Harrison, grandson of the Reverend Peter Cartwright. The other was named Greek Crafton, a young lawyer who studied law with Lincoln and Herndon. Harrison's father was rich, and Crafton's father was comparatively poor and yet highly respected. The village was in this county and called Pleasant Plains. There seemed to be a long-existing feud between the families of Harrison and Crafton, at least between the boys, young men about twenty-three years of age; they were young men of promise at that time. The young men met in a store in Pleasant Plains one day by accident and some hot words passed between the two. Crafton struck and gathered Quinn Harrison and threw him. Harrison in the scuffle got out his knife, cut and stabbed Crafton fatally; he lived a day or so and died of the wound. Harrison was arrested and a grand jury found an indictment against Harrison for murder. Lincoln, Logan, and others were employed by Harrison. Governor Palmer and the State's attorney prosecuted. The lawyers on both sides were among the ablest in the State. The case was one of intense interest all over the county. The case was opened and ably conducted on both sides; every inch of ground was contested, hotly fought. All the points of the law, the evidence, practice, and general procedure were raised and discussed with feeling, fervor, and eloquence. Lincoln felt an unusual interest in young Harrison, as the old man, Peyton Harrison, his father, had often accommodated Lincoln when help was needed. During the trial, which was a long one, a complex and a tedious one, the Court, Judge Rice, decided a question against Lincoln's views of the law. Lincoln argued the question of the law decided against him with ability, eloquence, and learning, as Lincoln had thoroughly studied the case in the facts, procedure, and the law. Lincoln submitted to the decision for a considerable time, but found that the point decided against him, and a material one, was one of the principal turning points of the case. Palmer was pushing his victory in the debate to its legitimate conclusion—the utter defeat and rout of Lincoln and the conviction of Harrison of the crime of manslaughter. Lincoln begged time of the Court to reargue the point. The Court granted time. Lincoln prepared himself well with law, came into court with an armful of books, and read the authorities plainly sustaining his view of the case. The Court was obdurate, clung to his decision, overruled Lincoln's objection, admitted the evidence, etc. Lincoln could not stand the absurd decision, for it was absurd and without precedent in the broad world; and in his anger he rose up and seemed inspired with indignation, mingled with a feeling of pity and contempt for the judge's decision. He actually was fired with indignation and spoke fiercely, strongly, contemptuously of the decision of the Court. Lincoln kept, in his anger and contempt, just inside the walls of the law, did not do anything, say anything, that would be a contempt of court; he was careful and yet the scoring that he gave the Court, through its foolish decision, was terrible, blasting, crushing, withering. I shall never forget the scene. Lincoln had the crowd, the jury, the bar, in perfect sympathy and accord. The Court's decision was ridiculed, scoffed, and kicked out of court. Lincoln was mad, vexed, and indignant. When a great big man of mind and body gets mad he is mad all over, terrible, furious, eloquent, etc. The Court at last was convinced or driven to pretend to believe that its decision was wrong, overruled his former decision, sustained Lincoln's views; and so now Lincoln had the field his own way, went to the jury, was able, eloquent, powerful, etc. Harrison, through Lincoln's courage, knowledge of the law and the facts of his case, was honorably acquitted—the verdict of the jury saying "justified." It was a proud day for Lincoln. Lincoln was a grand man, an imposing figure that day, I assure you. The Court was actually badgered by Lincoln into its final decision of the case. Governor Palmer couldn't stop Lincoln's force and eloquence. This was a grand trial and so paint it.

Your friend,
W. H. HERNDON.

Springfield, Ill., November 21, 1885.

Friend Weik:

It seems to me that in your article you *should* say something about Lincoln's nature, qualities, and characteristics; and so here goes. The predominant, the chief, qualities, etc., of Lincoln are as follows: He was morally and physically courageous, even-tempered and conservative, secretive and sagacious, skeptical and cautious, truthful and honest, firm in his own convictions and tolerant of those of others, reflective and cool, ambitious and somewhat selfish, kind to all and good-natured, sympathetic in the presence of suffering or under an imaginative description of it, lived in his reason and reasoned in his life. Easy of approach and perfectly democratic in his nature, had a broad charity for his fellow-men and had an excuse for unreflective acts of his kind, and in short he loved justice and lived out in thought and act the eternal right. The above is correct in Lincoln's *general* life. I do not say that he never deviated from his own nature and his own rules. His nature, the tendency of it, is as I state. I studied Lincoln critically for thirty-odd years and should know him well. Lincoln struggled to live the best life possible. This I know. Sometimes he fell short of his own ideal, as he has often told me; he has told me facts of his life that were not Lincoln's but poor human nature's *in* Lincoln. I shall never tell them to mortal man and of this be sure. Lincoln *as a whole* was really a most noble man.

You say that you intend to write two articles: one on Lincoln as a lawyer and one as politician. The idea is a good one and I approve of it. The fields are broad and good as I see it.

Your friend,
W. H. HERNDON.

I have weighed all my words well before I penned them.

H.

Springfield, Ill., December 1, 1885.

Friend Weik:

You wish to know if Mrs. Lincoln and the Todd aristocratic family did not scorn and detest the Hanks and the Lincoln family; and in answer to which I yell—yes. Mrs. Lincoln held the Hanks tribe in contempt and the Lincoln family generally, the old folks, Thomas Lincoln and his good old wife. Mrs. Lincoln was terribly aristocratic and as haughty and as imperious as she was aristocratic; she was as cold as a chunk of ice. Thomas Lincoln and his good old wife were never in this city, and I do not suppose that they were ever invited to visit Lincoln's house. Had they appeared, I doubt whether Mrs. Lincoln would have admitted them. A young lady by the name of Hanks—I think Dennis Hanks's daughter—came to this city about 1853 and went to school here; she boarded with Lincoln, but this created a fight, a fuss, between Lincoln and his wife. This young lady married a doctor by the name of Chapman, I think. She and her husband now live or did live in Charleston in this State; they are good people. While the young lady was here, Mrs. Lincoln tried to make a servant, a slave, of her, but, being high-spirited, she refused to become Mrs. Lincoln's tool. Mrs. Chapman is a lady; she and I used to correspond about the facts of Lincoln's life, etc. She by nature and in soul was a better woman than Mrs. Lincoln. I personally knew both. If you tell the story, keep Mrs. Chapman's name private, as she would not like it probably. I am glad to know that your *eyes are open* about Dennis Hanks; he is a grand exaggerator, if not a great liar. I believed nothing he told me unless he was—rather his story was—verified by John Hanks, as good a man as ever lived, an honest man and a truthful one. I am now busy in court and must dry up for a while. As facts come up in my mind, I will send notes to you of what

I *know*. You wish to know something of my visit to the abolitionists in 1858; will write you about this when I get time.

> Your friend,
> W. H. HERNDON.

How do you like Lamon's Life of Lincoln generally? It is the truest life that was ever written of a man in my opinion. I do not agree to all it says. I did not like the 19th chapter in all particulars. I think it is the 19th chapter.

Springfield, Ill., December 4, 1885.

To the Editor of the *Religio-Philosophical Journal:*

I have carefully read Mr. Poole's [1] address on Abraham Lincoln, published in the *Religio-Philosophical Journal* of November 28, 1885. Mr. Poole is a stranger to me, but I must say that he struck a rich golden vein in Mr. Lincoln's qualities, characteristics, and nature, and has worked it thoroughly and well, exhaustively in his special line.

I know nothing of Lincoln's belief or disbelief in spiritualism. I had thought, and now think, that Mr. Lincoln's original nature was materialistic as opposed to the spiritualistic; was realistic as opposed to idealistic. I cannot say that he believed in spiritualism, nor can I say that he did not believe in it. He made no revelations to me on this subject, but I have grounds outside, or besides, Mr. Poole's evidences, of the probability of the fact that he did sometimes attend here, in this city, séances. I am told this by Mr. Ordway, a spiritualist. I know nothing of this fact on my personal knowledge.

Mr. Lincoln was a kind of fatalist in some aspects of his philosophy, and skeptical in his religion. He was a sad man, a terribly gloomy one—a man of sorrow, if not of agony. This, his state, may have arisen from a defective physical organization, or it may have arisen from some fatalistic idea, that he was to die a sudden and a terrible death. Some unknown power seemed to buzz about his consciousness, his being, his mind, that whispered in his ear: "Look out for danger ahead!" This peculiarity in Mr. Lincoln I had noticed for years, and it is no secret in this city. He has said to me more than once: "Billy, I feel as if I shall meet with some terrible end." He did

---

[1] See the letter of January 5, 1886, to Poole.

not know what would strike him, nor when, nor where, nor how hard; he was a blind intellectual Samson, struggling and fighting in the dark against the fates. I say on my own personal observation that he felt this for years. Often and often I have resolved to make or get him to reveal the causes of his misery, but I had not the courage nor the impertinence to do it.

When you are in some imminent danger or suppose you are, when you are suffering terribly, do you not call on some power to come to your assistance and give you relief? I do, and all men do. Mr. Lincoln was in great danger, or thought he was, and did as you and I have done; he sincerely invoked and fiercely interrogated all intelligences to give him a true solution of his state—the mysteries and his destiny. He had great, too great, confidence in the common judgment of an uneducated people. He believed that the common people had truths that philosophers never dreamed of; and often appealed to that common judgment of the common people over the shoulders of scientists. I am not saying that he did right. I am only stating what I know to be facts, to be truths.

Mr. Lincoln was in some phases of his nature very, very superstitious; and it may be—it is quite probable—that he, in his gloom, sadness, fear, and despair, invoked the spirits of the dead to reveal to him the cause of his states of gloom, sadness, fear, and despair. He craved light from all intelligences to flash his way to the unknown future of his life.

May I say to you that I have many, many times thoroughly sympathized with Mr. Lincoln in his intense sufferings; but I dared not obtrude into the sacred ground of his thoughts that are so sad, so gloomy, and so terrible.

Your friend,
WM. H. HERNDON.

Springfield, Ill., December 10, 1885.

Friend Weik:

Your letter, dated the 6th *inst.*, is at hand. I am glad that you like Lamon's Life of Lincoln; it is the truest life that was ever written of [a] man. I gathered up the facts cautiously—carefully and critically. I know every person whose name is used in the book, I think. I know who were truthful, who were exaggerators, and who were liars, etc. Lamon gathered up a few facts.

Miss Owens is a Kentucky lady, is well educated, came to Illinois in 1836–37. Saw Lincoln at Able's. The lady's name is Mrs. Vincent [1] of Missouri. It is no exaggeration to say that Mrs. Vincent is an accomplished *lady*.

The dash of which you speak stands in the place of a woman. I cannot in honor answer further.

Lincoln came to this city in 1837 and from that time to 1843–44 he and Speed were quite familiar, to go no further, with the women. I cannot tell you what I know, especially in ink. Speed was a lady's man in a good and true sense. Lincoln only went to see a few women of the first class, women of sense. Fools ridiculed him; he was on this point tender-footed. John T. Stuart is dead. Between Lincoln and Stuart from 1843 to 1865 there was no good feeling of an honest friendship. Lincoln hated some of the ways of Stuart. Lincoln felt no jealousy toward Stuart. Stuart did toward Lincoln. Stuart in his heart hated Lincoln. John T. Stuart was seventy-seven years of age; he was a weak brother and a shy one, tricky, dodger; he and Lincoln did not agree in politics since 1853. Stuart was intensely pro-slavery, L. for freedom. S. and L. were in partnership only about two or three years.

Friend Weik, why, my good sir, I have given away twenty years ago all my Lincoln letters; he had not been buried before I was bounced for everything I possessed that Lincoln's fingers ever touched. I am a weak brother, you know, and I gave till I had nothing to give. You should have my letters of Lincoln if I had any, you know.

Your friend,
W. H. HERNDON.

Come and see me and I'll tell you much about men, times, women. I'll write to you as I get time; will write about my visit to Washington, etc., etc.

Springfield, Ill., December 16, 1885.

Friend Weik:

I have just thought of a new fact, which is as follows: Some time

---

[1] An error. She was Mrs. Vineyard, as explained in the letter of January 1, 1886, to Weik.

about 1855 I went into a bookstore in this city and saw a book, a small one, entitled, called, I think, *The Annual of Science.* I looked over it casually and liked it and bought it. I took the book to Lincoln and H.'s office. Lincoln was in, reading a newspaper of value; he said to me: "Well, Billy, you have got a new book, which is good, I suppose. What is it? Let me see it." He took the book in his hand, looked over the pages, read the title, introductions, and probably the first chapter, and saw at a glance the purpose and object of the book, which were as follows: to record, teach, and fully explain the *failures* and *successes* of experiments of all philosophies and scientists, everywhere, including chemistry, mechanics, etc. He instantly rose up and said that he must buy the whole set, started out and got them. On returning to the office, he said: "I have wanted such a book for years, because I sometimes make experiments and have thoughts about the physical world that I do not know to be true or false. I may, by this book, correct my errors and save time and expense. I can see where scientists and philosophers have failed and avoid the rock on which they split or can see the means of their success and take advantage of their brains, toil, and knowledge. Men are greedy to publish the successes of efforts, but meanly shy as to publishing the failures of man. Many men are ruined by this one-sided practice of concealment of blunders and failures." This he said substantially to me with much feeling, vim, and force. The last time that he spoke of the book to me he spoke in glowing terms.

Enclosed I send you a letter of mine, published in the *Religio-Philosophical Journal* of December 12, 1885.[1]

Your friend,
W. H. HERNDON.

Springfield, Ill., December 23, 1885.

Friend Weik:

Say in the early part of 1858 Mr. Lincoln came into our office in a dejected spirit. We passed the compliments of the morning, did some necessary and quite important business, etc., etc. Mr. Lincoln sat down on the sofa, seemed dejected, melancholic, spoke about politics, his chances for Senator, his hopes and his aspirations, spoke of the

---

[1] See the letter dated December 4, 1885.

dodging and wriggling of Douglas on the Kansas-Nebraska question, said kindly: "I think Greeley is not doing me, an old Republican and a tried anti-slavery man, right; he is talking up Douglas, an untrue and an untried man, a dodger, a wriggler, a tool of the South once and now a snapper at it—hope he will bite 'em good; but I don't feel that it is exactly right to pull me down in order to elevate Douglas. I like Greeley, think he intends right, but I think he errs in this hoisting up of Douglas, while he gives me a downward shove. I wish that someone could put a flea in Greeley's ear, see Trumbull, Sumner, Wilson, Seward, Parker, Garrison, Phillips, and others, and try and turn the currents in the right directions. These men ought to trust the tried and true men." This Mr. Lincoln said to me in substance, and I *inferred* from it, only *inferred* it, that Mr. Lincoln wished me to go and see these men, and see what I could do in the matter; he knew that I was with the most of these men in constant correspondence, and had been for years, long before Lincoln took his advanced anti-slavery grounds *on the stump*. So I bundled up, had plenty of money then, never supposing that I should want thereafter, and started east, on the *inferred* hint to see what could be done; landed in Washington; saw Trumbull, Seward, Sumner, Wilson; stated what I wished of them. They were all right and doing all they could to stem the rising tide of Douglasism. I then went to New York, saw Greeley, told him politely and cautiously my story, said to him that Douglas was a new convert, was not to be trusted, was conscienceless, and without political principles or honor, etc. I said to Greeley: "You do right in patting Douglas on the back, but wrong when you indirectly hit Lincoln, a true, real, and long-tried anti-slavery man, in order directly or indirectly to overthrow or kill Lincoln. Can you not assist Douglas and our cause by helping Douglas without stabbing Lincoln?" We had a long conversation, but this is the shell and substance of it. Greeley said to me, as I *inferred*, as I understood it, that he would most assuredly assist Douglas in all honorable ways; that he liked Lincoln, had confidence in him, and would not injure him; that he would somewhat change tactics, and be careful in the future. Greeley was kind to me, introduced me to many of the leading Republicans of New York City, had conversations with them about the way things were moving. Most of them said: "Greeley is all right, has a string to

pull, but will in the end show you his intents, etc., and will justify."
Greeley for some time acted up to the square thing, up to his promises as I *understood* them; wrote to Greeley that I thought he had
passed the line, etc. He and I had some hard words, but at last we
understood each other. He said something in his paper about me that
was not correct. I again wrote to Greeley correcting him; he apolo-
gized to me through the *Tribune*, i.e., he explained and withdrew the
charge, etc. From New York I went to Boston, saw Governor Banks,
Theodore Parker, Garrison, Phillips, and put them all right, if they
were not right before, which is more than likely. I was gone about
one month, returned home, paid my own expenses. I did not then think
that the trip was necessary at all, but to assure Lincoln, to pacify
him, to make him feel better, I went, and did all that I could for friend
Lincoln. When I got home I told Lincoln what I had seen and done,
gave him my opinion that the trend, tendency, and march of things
were all in his favor, and that all would come out right side uppermost; he seemed pleased, if not gratified, thanked me most heartily.
From the time that I saw these mentioned men and hundreds more,
including many newspapers, etc., I think now that things began more
and more to work for Lincoln's success. I say I think so, but do not
know the cause, unless it be my assurance that Lincoln, to the anti-
slavery cause, was as true as steel, as firmly set as Garrison, etc.

I saw many anti-slavery ladies, and their heads were stubbornly
for "Honest Abe." This cheered me, for I knew if the women were for
Lincoln that Lincoln was the coming man; many said: "Lincoln is not
radical enough, but he is a growing man, has a conscience that can be
educated, and the times will do that, if he has an ear to hear." I had a
good time of it, was treated well by all persons, saw the cities, etc. . . .

I may be mistaken in the year in which I went on my trip; it may
be I went in 1857 or in 1857–58. Correct me if I am wrong. It is now
thirty years since I went on the Lincoln business, and I may have
forgotten much of what was said, when, where, etc., etc. Probably, if
you will refer to Lamon's Life of Lincoln, it can aid you in dates and
the like. I may err in some things.

I am about pumped dry, dry as a sand desert.

Your friend,
W. H. Herndon.

Springfield, Ill., December 29, 1885.

Friend Weik:

I once had an excellent library which I was compelled to sell because I was too poor to hold it. I owed money and sacrificed it to pay my debts. I imported books from London, through the house of C. S. Francis & Co. When I heard of a good work, I ordered it, English, French, or German, if the two latter were translated. I kept many of my books in my office, especially the new ones, and read them. Mr. Lincoln had access to all such books as I had and frequently read parts of the volumes, such as struck his fancy. I used to read to him passages in the books that struck me as eloquent, grand, poetical, philosophic, and the like. I would talk in my own peculiar vein to Lincoln about what I read and thought; he would like or dislike what I read and thought, would discuss the subject with me, sometimes animatedly. Sometimes we would get into a philosophic discussion, sometimes on religious questions and sometimes on this question and on that. It was in the world of politics that he lived. Politics were his life, newspapers his food, and his great ambition his motive power. I have given you a list of the newspapers that we, one or the other of us, took from 1850 to 1861. Now let me give you the kind of books which Lincoln had access to and sometimes peeped into. I had all the following books, i.e., the writers of the works, their names, and the books, etc., they write. If I did not have all I had the most of them, quite all, and hundreds, if not thousands, of others; they are as follows:

Emerson	Darwin
Carlyle	Draper
Parker	Lecky
McNaught	Lewes
Strauss	Renan
Monell	Kant
Beecher	Fichte
Feuerbach	Conson [?]
Buckle	Hamilton
Froude	Spencer

I include publications up to 1861 only and the like; took the *Westminster Review*. All the above class of books I purchased as soon as out. If in German or French and *translated*, I sent for and got through the house of C. S. Francis & Co. of New York. I kept abreast of the spirit of the age till financial troubles overtook me in 1871–75. Since that time I have not read much. My poverty keeps my nose to the grindstone and it is now raw. I was of a progressive turn of mind and tried to get Lincoln in the same channel of thought. How I succeeded, time and criticism can alone tell. If I had any influence with him at all, it was along the line of the good, I hope and believe. Possibly I have helped the world a little in my way, hope so. I shall never state fully or otherwise what I did for Lincoln. I shall never do this in writing. I will talk to confidential friends somewhat in a *chat*, but never for use nor publication. I can now see Lincoln, his image before me; it is a sad beseeching look. I feel sad.

Your good friend,
W. H. HERNDON.

Springfield, Ill., January 1, 1886.

Friend Weik:

In my last letter I gave you a list of books which Lincoln more or less peeped into. I forgot some important ones on political economy; they are as follows: Mill's political economy, Carey's political economy, social science. McCullough's political economy, Wayland, and some others. Lincoln ate up, digested, and assimilated Wayland's little work. Lincoln liked the book, except the *free trade* doctrines. Lincoln, I think, liked political economy, the study of it. I had American and English works besides those mentioned above on political economy.

The following conversation between Lincoln and myself about 1858 is too good to be lost. One day I somewhat earnestly complained to Lincoln that he was not quick and energetic enough in a particular case to accomplish our ends and what I thought was needed in the case. In a very good-natured way he replied: "Billy, I am like a long strong jackknife doubled up in the handle. The extreme point of the blade has to move through a wider space before it is open than your little short woman's knife, which you hold in your hand, but when the jackknife is open, it cuts wider and *deeper* than your little thing. I am six feet two inches high and it takes me a good while to open and to act, so be patient with me. To change the figure," he said, "these long convolutions of my poor brain take time, sometimes a long time, to open and gather force, but like a long, well-platted, heavy, and well-twisted ox lash, when swung around and around high in the air on a good whip stalk, well seasoned, by an expert ox-driver and popped and cracked and snapped at a lazy ox shirking duty, it cuts to the raw, brings blood, opens a gash that makes the lazy ox sting with pain, and so, when these long convolutions are opened and let off on something, are they not a power and a force in action, as you say? You yourself have often complimented me on my force of expression and now in part you have the desired *why*." This Mr. Lincoln said to me, and the substance is his and many of the words are his just as he used them.

Lincoln's First Inaugural

Mr. Lincoln some time in January or February 1861 asked me to loan him Henry Clay's great, his best speech in 1850, and likewise told me to get him President Jackson's Proclamation against Nullification in 1832–33, I think, and the Constitution. I did loan him Clay's speech of '50, General Jackson's proclamation, and the Constitution of the United States. Lincoln was perfectly familiar with Webster's reply to Calhoun and Haynes in 1833, I think. Lincoln read Webster's reply to Calhoun and Haynes in 1834–35 in New Salem while deputy postmaster under Samuel Hill. Lincoln was thoroughly read up in the history of politics of his country. Lincoln, as soon as I got him what he wanted, went over to Smith's store on the south side of the public [square?], went upstairs above Smith's, his brother-in-law, and got his room and then and there wrote his first Inaugural. Lincoln thought that Webster's great speech in reply to Haynes was the very best speech that was ever delivered. It is my opinion that these books and speeches were all the things that he used in the writing of his first Inaugural.

Now about Mrs. Vineyard—not Vincent, as I wrote to you. I have not heard from her. However, I'll tell you where she lives, *if you will say to her that I referred you to her and that you are the only man, except Lamon*, whom I have mentioned her name to. This is the exact truth. Mrs. Vineyard, Mary, lives or did live in Western Missouri; she must be 78–80 years of age; she is, if living, an intelligent woman, well educated and refined.

One word about Dennis Hanks. When you see him, ask him, in a roundabout way, if Thomas Lincoln was not castrated because of the mumps when young. Dennis told me this often and repeated it. *Please* ask the question, won't you, and note it down.

If you see Mrs. Chapman and the doctor give them my best respects. You had better go down to Farmington in Coles and see Mrs. Moore, if living; she is Lincoln's stepsister, as I remember it. As you live in Indiana, you had better go and see Miss Jones of Gentryville. Lincoln kept store or worked for Jones. When you come up here, I have an idea to suggest to you.

Excuse this paper and my blunders on it.

Your friend,
W. H. HERNDON.

Springfield, Ill., January 5, 1886.

Mr. C. O. Poole.

My dear Sir:

In the first part of the nineteenth century a great and noble man was born to America specially and to the world generally. His life was a grand success and his name stands high up among the mountain men of the world. Mr. Lincoln thought too much and did too much for America and the world to be crammed into an epigram or shot off with a single rocket; he was too close to the touch of the divine everywhere and too near to the suggestions and whisperings of nature for such quick work, done with a flash. It is said that he was a many-sided man. It will take close, severe, and continuous thought through an analysis of his character to understand him or give a just idea of the man. Mr. Lincoln was a riddle and a puzzle to his friends and neighbors among whom he lived and moved. You wish to see this puzzle solved and this riddle unriddled. You and the world wish, crave, to know the elements of Lincoln's great and honored success. You desire, you wish, for a knowledge of the causes of his power and the secrets of his success. Having been acquainted with the man for more than thirty years, twenty years of which he was known by me closely and intimately, I have formed a settled opinion, founded on my own observation, experience, and reason, of the man, and the causes of his power and the secrets of his success, and I propose to give to the world my opinion of them. This is done, *first*, because the man was hard, very difficult to understand, even by his bosom friends and his close and intimate neighbors among whom he associated, and, *secondly*, because the reading and thinking world does not know him today. I really and dearly wish to aid the good people in forming a good, a correct and just opinion of the man. If Mr. Lincoln could speak to me this day, in reference to my purpose in writing this letter, he would say : "Tell the truth and don't varnish me," and I shall follow its spirit.

First: Mr. Lincoln's success in life rested on his qualities, characteristics, and nature, which are as follows : *First:* he had great reason, pure and strong; he lived in the mind and he thought in his life and lived in his thought. Lincoln was a persistent thinker, and a profound analyzer of the subject which engaged his attention. Politics were his life and his ambition his motive power, newspapers his food. What he read he read for a proximate, near end ; he was not a general reader ; he was embodied reflection itself ; he was not only reflective but abstracted. These wrought evils on his intellectual and physical system ; he was a close, persistent, continuous, and terrible thinker ; he was self-reliant, self-helpful, self-trustful, never once doubting his own ability or power to do anything anyone could do. Mr. Lincoln thought, at least he so acted, that there were no limitations to the endurance of his mental and vital forces. In his case from a long, severe, continuous, and exhaustive study of the subjects which he loved, generally taking no stimulative food nor drinks, there followed as a consequence physical and mental exhaustion, a nervous morbidity and spectral illusions, irritability, melancholy, and despair. Hence, I think, comes a little of his superstition.

Secondly, Mr. Lincoln had an active, breathing, and a living conscience that rooted itself deep down in his very being, every fiber of which twisted around his whole nervous system. This conscience of his was a positive quality of him, and it sent its orders and decrees to the head to be executed there ; it was the court of courts that gave final judgments from which there was no appeal, so far as he was concerned ; he stood bolt-upright and downright on his conscience. What that decreed the head and tongue and hands obeyed unhesitatingly, never doubting its justice. Lincoln lived mostly in the conscience and the head ; and these two attributes of his were the two great ones of his nature, the ruling and predominant ones of his whole and entire life. It is thought by some men that Mr. Lincoln was a very warm-hearted man, spontaneous and impulsive. This is not the exact truth. God has never yet made and it is probable that He never will make any man, any creature, all head, all heart, and all conscience. His types are of the mixed elements compounded to suit Himself. Mr. Lincoln was tender-hearted *when in the presence* of suffering or when it was enthusiastically or poetically described to him; he had great charity for the weaknesses of his fellow-man; his nature was merciful and it sprang into manifestations quickly on *the presenta-tion* of a proper subject under proper conditions; he had no imagination to invoke, through the distances, suffering, nor fancy to paint it. The subject of mercy must be presented to him. The main question with Mr. Lincoln was: "Is the thing right, is it just?"; and if a man was the subject of his attention, the question which he put to himself was: "What great truth, what principle, do you represent in this world?" If the thing was just, he approved of it, and if the man was a sham, he said: "Begone." He was a man of great moral and physical courage and had the valor and bravery of his convictions and dared cautiously to do what he thought was right and just; he was cautious and conservative in his nature, was prudent and wise in his acts, and I have often thought over-cautious, sometimes bordering on the timid. Sometimes he stood long hesitating between the thought and the deed.

Thirdly: Mr. Lincoln's heart was sufficiently warm and he [was] sufficiently impulsive and spontaneous for the broad field and noble sphere of his action, his and the nation's destiny. A governor, a judge, a president in office, has not legally much to do with the heart, but has all to do with conscience and reason, right and justice as defined by law. Had Mr. Lincoln been a man of no will and all heart, this great government would have gone to wreck in 1863 or before. Come, was not Mr. Lincoln built and organized for the occasion? Was he not the right man in the right time, in the right place? Would you have made him different? How would you have grouped the atoms or mixed and mingled the elements of his make-up?

Mr. Lincoln was a sad, gloomy, and melancholic man and wore the signs of these in every line of his face, on every organ and every feature of it; they were chiseled deep therein, and now the question is: What were the causes of these? The causes were, *first*, possibly heredity, and, *secondly*, his physical *organization*. Mrs. Thomas Lincoln, Abraham's own mother, was an uneducated, somewhat rough, but by nature an intellectual, sad, and sensitive woman. It is quite possible that Mr. Lincoln inherited this sadness and sensitiveness from his mother; he was in some particulars a very sensitive man. It is probable that his physical *organization*, which functioned slowly and feebly, gave rise to feelings of uneasiness, nervousness, and irritability, gloom, melancholy, and despondency, if not sometimes of despair. Both of these, heredity and organization, may have acted as causes. These states, however caused, made him a fatalist in philosophy and a skeptic in matters of religion. His philosophy was: "What is to be will be, and no wish of ours nor prayers can change nor reverse the inevitable decree." Lincoln's sad hopeless declaration to his friends in Washington, who advised him to be more careful of his person in the future than he had been in the past, in substance was: "My dear sirs, [if] it is writ, it is writ." The very idea that he was in the hands of an invisible, irresistible, and inevitable deaf power which moved as an omnipotent force evidently harassed and worried him. There are two other minor causes that may have intensified his states, his melancholy, and the like; they were, *first*, his intense love for, courtship of, and untimely death of, Ann Rutledge, the handsome, sweet, and lovely girl of New Salem, and, *secondly*, his courtship and marriage to Miss Mary Todd. Lincoln's married life was a domestic hell on earth. The whole sad story *shall* be told sometime. Twice in this man's life he walked that sharp and narrow line that divides sanity from insanity.

Men at once, at first blush, everywhere saw that Lincoln was a sad, gloomy man, a man of sorrow. I have often and often heard men say: "That man is a man of sorrow, and I really feel for him, I sympathize with him." This sadness on the part of Mr. Lincoln and sympathy on the part of the observer were a heart's magnetic tie between the two. This result gave Lincoln a power over men, rather it was self-inspired. All men and women always and everywhere treated him under all conditions with great and profound respect, and a close observer of human nature could see, detect, that much of that deep respect issued from the heart. Let me translate such acts of respect and deference of those who ever saw him into my own words. Those words are: "I beseech you, let me respect and favor you." Men who do not know Mr. Lincoln, and never did, have paraded his hardships and struggles in his younger days in glowing words, or sad ones. Such an idea, such a description of the man, is not exactly true; he never saw the minute, the hour, nor the day that he did not have many financial friends to aid him, to assist him, and to help him in all ways. His friends vied with each other for the pleasure or the honor of assisting him. Lincoln deserved all this respect and confidence; he was all honor and integrity, spoke the whole truth and acted it; he, like all boys in the great West as well as elsewhere, had to study in order to learn. Life in his case was a comparatively easy life, as compared with the struggles of the ambitious young man of the East. There the struggle for life is the fiercer. Lincoln was the favorite of everybody—man, woman, and child—where he lived and was known, and he richly deserved it. Lincoln generally rejected all help, his idea, motto, being: "Those who receive favors owe a debt of gratitude to the giver and to that extent are obedient and abject slaves."

First, now if the reader will but put these four qualities of Lincoln together: *first*, namely, his great reasoning power with a profound judgment, if he had time to fully evolve and apply his ideas to the facts of life; *secondly*, a deep and living conscience, with a tender heart *in presence* of suffering or want; *thirdly*, his spirit of prudence and his genius for practical sagacity; and, *fourthly*, a sadness, a gloominess, with somewhat of fatalistic ideas in his philosophy and skepticism about his religion or beliefs, authority, creeds, and forms of religion; *and run them out as causes* into his daily life, he will have the causes of his power and the secrets of his success. These have influenced me and thousands, if not millions, of others. I felt these influences when he and I were younger, and I feel them now. Because of Lincoln's great reason, his conscience, his heart, his sadness, his prudence and practical sagacities, women, men, the people, and the nation voluntarily and trustfully threw themselves into his arms, clothed with an almost infinite power, and as calmly and as confidingly and as trustfully rested there as when an infant goes to sleep in its mother's loving, tender, and watchful bosom. Lincoln deeply impressed this trustworthiness upon the people, and they were never deceived; they were an impressible mass and he stamped it deep with the word—*Trust*.

Secondly, Mr. Lincoln continuously lived in three worlds, states, or conditions of his existence. *First*, he lived in the purely reflective and thoughtful; *secondly*, in the sad, thoughtless, and gloomy; and, *thirdly,* he lived in the happy world of his own levities. He was sometimes in the one state and then in another, and at times the transition was slow and gradual and at times quick, quick as a flash. Writers, respected ones, and biographers have said that Lincoln was a many-sided man. If they mean that he was sometimes reflective and thoughtful, sometimes thoughtless, and sometimes cheerful and happy, then I have no objections to the idea of his many-sidedness. I would suggest a better and a more accurate idea, and that is that Mr. Lincoln was a many-*mooded* man. To form a perfectly true idea of the man, take the first four qualities as last mentioned above and the three last mentioned and bunch them, and the reader has a true analysis of Lincoln's nature and a good insight into the inner man. Every feeling that Lincoln felt, every thought of his, every willing and action of the man, issued, burst out of and from the qualities, attributes, and states above given. His thoughts were tinged and colored and his acts fashioned by his moods. These must all be considered and taken as a whole when Mr. Lincoln is to be thoroughly understood by anyone.

Wishing to help the people to understand Mr. Lincoln, they must indulge me in a repetition of another idea so as to keep the full train of thought in view. He thought, at least he so acted, that there were no limitations to the force and endurance of his mental and vital powers. In his case, from a long, continuous, severe, persistent, and exhaustive thought of the subject which he loved, as a general rule taking no stimulative food nor drinks, there necessarily followed, as a consequence, physical and mental exhaustion, a nervous morbidity, a sadness, a gloom, a melancholy, spectral illusions, irritability, and despair. Hence it may be comes his superstition. I state this that men see Mr. Lincoln as I saw him and knew him. This is the sole reason.

In what Mr. Lincoln said he suppressed no fact and suggested no falsehood; he told the truth and the whole truth, and this truthfulness and sincerity were written on every organ and feature of the face. The observer saw this and firmly and fixedly believed and trusted what he saw and felt. I do not wish to be misunderstood. I have said and now say that Mr. Lincoln was a secretive, silent, and a very reticent-minded man, trusting no man, nor woman, nor child with the inner secrets of his ambitious soul. This man was easy of approach and perfectly democratic in his nature. No man, however humble, ever felt uneasy in his presence. Lincoln was an odd man, a singular man, awkward, uncouth, graceless, and somewhat unsocial. But these, to some repulsive, aspects of his nature, like the lesser stars in the heavens, were driven into the dark infinite background by the greater and brighter flaming ones of his good intents beaming o'er his face.

This great man, for great he was, has given to the world a great, a grand character, and let us all lovingly cherish it forever. Mr. Lincoln is a true and faithful expression of this, our age and a good representative of it. Our generation and our times will eloquently speak to the great infinite future generations and times, through our good and great man, who will teach them our arts, sciences, civilization, and philosophies. The good deeds of today will run through the race and knit us all together by silver threads, along the lines of which we of today and of this generation shall speak through all times and to all generations of men.

Your friend,
WM. H. HERNDON.

Springfield, Ill., January 7, 1886.

Friend Weik:

I wish to say a few words about Lincoln's education or the probabilities in him of a college and classical education. Mr. Lincoln was by nature a man of peculiarities and of strong individualities. His expressions were strong, gnarly, and original; he had an exact and keen perception, the precise seeing of the thing or idea, and had the power of expression; he studied expression, the keen, clear power of exact utterance to convey his idea. Had he gone to college and *half* graduated, or wholly so, and before his style was crystallized, or had [he] been educated after he had read our rounded, flat, dull artistic style of expression, writing or speaking, he would have lost, and the world would have lost, his strong individuality in his speech, his style, manner, and method of utterance. He would have been a rounded man in an artistic way, would have sunk into the classic beautiful. But it so happened, was so decreed, that his style, manner, method or utterance, expression, its strength, its simplicity, and rugged grandeur, were crystallized long before he became acquainted with the smooth, weak, and artistic style of today. Lincoln was Lincoln and no one else; and he spoke and wrote in Lincolnisms. Polish, art, and literature grind down our peculiarities, personalities, and individualities and make us alike in expression. We sacrifice strength and grandeur to art and beauty. If you remember, I told you that the process, way, of Lincoln's mental evolution was through thought to Æsop's fables, through these to general maxims, from maxims to stories, jokes, jests, and from these to clear, strong Anglo-Saxon words of power. In his mental evolution he passed through all these phases. I have heard Lincoln substantially state this, including the probabilities of the weakening process, methods, etc., of a classical or college education; so I was told this by all his friends in Indiana and his early friends in Illinois.

The flunky, smooth, sickly, weak artistic literature of the day, ocean wide and as shallow too, would, like the rising tide and reflow, the pulses and surges of the sea, have ground the sharp, jagged, and rough corners off the man like the ground pebbles into a round polished thing, like the pebbles on the beaches of the ocean, all quite alike.

Lincoln, you know, was a complete success in law, in politics, and as a ruler, as President of the United States; he was a flat failure as inventor, eulogist, and lecturer; he once tried to demonstrate the undemonstrable; he thought that he could completely demonstrate, square rather, the circle; he purchased tools, etc., with which to make the attempt, but failed. Lincoln was keenly sensitive to his failures, and it would not do to mention them in his presence. Mr. Lincoln, had he taken up the idea, had he thought it necessary, would have taught the graces of motion, civilities of life, etiquettes of society and its fashions. Lincoln thought that he could do anything that other men could or would try to do; he had unbounded confidence in himself, in his capacities and powers; he asked no man's advice and sought no man's opinion, as a general, quite universal rule.

These peculiarities and failures show that Lincoln had narrow and shallow shoals in the river of his being o'er which the waters danced and rippled, but which broke in the flashing sunlight into millions of flashing mirrors, reflecting wondrous beauty to the human eye, and yet these narrow and shallow shoals only proved that above them and below them there were deeper waters all up and down the great stream of his grand life that flowed onward and onward to the deep inner seas of the Eternal. Such was Lincoln.

It is now late and in the night, am tired from my daily toil. Will you have the kindness to write me out a copy of this and send it to me? I have no time to do it, want said copy for a friend in New York. So good night, my friend.

Your good friend,
W. H. HERNDON.

Springfield, Ill., January 8, 1886.

Friend Weik:

I have heard Lincoln tell the following *facts* on himself. In 1850 Mr. Lincoln was an applicant, under Fillmore's administration, for Commissioner of the General Land Office; he made arrangements to start for Washington and started from Ramsdell's tavern in this city; he had a companion in the stage, for it was in old stage times, who was a gentleman from Kentucky, educated, cultured, and a man of accomplishments, but, like all warm and good-hearted men, he loved the good and cheerful. The two men, Lincoln and his friend, started for Washington early in the morning, eating their breakfast before day. After they had got in the stage and had ridden some miles, the Kentucky gentleman pulled out of his pocket a small plug of the very best tobacco from the "sacred soil of Virginia," and handed it to Mr. Lincoln, with a fine tortoise-shell penknife, and said to Lincoln: "Stranger, will you take a chew?" and to which Mr. Lincoln said: "Thank you, I never chew." The two rode on for some miles. When they got near Taylorville, some twenty-five miles from this place and east of it, the Kentucky gentleman pulled out a fine cigar case filled with the very best and choicest of Havana cigars, opened it, got out his lighter, and said to Lincoln: "Please have a fine Havana cigar," and to which Mr. Lincoln replied in his kindest manner: "Thanks, stranger, I never smoke." The gentleman lit his cigar and very leisurely rode along thumping and bumping over the rough road, smoking and puffing away, conversing all the while. Lincoln and his Kentucky companion became very much attached to each other. Lincoln had told some of his best jokes and the man had spun out his best ideas. They were really much pleased with each other, seemed to fit one another. The Kentucky gentleman was graceful and Lincoln graceless, but somehow or other they fitted each other like brother chums. They rode on merrily and pleasantly for a long, long while to them, for it was a tiresome journey. The stand where the two were to eat their dinners was being approached, was seen in the distance. The Kentucky man threw out of the stage the stub of his cigar, opened his satchel or other thing, and took out a silver case filled with the very best French brandy, took out the cork, got a silver cup, and handing them to Lincoln, saying: "Stranger, take a glass of the best of French brandies, won't you?" and to which Mr. Lincoln said: "No, I thank you, mister, I never drink." This peculiarity seemed to amuse the Kentucky gentleman very much; he threw himself back against the front of the stage and good-naturedly and laughing said: "See here, stranger, rather, my jolly companion, I have gone through the world a good deal and have had much experience with men and women of all classes, and in all climes, and I have noticed one thing—" Mr. Lincoln, here breaking in anxiously, asked his companion: "What is it, what is it?" "It is this," said the Kentucky man. "My observation, my experience, is, among men, that those who have no vices have d——d few virtues." Lincoln was fond of a joke as you know, looked at his friend sharply to see if it was a joke or was intended for an insult, intending to pitch him out of the stage if it was an insult, and to laugh over it if a joke. Lincoln was quickly convinced that the man was good-natured, kind, gentlemanly, etc.; and then he burst out into a loud laugh saying: "It's good, it's too good to be lost, and I shall tell it to my friends." Lincoln really laughed himself tired, kicked out, in fact, the bottom of the stage, tore out the crown of his hat by running his hand through it, etc., etc. The two friends became bosom ones and landed in Washington together. The Kentuckian got what he wanted and Lincoln got defeated, etc.

Your friend,

W. H. Herndon.

Springfield, Ill., January 8, 1886.

Friend Weik:

It was the habit, custom, of Mrs. Lincoln, when any big man or woman visited her house, to dress up and trot out Bob, Willie, or Tad and get them to monkey around, talk, dance, speak, quote poetry, etc., etc. Then she would become enthusiastic and eloquent over the children, much to the annoyance of the visitor and to the mortification of Lincoln. However, Lincoln was totally blind to his children's faults.

After Mrs. Lincoln had exhausted the English language and broken herself down in her rhapsodies on her children, Lincoln would smooth things over by saying: "These children may be something sometimes, if they are not merely rare-ripes, rotten ripes, hothouse plants. I have always noticed that a rare-ripe child quickly matures, but rots as quickly." Lincoln was proud of his children and blind to their faults. He, Lincoln, used to come down to our office on a Sunday when Mrs. Lincoln had gone to church, *to show her new bonnet,* leaving Lincoln to care for and attend to the children. Lincoln would turn Willie and Tad loose in our office, and they soon gutted the room, gutted the shelves of books, rifled the drawers, and riddled boxes, battered the points of my gold pens against the stairs, turned over the inkstands on the papers, scattered letters over the office, and danced over them and the like. I have felt a many a time that I wanted to wring the necks of these brats and pitch them out of the windows, but out of respect for Lincoln and knowing that he was abstracted, I shut my mouth, bit my lips, and left for parts unknown. Poor boys, they are dead now and gone! I should like to *know* one thing and that is: What caused the death of these children? I have an opinion which I shall never state to anyone. I know a good deal of the Lincoln family and too much of Mrs. Lincoln. I wish I did not know as much of her as I do; she was a tigress. I can see poor Lincoln woman-whipped and woman-carved [?] and yet sometimes he would rise and cut up the very devil for a while, make things more lively and "get." This woman was once a brilliant one, but what a sad sight to see her in any year after 1862 and especially a year or so before she died; she refused to see any and all ministers of the gospel, any preachers, about her hopes of heaven or fear of hell, about God or her own salvation. I guess her religion was like her husband's, rather infidel, agnostic, or atheistic, etc., etc., according to moods or whims.

You state to me that I am the only one of Lincoln's friends, contemporaries, that is willing to tell anything or much about Lincoln or his family. There are two good reasons for this: first, he was well and perfectly known by many, and, secondly, he trampled too often and too hard on the toes of those who did know him. Lincoln outstripped his contemporaries and companions and they feel a terrible jealousy against the man who overheaded, outstripped them. I have seen this meanness often. I have often said to you that Lincoln was terribly ambitious and to that extent he was egoistic, selfish, cold. The ruling people here, say from 1856 to 1861, do not, as I think, do right; they are mum about him except they are forced to say something good of him occasionally. The people, the middle-class, worship Lincoln, and the very bottom class blindly fall in the currents. I feel it my duty to state to all people my ideas of Lincoln and my knowledge of the facts of his life so far as I know them. This is my religion, has been for twenty years, and will be probably for ten more years. I want the world to know Lincoln.

Your friend,

W. H. HERNDON.

Springfield, Ill., January 9, 1886.

Friend Weik:

Justice North of this city was once in St. Louis hunting up an auctioneer. North kept in this city an auction room and wanted a number one auctioneer, a practical and a good one. Some gentleman in St. Louis recommended one Charles Lewis, if I have not forgotten the name; he was somehow a nephew of Mrs. Lincoln or probably other relative. North and Lewis made a contract. Lewis came up to this city as North's auctioneer; he had money and asked no favors, got $60 per month from North for his services. As soon as he landed here, he as a relative of *Mrs.* Lincoln thought it his duty to call on his *aunt.* So he went to see her, knocked at the door, was coldly admitted, told Mrs. Lincoln who he was, etc., etc. Mrs. Lincoln's avarice at once arose and she told the young gentleman in coarse, cruel, and brutish language that she did not wish her poor relatives to pile themselves on her and eat her up. The young man tried to explain to her that out of respect he had called to see her, said he had plenty of money and had a good position and did not need her charity and did not deserve her coarse, savage, and brutal language; he quickly left the house, deeply mortified, leaving Mrs. Lincoln in one of her haughty, imperious, and angry states. When Mr. Lincoln returned home in about two hours, he at once saw that Mrs. Lincoln was standing square on her ears. Lincoln asked Mrs. Lincoln what was the matter; she told him; he knew that she had acted the fool and the savage. Mr. Lincoln instantly went down to North's auction room, expecting to find rather a rough young [man]—but unexpectedly he found a rather accomplished fellow—in order to apologize to the young man for the cruel treatment he had received at the hands of his wife. The young man made his statement to Lincoln; Lincoln at once saw how it stood, apologized to the young man, talked to him tenderly and in a fatherly way, offered to assist him in all ways, loan him funds, if the young man needed it, invited him to his house, etc., etc. The young man thanked Mr. Lincoln and told him that he did not need his assistance, but was much obliged to him, etc.; he never went to see Mrs. Lincoln again. The young man was heard to say: "Uncle is one of the noblest of men, but Aunt (or Cousin) is a savage." This story illustrates the difference between Lincoln and Mrs. Lincoln. This was about 1858, probably 1860. Lincoln as a general rule dared not invite anyone to his house, because he did not know what moment she would kick Lincoln and his friend out of the house. This woman was to me a terror, haughty, poor when she married Lincoln, imperious, proud, aristocratic, insolent, witty, and bitter; she was a gross [?] material woman as she appeared to me. Look at her picture and you can see what I have seen. In her domestic troubles I have always sympathized with her. The world does not know what she bore and the history of the bearing. I will write it out some time. This domestic *hell* of Lincoln's life is not all on one side. I do not and cannot blame Lincoln, and do not wish you to suppose that I could censure him, for I could not. Wait patiently for all the facts. Mrs. Lincoln acted out in her domestic relation the laws of human revenge; this is somewhat of my meaning, sit still and "wait for the glory of the Lord."

You will please take my notes, called letters, just as they are. I have no time to read them and correct them. When you copy all or parts, please correct. I have to write in a run and a rush, as you know the facts of my business and the conditions of my life. I have to struggle today for my tomorrow's bread.

Your friend,
W. H. HERNDON.

Springfield, Ill., January 9, 1886.

Friend Weik:

I know a man now living, or did live, in Menard County; he, if living, must be eighty [1] years of age. The name of the man is Mentor Graham; he was an intelligent man, a good and a truthful man, and yet in some things he was "sorter cranky." About the year 1817 he was traveling from —— to Elizabethtown, Kentucky. In passing from —— to the latter place he saw at a little place a crowd of men, stopped, hitched his horse, and went among the crowd, soon found out that a man had killed his wife. Persons were expressing their horror of the act. Soon after Graham had stopped Thomas Lincoln and his boy Abraham came along and stopped, went among the crowd, found out what was the matter, had some conversation with the crowd, and now comes the nib of this letter. After all the people had expressed their ideas, one of the men said to Abraham: "My little boy, what do you think of such a deed?" The boy studied a moment, and gave a terse and eloquent idea of the cruel deed. Graham says that the boy was very sad, that his language was eloquent and feeling for one so young. The remarks which he made astonished all present, were pronounced good, plain, terse, and strong, and says Graham: "I have now known Mr. Lincoln for more than fifty years and I can see the same trait of character and the same style now in Lincoln that I did in 1817 in Kentucky; he studies to see the subject matter clearly and to express it tersely and strongly. I have known him down here in Menard study for hours the best way of any of three to express an idea; he was a strong man and an honest one. I knew Lincoln's relatives way back in 1802–4. Thomas Lincoln was a blank, but a clever man, a somewhat social creature. How he raised such a boy as Abe the Lord only knows."

The above I know to be true so far as this: Lincoln always struggled to see the thing or the idea exactly and to express that idea in such language as to convey that idea precisely. When a young boy he read pretty much all the books in the neighborhood, and they were not more than a dozen. If he found anything worthy of his thoughts, he would write it down, commit it to memory, then analyze it while he held it firmly in *consciousness*, in his mind. When this was done, he would tell it o'er and o'er to his stepmother and friends; and I can say the same thing with this addition: that he used to bore me terribly by his methods, processes, manners, etc., etc. Mr. Lincoln would doubly explain things to me that needed no explanation. However, I stood and took it out of respect for the man; he was terribly afraid that I

---

[1] Herndon must have meant ninety.

Henry C. Whitney
Collection of Herbert Wells Fay

Truman H. Bartlett
Collection of Prof. H. W. Gardner

Jesse W. Weik

Ward Hill Lamon

HERNDON'S CORRESPONDENTS

John T. Stuart

Stephen T. Logan

Joshua F. Speed

James H. Matheny

Collection of Herbert Wells Fay

LINCOLN'S LAW PARTNERS AND EARLY FRIENDS

did not understand him when I understood even his thoughts at it. Lincoln despised "glittering generalities" and even hated the man that used them. Mr. Lincoln was a very patient man generally, but if you wished to be cut off at the knee, just go at Lincoln with abstractions, glittering generalities, indefiniteness, mistiness of idea or expression. Here he flew up and became vexed and sometimes foolishly so; his mind was so organized that he could not help it, and so we must excuse him. Lincoln's ambition in this line was this: he wanted to be distinctly understood by the common people; he used to say to me: "Billy, don't shoot too high, shoot low down, and the common people will understand you; they are *the ones* which you wish to watch, at least they are the ones whom you ought to reach. The educated ones will understand you anyhow. If you shoot too high, your bullets will go over the heads of the mass, and only hit those who need no hitting." This Lincoln has said to me many times when I was on the stump or at the bar, or writing leaders for our newspapers, which I did from 1854 to 1861, advocating Liberty and Lincoln.

Your friend,
W. H. HERNDON.

Springfield, Ill., January 11, 1886.

Friend Weik:

You wish to know more about Lincoln's domestic life. The history of it is a sad, sad one, I assure you. Many and many a time I have known Lincoln to come down to our office, say at 7 a.m., sometimes bringing with him his then young son Bob. Our office was on the west side of the public square and upstairs. The door that entered our office was, the up half, of glass, with a curtain on the inside made of calico. When we did not wish anyone to see inside, we let down the curtain on the inside. Well, I say, many and many a time have I known Lincoln to come down to our office, sometimes Bob with him, with a small lot of cheese, crackers, and "bologna" sausages under his arm; he would not speak to me, for he was full of sadness, melancholy, and I suppose of the devil; he would draw out the sofa, sit down on it, open his breakfast, and divide between Bob and himself. I would as a matter of course know that Lincoln was driven from home, by a club, knife, or tongue, and so I would let down the curtain on the inside, go out, and lock the door behind me, taking the key out and with me. I would stay away, say an hour, and then I would go into the office on one pretense or another, and if Lincoln did not then speak, I did as before, go away, etc. In the course of another hour I would go back, and if Lincoln spoke, I knew it was all over, i.e., his fit of sadness, etc. Probably he would say something or I would, and then he would say: "Billy, that puts me in mind of a story," he would tell it, walk up and down the room, laughing the while, and now the dark clouds would pass off his withered and wrinkled face and the God-blessed sunshine of happiness would light up *those* organs o'er which the emotions of that good soul played their gentle dance and chase. Friend, I can see all this now acting before me and am sad.

Your good friend,
W. H. HERNDON.

Springfield, Ill., January 15, 1886.

Friend Weik:

There was a curious streak in Lincoln and it was that of a *seeming* ingratitude. Lincoln came to this city in 1837, and Joshua F. Speed gratuitously took him into his room, gave him bed and house room, etc. William Butler was a man of some wealth for the time, was successful in business, was making money, etc.; he took Lincoln to his house, gave him a bed, sleeping room, and boarded him from 1837 to 1842, when Lincoln got married to Miss Todd, *the female wildcat of the age.* Butler was a Whig and so was Lincoln. Butler did not charge Lincoln one cent for the board for years, lodging, etc., etc. Butler saw in Lincoln a gloom, a sadness, melancholy, etc., and deeply sympathized with him, wanted to help him. Lincoln is painted by men who do not know him as having a hard time of it in his struggles for existence, success, fame. This is all *bosh,* nonsense. No man ever had an easier time of it in his early days, in his boyish, in his young, struggles than Lincoln; he had always had influential and financial friends to help him; they almost fought each other for the privilege of assisting Lincoln; he was most certainly entitled to this respect. I have watched men and women closely in this matter. Lincoln was a pet, a faithful and an honest pet in this city; he deserved it. Lincoln was a poor man and must work his way up; he was ambitious, fired by it; it eclipsed his better nature, and when he used a man and sucked all the uses out of him, he would throw away the *thing* as an old orange peeling. This was not always the case, probably not Lincoln's general rule. Lincoln was elected to Congress in 1847, I think; he had some patronage to bestow and his old friend Butler applied to him for the office of the Register or receiver of public monies in this city. There was another applicant for the same office by the name of King, a kind of worthless man, in my opinion, and Lincoln gave the office to King over the head of Butler. Butler and Lincoln did not speak for years. Butler opposed Lincoln in all his aspirations for office from 1847 till about 1858. Butler frequently with others defeated Lincoln's schemes. Lincoln thought it best for himself to bury the hatchet, as I suppose. Lincoln was again, say in 1862–63 approached by Butler for an office, and Lincoln *did* give it to him, and out of which he made a fortune. Such are the tricks and ways of politicians in this world. . . . I saw Judge Matheny this morning and asked him his remembrance of the facts, and he remembers it substantially as I do, and as stated herein. History, if it is worth writing, is worthy of true writing and so I give you this note. I hope that you may never be a politician, pray so.

You may think that because I cut men, state the truth of them, that I am a soured disappointed man, and in thus thinking you are mistaken. I never was ambitious along the lines of politics, and on this line even I have been successful. My ambition was not for office, nor money, nor fame. My ambition in this life was to be an intelligent man, and a doer of good to my fellow-man. Today I am a progressive and an advanced little thinker, a reformer, an optimist, an altruist, believing in an infinite Energy, Universal Soul, God, in universal inspiration, revelation—sons of God. I am credulous to this extent, am broad and generous in my views. This infinite energy has no *pets*, rules mind and matter by laws, absolute, universal, and eternal. Now you have my philosophy and religion. I am today under my beliefs a contented and a happy man, and always have been and expect, hope, to remain so.

It seems to me that I have written to you enough matters to make a respectable Life of Lincoln. I feel that I am about pumped dry. However, I shall continue to send you well-authenticated facts and *only such*. Had you not better change your plans and issue a little Life of Lincoln yourself? Answer this last idea. We have had a terribly cold snap; weather has changed and it is now snowing.

Your friend,

W. H. HERNDON.

Springfield, Ill., January 16, 1886.

Friend Weik:

Your kind letter, dated the 12th *inst.*, is just handed to me, and in reply to past would say that I *never* told you that *Mrs.* Lincoln wanted to marry Douglas. I *did* say to you that Douglas wanted to marry Mrs. Lincoln when a girl. Mrs. Lincoln, when a girl, was courted by Douglas and Lincoln at the same time. Mrs. Lincoln was a keen observer of human nature, an excellent judge of it, none better; she was a terrible woman, but I must give her credit for a keen insight into men and things. Had *hell* not got into her neck she would have led society anywhere; she was a highly cultured woman, witty, dashing, pleasant, and a lady, but hell got in her neck, which I will explain to the world sometime, if I live. This will be a curious history. When all is known, the world will divide between Mr. Lincoln and Mrs. Lincoln its censure, as I believe. Mrs. Lincoln saw in Mr. Lincoln honesty, sincerity, integrity, manliness, and a great man in the future. Mrs. Lincoln saw in Douglas a rake and a roué by nature, a demagogue and a shallow man. This I *know*. Probably I know too much of all these things. Mrs. Lincoln chose Lincoln, and the choice showed her insight and her wisdom. I *know* the whole story from beginning to end. I know that Mrs. Lincoln acted badly, but hold your opinion for a while. I have always sympathized with Mrs. Lincoln. Remember that every effect must have its cause. Mrs. Lincoln was not a she-wolf, wildcat, without a cause.

I am glad that you save and have saved all things written to you by me. I want them saved, because they will have much in them probably that the world will want. I am willing to be tested by them during all coming time, by the severest criticism. If I misrepresent willfully, the world will know it; and if I am honestly mistaken, the world will know that; and if I am true, they will know that too. We cannot escape criticism if we are worthy of it.

Your friend,

W. H. HERNDON.

In a day or so will write you more about Lincoln's domestic relations.

January 16, 1886.

Friend Weik:

Let me give you an exact idea of Miss Todd, Mrs. Lincoln afterwards. I said to you and now say to you that, when Mrs. Lincoln was a young and unmarried woman, she was rather pleasant, polite, civil, rather graceful in her movements, intelligent, witty, and sometimes bitter too; she was a polished girl, well educated, a good linguist, a fine conversationalist, was educated thoroughly at Lexington, Kentucky; she was poor when she came here about 1839, a little proud, sometimes haughty. I have met Miss Todd many times at socials, balls, dances, and the like, have danced with her. I think that Miss Todd was a very shrewd girl, somewhat attractive; she discreetly kept back the fundamentals, the groundwork of her organization; she was a shrewd girl and a sharp one, a fine judge of human nature and of the appropriateness of conditions. However, after she got married she became soured, got gross, became material, avaricious, insolent. The wolf, I guess, was in her when young and unmarried, but she unchained it, let it loose, when she got married. Discretion when young kept the wolf back for a while, but when there was no more necessity for chaining it, it was unchained to growl, snap, and bite at all. But remember that in finite things, that every effect has its appropriate cause. Keep your judgment open for subsequent facts.

I intended to say that, in the Butler note, Butler gratuitously, freely, and without charge boarded Lincoln from 1837 to 1842, when Lincoln got married. I think that in my hurry I forgot to state this fact distinctly. I now say it. The reason why Lincoln appointed, had King appointed, was that King lived in a northern county in this State. This county Lincoln wanted and King could carry it. Butler lived in this county and couldn't be of any use north to Lincoln. Hurrah for politics and politicians. Politics rob us of our better nature and politicians rob us of our money, etc. Hurrah for politics and politicians.

Your friend,
W. H. HERNDON.

Religiously private.   H.

Springfield, Ill., January 19, 1886.

Friend Weik:

You once asked me for a history of Lincoln's paternity and, as I remember it, I promised to give it to you sometime, if I had the time to do it. The facts are about as follows: Lincoln once told me that his mother Nancy Hanks was the illegitimate child of a Virginia planter; he told me never to tell it while he lived, and this I have religiously kept and observed. This is *one* fact in the chain of *inferences*. Thomas Lincoln, the father of Abraham, in the spring of 1805 commenced going to see Sally Bush; he courted this finely developed and buxom girl; she refused him, did not at all reciprocate his love. This lady, whom I knew, was far above Thomas Lincoln, somewhat cultivated and quite a lady. Mr. Lincoln, Thomas, then—say in the summer of 1806—commenced going to see Nancy Hanks, Abraham's mother. Nancy Hanks accepted Thomas Lincoln's hand; they were actually married in Washington County, Kentucky. The marriage took place September 23, 1806, and the first child born to Mrs. Lincoln was on the tenth day of February 1807, a little less than five months from the day of the marriage. This is the *second* fact which you must carry along in order to draw correct inferences. About 1815 one Abraham Enloe was caught by Thomas Lincoln in such relations and under such conditions with his wife that he was convinced that his wife was not, like Cæsar's wife, above suspicion. Thomas Lincoln jumped on and into Enloe for what he had been doing, as Lincoln supposed. Lincoln bit off Enloe's nose in the terrible fight. This is fact number *three*. Lincoln, Thomas, was so annoyed with Enloe's visits and conduct that he was driven from Kentucky; he moved from there, to Indiana, about 1816–17. While *Mrs.* Lincoln bred like a rat in Kentucky, she had no more children in Indiana. This is fact number *four*. Mrs. Lincoln died about 1818–19 in Indiana. In about one year thereafter Thomas Lincoln went back to Kentucky to see Sally Bush, who had in the meantime—say in 1807–8—married to one —— Johnston. Johnston and Mrs. Johnston had two children or more. I knew them both. Johnston died about the time that Mrs. Lincoln did—one died in Indiana and the other in Kentucky. Miss Bush, now Mrs. Johnston, was a finely developed woman and so was Mrs. Lincoln. The reputation of Mrs. Lincoln is that she was a bold, reckless, daredevil kind of a woman, stepping to the very verge of pro-priety : she was badly and roughly raised, was an excellent woman and by nature an intellectual and sensitive woman. Lincoln, Abraham, told me that his mother was an intellectual woman, sensitive and some-what sad. I distinctly remember what Lincoln told me and the cause of the conversation. Lincoln said to me on that occasion this: "All that I am or hope ever to be I got from my mother, God bless her"; and I guess all this—what Lincoln told me—was the truth. Thomas Lincoln went back to see Mrs. Johnston, as said before, and they were married in Elizabethtown, Kentucky, about the year 1819. Remem-ber that Mrs. Johnston had children by Johnston. This is a *fifth* fact. Mrs. Johnston, now Mrs. Lincoln, went to Indiana with Thomas and there had no children while in the prime and glory of her good life; she was a good woman, a kind, clever, and polite one. I knew her. Mrs. Thomas Lincoln, his second wife, now took possession of things in Indiana, dressed up, taught, and kindly cared for Thomas Lincoln's two children by his first wife—Abraham and Sarah. Mrs. Lincoln, Thomas's second wife, had no more children while in Indiana, though she bred, had children, in Kentucky by Johnston. Here is the *sixth* fact. The two [children] by his first wife and the two by his last wife —Johnston the father—were raised up together and actually loved one another. In other words Lincoln had two or three children by his first wife, and none by his last. Mrs. Johnston had two or three children by her first husband and none by Thomas Lincoln. The four children were raised up, vegetated together.

In addition to all the above facts, or supposed ones—for I give no opinion—Dennis Hanks told me that Thomas Lincoln, when tolerably young, and before he left Kentucky, was castrated. Abraham Enloe said, often said, that *Abraham Lincoln was his child.* All these facts, if facts they are, I received from different persons, at different times and places. I reduced much to writing at the time, have letters on the subject from Kentucky and some of the facts I remember, i.e., I well remember what was told me, though I did write all down.

Now let me give you something on the other side. The clerk of the court of Elizabethtown—Winterbottom, I think is his name—wrote to Mr. Lincoln in 1859–60 something about his mother, and Lincoln said in reply: "You are mistaken in my mother." I have seen Lincoln's letters to the clerk, whatever may be his name. The clerk and I corresponded some little, but I may miss his name. Here is the whole story as it has been told to me, and I give you no opinion of fact nor inference. You must judge for yourself. It's a curious story, and may all be true.

> Your friend,
> W. H. HERNDON.

Please send me an exact copy of this, breaking it into paragraphs if you can.

> H.

Keep this religiously private.   H.
> *Springfield, Ill., January 23, 1886.*

Friend Weik:

. . . I have read the Allen letter and know all about it. Allen was a great blow, a suggestor, a wild exaggerator, and somewhat of a l——r. Mr. Lincoln knew the man and shot off his caricature, burlesque of Allen. Lincoln, when he wrote the letter, was in one of his best joking moods. Did you take it as all done in good faith? Allen's idiotic son, weak-minded son rather, after his father's death and not knowing the facts as well as the people here, the old settlers, published the letter, a most foolish thing. Had he consulted friends, his father's old ones, it, the letter, would never have seen the light.

I wish to state some facts about Lincoln's domestic relations which I do not want to be forgotten. About the year 1857 a man by the name of Barrett was passing along Eighth Street near Lincoln's house; he saw a long, tall man running and saw a little low, squatty woman with a butcher knife in her hand in hot pursuit; he looked and saw that Lincoln was the man and Mrs. Lincoln was the woman. Lincoln's house on Eighth Street fronts westward. He ran eastward down the walk in his own lot. Stephen Whitehurst lived in the same block. His house fronted east, the house being east of Lincoln's. The consequence is that the back doors looked into each other. Whitehurst was on that day—Sunday if I recollect the time, the day—standing in the back door of his own house and saw what happened. Lincoln ran down the walk in his own lot but, seeing the people coming from church or going to it, he stopped short and quick and wheeled around, caught Mrs. Lincoln by the back of the neck and at the seat of her drawers, carried or pushed her squealing along the walk back to the house—Lincoln's house—got her to the door of the kitchen, opened it, pushed her in, at the same time, to use Whitehurst's expression, gave her a hell of a slap on her seat, saying to her: "There now, stay in the house and don't be a d——d fool before the people."

Again in the winter of 1857 the Supreme Court was in session and Lincoln had an important suit to argue. He came in the clerk's office, the law library room too; his nose was plastered up, fixed up with court plaster. Now for the facts. Lincoln had on the day before become somewhat abstracted, thoughtful, and let the fire in Mr. and Mrs. Lincoln's sitting room nearly die out. Mrs. Lincoln came to the door of the sitting room from the kitchen and said: "Mr. Lincoln, put some wood on the fire." Lincoln did not hear her and neglected the repair of the fire. Mrs. Lincoln came to the sitting room again and said: "Mr. Lincoln, mend up the fire," it having got low down. Lincoln did not hear Mrs. Lincoln; she came in again and picked up a stick of wood and said: "Mr. Lincoln, I have told you now there three times to mend the fire and you have pretended that you did not hear me. I'll make you hear me this time," and she blazed away at Lincoln with a stick of stovewood and hit him on the nose and thus banged it up. Someone in the courtroom asked Lincoln what was the matter; he made an evasive reply in part to the question. Lincoln's girl stated this, if others did not know it. From what I know of the facts, it is more probable that it is true than untrue. I believe it; it went around among the members of the bar as true. Many such quarrels did take place between Lincoln and his wife. Lincoln's domestic life was a home hell on this globe.

Your friend,
W. H. HERNDON.

Springfield, Ill., February 18, 1886.

Friend Fowler: [1]

It may help you to understand Lincoln somewhat thoroughly by stating to you his philosophy. Mr. Lincoln believed that what was to be would be, and no prayers of ours could arrest or reverse the decree; he was a thorough fatalist, and thought the fates ruled the world; he believed that the conditions made the man, does make the

---

[1] Probably the Senator Fowler referred to in Herndon's letter of October 5, 1889.

man; he believed that general, universal, and eternal laws governed both matter and mind, always and everywhere.

This philosophy as a whole will account for much of the facts and laws of his splendid life. Things that were to be, *would* be, and hence he patiently waited on events; his charity for men, their feelings, thoughts, willings, and acts sprang out of his philosophy, that conditions made them; his want of malice sprang out of the same. Lincoln neither hated nor did he love; he never but once or twice eulogized men, nor did he ever curse them. Men were mere tools in the hands of fate, were made as they are made, by conditions; and to praise or blame men was pure folly. Men were not entitled to credit for what they were or did, what they thought or said, how they felt or acted. The thing was to be, and no prayers of ours could arrest or avert the decree; men are made by conditions that surround them, that have somewhat existed for a hundred thousand years or more.

Man is compelled to feel, think, will, and act by virtue and force of these conditions; he is a mere child moved and governed by this vast world machine, forever working in grooves, and moving in deep-cut channels; and now what is man? He is simply a simple tool, a cog, a part and parcel of this vast iron machine that strikes and cuts, grinds and mashes, all things that resist it. The fates had decreed it and what they decreed is irresistible and inevitable. Here human prayers are blank absurdities. What a man is, he is because of the great world's eternal conditions, and is entitled to no credit for virtue nor should he be blamed for vice. "With malice toward none and charity for all"—I live for men—was Lincoln's feelings, thoughts, wills, and acts. Man does but what is commanded by his superiors.

Lincoln used to quote Shakespeare's philosophy:

> There's a divinity that shapes our ends,
> Rough-hew them how we will.

If a man did him an injury, or grievous wrong, the man was a mere tool and obeyed the powers; and if the man did him a great good, blessed him and made him happy, still he but obeyed orders, and he was not to be censured for the wrong nor praised for the right. Everything, everywhere, is doomed for all time. If a man was good or bad, small or great, and if virtue or vice prevailed, it was so doomed. If bloody war, deathly famine, and cruel pestilence stalked over the land, it was to be and *had come,* and to mourn for this, to regret it, to resist it, would only be flying in the face of the inevitable.

Lincoln was patient and calmly waited on events; he knew that they would come in their own good and appointed time; he was not surprised at their coming nor astonished at their extent, nor depth, nor fury. The fates and the conditions were *the* powers. Laws ruled everything, everywhere, both matter and mind from the beginning to the end, if there was a beginning and an end.

Such was Lincoln's philosophy; he was in religion a *Liberal*—naturally and logically so. Do not misunderstand me—probably Lincoln *did not* believe that Brutus was specially made and ordered to kill Cæsar with a dagger in the Senate Chamber; and yet he fully believed that Brutus and Cæsar stood in the line of the rush of the forces of nature let loose millions of years ago and let go at full play.

I hope that these remarks will assist you in finding Lincoln, the real man as he lived among us.

You spoke in your eloquent letter of Emerson and Lincoln; they differed widely. Emerson had the genius of the spiritual and ideal; Lincoln had the genius of the real and the practical. Emerson lived high among the stars; Lincoln lived low among men. Emerson dreamed; Lincoln acted. Emerson was intuitional; Lincoln reflective. Both were Liberals in religion and were great men.

Your friend,
W. H. HERNDON.

Springfield, Ill., April 14, 1886.

Mr. James W. Keys.
My dear Sir:

You ask me for a short account of my acquaintance with Abraham Lincoln. I became acquainted with Mr. Lincoln in 1834, and from that time to the day of his death, I knew the man well—I may say, intimately. He moved to the city of Springfield in 1837; it was then but a small town or village—now quite a city. I studied law with Logan and Lincoln, two great lawyers—in 1842–43. In 1843 Mr. Lincoln and I became partners in the law business in Springfield, but did business in all the surrounding counties. Our partnership was never legally dissolved till the night of his assassination—his death. The good man, the noble man would take no money of my fees made in the law business after his election to the Presidency. Mr. Lincoln was a safe counselor, a good lawyer, and an honest man in all the walks of life. Mr. Lincoln was not appreciated in this city, nor was he at all times the most popular man among us. The cause of his unpopularity, rather the want of popularity, here arose out of two grounds. First, he did his own thinking, and, second, he had the courage of his convictions and boldly and fearlessly expressed them. I speak generally, and especially of his political life. Mr. Lincoln was a cool, cautious, conservative, and long-headed man. Mr. Lincoln could be trusted by the people; they did trust him, and they were never deceived. He was a pure man, a great man and a patriot.

In the practice of the law, he was simple, honest, fair and broad-minded; he was courteous to the bar and to the Court; he was open, candid, and square in his profession, never practicing on the sharp nor the low. Mr. Lincoln met all questions fairly, squarely, and openly, making no concealments of his ideas, nor intentions, in any case; he took no snap judgments, nor used any tricks in his business. Every man knew exactly where Mr. Lincoln stood, and how he would act in a law case. Mr. Lincoln never deceived his brother lawyers in any case. What he told you was the exact truth. . . .

The desk made of walnut with four shelves in it, with two leaved doors belonged to Lincoln and myself in our early practice. The desk contained most of our books for years. The table is made of walnut with two drawers; the desk and table were placed in our office on the same day, say as early as 1850, probably before. You now own the desk and table that Lincoln once owned; he gave me the desk and table, and what you have is genuine and true. They have never been out of my sight since they were delivered to Lincoln and myself. Please take good care of the sacred things, mementos of the noble man Abraham Lincoln.

Most respectfully,
WM. H. HERNDON.

Springfield, Ill., July 10, 1886.

Friend Weik:

. . . In answer to your question, let me say that Mr. Lincoln was *not* at Chicago, nor nearer there than this city, during the week, time, of his nomination for the Presidency in 1860. Mr. Lincoln was in this city during the convention, all the time of it, playing ball and drinking beer with the boys. He was nervous that day and played ball and drank beer to while away the time; he hoped and despaired that day in this city. I was in Chicago during the time of the convention, but Lincoln was not there; he was *here* and had *not* been in Chicago for months, probably, before the convention.

Your friend,
W. H. HERNDON.

Springfield, Ill., October 9, 1886.

Friend Weik:

. . . I have received no reply from the publishing company as yet in answer to mine, my last. When I get an answer, I will send it to you. You and I can write the biography wanted. My letters to you are half of the biography, ready-made to hand. I have probably all the *original* papers, the important ones *out of which* Lamon wrote his Life of Lincoln; he never had the originals. I only sold him copies of the originals. I kept the originals and have them at my house in the country. Some few things may be lost.

I referred to you as my literary friend, because the publishing company asked for the name; and I thought it due to you to say so. I explained to them that you were just entering the literary field in my last. It's all right. You need not fear that the publishing company will dispense with your services. I'll see to that, my friend.

Your friend,
W. H. HERNDON.

Chicago, December 1, 1886.

Friend Weik:

I have sent you some cards and pamphlets explaining the purposes and scope of the Lincoln Memorial Collection owned by Messrs. Keys and Munson of this city, and if anything more comes out, I'll send to you. I am here to assist them in starting their valuable collection of Lincoln relics to the public view. I am not here expressly to lecture. However, I do not know what will happen in this world of rushing events. I am pushing the collection along as well as I can, do not know when I shall go home, am as fat, hearty, and jolly as a pig; I am not run and kicked to death, have a little time to laugh and be merry.

The word "Sarah," I think, refers to Mrs. Edwards as I now recollect it. When I see you [I shall] refresh my memory by looking at the papers. When an opportunity presents itself and at the proper time, I may say something to the leading men and houses here about our intentions of writing, etc. Let us push things along somewhat before we talk to publishers. I am glad that you are pulling the wires in Boston and New York. I have a friend in New York who will help us, if you give me the privilege, give your consent that I should write him on the subject. Give me by letter the substance of what you want said and I'll write to him; his name is C. O. Poole, who has written to me three or four times on this very subject, but I would evade the question, skip over suggestions.

I am not surprised at all that Nicolay and Hay will be attacked for willful suppression of facts; they know all about Lincoln's ancestry, Nancy Hanks, Enloe, Lincoln's paternity, etc., etc., just as fully as I do or you do. Mr. A. W. Drake, the artist of the *Century*, intimated to Messrs. Keys and Munson as much, in fact told them the whole story as they told it to me long, long before I ever intimated such a thing to them. The thing comes straight to me, no earthly doubt. Nicolay and Hay tell the truth, as I now remember it, as far as they go, but skip the point, suppress facts. Write me often as I am lonesome and love to read your letters.

Your friend,
W. H. HERNDON.

Chicago, December 5, 1886.

Friend Weik:

On yesterday I finished reading the December number of the *Century* and am astonished at the length and dullness of Nicolay and Hay's second article. If *that* article is a sample of *what is to come*, I make a prediction that the whole thing will fall stillborn, dead; it is too long a piece to say nothing in, too much little unimportant stuff in it for the length of it. If what has been said in the two articles were condensed into a short chapter, then it would do. Are Nicolay and Hay going to suppress the story of Ann Rutledge, the finest story in Lincoln's life? What do you think of the two articles? What does the world say? What do the critics say? I want to make you a bet; I will bet you a chicken cock that Nicolay and Hay's book will tire out the public by its length and its unimportant trash. You mark what I say unless a change is made by N. and H.

I am glad that you are in earnest about our book, hope you will keep so. By the way, if your literary friend wants to see our papers in order to write something about Lincoln, Nicolay, and Hay, give him access to the memoranda if you see proper. Do so to any good friend if you wish. My *private* letters are private and no one is to see them except yourself. I mean mostly those letters written *to me* by others. Act in all cases according to your best judgments and I'll sanction.

I hope that you will think better of my arrangement with Keys and Munson. I did for the best. My word is out to them and I can but perform. Good will come out of it. . . .

Your friend,
W. H. HERNDON.

Chicago, December 8, 1886.

Friend Weik:

. . . I shall write to C. F. Black, *the real author of Lamon's Life of Lincoln,* and get him to help us to launch our book upon the public sea; he knows the ropes or ought to; he is a man of influence, Lieutenant Governor of Pennsylvania, and can help us. Keep your eyes open as to Mrs. Garrison's propositions. It seems that she wants us to secure her a fee as soon as she gets a publisher for the book. Can't she wait till it is published? The name which you propose to give the book is very good and I approve of it. . . .

Your friend,
W. H. HERNDON.

Chicago, December 9, 1886.

Friend Weik:

I am here and somewhat lonesome and I will have to talk to you, make a companion of you. You were quoted Judge Davis on me to the effect that Lincoln was a *great* lawyer. That I never denied, but I said that he was not a first-rate *nisi prius* lawyer. I further said that he was not a learned lawyer, and that he was a case lawyer, etc. Just hear what Judge Davis does say: he says of Lincoln: "He could hardly be called very learned in his profession, and yet he rarely tried a cause without fully understanding the law applicable to it." This I agree to and now the question: Come, how was he a *great* lawyer? Says Judge Davis: "*He read law books but little*, except when the cause in hand made it necessary." The next question comes: What books did he resort to to get his information? He went to the reports and hunted up like cases; he was a case lawyer and that only; he never as a general rule went to the textbooks, and he was ever ready to attend in a masterly way all cases that came before him, right or wrong, good or bad, ready or not ready, except *ever* ready through his legal love and his own sagacity. Now you have my opinion right or wrong, wise or foolish.

You have never told me how you liked my Lincoln records now in your possession. How do you like 'em? Nor have you ever said how you liked Nicolay and Hay's two articles in the *Century*. The opinion here is generally good, somewhat mixed up. Tell me all about what you think of the two pieces, etc. Come, give me your ideas.

I shall write to Poole and to Governor Black ere long and get 'em to help us to launch our little craft on the great public sea.

Your friend,
W. H. HERNDON.

Chicago, December 13, 1886.

Friend Weik:

I received a letter from Governor Black, the author of Lamon's Life of Lincoln; he says that someone is writing severe criticisms on N. and H.'s life of L.; he thinks it is Lamon who does it but does not know it absolutely. Black says he will write me soon and tell me all about it; his letter to me is dated the 8th *inst.*; he further says that Lamon is soon to publish his second volume of the Life of L. and will reprint the first volume. Lamon is in Washington now, and I shall write to him, asking him to send me his criticisms or others; he will

Leonard Swett

Horace White

Collection of Frederick H. Meserve

David Davis

Norman B. Judd

Collection of Harry MacNeill Bland

POLITICAL ADVISERS OF LINCOLN

Big Me

My parents

Come from Virginia about the year 1808 and settled in Green
County, Kentucky, — was born in Greensburg Ky on deer 25th
1818, a few months after Illinois was admitted into the Union
— moved to Illinois in 1821 and settled near Springfield
Illinois — moved to the town in 1823 — father went to merch-
andizing in '26 — was clerk in my fathers store for years,
& except when going to school, — went to the Schools where
each parent paid for his children's tuition — reading-writing,
Ciphering — geography — grammar and some of the higher branches
were taught — went to a most excellent high school in the
City, for two or three years — say from '34 to '36 — went to Illinois
College in Jacksonville for one year '37 — clerked in a store from
'37 to '41 — was married in '40 to Miss Mary Maxcy, daughter of Col Maxcy — kept store, clerked, from '41 to '43 when
I commenced to study the law regularly with Logan & Lincoln —
before this studied law of nights after business hours — was
admitted to the bar in 1843 — entered into partnership with
Lincoln in '43 and was such partner till the death of Mr
Lincoln — was studious — too much so for my own health —
Studied from 12 to 14 hours a day — had a wish to supplant —

FACSIMILE OF A PAGE OF "BIG ME"

send to me quickly and I'll send to you if I get any, will tell you what Black says.

Can you not block out the first and second chapters of our Life of L. before I come to see you? Come, try and do it, will you? By the way, have you seen any criticisms on N. and H.'s work? If you have, what are they in substance? I am so tied up here that I have no time much to read the papers. I have to explain to visitors the nature, history, etc., of the Lincoln Memorial Collection; it keeps me blabbing all the time. The thing is new here and not a great many people visit it as yet though the promises are good. The collection will be a good thing in the near future, as I think. Lincoln is growing in the estimation of the people; and the older the relics of him, the more valuable the collection will be and the more eager to see what Lincoln saw and had, felt and thought, dreamed and acted. The people are crazy for autographs. One man, Mr. Lindman, paid $1000 for the autograph of Shakespeare. Lincoln's autographs bring from $10 to $20. I could get that for each autograph of L. if I had any. It is a curious phenomenon of our nature, this craving of autographs. A candy man here, Mr. Gunther told me, had $40,000 worth of autographs in his safes. I have forgotten the man's name; he is the great wholesale candy man of this city, sent me a fine box at Springfield some little time since; went to see him and his house since I have been here; he is wild on autographs.

I think that Mrs. Garrison needs watching; she seems to me to be avaricious and selfish in this extreme; she seems to understand the ropes and herself, including the meanness and frauds of the publishing business. Black could tell you a story that would shock you. We will have to keep both eyes and ears open or we are gulped down, swallowed up body, breeches, and soul. How do you feel about the matter? I hope that we shall succeed somehow and with someone.

In one of your letters to me you state that we are to write the Life of L. honestly, fairly, squarely, telling the whole truth and suppressing nothing, up to 1860, and there leaving him a grand figure standing up against the clear deep blue sky of the future. This is a good idea and I approve it in toto. Would it not be a good idea to have a *short* concluding chapter on him, not going into the details of his administration, the war, the reconstruction measures, etc., etc.? We would thus give a full life of the man and yet leaving him standing up against the deep blue of the future. I am simply suggesting, not dictating. Think of the suggestion. I am not particular as to the *where* in L.'s life that we shall leave him full to the gaze of the people. Write to me often and tell me your thoughts and your *dreams*.

Your friend,

W. H. HERNDON.

Chicago, December 22, 1886.

Friend Weik:

Your letter, dated the 19th *inst.*, was duly received. I regret to hear of your good grandmother's death. I once had an excellent old grandmother and I know how I felt the loss of her. She was a good old Virginia lady.

I hope that you and Wartman will find new matters of interest in Indiana, and I do hope that you will get the "Chronicles." The man who had them while I was in Spencer County would not spare them under any consideration. I had no money *with which to coax him.* As to the anonymous letter, I never paid much attention to it, because, as I recollect, the fact is that Sarah Lincoln was the oldest child of Mrs. Lincoln, Nancy Hanks, and hence Abraham may have been the child of Thomas, upon the condition that Thomas was not castrated and upon the further condition that Enloe never had connection with Nancy at any other time thereafter. I do not like anonymous letters anyhow. However, push your investigation with vigor, for something may come of it.

It would be prudent and wise for you to go into New York, now when the book is ready. You judge of the time and other circumstances. If I hear from Black or anyone else touching our business, let me assure you that I'll write to you. I am well and hearty as a pig, am contented, and, by the way, I talk a good deal to the people about Lincoln. Without knowing what you and I are about, they hope that I'll write the life of L. The people here have confidence in what I say; they know that I *knew* Lincoln. It is dark in the room in which I'm writing and hence excuse crowdedness of lines, etc. Enclosed you will find a copy of the Campbell letter which you wish. I shall write out fully L.'s philosophy and his religion in short when I get time; have said enough about his religion, and yet some general remarks must be made in his biography. What say you?

Your friend,
W. H. HERNDON.

Chicago, December 24, 1886.

Friend Weik:

I have just received a letter from Mr. Poole in which he uses the following words about N. and H.'s life of Lincoln: "Yes, I have read some of Nicolay and Hay's on Lincoln. The environment, etc., etc., of these men *at present* is very much against them, showing Mr. Lincoln as he was. They are aiming to do, first, a superb piece of literary work; secondly, to make a story popular with the '*classes*' as against the '*masses*.' It will result in delineating the real Lincoln about as well as does a wax figure in the museum."

There is a good deal in this criticism, I assure you. The suppressions of the truth by N. and H. will injure them. I am of the opinion, of the growing opinion, that we will have to state facts, leaving each man and woman free to draw their own conclusions. I wish to state in full Mr. Lincoln's philosophy, objective and subjective. I wish to say a few words on L.'s religion. This is all. I do not wish to suppress the truth, nor to suggest a falsehood in the life of Lincoln. The whole facts must come out sooner or later. Shall we take the lead or play the coward? This is my idea, i.e., take the lead and think about it, if you please, my good friend. I do not think that it is necessary for you to come here. We can see each other in Springfield or Greencastle when the time comes. If you go anywhere this winter, go into Kentucky, go to *Elizabethtown* and to *Springfield*, Kentucky, to Paris, and to other places, and dig out the facts. Lincoln, Thomas, was married, as I remember it, in Washington County, Kentucky. Go there and scratch out the facts as a dog digs out a rabbit, corn, or ground hog. I like your pluck and energy, your industry and persistency. I will send you all the news about Lincoln, N. and H. criticisms, etc., when and as they come to hand.

Your friend,
W. H. HERNDON.

Chicago, January 2, 1887.

Friend Weik:

Have you read the January number of the *Century?* If you have, you will see that N. and H. have suppressed many facts, material facts, of Lincoln's life, and among them are L.'s genealogy, paternity, the description of Nancy Hanks, old Thomas Lincoln, the Ann Rutledge story, L.'s religion, L.'s insanity, the facts of L.'s misery with Mary Todd, L.'s *breakdown* on the night that he and Mary Todd were to be married, etc., etc. I do not say that they did not mention some of these things in a roundabout way, but I do say that the kernel, "nib," and point of things have been purposely suppressed. N. and H. do *know* the facts fully, as I am informed on good authority. Mr. Drake told them to Keys and Munson tolerably plainly. Do you call this history, do you call it biography? No wonder that L. had a contempt for all history and biography; he knew how it was written; he knew the motives and conscience of the writers of history and biography. Lincoln wanted to know the whole truth and nothing less. This I know. N. and H. write correctly, as far as they go, or probably *dare* go. The reading world is not ready to hear the whole truth, if it is an unpleasant thing; they love to be put to sleep by pleasant stories or humbugged by falsehood. Barnum is the beau ideal of the American. Nothing succeeds like success, this is what the general American worships, it and the ring-roll and glitter of the almighty dollar. Probably this idea moves N. and H. to do what they are doing. N. and H. handle things with silken gloves and "a camel-hair pencil"; they do not write with an iron pen. If some sharp critic knew what you and I know, he would shiver the future of N. and H.'s biography in a minute. I say that the boys write well and tell the truth very correctly as far as they go. Who is to blame, the people or N. and H.? I am of the growing opinion that we must *state facts* while we give no opinion, leaving all men and women open to form their own opinion *on the facts.* This I have stated to you before, and now I should like to have a hint of your ideas and feelings. What say you? Come out with them in fun. I used to tell Lincoln in my wild way in 1858–59–60 this: "Lincoln, you must take an advanced step if you wish to be successful in your hopes and your ambition." I thought that he was too conservative at that time. *He moved and won.* If you wish to succeed in our Life of L., you must take *an advanced step.* You must strike the world with a grand surprise. This is just what the world demands and without such a strike the people will go to sleep over your biography. This is my opinion. To tell the whole truth about L. would be a grand surprise. Now you have my opinion in full, good or bad, wise or foolish. . . .

Your friend in haste,
W. H. HERNDON.

Chicago, January 6, 1887.

Friend Weik:

Mr. Lincoln was employed in 1855 by a man by the name of Manny to go to Cincinnati, Ohio, and defend for him a case before Justice McLean, a case for an infringement of a patent and wherein McCormick was the plaintiff and Manny was defendant. The case was an important one, and big attorneys were employed on both sides, Seward, Stanton, and others. Mr. Lincoln went on to Cincinnati to attend to the case. Probably Manny came out to Illinois and accompanied Lincoln to Ohio. This is only my recollection. Mr. Lincoln landed in Cincinnati on time. Manny accompanied Lincoln in the morning after Mr. Lincoln had arrived in Cincinnati to Stanton's office, was ushered into the anteroom. Manny left Lincoln for a moment in the anteroom, went and said a word or two to Stanton. Between the anteroom and Stanton's office there was a door with a large glass in it, so that Stanton could look through and see Lincoln. Stanton did look through the glass and did see Lincoln, who was rather illy clad according to Stanton's notions of what great lawyers ought to wear. Manny was in Stanton's room and Stanton contemptuously and grossly said to Manny: "Why did you bring that d——d long-armed ape here for? He does not know anything and can do you no good." Manny was surprised. Lincoln distinctly heard what Stanton said; he was deeply insulted and felt indignant; left the room and never appeared in the case any more; stayed in Cincinnati a few days till the trial was over, as some say, and, as others say, he left Cincinnati instantly in high anger. My recollection is that he stayed in Cincinnati till the trial was over, though he did not have anything to say in his case. The lawyers with Lincoln treated him badly, discourteously, and meanly from the beginning to the end. When Mr. Lincoln came back to Springfield, he looked sad and sour and gloomy, and I never asked him how his case ended, thought probably that he had lost his case and felt badly over it.

Your friend in haste,
W. H. HERNDON.

In this case, too, Lincoln sank his private griefs, wrongs, etc., out of view; appointed Stanton Secretary of War for the public good.

Chicago, January 7, 1887.

Friend Weik:

I am instructed by Messrs. Munson and Keys to write to and ask you if you would dispose of the old Bible record of which you sent me a copy, the one that Dennis Hanks tore out and wore out, and that Mrs. Chapman gave you. They likewise would like to know if you would dispose of the leaf of Lincoln's copy or exercise book which I gave you several years since and has some Lincoln poetry on it. If you would dispose of these things they would like to know your terms.

The articles by N. and H., so far as they go and *when they touch* Lincoln at all, when they got *in view* of him, are very wonderfully correct as I recollect Lincoln's history. The evasions, suppressions, and dodgings of N. and H. show that they are afraid to *speak out the truth*. The story of Ann Rutledge is one of Lincoln's best episodes, best episodes in L.'s life. I guess you are right in this, that N. and H. were praised too much, blew too big a horn, tooted too loud, can't hold the attention of the people to the grand starting blast, fear this. Wait, and probably N. and H. will put in Mrs. Lincoln's photo; they will do wrong to neglect it. Possibly Mrs. Lincoln offended the "boys" while in Washington; guess she did and they are revenging themselves. Wait, probably they, N. and H., will put in Mr. and Mrs. Edwards's yet. I'll get all the photos that I can, and send or bring to you. I'll see Mather and get his story if I can, hope that you'll get Mrs. Vineyard's photo. Read up, outline, and let me hear from you again and often. I have got Barrett's Life of Lincoln, Arnold's, Lamon's, Holland's, and the everyday Life of Lincoln by Brown; will bring or send you any of these which you want. No, I have not seen Robert Lincoln and don't expect to, don't care to do so. I think that Robert hates me because I tell the truth, have told the truth about his mother and father. Bob's a Todd, not a Lincoln; he's a little man with good intentions probably.

W. H. HERNDON.

Chicago, January 8, 1887.

Friend Weik:

Enclosed you will please find a letter from Mr. Lamon of Indiana. The story, as I related it to you once, is this: One of the Grigsby boys married Lincoln's sister; Lincoln thought that the Grigsbys mistreated her, and the Lincolns and the Grigsbys fell out, one with another, etc. The two Grigsby boys were subsequently married on the same night and *probably to two sisters*. Old man Grigsby, for the two boys, had and held an infair, as was the custom at that time, at his house. The neighbors were invited except Abraham, and all went along as merry as a Christmas bell. Abraham got the ears of some of his chums who were in the house and *at the infair*. Abraham was not invited and *so he felt huffy and insulted*. He therefore told the boys inside this: "Let's have some fun." "Well," said the boys inside. It was arranged between the insiders and outsiders that the two married couples should be put to bed, but A's husband was to be put in B's bed and C was to be put in D's bed, all changed around and in the wrong places. Both husbands got in the wrong bed by direction, made between Abraham and the invited insiders, so it was arranged and so it was executed. The girls were aloft when they and their husbands were put to bed. Soon, however, a scream and a rattling of boards aloft were heard and all was "confusion worse confounded." A candle was lit and things found out and explained to the satisfaction of the women and the men. Probably the women knew the voices of their loved ones, and by that means the terrible mistake was found out, but who caused it and what for were not found out for some time. Here is Abraham who was joyous and revenged that night, the good saint at one of his *jokes*. I have forgotten the names of the boys, their given names, and likewise the girls' given and surnames. You will get the names when you go to Indiana. The story was told to me by one of the Grigsbys. Root out the story. It's true. Can you read this?

Your friend,

W. H. HERNDON.

Think the name of the boys was Charles and Reuben Grigsby.

Chicago, January 14, 1887.

Friend Weik:

Enclosed you will find Badeau on Mrs. Lincoln and Garrison on the same. I sent you your Indianapolis paper, but for fear it would not reach you, I send the slip. You may not have seen Garrison's estimate of L., and therefore I send it. Garrison stayed with me about eight days some years since; he was a perfect gentleman and a very social man. My wife loved the man; she was once a pro-slavery girl, but I took that out of her by fair argument and reason pretty quick after marriage; she is now a rabid Liberty woman in every direction. I shall start for home tomorrow evening, nothing preventing, and will send you those books according to your wish and see the people you told me to see, etc., etc.

From the criticisms of the press it would, it does, appear that the reading world wants to know every and all events, facts, incidents, thoughts, feelings, and adventures of Lincoln, including the books he read and the girls he "hugged," and the like, upon the fact of human experience that the man grows out of the boy and the boy out of the child. The foundations of manhood are laid in the boy, deep down in the boy. Mrs. Thomas Bush Lincoln did her job well in making Abe; she is the good angel who did it; she had, too, *choice material.* Now when you go to the southern part of Indiana, or when you go to Kentucky, gather up all the facts, dig 'em out, run 'em down, of L.'s youth, and when I go to court in Menard County, I shall do the same, will go there in March. The second thing will be to get a perfect description of Tom L., Nancy H., Sarah Bush L., Abraham L., which you will find in *Six Months in the White House.* There is an old man who knows Nancy. You will see him in the *Century.* I had nothing else to write, and so gabbled along, wanted to send slips of paper most.

Your friend,

W. H. HERNDON.

Springfield, Ill., January 22, 1887.

Friend Weik:

I am at home once more and I am glad of it, and I suppose that you are, because I can have more time to write my notes. In a few days I shall send to you the books on Lincoln which I wrote to you about, some time since. By this time, I guess that you have read my letters, evidences, etc., about Lincoln; and by the way let me ask you a question, which is as follows: How did you like my Ann Rutledge lecture, as a whole and especially that part which talks about the old settler? There was not much of "*the malaria*" in them nor any of "*the miasmatic*" sickly indolence in them, as H. and Nicolay write; they were a brave, generous, hospitable, jolly, rollicking set of boys, I assure you; these people were the very devil for fun and were warmly social; they were the most social of creatures, these people in and about New Salem; they were rude and rough, it is true, but full of truth and honesty; they were not a gloomy nor a sad people; they were full of life, over-souled, and that is all. These people were not touched by "the malaria" nor dwarfed by "the miasma." The "boys" say this in order to show that the sadness of Lincoln was of the forest. This is all nonsense. Lincoln's sadness, gloominess, etc., were the result of his *organism* and facts subsequent to his birth; he knew a great deal of his birth, etc., more than one thinks. *Forest* life does not make a man sad, nor gloomy, nor melancholic; it makes a man sincere, earnest, thoughtful. Away with "the malarial" and "miasmatic" idea; it is nonsense or worse than that.

I understand that the *Nation* is giving the "boys" a considerable lashing. The editor sees, as all men and women see, that the "boys" are covering up things, evading sharp facts, suppressing important things, facts, and events in Abraham's young life. Some of the finest episodes in L.'s young life are omitted or evaded or smothered up in *words*. Read in H. and N. Lincoln's courtship with Miss Todd and what came of it, and then tell me, if you possibly can, the *real* facts of that sad, terrible event. Can you tell me anything about, can you tell to the inquiring soul anything about, the facts of Lincoln's courtship of Miss Todd and what came of it? It is apparent to all persons who read the article spoken of that something is kept back, facts smothered by many, *many words*. The boys had better have told the truth or kept wholly silent on the subject, for the tendency of veiled things, stories, is to magnify the thing half concealed. Men and women are inquisitive, and hint a thing to them only and they will flash the story falsely seen to suit the demands of the mind. I once wrote a piece on this very question for Mr. Thorndike,[1] of the *North American Review*, which talks out in school. I wish that Thorndike

---

[1] Allan Thorndike Rice.

would publish it now while the fever is up; it would put the story right and convince the people that there was one man in America who dares to tell the truth who was not writing the life of Lincoln under the surveillance of "Bob" Lincoln. H. and N., in my opinion, are afraid of Bob; he gives them materials and they in their turn play *hush*. This is my opinion and is worth no more than an honest opinion.

There was a story current here some years since that Lincoln courted a young lady here by the name of Rickard. My wife's step-mother was a Rickard and the sister of the courted girl. My wife says that her stepmother told her that Lincoln wanted "Sue," that is, Susan Rickard; she is still living here and I'll try and get the truth out of her. Women, as a general rule, do not love to blab about these things, especially to the general public. I once had Miss Rickard's confidence and I think I hold it yet. I'll see about the matter when I have time and the fruit sought is ripe. I *do* want to get at the exact truth of all the Lincoln facts. I have tried to do so for twenty years or more and will to the very end. The reading world is entitled to truth; it is their right to have it, and it is our religious duty to tell it.

I will see Mrs. Francis and Mrs. Edwards and get out of them some facts which I want and they know—at least I think they do know what I want. Mrs. Francis once was quite a woman, a shrewd one, a friend of Miss Todd and Mr. Lincoln; it was she who patched up Miss Todd's and Lincoln's grievances. Mrs. Francis belonged to the aristocracy of this city till she moved to Oregon, or to the great open wide wild West from which she has returned to her old nest to die.

If you will look at your Indiana paper, you will see that it makes this criticism, namely, that one of Lincoln's biographers makes a statement of a fact and that all others simply follow in his wake, fol-low in detail what the first one uttered, a mere flock of sheep following where the ram goes, and this is to a certain extent very true; and yet it is equally true that there must be *a thread* to every narrative of facts, if of considerable length. Now the question comes, is, how to avoid the just criticism and yet keep in view *the thread* of the narra-tive? Take the killing of Abraham Lincoln's grandfather as an illus-tration; shall we go over the same old story in length, *in detail,* or shall we simply say that he was killed by stealth in Kentucky while opening a farm about the year 1781 or 2? Lamon first tells the story and then Arnold and then H. and N. and then shall we? I think it

best to cut the story short but keep in view *the thread of the narrative.*
Friend, *keep a keen lookout for criticisms,* and we will avoid much
fault-finding. We ought to condense. We ought, as the diamond-seller
says, to give a fine color, a keen and sharp cutting, and a gem full
of fire to our production. In better words, let our gem have a fine
color, a sharp and keen cutting, and filled with blazing fire. We should
keep *Truth* always before us and then fire it.

Hay and Nicolay say in the January number of the *Century* substantially this: that Speed was the *only intimate* friend that Lincoln
ever had, and that Speed and Lincoln poured out their souls to each
other. Possibly I do not understand what they mean by the word
intimate. If they mean to say that Lincoln had no friends, after
Speed, to whom he poured out his soul, then it *may* be true, but the
question comes: Did he pour out his soul to Speed? Lincoln's nature
was secretive, it was reticent, it was "hush." Did Lincoln violate that
whole nature? He may have opened to Speed *in one direction under
conditions.* He was courting Miss Todd and Speed was—well—you
can guess. These facts brought the two close together, and on the love
question alone Lincoln opened to Speed possibly the whole. Did Lincoln tell Speed his love scrapes with Ann Rutledge as well as others?
He did not. See Speed's letter to me in Lamon's Life of Lincoln. . . .
Still another question comes: Did Lincoln and Speed or either of them
open the facts, their minds, to Hay and Nicolay about the *intimate*
friendship? Who authorizes H. and N. to assert what they do assert?
How do H. and N. know that Lincoln and Speed poured out their souls
to one another? If to tell a friend some facts in *one line* or direction
constitutes *intimate* friendship, then Lincoln always, before and after
Speed left Illinois, had *intimate* friends, and if Lincoln's refusal to
tell all the secrets of his soul to any man shows a want of intimate
friendship, then Lincoln never had an intimate friend. Poetry is no
fit place for severe history. I think the truth is just here, namely, that
under peculiar conditions and under *lines of love* and in that direction they were *intimate* friends. No man pours out his *whole* soul to
any man; he keeps millions of secrets in his own bosom, with himself
and God alone; he would keep them secret from God if he could. Such
broad assertions as H. and N.'s are lies and nothing less. Did H. and
N. enter Lincoln's and Speed's minds and read the story? Nonsense.
Let us keep shy of poetry or poetical license in our book, if we can.

Let us ever keep in mind facts, truths, and then write tersely and to the point, plainly to the understanding of the great mass of men, to the common people. Lincoln has often said to me: "Don't shoot too high, aim low."

Enclosed, with this is a letter which I wrote to Mr. Poole [1] in '86, which you can read and file away. In the letter I say, and now affirm, that Mr. Lincoln was a riddle and a puzzle to his neighbors generally. Some few knew the man inside and outside; he was at once a many-*sided* and a many-*mooded* man. At times he had his spells in which he seemed to be destitute of reason. In the Poole letter, in my hurry while writing it, I may have pressed the idea of *heredity* too far or given it too much force. I shall correct the letter and the idea some-time when I write to you. The letter was in fact hurriedly written and I had no time to correct nor rewrite it. Read it and tell me how you like it in general. I do not in fact pride myself on the letter.

Your friend,
W. H. HERNDON.

January 22, 1887.

Friend Weik:

You must expect some repetition where I write so many different letters to different men all over the Union, east and west, north and south. I cannot help it entirely and no man could. What I cannot help I am not to be censured for.

Your friend,
W. H. H.

Springfield, Ill., January 1887.

Friend Weik:

Judge Matheny tells me this story of Mr. and Mrs. Lincoln; the story was told him by one of the parties to it. About the year 1850 there lived in this city a man by the name of Tiger, who was a personal friend of Lincoln; he was a kind but a powerful man physically. Tiger heard that Mrs. Lincoln was without help and, knowing that Mrs. Lincoln was a tigress and could not for any length of time keep a

---

[1] See letter of January 5, 1886.

girl, thought that he had a niece, who was a fine girl, industrious, neat, saving, and rather handsome, who could satisfy anybody on earth. So he sent the girl down to see Mrs. Lincoln; she, Mrs. L., was anxious to get a girl, and arrangements were made between the two that Sarah, the girl's name, should stay and help Mrs. L. Everything went on well for some time, Mrs. L. bragging of her Sarah all the while to her neighbors and visitors. Sarah herself was no common hired girl, but a fine woman and rather intelligent, pleasant, and social. Mrs. Lincoln at last got on one of her insane mad spells, insulted and actually slapped the girl, who could and would not stand it. So she quit Mrs. Lincoln, went home to her uncle Tiger's, and told her story, weeping and crying all the while. Tiger felt bad about the matter but, knowing that all quarrels generally have two sides to them, he was determined to find out the truth of the matter. So he went down to Lincoln's and, when he got there, he saw that Mrs. Lincoln had thrown the girl's trunk and clothes out of the house and on the pavement in the street. On approaching the house, he saw the things; and just in the yard stood Mrs. Lincoln ready for a fight. Tiger advanced and spoke to Mrs. Lincoln in a kind and gentlemanly way; said he came to see her and find out who was in fault, and what was the matter, all about it. Mrs. L. at once blazed away with her sharp and sarcastic tongue, having her insane mad spell on her, abused Tiger shamefully, calling him a dirty villain, a vile creature, and the like. Tiger stood still, waiting for an opportunity to pitch in a word of peace and reconciliation, but to no purpose. Mrs. Lincoln got madder and madder, boiled over with her insane rage, and at last struck Tiger with the broom two or three times. Tiger now got mad, but said nothing to Mrs. Lincoln, not a word, stood the licking as best he could. Tiger at last gathered up the clothes of the girl and, being a strong man, threw the trunk on his shoulder and carried it and the girl's clothes home to his niece. The older the thing—his licking by Mrs. L.—got, the madder Tiger got, and so he swore to himself that no man's wife should thus treat him and go free from a whipping or at least the husband should humiliatingly apologize for the wrong done him by his wife. The longer the thing stood in Tiger's mind, the more furious Tiger got, and so he went down into the city in search of Lincoln, in order to make him correct the thing or to whip him, to apologize or to stand a thumping, licking, a severe whipping; he after some considerable search found Lincoln in Edwards's store reading on the counter, telling one of his best stories. Tiger caught part of the story that tickled him very much. However, Tiger, being a man of *will*, called Lincoln out of the store and told him the facts of the fight between the women, and his licking by Mrs. Lincoln, and said to Lincoln that he must *punish* Mrs. Lincoln and apologize to him, Tiger, or . . . and just here Lincoln caught what was coming, looked up to Tiger, having held his head down with shame as Tiger told the story of his wrongs done him by Mrs. L., and said calmly, kindly, and in a very friendly way, mingled with shame and sadness: "*Friend* Tiger, can't you endure this one wrong done you by a mad-woman without much complaint for old freindship's sake while I have had to bear it without complaint and without a murmur for, lo, these last fifteen years?" Lincoln said what he did so kindly, so peacefully, so friendly, so feelingly, so apologetically in manner and tone, and so sadly, that it quickly and totally disarmed Tiger, who said to Lincoln: "Friend, give me your hand. I'll bear what has been done me by Mrs. Lincoln on *your* account and *your* account alone. I'll say no more about the matter, and now, Lincoln, let us be forever what we have been, friends." Lincoln instantly took and grasped, warmly grasped, Tiger's hand and shook it in a real friendly, Western style, saying: "Agreed, friend Tiger, and so let us be what we have always been, warm personal friends," and they ever were afterwards. Thus ended in the very best feeling and warmest friendship what at one time threatened to be a terrible personal fight. Both men were physically powerful and personally brave, and it is very doubtful which of the men was the most powerful. Lincoln was wise in not letting Tiger say what he intended to say, which was: "I'll punish, whip, you for your wife's wrong." That would have offended Lincoln and a fight would have certainly ensued. Lincoln tapped the cloud before the bolt came. I say that Lincoln was wise in the right, exact moment where wisdom was most needed and coolness. This little story brings out one of Lincoln's best characteristics—patience, peace, shrewdness, and practical wisdom; it affects me as much as any little story that I ever heard of Lincoln. God bless the man. He has blessed him as He has blessed no other man. Sometimes I can see Lincoln standing before me as I write about him, and so it is just at this moment I see Lincoln, the sad, the noble man.

I hope that you can read this fine little story, ending in peace and lasting friendship between two old personal friends. It is a good story and one that can be relied on; it comes from the right quarters and through men who know what they are talking about, men of truthfulness, honor, integrity.

Your friend,
W. H. HERNDON.

Mrs. Lincoln had the insanity of madness and not the madness of insanity before she left for Washington.

H.

Springfield, Ill., January 30, 1887.

Friend Weik:

I wish to, as it were, repeat some things in order to make my ideas clean and clear. I have tried to understand some of the philosophy of N. and H. They say in the January number of the *Century* at page 378, I think, that Lincoln's sadness, gloom, and melancholy were caused by his constitutional tendencies *slightly*—"taint," to use their expression—and that that constitutional tendency was intensified by the *malarial and miasmatic* idea; they further say, to add to the force of the argument, that we of the great West in an early day lived a forest life, and that a forest life made us *sad, gloomy, and melancholic,* and hence Lincoln's sadness, gloom, and melancholy; they use the three words—sadness, gloom, and melancholy—as I remember it. I have not the January number of the *Century,* having loaned it to my son. N. and Hay further state that we of the great West of an early day were unsocial and never *smiled,* only laughed. Now all this is but to prove that Lincoln was sad, gloomy, and melancholic, *slightly* through his organism, which *slightness* was intensified by the malarial and forest life idea. Let me see as to this argument. What is sadness, gloom, and melancholy? They mean a state of *sorrow, dejection,* and *an idea that bodes an evil,* which throw their shadow over the face of the man. That Mr. Lincoln was a sad, gloomy, and melancholic man, I admit; his sadness, etc., were *principally* and *chiefly* caused by his organism, his make-up and his constitution, which certain tendency of it was intensified by a series

of facts happening to him in his after life and a knowledge coming
to him of the lowness of his origin, his mother's illegitimacy, his
aunt's looseness, his father's loss of manhood possibly, and doubts
of his own paternity, etc., etc. These, with the untimely death of
Ann Rutledge, and his unfortunate marriage to Miss Mary Todd,
and the hell that came of it, caused Lincoln's sadness, etc., i.e., intensified his original nature. Lincoln's philosophy was a gloomy belief—
terribly so. But let me continue. Does a forest life make man and
woman sad, gloomy, and melancholic? Remember what I said as to
the nature of sadness, etc. That a forest life makes men and women
sincere, thoughtful, earnest, sedate, reticent, contemplating, determined, which appear on the face, there is no doubt; and this state has
been called *sadness, gloom,* and *melancholy* by N. and H. Nonsense.
A nation may probably be sad alone, not dejected, not feeling, not
having the idea on the face of a coming evil, a boding desolation. A
people may be sad, that is, be serious, earnest, etc., and this is the
case with the American people. The Americans are comparatively a
sad people. They have an unconscious destiny before them, and that
makes them sad. Again N. and H. say that we of the great West
in early times never *smiled*, only laughed. Had these gentlemen been
raised in the wild, wide West where Lincoln was raised, they would
never have talked so wildly. Had they been here in an early day,
they would have seen men and women smile and laugh at every dance
and at every corn shucking, at every social gathering, and at every
hoe-down, at every muster and at every election, at every camp meeting and shooting match, at every fireside and on every highway; they
would have seen, had they been here, a social, jovial, cheerful, generous, and an honest people, smiling and laughing everywhere as
occasion demanded. To *smile* is but a half-tickling, but to laugh is the
highest outburst of the human soul in the line of joyous feeling. The
boys should not speculate; they should stick to facts. Lincoln's sadness in short, etc., were constitutional, and those states were intensified by facts and knowledge of his after life, by his conditions and
his environments, socially, morally, mentally, the death of Ann Rutledge and his marriage to Miss Mary Todd and the hell that grew
out, came out of it. Lincoln's philosophy played its part in his
gloomy states. I'll explain. Lincoln's marriage was a policy marriage

and he paid the penalty of it, and the payment of that penalty wrote its receipt on his face.

Your friend,
W. H. HERNDON.

Would it not be a good idea to get our Springfield papers to say in a short way that they understand that Herndon & Co. are writing about the life of Lincoln?

Springfield, Ill., February 5, 1887.

Friend Weik:

It is said by some of the biographers of Lincoln that "he never drank a drop of liquor in his life" and that he never chewed nor smoked a cigar or pipe. It is not true that Lincoln "never drank a drop of liquor in his life"; it is true that he never smoked or chewed tobacco. Mr. Lincoln did sometimes take a horn; he played ball on the day of his nomination at Chicago in 1860 with the boys, or the day before that, and did drink beer two or three times that day and during the game or play; he was nervous then, excited at that particular time, and drank to steady his nerves. Lincoln has been often heard to say that "I never drink much and am entitled to no credit therefor, because I hate the stuff." A friend once asked Lincoln this question: "Don't you like liquor, Lincoln?" and to which L. replied: "No, it is unpleasant to me and always makes me feel flabby and undone." Lincoln had a low or slow circulation of the blood, and hence he had not much wear and tear of the tissues of the body; and hence no very strong thirst or appetite for stimulating drinks, nor other tonics; he had a good but moderate appetite for food, and was satisfied with almost anything that would satisfy hunger, anything with which "to fill up." Lincoln in thought and in act moved slowly, mentally and physically. He reasoned from the simple to the complex, from the concrete to the abstract, from fact to principle, from these to laws, through analogy; he was a worshiper of principles and laws. To him everything was Law. These persons generally who have a rapid circulation and [are] somewhat nervous, who think quickly and act quickly, have much of the wear and tear of the tissues of the body, and consequently desire stimulants—tonics, and sometimes unfortunately much of them, to restore the loss of tissues, or to arrest further loss or destruction of them. Such men generally love strong food, heat-giving food, and demand it, are somewhat dyspeptic, because of the strong food, and the excess of it, and their bad digestion. Lincoln had a good appetite and good digestion, ate mechanically, never asking why such a thing was not on the table nor why it was on it, if so; he filled up and that is all; he never complained of bad food nor praised the good. Lincoln was rather silent at the table, holding but little conversation there with anyone. I, on the circuit, have sat down with Lincoln a thousand times, it may be, at the table, and he never made any fuss about the food on the table; he ate and went about his business, though the food was "cussed bad," as eight out of ten at the table would say. Some would swear at it and others would laugh at their misfortunes in not getting "goodies." Lincoln did drink when he thought that it would do him good; he was never seen under the influence of liquor more than once or twice in his younger days when it, liquor, was quite in universal use.

Lincoln was a riddle and a puzzle sometimes; he loved best the vegetable world generally, though his food was of a mixed kind; he loved a good hot cup of coffee; and especially did he love apples; he would wrap his forefinger of his right hand and his thumb around the equatorial part of the apple and commence eating it at the blossom end, never using a knife to cut or peel the apple. I have seen him read, study his case and the law of it intently, while eating his apple. His table at home generally was economized to the smallest amount; he never dared as a general thing to invite his friends to his house. Judge Davis told me that Lincoln never invited him to his house, and have heard many others of Lincoln's best friends say the same thing. Mrs. Lincoln was a very stingy woman and yet she would occasionally have parties. Lincoln himself had none of the avarice of *the get* and yet he had a tinge of it in *the keep;* he was not generous in his money matters, unless he had some view in end. Mrs. Lincoln was the cause of his poor tables; she economized here to swell otherwise. Poor unfortunate woman! Wish that she had done better. The world will better understand the woman and the cause of much of her and Lincoln's troubles when Thorndike Rice of the *North American Review* publishes my article on Lincoln, his marriage, etc., until which time, form no crystallized unchangeable opinion. Rest easy and be content.

Your hurried friend,
W. H. HERNDON.

Springfield, Ill., February 6, 1887

Friend Weik:

That Lincoln had his peculiar *states* above described no one doubts, and that they sprang out of his organism admits of as little doubt. There is a physical organism and an intellectual one in every human being. Minds are of different kinds. Some minds require much evidence before believing and some less. Every mind must believe or fail to believe on certain evidence and some minds are credulous and some incredulous. This difference comes out of the intellectual organism, as we call it for the sake of an idea. Mr. Lincoln's mind required much evidence to produce conviction: it was an incredulous mind and naturally disposed to doubt, deny, was skeptical. Now the question comes: "Did Lincoln's gloom, etc., come out of his intellectual organism, or his physical?" Or put in different words: "Did his mind with his philosophy make him such—gloomy, etc.—or did his physical organism alone make him so?" It was his physical side that did it.

Lincoln's philosophy grew out of his mind, which was bottomed on the physical as a boy grows out of a man, an oak out of an acorn: it *had* to be just as it was and could not be otherwise by any means; and now another question comes: "Did his philosophy make him more such, etc., than he otherwise would have been?" His philosophy may have tinged, have colored or intensified, his sadness somewhat, a little, but it did not cause his sadness, etc. What was Lincoln's philosophy? He was honestly a fatalist and has been often heard to say: "I always was a fatalist," and quoted Shakespeare as follows:

> There's a divinity that shapes our ends,
> Rough-hew them how we will.

He believed in predestination, foreordination, that all things were fixed, doomed one way or the other, from which there was no appeal. He has often said to me: "What is to be will be and no efforts nor prayers of ours can change, alter, modify, or reverse the decree." Lincoln was somewhat superstitious, had a kind of foreboding of his fate; he said to me more than a dozen times this: "I feel as if I shall meet with some terrible end"; and then would become more sad. Lincoln always, to me in our private conversations, said that there was no freedom of the will, rather the mind as a whole; he maintained that there was no conscious act of any man that was not moved by a motive, first, last, and always. Finally Mr. Lincoln believed in constant modes of operation in nature, continuous and unchangeable ones eternally, Law, in short, that ruled both matter and mind. This philosophy of Lincoln I have heard him state many, many times in our philosophical discussions, private office conversations. Mr. Lincoln was a natural, necessary, and inevitable-doomed Infidel—*logically* and *absolutely* so; he was under his law; and it is all folly for any man to say that Mr. Lincoln was a Christian and believed in the efficacy of prayer. You might put the following words in Lincoln's mouth and they would be substantially true: "What can I do—what can any man do—what can the whole race molded into one man do—to arrest the workings of this terrible, this iron, this all-powerful machine that by decree and doom moves in its inevitable and omnipotent way to its own ends, working *out* new life and grinding *in* death forever? What [can] change this power and arrest its operations, which are certain, absolute, and eternal! This vast iron machine moves in no mysterious way, moves with an omnipotent force. I cannot act against it. No, I cannot even *think* against it!" Here you have Lincoln's philosophy, his religion, and his thoughts. Lincoln in his younger days tended toward scientific materialism, that is, he believed that behind all these phenomenal manifestations of the universe there was a *power* that worked for righteousness, as seemed to us. He would not call that *power* God. He called it *Maker*. In after life he used the familiar language of the day, and called it *God*. He did not use the word God in any religious sense, Christian sense rather. He was most emphatically an Infidel, was so logically, naturally, inevitably so, as his philosophy reveals—and demonstrates.

Your friend,
W. H. HERNDON.

Springfield, Ill., February 9, 1887.

Friend Weik:

I have read the February number of the *Century*, the article by H. and N., and find it a rather poor thing; it is wordy and windy and takes no note of time for the benefit of the reader in this short life of ours. I [can], and so can anyone, write the substance of the article, so far as a knowledge of Lincoln is concerned, in ten lines. The writers say, tell, a good truth when they state that "Lincoln received every-body's confidence and rarely gave his own in return." This is most emphatically Lincoln. Again the "boys" state another fact—namely, that Mr. Lincoln had great individuality which he never sank in the mob nor mixed it with any class of men; his individualism stood out from the mass of men like a lone cliff over the plain below. Again the "boys" say that Mr. L. had a great dignity, and that is the truth. I do not use the word "boys" in any contemptuous sense. I respect them very much; they are doing a good thing. Mr. Lincoln was a very plain man and of—to a certain point—easy approach, quite democratic, somewhat social, but beyond a certain ring of self-respect which sur-rounded and guarded his person no man ever dared go without a silent but powerful rebuff. Lincoln kept aloof from men generally, few knew him; he would be cheerful and chatty, somewhat social and communica-tive, tell his stories, his jokes, laugh and smile, and yet you could see, if you had a keen sense, perception of human character, that Lincoln's soul was not present, that it was in another sphere; he was an ab-stracted and an absent-minded man; he was with you and he was not with you; he was familiar with you and yet he kept you at a distance, substantially saying to himself: "This nature of mine *is mine alone,* and it is sacred ground on which no man shall tread." It is well to note this peculiarity of Lincoln. This peculiar nature of Lincoln will ex-plain to you why it was that Holland never found out anything while here gathering up facts of Lincoln's life; and it further explains why there was such a disagreement among the citizens of Springfield gen-erally as to the nature, qualities, and characteristics of L. Turn to my long article which I sent you—the one prepared for the *Tribune*—and you will see what Holland says as to the opinions of the good people of this city about L. Few knew the man and the many were ignorant; and hence the disagreement among ourselves as to the man. Lincoln was reticent, secretive, incommunicable, in some, many, lines of his charac-ter. The "boys" do not say all that I repeat here to you; and it is well to note what I say, if you wish to know the man which you are soon to write about. I have seen and felt all this in Lincoln a thousand times. I have stated all this many, many times to the reading world. See *Six Months in the White House,* see *Truth Seeker,* etc., etc., and other let-ters scattered through the papers from 1865 to 1887 and including my letters to you. What I say here is but a repetition, but it is well enough *to say it again and again*. Lincoln's individualism was great, so was his dignity, so was his reticence, abstractedness and absent-mindedness—a peculiar man, this Abraham was.

You ask me some questions. I never was in Kentucky, except along the line on the Ohio River, since the assassination of Mr. Lincoln. The Speeds live about four miles from Louisville. The picture which Speed told me about was, as I remember it, a painting, a painting possibly full-size, by Carpenter. The little book of which you speak is now in Lamon's hands; he will not give it back to me; it was only loaned to him. I'll tell you all about it when I see you, can't risk the substance in a letter—too long and too much of it. Mrs. Dale did, I think, one day go to my private drawer and read part of the book, as I am informed. She didn't see the beautiful if she did. It is probable that I let her see the book—it's a good long time since, and I cannot recollect everything exactly as it was in minutiæ though I can in substance as well as I ever could, though sixty-nine years of age. I am glad that you have the picture of Mrs. Vineyard.

I am not acquainted with Washburne much, though I may write to him or get someone to do it; he would be a good man for our purposes and plans. It is prudent probably that we should not press our venture till we can see the publisher face to face with our manuscript in our hands and then, as you well say, "We can talk business," and not well before. We will find in good time a publisher, fear not, despair not.

I am glad that you are going to Kentucky in search of new facts and old ones, if true, on Lincoln. The Enloe business should be probed to the bottom, including the character of Nancy Hanks. I once saw a letter published, it was in some Kentucky paper, in which Miss Hanks was described as a cheerful, rollicking, daring, reckless "gal," breaking through all rules of propriety or forms, etc., in society, and that she became sad while in Indiana. The man is now living and in Kentucky who wrote the letter, think his "fiz" is in the *Century*. However, you can get lots of evidence on this ground. I was told that Ben Hardin, old Ben of Kentucky, used the "gal" when he pleased. When you are done in Kentucky, if you go there first, go into the southern part of Indiana, taking with you, if you want to, my friend Wartman of Evansville. I am going to Menard court in March and I'll see what I can and take notes, and then write to you. I shall see Mrs. Francis, Edwards, Susan Talbott, and other people, and catch up what I can.

I shall do at all times and places just what I promise you that I will do. I am "sorter" insane on the question of telling the truth, and doing what I promise if I possibly can. In the meantime, rest easy. I cannot do all things "right" off, for I have to fight for bread and butter, and this, you know, takes time. I am busy on my farm and only write to you in the night or on rainy or bad days, when I cannot work.

Your friend,

W. H. HERNDON.

Springfield, Ill., February 11, 1887.

Friend Weik:

Mr. Lincoln was not at all times the popular man in Sangamon County, the capital county of this State, L.'s home, and there is a good reason, many reasons for it. In the first place, he was not understood by the mass of men; in the second place, he was not a social man, not being "hail fellow well met"; and, in the third place, he was a man of his own ideas, had the courage of his convictions and the valor of their expression. Lincoln was social in spots, at courts on the circuit as we traveled around with the judge; he was courageous in his ideas everywhere and at all times. Mr. Lincoln was not a warm-hearted man, positively so; he was abstracted and absent-minded. When in one of his moods he was abstracted and absent-minded and would not notice a friend on the street, though spoken to pleasantly; he would straddle along, stride along, not noticing his friends nor reply to any good-morning salutation. All this was taken for *coldness, dignity, pride,* etc., etc., by some, and hence by that some and his friends Lincoln was misjudged and disliked. These moods of Lincoln, when I have met him on the street, caused him to pass me unnoticed, though spoken to warmly and kindly, and yet I know the man so well that I paid no attention to it, rather I have felt for him, sympathized with the suffering, sorrowful, sad man. *Hell* was to pay in his family frequently, and this intensified his *states.* Lincoln was a many-*sided* man and a many-*mooded* one, and how do you expect the mob to understand greatness in misery? I was the firm, devoted friend of Lincoln from 1833 to 1865, and nothing could move me from my convictions of Lincoln's goodness, honesty, and greatness. I voted for him all the time against the world. I helped for years to write him up in our *Illinois Journal* and other papers in this and other States. Lincoln and I frequently disagreed on measures and men, never on principle, as I now recollect it. Before Lincoln was assassinated, I doubted the policy and the principle of a tariff except for revenue alone, and today I am a radical free trade man. In 1847–49 I saw that Lincoln would ruin himself about the Mexican War, and his opposition to it, and so, being his friend and not seeing the question as he did, I tried to prevent Lincoln's destruction. I wrote to him on the subject again and again and tried to induce him to silence, if nothing else; but his sense of justice and his courage made him speak, utter his thoughts, as to the war with Mexico. Lincoln and I had many hot disputes in our office, and yet those disputes were friendly ones. He was never insulting nor dictatorial to me. No politician in America can vote and live if he opposes war in which the spread eagle is concerned, America. When Lincoln returned home from Congress in 1849, he was a politically dead and buried man; he wanted to run for Congress again, but it was no use to try.

Judge Logan tried his hand as successor of Lincoln, but Logan was a failure, and a fizzle. Here was a cold, avaricious, and little mean man for you as the people saw him. Lincoln from 1849 to 1855 became a hard student and read much, studied Euclid and some mathematical books, read much in the political world. The repeal of the Missouri Compromise Acts roused Lincoln, waked him up to his new opportunities, and he seized them, and you know the result. Lincoln was born out of the war and given to the manhood of glory, such is life with an opportunity, verily

> There's a divinity that shapes our ends,
> Rough-hew them how we will.

Now, as to Lincoln's ideas, the courage of his convictions, and the valor of their expression. *First*, Mr. Lincoln as early as 1836 issued a political handbill in which he declared himself for woman's rights. His keen sense of justice could not refuse woman the rights which he demanded for himself, said to me often that that question was one of time only. *Secondly*, he in 1835–36 wrote a little book against Christianity, which was burned by Samuel Hill, his friend; he often in conversations as late as 1850 aired [?] his ideas in this city. I have heard him, so has Judge Matheny, Stuart, and many others. *Thirdly*, in 1844, I *think*, he advocated temperance in 1844 before the Washingtonian Society, both temperance and the society being somewhat unpopular at that time. The Washingtonian Society was formed by a dozen or more drunkards; and the élite and Christians of this city more or less turned up their nice noses at the men and what they advocated. Nearly all men drank during those days, and hence to run up against custom and habit quite universal was unpopular. *Fourthly,* Lincoln bitterly opposed the Mexican War, as you know; he did so while political death stared him in the face; it buried him and yet "he arose on the third day" and became our national savior. *Fifthly,* he opposed slavery everywhere and at all times when to oppose it was political death. From 1820 to 1860 it was a time of "doughfaces" in the North. Lincoln turned his face to flint on this question and stood firm on his conscience. *Sixthly,* he opposed the repeal of the Missouri Compromise of 1819–20 with all his soul, first, on the grounds of policy and, secondly, on principle. The repeal was for a time Democratic, pro-slavery, and popular; but Lincoln with others made the repeal unpopular and justly odious. This repeal was his grand opportunity, and he seized it and rode to glory on the popular waves. *Seventhly,* he advocated the policy of free immigration of foreigners and their right to vote, when Americanism here was popular and rampant. The question arose in this city as to the right of foreigners, who had not been naturalized, though they had lived in this State as residents for six months or a year as the case might be, to vote at our city election. I was city attorney at that time, as I now remember it, and it was my duty as such officer to see that no one illegally voted and to have them punished for such violation of the charter and ordinances of the city. The question was a doubtful one, one in which different but honest opinions could be expressed. I spoke, as attorney of the city I think, to Lincoln about the question, showed him the laws of the State, the charter of the city, and its ordinances, with changes *in the State law,* and asked him his opinion of the law. After looking over the matter and taking his time, he said to me: "The question is a doubtful one, and the foreigner is taxed by the city, and it is but justice that they should vote on all questions of city policy or interest." The precise question was: Does a general law passed by the Legislature repeal a city charter without including it, naming it directly or by just inference? I said "no" and this cut off many votes; it was compromised at last, however. The Whigs, Lincoln being one, were opposed to the foreigners' right to vote in city matters. Lincoln dared be just and stand bolt upright. *Eighthly*, Mr. Lincoln opposed Know-Nothingism in all its phases, everywhere, and at all times when it was sweeping over the land like wildfire; he and I stood shoulder to shoulder on this as well as all the questions mentioned herein except as stated. *Ninthly*, Mr. Lincoln had the courage to issue his Proclamation of Emancipation when one side of the Republican party said that he was too cowardly to do it, and the other side said that the issue of the proclamation at this time would lose the fall election for the Republican party; he had decided to issue it and he decided this time. The proclamation came as by doom. He had the courage in his Greeley letter to say that what he did or failed to do about emancipation, etc., etc., was not done for the Negro, was done to save the Union. Nor could the Senate of the United States drive Lincoln to dismiss Secretary Seward; and, *tenthly* and lastly, when Mason and Slidell had been arrested by Captain Wilkes of the *San Jacinto* and the press and the people all over the land were wild with enthusiasm over the glorious event, demanding the punishment of these traitors, when the Secretary of War, the Secretary of State, and his Cabinet were wild and furious for the punishment of these men, one cool head and one brave heart rose up and said substantially: "This must not be, these men must be released, one war at a time. To punish these men now would cause a war between England and America, and that is just what the South wants. Take off the shackles from these men, open the doors of their prison, and apologize to England," and so it was done, though a bitter pill to take under the circumstances. England will some day rue her course. Here stands Lincoln a brave and a great soul who had the courage of his convictions, his ideas, and the swift valor of their expression. How do you like the man, friend Weik?

Your friend,
W. H. HERNDON.

Had not Mr. Lincoln been assassinated just when he was, he would have *governed* the Republican party during his second term or it would have crushed him if it could. There would have been a struggle over policies and measures.

H.

Lincoln's ideas with his courage made him at times unpopular.

Springfield, Ill., February 16, 1887.

Friend Weik:

Probably I have told you this story before and, if so, excuse me. From the time that Lincoln and I entered into partnership in the fall of 1843, I was quite a reader in biographical literature. Seeing a notice of a fine Life of Burke, the English orator and statesman, I ordered it from C. S. Francis & Co., of New York. I read it carefully, two weeks, and liked it very much. One morning I had it on our table and was looking over some few pages, which I was desirous of reading again, when Lincoln came into our office; he looked rather cheerful and pleasant. We spoke kindly to each other, passed the compliments of the morning, etc. I said, still thinking of the book: "Lincoln, do you not wish to read an excellent and eloquent Life of Burke, the English orator and statesman?" and at the same time handing him the book; he took it in his hands and hastily ran over some of the pages of it, reading a little here and there, and then, handing me back the book, said: "No, I don't want to read it. Biographies as written are false and misleading. The author of the Life of his love paints him as a perfect man, magnifies his perfections and suppresses his imperfections, describes the success of his love in glowing terms, never once hinting at his failures and his blunders. Why do not," said Lincoln, "book merchants and sellers have blank biographies on their shelves always ready for sale, so that, when a man dies, if his heirs, children, and friends wish to perpetuate the memory of the dead, they can purchase one already written, *but with blanks,* which they can fill up eloquently and grandly at pleasure, thus commemorating a lie, an injury to the dying and to the name of the dead?"

This Mr. Lincoln said to me in substance just as I have it. I felt the force of what he said, because I had thought the same. I may sometimes repeat stories to you, not keeping any record of what I do write. In writing so much to you, how can I help it? Could you, if you kept no record?

[W. H. HERNDON.]

Springfield, Ill., February 18, 1887.

Friend Weik:

. . . On Saturday evening I was called out to write the will of Benjamin Bancroft, and at the house of Bancroft I found an old friend of Lincoln, whose name is Fisk; he told me the following story, which is correct. A man by the name of Pollard Simmons was a good friend of Lincoln in 1834–36. John Calhoun was the surveyor of Sangamon County, was "the candle-box Calhoun" and a Democrat in 1834–36. Simmons loved Lincoln, who was very poor at that time, and he tried to get Lincoln in some business; he applied to Calhoun as the friend of Lincoln to give him a deputyship in the surveying business. Calhoun, as Simmons remembers it, gave Lincoln a deputyship. Simmons got on his horse and went on the hunt of Lincoln, whom he found in the woods mauling rails. Simmons said: "Lincoln, I've got you a job," and to which Lincoln replied: "Pollard, I thank you for your trouble, but now let me ask you a question. Do I have to give up any of my principles for this job? If I have to surrender any thought or principle to get it, I wouldn't touch it with a ten-foot pole." "No, you do not, Lincoln," said Pollard Simmons, and to which Lincoln replied: "I'll accept the office, and now I thank you and my superior for it."

You wish me to state some of Lincoln's customs and habits about the office in Springfield. Well, when he got to the office about 9 o'clock in the morning, the very first thing that he did was to pick up some newspapers, if I had not hidden them, and read them aloud, much to my discomfort; he would spread himself out on the sofa, one leg on a chair and another on the table or stove. I have often said to Lincoln: "Why, Lincoln, do you always read aloud?" and to which he said: "When I read aloud, my two senses catch the idea. First, I see what I am reading and, secondly, I hear it read, and I can thus remember what I read the better." Sometimes Lincoln would read something in the papers and that would suggest to him an idea and he would say: "That puts me in mind of a story that I heard down in Egypt in Illinois"; and then he would tell the story, and that story would suggest another, and so on. Nothing was done that morning. Declarations, briefs, pleas, and demurrers were flung to the winds. It was useless to attempt to read any more that morning. Sometimes Lincoln would, when his wife had gone to church or when she had kicked him out of the house, bring to the office Willie and Tad—*these* little devils to me, so bad were they, but now little angels, I hope. These children would take down the books, empty ash buckets, coal ashes, inkstand, papers, gold pens, letters, etc., etc., in a pile and then dance on the pile. Lincoln would say nothing, so abstracted was he and so blinded to his children's faults. Had they s——t in Lincoln's hat and rubbed it on his boots, he would have laughed and thought it smart. Lincoln was a fool in this line. Lincoln was a selfish man generally and especially in the political world but was blindly generous to his *own*. He worshiped his children and *what* they worshiped; he loved what they loved and hated what they hated—rather, disliked what they hated, which was everything that did not bend to their freaks, whims, follies, and the like. But poor Lincoln and Willie and Tad. I am now sorry that I used to hate the children. I regret it, but human flesh could not have borne it better than I did. I did it out of pure and perfect respect for Lincoln.

In our disputes on law points—on principles in any line—Lincoln was never *to me* insulting nor domineering; he was cool and patient, kind and tender. We used to discuss philosophy, which I have written to you so much about. Lincoln never read much law, and never did I see him read a law book through, and no one else ever did. Politics were Lincoln's life and newspapers his food. I'll keep on this line a little while.

Your friend,
W. H. HERNDON.

A law office is a dry place for incidents of a pleasing kind. If you love the stories of murder, rape, fraud, etc., a law office is a good place, but, good Lord, let me forget all about a law office.

H.

Springfield, Ill., February 24, 1887.

Friend Weik:

As I said to you, a law office is a dry place. There is nothing in it but work and toil. Mr. Lincoln's habit was to get down to his office about 9 a.m., unless he was out on the circuit, which was about six or eight months in the year. Our office never was a headquarters for politics. Mr. Lincoln never stopped in the street to have a social chat with anyone; he was not a social man, too reflective, too abstracted; he never attended political gatherings till the thing was organized, and then he was ready to make a speech, willing and ready to reap any advantage that grew out of it, ready and anxious for the office it afforded, if any in the political world. If a man came into our office on business, he stated his case, Lincoln listening generally attentively while the man told over the facts of his case. Generally Lincoln would take a little time to consider. When he had sufficiently considered, he gave his opinion of the case plainly, directly, and sharply; he said to the man: "Your case is a good one," or "a bad one," as the case might be. Mr. Lincoln was not a good conversationalist, except it was in the political world, nor was he a good listener; his great anxiety to tell a story made him burst in and consume the day in telling stories. Lincoln was not a general reader, except in politics. On Sundays he would come down to his office, sometimes bringing Tad and Willie and sometimes not, would write his letters, write declarations and other law papers, write out the heads of his speeches, take notes of what he intended to say. How do you expect to get much of interest out of this dry bone, a law office, when you know that Lincoln was a sad, gloomy, melancholic, and an abstracted man? Lincoln would sometimes lie down in the office to rest on the sofa, his feet on two or three chairs or up against the wall. In this position he would reflect, decide on what he was going to do and how to do it; and then he would jump up, pick up his hat and run, the good Lord knows where. Judge Davis was judge over, I think, ten counties, and it generally took him six to eight months to go around this circuit twice a year. Lincoln would never come home while the court was grinding out justice on the circuit, to see his wife or family; while all other lawyers, every Saturday night after court hours, would start for home to see wife and babies. Lincoln would see us start home and know that we were bound to see good wife and the children. Lincoln, poor soul, would grow terribly sad at the sight, as much as to say: "I have no wife and no home." None of us on starting home would say to Lincoln: "Come, Lincoln, let's go home," for we knew the terrors of home to him. I can see poor Lincoln now as we turn our backs on each other, one bound for home and one back to the courthouse. It's too sad to think about. I wish I did not know it all. Lincoln, you know, was not a social man, and hence those little *incidents* in his office and around his hearth which you want so much are hard to gather and to get, for they are few and far between. You know the relation between Mr. and Mrs. Lincoln and you ought to know by this time that the *rich incidents* at that house were those of an unpleasant nature. You had better see Mrs. Chapman of Coles County on the subject, the question of rich incidents. I know that she can tell you much about the customs, habits, methods of life, etc., about Lincoln's home.

You wish me to state what year Lincoln and I entered into partnership; it was in the fall of 1843, and that partnership was never dissolved till the evening of his assassination. . . . You further wish me to state what the motives were that actuated Lincoln in taking me into partnership. I answer, I don't know and no one else does. The Reverend J. A. Reed of this city *knows* all about *God*, and why does he not *know* all about *Lincoln?* Reed is simply foolish in his attacks on me, because I said and published that Lincoln was an Infidel. Reed is a little bitter Christian and that's all there is of it. . . .

Your friend,
W. H. HERNDON.

Mr. Weik, I do not like to talk about myself, have never followed that practice, and never will. I may say to you that Lincoln never regretted our partnership and that's enough.

H.

The Hon. John T. Stuart got mad at Lincoln and myself because Lincoln did not take him into partnership in 1843, and he pursued us all his life with more or less bitterness on the sly.

H.

Springfield, Ill., February 25, 1887.

Friend Weik:

I want this to go in our book, at least in substance. Mr. Lincoln's philosophy was as follows: First, he believed that what was to be would be and that no prayers of ours could arrest or reverse the decree. Secondly, he was a fatalist and believed that fatalism ruled the world. Thirdly, he believed that conditions made and do make and will forever continue to make the man and not man the conditions. Fourthly, he believed that there was no freedom of the human mind; and, fifthly, he believed that universal, absolute, and eternal laws ruled the universe of matter and of mind, everywhere and always. Mr. Lincoln also contended that motives moved the man to every voluntary act of his life. If the above was Lincoln's philosophy or a part of it, then many acts of his life may be justly interpreted and the man better understood by it. Lincoln's patience sprang from his philosophy; his calm quiet waiting on the events of the times, his coolness, calmness under the times of terrible bloody war, his charity for men and his want of malice for them everywhere, all grew out of his peculiar philosophy. Lincoln neither loved nor hated, never admired and never censured, never eulogized and never condemned man. I speak of Lincoln's general nature. Is this true and, if so, why is it true? Men had no free choice; things were to be, and they came, irresistibly came, doomed to come; men were made as they are made by superior conditions over which they had no control; the fates settled things as by the doom of the powers, and laws, universal, absolute, and eternal, ruled the universe of matter and of mind. Men were but simple tools of fate, of conditions, and of laws, and to praise men on the one hand or censure them on the other was in the abstract wrong in principle at all times. The thing, the event, was to be just as it had come, and no right and no wrong and no virtue and no vice should in truth be attached to it. The man, the people, but obeyed their superiors. The man, the people, and the whole race are made by forces, conditions, environments, around them, set in motion a million years or more ago, sweeping swiftly around the universe every instant of time, never flagging, ever onward. . . .

Man is compelled to feel, think, will, and to act subject to the influences of these conditions; he, man, is a mere child moved and made by this vast world machine, working in grooves and moving in deep-cut channels forever and forever; and now what is man? He is simply a *simple tool*, a mere cog in one wheel, a part, a small part, of this vast iron machine that strikes and cuts, grinds and mashes, all things, including man, that resist it. Events, the fates, decreed them, and what they decree is irresistible and inevitable, and *no prayers* of ours can arrest or reverse the decree. What a man is, he is because of the conditions of the universe and is entitled to no credit and should have no blame attached to him for the deed. If a man did Lincoln a grievous wrong, the man was a mere tool, and did but obey his superiors. If the man did him a good, he but obeyed the powers and should not suffer for the wrong nor [be] praised nor paid for the right. The man was compelled, driven, to do what he did do. It was to be and had come. If a man was good or bad, small or great, successful or unsuccessful, filled with virtue or overflowing with vice, and if war, pestilence, or famine stalked abroad over the land, it all was doomed from the beginning. Lincoln was patient and calmly waited on events; he knew they would come, because cause and effect, antecedents and consequents, are ever in action following laws. Every event in the universe was preceded by some prior cause and gave guarantee of some subsequent event flowing therefrom. It is possible that Lincoln did not fully believe that Brutus was specially made to kill Cæsar in the Senate Chamber of Rome with a dagger and that Cæsar was specially made to be killed by Brutus; and yet he would believe, because it is true, that both Brutus and Cæsar were forced by conditions over which they had no control into the inevitable paths and center of forces that destroyed Cæsar and made in one short moment a criminal of Brutus and a murderer.

Now one word as to Mr. Lincoln's religion. From Mr. Lincoln's tender heart and large head, from his philosophy and from his feelings, his thoughts, his determinations, his willings, and his acts throughout life, one is compelled to say that Lincoln's religion was of a broad and noble kind—a liberal, an infidel, one who did not believe that the Bible is God's special and divine revelation.

This is all that I propose to say, where I have the say, about Lincoln's philosophy or his religion; it is a good condensation of all that I have said to you on that subject; and all that is necessary to say. What is said is true and will offend no one, as I see it. The truth ought not to offend, where that truth is stated in a kindly and gentle, manly way, said to explain the nature, qualities, and characteristics of one of God's great men, who once was with us and for us.

Your friend,

W. H. HERNDON.

This is a good condensation of all that I have said to you on the special subjects herein; and will probably supersede all other letters, lectures, etc. This does not exclude Lincoln's sadness, etc., and the philosophy of it. I'll explain when I see you.

Springfield, Ill., March 16, 1887.

Friend Weik:

Enclosed you will find a good notice of Nicolay and Hay's work which I cut from *Puck* of March 9, 1887; it is an excellent thing and shows plainly that N. and H. have introduced too much collateral and unimportant matter that does not touch any part of Lincoln's life, fact, philosophy, religion, qualities, characteristics, etc. N. and H.

have entered too deeply in trash, nonsense, collateral facts, unimportant events and persons; they have wearied the people, tired them out. In writing our book let us avoid this step—this fatal step. Let us see the mark and shoot for that directly as with a rifle for the center. In other words let us write directly of Lincoln and Lincoln alone, leaving off facts and principles that do not touch Lincoln. Strip Lincoln naked and write of him and of him alone. All facts that explain Lincoln's life, his religion, philosophy, his politics, his domestic life, etc., etc., should be directly stated, honestly—fairly and impartially. Throw light on this great man and not cloud him by verbiage, nor bury him under a mass of unimportant facts and persons—this is our duty. This is my idea. The people in this city are getting tired of N. and H.'s Life of Lincoln; they laugh at it in Menard where I have been. I will soon send you some information that I got while in Menard; was sick during court and couldn't do much. I saw Mrs. Bell and she is to make us out a copy of the quilt on which Lincoln stuck a stitch or two, with a $\frac{1}{2}$ eye on the needle and $1\frac{1}{2}$ eyes on Ann Rutledge. It is the universal opinion of the old folk of Menard that Lincoln and Ann were engaged to be married absolutely. I have examined the right ones on this question—people that *know* and who are truthful.

Your friend,

W. H. HERNDON.

Springfield, Ill., April 16, 1887.

Friend Whitney [1] :

Your very kind letter, dated the 3d *inst.*, was duly received. On going to the city late on Saturday, one week ago, I found your letter awaiting me. It was late in the evening and I had to go home six miles from the city, and this state of facts is my excuse for long, long delay to you. I have carefully read your note and I see nothing in it that is not true. You hit Lincoln very well. He was a curious man and was moved by his words. Lincoln had *no home*, just as you say. He had a domestic hell that he did not like and went there only to eat and sleep. Lincoln ought never to have married anyone. He had no quality for a husband. He was abstracted, cool, never loved, and could not from his very nature. What you say about Lincoln is substantially correct.

I cannot now tell you where you can get any of my four or five lectures on Lincoln. I never thought enough of them to preserve them, though others stenographed them and were thus sent over the country. Nicolay and Hay are failing and, as you will say, are getting "worse and worse." As to Lincoln's stories I do not remember any that would do to state to a mixed audience in a lecture. They would cut someone on some point.—Yes, I am going to write the Life of Lincoln as I saw him, honestly, truthfully, courageously, fearlessly, cut where it may. What you say about Lincoln's gloom, sadness, high exaltation, is substantially correct. Lincoln felt the *Honor* and the *Burden*, but he was Lincoln still. The exaltation made him more thoughtful and more abstracted and more gloomy and to that extent more miserable. Lincoln once said to me this: "I fear that I shall meet with some terrible end," and this cloud always hung over him. I will answer your note, the parts unanswered, as soon as I can.

Your friend,
W. H. HERNDON.

Hope you success in your lectures.

H.

---

[1] An attorney in Chicago. See reference to him in the letter to Bartlett of July 27, 1887, below.

Springfield, Ill., June 8, 1887.

Mr. Bartlett.

My dear Sir:

Your letter dated the 27th *ult.* was duly received and in reply to which let me say: I have a photograph of President Lincoln. The one I have is taken with the right cheek, the right side of the face, to the observer, hair tossed upside down, necktie on and collar turned down. If you have not got this, I can possibly send you one or I will loan you mine or give it to you if I must. This photo was taken in Chicago, as I understand it, in 1857.

I am glad to know that you are an artist and will assist you all I can in photos or otherwise. I have carefully read the criticisms or notices of your Life of Rimmer, the artist. The notices are good and written in good taste. By the way, about twenty-five or thirty years ago I saw a notice of a work in art, published in some Boston paper. I sent for the work, got it, read it with pleasure and profit. It was enthusiastically written. I admired the book. Was it written by Rimmer? It may be that you were the author. I am not an artist but a lover of the beautiful in every direction. I hope that you are executing a bust or something of the kind of Lincoln.

Let me subscribe myself,

Your friend,

W. H. HERNDON.

Springfield, Ill., June 24, 1887.

Mr. Bartlett.

My dear Sir:

Your kind letter, dated the 14th *inst.*, was duly received. At the time I received your letter I got the photo of Lincoln from the steel engraving by T. Dewey, and with it came your photo of your sketch in clay. The steel engraving is very good and so is your sketch in clay. The photo from the steel engraving and the one I have are alike excepting the one I have has no whiskers on it. I today send you the one which I have and which you are welcome to. I send you the photo from the steel engraving likewise, as you may need it. What I meant when I said that I would assist you was this: I would if you wished gather up for you photos, ambrotypes, etc., such as I could find here. I am glad that you have a copy of Mr. Lincoln's life mask and admire your determination in going to Paris, the city of science. I hope that the artists and physiognomists of Paris will give you a scientific and candid judgment which will be a revelation of Lincoln, objectively and subjectively. Lincoln was a mystery, a wonderful man. I hope that you will give voice to your own thoughts about Lincoln when you get ready. I once delivered in this city three or four lectures on Lincoln in which I gave my poor opinion of the man, and if you will get a copy of *Six Months in the White House* by the artist Carpenter, you will find, toward the end of it, my views in substance. It is a small book and indexed. The substance was stenographed by a friend. I *think* that the book will help you. I knew Lincoln well for more than a quarter of a century and I studied the man inside and outside as well as I could. You speak of Mr. Lincoln's fine physical nature, but to see and study the man you would say that Mr. Lincoln's physical nature was comparatively low, coarse, and not fine and high. He seemed to have no blood in his frame, his flesh was dark, wrinkled, and folded; it looked dry and leathery, tough and everlasting; his eyes were small and gray; head small and forehead receding; but when this great man was moved by some great or good feeling—by some idea of liberty or justice or right—then he seemed an inspired man. It was just then that Lincoln's nature was beautiful and in complete harmony with the laws of the great Eternal. I have seen him in this enshrined condition and thought that he was molded in the spirits but mad. Lincoln was a great man, a good man, and a pure one, and beneath his rough exterior nature wove her fine network of nerve. In *Six Months in the White House* I tried to describe Lincoln. This book *may* assist you; it will not do you any harm. . . .

May I say to your private ear that I am engaged in writing the Life of Lincoln, the special purpose of it being to fill a blank, as I see it? I could tell you much about Lincoln if I could sit down and talk with you for a day or so, but we are too far apart to sit down in chairs and chat. I forgot to say above that in my poor opinion Lincoln had not arrived, when he was assassinated, at the meridian of his intellectual power.

Your friend,
W. H. HERNDON.

Springfield, Ill., July 8, 1887.

Mr. Bartlett.

My Friend:

I received your letter and note dated the 28th *ult.*, for which please accept my thanks. At the time that the letter and note came to hand I received the two photos of Mr. Lincoln. I thank you for them too. The history of the photo in Garrison's possession is, *I think*, as follows: Mr. Garrison, even after Mr. Lincoln's assassination, came out to Illinois, came to my house and stayed with me some seven or eight days; he and my wife seemed to enjoy each other's company. Garrison and I went out to see Lincoln's monument, etc., etc. While he was my guest he presented me with the photos of himself and wife, that is, he gave them to my wife; they are now in her album and in her possession. My wife says that she in return gave Garrison Lincoln's photo, thinks that she recognizes this as the one, the original now in Garrison's possession. My good wife dearly loved Garrison and is now in the prime of her life. I do not think that she is mistaken as to the facts, though she may possibly be. It is a *fact* that she did give Garrison Lincoln's photo. By the way, the photo about which I am talking is an excellent one of Lincoln, the very best one ever taken of him. The artist caught him in a good humor, state, mental condition, feeling, thought, or what you will. Again I thank you for it. As soon as I can get time I will go into our photo galleries and look over the photos, and if I see any thing good or bad, I'll send it to you, if I can get it. I am busy right now. I had to deliver a Fourth of July notice in an adjoining court on the Fourth and hence got a little behindhand—will soon catch up.

(In your letter of the 28th *ult.* you state in these words: "When I spoke of Lincoln's fine physical nature I meant it from a physical point of view, that is, I would say he had a fine physical nature, was tall, healthy, strong, mobile in movement, and of good proportion." I understood you, and now you will pardon me if I state that he was not of good proportion, was six feet four inches high in his sock feet, was thin, wiry, sinewy, not MUSCULAR, weighed from 160 to 180 pounds; and if you mean by the word *mobile*, nimbleness of motion, ease of movement, grace of movement, you are mistaken. If you mean to say and I do not so understand you that, by the word *mobile*, you mean that Lincoln had mutability of temper, then you are correct. There were *great contrasts* in Lincoln's life, mysterious ones. Sometimes Lincoln was great, very great, and sometimes small. He was strong and he was weak; he was sad and cheerful by turns; he was good-natured generally, but it was terrible to see him mad; he was all honor, full of manly integrity, sympathetic, practically wise, politically sagacious, never moved nor acted from mere *feeling*, but from thought, reason; he was cool, conservative, and courageous, was truly a noble man. When you read *Six Months in the White House* by Carpenter, *please tell me what impression it had on you as to Lincoln.* You are correct when you say that Lincoln's brain was one of QUALITY and not size.) Will you please pardon me for being so plain, outspoken? You ask me if I ever saw in this great wild West many men of Lincoln's *type*, and to which I answer, *yes*. The first settlers of *central* and southern Illinois were men of that type. They came from the limestone regions of Virginia, Kentucky, Tennessee, etc., and were men of giant strength, physically fine and by nature were mentally strong. They were originals, were individualists. They had no education and no culture, but good nature helped them. The strong *alone* from 1818 to 1830 could get here, and the strong *alone* could survive here. Some of these men were politicians, some lawyers, some farmers, etc. No one was like Lincoln, and yet many men were of his type. I cannot now further explain than to say that conditions made this class of men—may explain to you sometime. Limestone water, so scientists say, gave us big frames, and the struggle for life in this *urbanship* and the South gave us, if you please, mental fire. A forest life makes us sad—and thoughtful. I think that by nature we were a great people. We were rude and rough, had no polish, no culture. Each man and woman was himself or herself individually; distinct individuality was the rule. Each followed his inclinations and despised imitation. Lincoln was Lincoln, Grant Grant, Douglas was Douglas. Had Lincoln been a man of high culture, polish, of literary taste, habits, etc., etc., he may have been a good country lawyer—that's all. I hope that you understand me; can't by letter fully explain.

(You are entirely correct about the study of Lincoln; he was a man of "extraordinary contrasts"—he was Lincoln and Lincoln alone, and none exactly like him. You must study him by himself and from himself. The reason why I stated so much about Lincoln in my former letter was this: Give a sculptor one fact, a leading physical fact, and that suggests to him another in complete harmony with the other. Lincoln had large hands and feet—foot flat. Hence a large frame, etc., etc. Lincoln's religion was practical and hence materialistic, and hence to a certain extent was his organization, etc. I speak generally. You would not look for a well-minded man in such a description. I have studied Lincoln inside and outside. Pardon me. I describe him to you as I saw him and knew him. I loved the man and worship, as it were, his memory. I owe to truth a fidelity and mean to pursue that course to the end.)

I hope that your son will succeed to his and his father's satisfaction. I and my countrymen shall be proud of him, glad to know that he pleased the jury of French artists. I have often thought that the age of the sculptor was gone, but I hope not; so I have thought of painting and poetry, but I hope not, hope that I am mistaken.

You state one fine truth as the world thinks and moves; and it is this: "It is a sorry fact of human nature that the great truth about a man is not preferred to an artificial estimate of him, even by those who are supposed to love him best." Hero worship, the worship of the ideal in man, is the spirit of the age. Fact gives place to the ideal and truth; *solid fact* gives place to the imagination, and firmly revels in the unreal. I have been much abused for telling the truth about Lincoln; and this I shall continue to do. Lincoln will rise in the estimation of mankind the higher, the more thoroughly he is known, because that estimate will be formed from facts truthfully and courageously told. When public opinion is thus formed, it never changes; it rests on fact —on eternal verities.

Your friend,
W. H. HERNDON.

Springfield, Ill., July 11, 1887.

Mr. Bartlett.
My dear Sir:

On going to the city from my country home on Saturday last I found awaiting me your very kind letter, dated the 4th *inst.*, and the *Art Life of William Rimmer*. I am much obliged to you for the letter and the precious book. The typography, the mechanical execution of the book, is excellent. The literary, the thought department, must be as good or better. I shall read the book carefully and preserve it forever. Poor

William Rimmer, how he felt the shock and sting of this, to some, cold world! William was a genius. Genius always flutters around the pivot of insanity, is shy, somewhat unsocial, retired, sensitive, with a heart, head, tuned to the harmony of the universe; but how it suffers!

The article which you sent me about Lincoln and Douglas is untrue in part, in the main part. Mr. Lincoln only corrected his speeches, made them talk as he had talked on the stump. This he did and no more. His corrections were only verbal and not otherwise. Mr. Lincoln told me how it was. I will refresh my memory and correct the note some time. You ask me to state to you Mr. Lincoln's attitude, pose, look, acts, gestures, etc., etc., while in the act of speaking, addressing bodies of people. I will do so just as soon as I can see some old friends who were close observers of Mr. Lincoln. We will have a talk and then I will write to you in full. I have seen Mr. Lincoln in every possible human attitude, have heard him speak for many years.

I am glad that you like my stenographed lecture in *Six Months in the White House* by Carpenter. I thank you for the compliment in your letter. I hope that will excel my poor effort in your work, and think you will. I will give you when I can the causes of Lincoln's sadness, gloom, and melancholy, his suffering, etc., but it must be kept a private matter for a while.

Your friend,
W. H. HERNDON.

I will gladly receive any photos you may send me and in looking over them I will give you my opinion. The Garrison one will be among the best, as I think. Hurriedly, H.

Springfield, Ill., July 17, 1887.

Friend Whitney:

In your last letter to me, dated the 4th *inst.*, you state that Hesler has three photos of Lincoln—one taken in Chicago in 1857, one in this city in 1860, and one in Washington in —— taken with *whiskers*. As I understand, you say that you can send me one. I will thank you for the one in '60; and if you can send me the one in '57, and for which I shall be under many obligations to you.

I will willingly, as I have time, give you any opinion which I have of Lincoln. The truth and the whole truth about Lincoln will never injure him. He will grow larger under the blaze of truth and the sharp-est criticisms of the iron few. He was too great, too good, and too noble to be injured by truth. He had his faults, more negative ones, and who has not some of these spots? The blazing sun has them and so did Jesus have them. What would you give for a true life of Washington—the *inside* life of him? The great reading growing world shall have one of Lincoln, if I live, but I will catch the devil for so doing. The world demands truth and truth it shall have. Lincoln was a curious, wonder-ful, mysterious man, incomprehensible by the mass of men. I studied Mr. Lincoln for twenty-five years, inside and outside. He was a man of opposites, of terrible contrasts. One man today would see Lincoln in one state and the man would say this was Lincoln. Tomorrow this same man would see Lincoln in a totally different state and say this was *not* Lincoln, and yet it was, for Lincoln *was under his law*, and that ruled him with the iron of logic. This caused, these contrasts in Lincoln caused, the differences of opinions among men in relation to Lincoln.

Your friend,
W. H. HERNDON.

Mr. Lincoln was a many-mooded man. One man would see *this* mood and one man *that*, and from seeing Lincoln in one mood each man would form his opinion on one phase of L., and hence the errors of judgment among the people as to L.

Springfield, Ill., July 19, 1887.

Mr. Bartlett.

My dear Sir:

I will now answer your questions put to me in your letter of the 4th *inst*. In this State and especially about the center of it we have no tables, boxes, stands, behind which we address and speak either to jurors or to crowds. It is open before us and we speak from the level floor where we address the jury and about on a level with them. Some-times the jurors are raised a little, the back seat being higher than the front, so that those behind can see and hear. We speak from stumps in the woods, if no better can be had, from boxes, from rude and tem-porary platforms erected in groves, woods, or public squares in cities or villages. Everything is open, visible, and clear. We have no tables, boxes, boards, planks to hit, beat, and to bang. The speaker stands out fully to public view, and the crowd is seen plainly by the speaker—so much for circumlocution to catch an idea.

Mr. Lincoln was six feet and four inches high in his sock feet; he was consumptive by build and hence more or less stoop-shouldered. He was very tall, thin, and gaunt. When he rose to speak to the jury or to crowds of people, he stood inclined forward, was awkward, angular, ungainly, odd, and, being a very sensitive man, I think that it added to his awkwardness; he was a diffident man, somewhat, and a sensitive one, and both of these added to his oddity, awkwardness, etc., as it seemed to me. Lincoln had confidence, full and complete confidence in himself, self-thoughtful, self-helping, and self-supporting, relying on no man. Lincoln's voice was, when he first began speaking, shrill, squeaking, piping, unpleasant; his general look, his form, his pose, the color of his flesh, wrinkled and dry, his sensitiveness, and his momentary diffidence, everything seemed to be against him, but he soon recovered. I can see him now, in my mind distinct. On rising to address the jury or the crowd he quite generally placed his hands behind him, the back part of his left hand resting in the palm of his right hand. As he proceeded and grew warmer, he moved his hands to the front of his person, generally interlocking his fingers and running one thumb around the other. Sometimes his hands, for a short while, would hang by his side. In still growing warmer, as he proceeded in his address, he used his hands—especially and generally his right hand—in his gestures; he used his head a great deal in speaking, throwing or jerking or moving it now here and now there, now in this position and now in that, in order to be more emphatic, to drive the idea home. Mr. Lincoln never beat the air, never sawed space with his hands, never acted for stage effect; was cool, careful, earnest, sincere, truthful, fair, self-possessed, not insulting, not dictatorial; was pleasing, good-natured; had great strong naturalness of look, pose, and act; was clear in his ideas, simple in his words, strong, terse, and demonstrative; he spoke and acted to convince individuals and masses; he used in his gestures his right hand, sometimes shooting out that long bony forefinger of his to dot an idea or to express a thought, resting his thumb on his middle finger. Bear in mind that he did not gesticulate much and *yet it is true* that every organ of his body was in motion and acted with ease, elegance, and grace, so it all looked *to me*.

As Mr. Lincoln proceeded further along with his oration, if time, place, subject, and occasion admitted of it, he gently and gradually warmed up; his shrill, squeaking, piping voice became harmonious, melodious, musical, if you please, with face somewhat aglow; his form dilated, swelled out, and he rose up a splendid form, erect, straight, and dignified; he stood square on his feet with both legs up and down, toe even with toe—that is, he did not put one foot before another; he kept his feet parallel and close to and not far from each other. When Mr. Lincoln rose up to speak, he rose slowly, steadily, firmly; he never moved much about on the stand or platform when speaking, trusting no desk, table, railing; he ran his eyes slowly over the crowd, giving them time to be at ease and to completely recover himself, *as I suppose.* He frequently took hold with his left hand, his left thumb erect, of the left lapel of his coat, keeping his right hand free to gesture in order to drive home and to clinch an idea. In his greatest inspiration he held both of his hands out above his head at an angle of about fifty degrees, hands open or clenched according to his feelings and his ideas. If he was moved in some indignant and half-mad moment against slavery or wrong in any direction and seemed to want to tear it down, trample it beneath his feet, and to eternally crush it, thus he would extend his arms out, at about the above degree, angle, with clenched big, bony, strong hands on them.

If he was defending the right, if he was defending liberty, eulogizing the Declaration of Independence, then he extended out his arms, palms of his hands upward somewhat at about the above degree, angle, as if appealing to some superior power for assistance and support; or that he might embrace the spirit of that which he so dearly loved. It was at such moments that he seemed inspired, fresh from the hands of his Creator. Lincoln's gray eyes would flash fire when speaking against slavery or spoke volumes of hope and love when speaking of liberty, justice, and the progress of mankind. Such was this great man *to me,* and I think, I know, such he was to thousands, if not to millions of others. I speak from long knowledge, observation, experience, but with my poor reason impartially. You know my criticisms of Lincoln as published in Carpenter, and *now take this letter and that criticism* and you have my exact ideas of Lincoln in the fields touched upon.

What is here written is written after thought and after investigation among close observing friends, my own knowledge, observation, and experience included, and if these hasty words will give you any idea of Lincoln's methods, ways, manners, etc., etc., of speaking, etc., etc., I shall be amply paid.

I have this morning just returned from our Menard circuit court, where I was attending to my professional duties. It is hot and I am tired.

Your friend,

W. H. HERNDON.

P.S. In Carpenter's book and in my lecture I said that Lincoln had no dignity "*so called.*" I used *that* word. I did so meaning that Lincoln had no pride, haughtiness, self-conceit, poorness of carriage. Lincoln was a man of great dignity and yet democratic, easy of approach. He would up to a certain point allow any approach, but go beyond *that*, and his dignity soon protected itself, and wilted the man who dared go beyond the proprieties of the occasion.

H.

I distinctly remember what is said herein though I conversed with others to be sure.

Springfield, Ill., July 27, 1887.

Mr. Bartlett.

My dear Sir:

I promised to answer your letter of the 15th *inst.* and will try and do so now. It is a hard and a difficult matter for two men living at a distance from each other, by running letters, to understand one another, especially so if they follow different pursuits and use local words, words of art, law, science. When I said that Lincoln was not of a good proportion, I compared him with others, the *general* man. When you said that he was a man of good proportions, you looked at him alone and compared his parts, organs, one with another—Lincoln's legs with Lincoln's arms, etc. Now you see where we differed. We are both correct. Lincoln was a man of good proportions when we look at him alone and not by comparison with the *general* man, the great mass of men. Lincoln was out of proportion when compared with the mass of men. The world is full of fuss and fight simply because men do not understand one another. You are correct when you say that Lincoln was *mobile* when looked at alone, one of his parts compared with another of his parts. This I confess. You will find the plains, mountains,

and outlines of Lincoln's head and face hard to catch ; they are so sub-
tle. In this you are clearly correct. You will have to use many photos
—side views, half-side views, and front views to catch the man and the
spirit of him. I said that your statue in clay is good ; and I say so now.
I have it in my hands while writing this. Lincoln had the grace of pose
and action. In my poor lecture in Carpenter, a mere sketch of two or
three lectures, I said that he walked so that he seemed to pocket time,
walked easily, and to that extent walked gracefully. This is what I
meant and so you will perceive that we do not much disagree. I try to
understand men's positions, natures, surroundings, etc., etc., and I
think I understand you. Again you are correct when you say that the
photographers—ignorant, unscientific men, men of no taste, no judgment—wishing to make a show of art, ruin the photos which they do
take by pencil, paint, coloring, etc. I would give a good many dollars
for a number one photo of Lincoln, but there is none, as it appears to
me. By the way, I have just received a letter from Mr. Whitney, an attorney and a friend of mine in Chicago, stating that Hesler has found a
new picture, a first-class photo of Lincoln, hidden or laid accidentally
away for twenty-seven years. Mr. Whitney says that this found photo
is the very best photo ever taken of Lincoln—he knew Lincoln well—
he says he will get and send me one in a few days and I'll loan it to you,
will give you my opinion of it. In your last letter to me you state that
it is possible that you will come to Illinois and see the great West, your
friend included. I would be glad to see you and happy if I can give you
an idea of L. After the first of August I shall be in Greencastle, Indiana, where a friend will assist me in writing the Life of L. The book
will *not* detail the general history of L. but will deal with him as an
individual, as a neighbor, domestically, as lawyer, as politician, statesman, etc. A mere thread of his general history will be kept up and no
more. In one of my letters to you I said of us Western people, especially of the old settlers, say from 1818 to 1845, that they had no culture, and in reply to which you state that that expression in your section means a college education, etc., and not the culture that comes of
observation, experience, and reason. The old settlers from 1818 to '45
were men of culture—so were the women, God bless 'em. If culture in-
cludes sharp observation, quick and broad experience, and a manly
reason of or about men, commerce, laws, institutions, human nature,
and the world and its affairs generally, excluding college education, I

have never seen such a people. I have been in your State and know many of your men personally and all the great ones of reputation, but for good horse sense our people, the old settlers, were your equals, if not your superiors as a mass. You ask me if I know Walt Whitman. I do by reputation, have read his *Leaves of Grass*, etc. He is a poet truly and indeed. I know Whittier and other of your poets by reputations. I like the heart and sympathy of Whittier and the bold originality of Whitman. I knew Phillips, Parker, Garrison, and other of your great men personally. One more word, you speak of Lamon's Life of Lincoln. May I say to you that, take it as a whole, it is one of the truest Lives ever written of a man? I do not agree to all it says.

Your friend,
W. H. HERNDON.

Greencastle, Indiana, August 4, 1887.

Friend Bartlett:

. . . I duly received the photo taken from an oil painting as large as life made by Artist Hunt. I thank you for it and its history. . . . I landed here on Monday night last and I am hard at work on my inner, subjective Life of Lincoln, his nature, characteristics, etc., etc. It is extremely hot and dry here—everything is burning up, and much suffering this winter is predicted here on that account. As soon as I get time and the weather cools, I will make notes of the photos which you sent me and send them to you. . . .

Your friend,
W. H. HERNDON.

Greencastle, Indiana, August 7, 1887.

Mr. Bartlett.

My dear Friend:

Your letter, dated the 30th *ult.*, is just received and I thank you for it. I am glad that you and I *now* agree about Lincoln's physical form, and now for the relationship between his physical and mental make-up. Keep in view Mr. L.'s form, including shape, etc. (He was a great big, angular, strong man, limbs large and bony; he was tall and of a peculiar type. I said to you once that Mr. Lincoln had not arrived at maturity in 1865, and I *say so now*. Mr. Lincoln was of a lower slow mechanical power, inside of him; his blood ran slowly, had low or slow circulation and consequently a slow build-up. As he had a slow build-up, he had a slow development: he grew up like the forest oak, tough, solid, knotty, gnarly, standing out with power against the storm, nearly defying the lightning. Hence I conclude that he had not arrived at his highest point in 1865. You see the value of getting some leading fact, great fact, of the physical man. No other man on the continent could have stood what Lincoln did in Washington; he had a frame of *iron*. Now for the mind. As Mr. Lincoln had a slow circulation and a slow build-up, so his mind acted slowly and his mind was tough, solid, knotty, gnarly, more or less like his body; he was angular in body and angular in thought, in idea and speech; he was a tall and big-boned man and his speech was tall, strong, and big-boned and enduring. The convolutions of his brain were long; they did not snap off quickly like a short thick man's brain; they had to have their time, but when those convolutions opened and threw off an idea it *was* an *idea*, tough, solid, gnarly, big, angular. Tallness, height, generally indicates power in the man. Mr. Lincoln was not what is called muscular, but was sinewy, wiry. The enduring power of Mr. Lincoln's brain, thought, was wonderful: he could sit and think without rest or food longer than any man I ever saw. Please see Lincoln's strong, terse, knotty, gnarly, and compact words, driven together as by a sledge hammer; his sentences, his thoughts as uttered—are they not grand types of informal expression? What say you? It is the force of the inner build-up power, mechanical or spiritual, just as you please, which makes the physical and intellectual man. I have given you the correspondencies in my own rude rough way. The key of the know I have given you, that's certain, and by running throughout, with the assistance of that key, you can see Lincoln as I saw and knew him.)

I am very busy here writing my memoirs of Lincoln and have no time to run things out for you. You are enough for that—my superior, I know.

I will keep my friends always, if I can. I am glad that you wish to know Lincoln and I'll assist you to know the man, if I can, but I must have a little time. I'll more fully hereafter answer your letter of July 30. Write to me as often as you please and I'll answer as well and as quickly as I can. Possibly I can help you some. I am a weak brother but will assist others with that weakness to the best of my heart and head.

Your friend,
W. H. HERNDON.

Greencastle, Ind., August 9, 1887.

[To Bartlett.]

Friend:

Your last letter and photo are this minute handed to me—much obliged. Enclosed is a poor lecture of mine—just found among the rubbish—which I delivered in the city of Springfield in '66. The object of the lecture was to show Lincoln's environments—physical, mental, moral—those things that influenced his after life, it may be. You will probably be pleased with my description of the *Pioneers* of Illinois. I came from Kentucky a boy, in '21, and know by observation and experience the men and things written about. The lecture, to me now, is wordy and somewhat strained, and yet it is true to the letter. I have seen all the persons and thousands of others, pioneers, mentioned in this except one or two men—think one only as now remembered. You once asked me this substantially: "Did you ever see a man of Lincoln's type?" The lecture will answer: "Yes, it may be a thousand." I wanted to get out Lincoln's love story and his insanity, etc., badly, before I fizzled out. No one else knew it as I did and no one who knew part of it could write. Hence the lecture, good or bad. Towards the conclusion you will see that I maintain that creative activity is the law of the *mind.* You have an idea of Lincoln. You through mental creative activity create a sketch in clay, the counterpart of the idea. We receive a sensation and we through the laws of the mind create a concept and out of that a complete, well-cut idea. What the law of the *brain* may be is another and distinct question. Read the pioneering part especially. Excuse me—am hurried and have no time to correct or rewrite. Some day I may sit down and write you a good letter, that is, if I can. After reading the pioneering part write to me, telling me how the people, the description, strikes you.

Your friend,
W. H. HERNDON.

Greencastle, Indiana, August 11, 1887.

Mr. Brisbin.

My dear Friend:

. . . I am here finishing writing the life—a peculiar one—of Lincoln, and those who love "God's naked truth" *may* like it. Possibly so.

You write to me a very kind letter indeed—and how different is your letter from those that I generally receive from ministers of the Gospel. I am in excellent health, have no vices, and take care of myself. Yes, I have one vice, I smoke. Speaking about my book, let me say that it is thought that it can be got ready by January '88—hope so; it will search Lincoln's life in some particulars thoroughly. . . .

Your friend,

W. H. HERNDON.

Greencastle, Indiana, August 14, 1887.

Friend Whitney:

Some time since you wrote me a letter in which you gave me a theory or a fact, if you please, about the *cause* of Mr. Lincoln's sadness, melancholy, etc. You said that those states of Lincoln's being were antenatal. You further said, in substance, that Lincoln's mother had fears, thumps, kicks, strokes, knockdowns, etc., etc. I do not use your words, but your ideas. Have you any facts on which to rely for your belief? If you have, *please* tell me all about them, when, where, and by whom done, etc., etc. Please answer me soon.

Your friend,

W. H. HERNDON.

Greencastle, Indiana, August 16, 1887.

[To Bartlett.]

My Friend:

Your letter of the 10th *inst.* was duly received and I shall proceed at once to answer it. I did not intend to say that Lincoln's organization was a *low* animal organization. What I meant to say was that it was a slow-working machine—blood ran slowly, and the like. Let me tell you some facts, in addition to the above. Lincoln's flesh was coarse, pimply, dry, hard, harsh, color of his flesh saffron-brown, no blood seemingly in it, flesh wrinkled. Mr. Lincoln had an evacuation, a passage, about once a week, ate blue mass. Were you to read his early speeches thoroughly and well, you could see his, then, coarse nature, his materialism, etc. He grandly rose up more spiritualistic, and this is one of the reasons why I say that Lincoln was not fully developed, in mind, at least. He may have just entered the field of his power, intellectual power, but he had not got to the center of it. If I were you, I would consult some of the best of Boston's physicians on the very question of *low* organization. I have a kind of imperfect idea on this point. If your physicians give you an opinion, please write to me. Lincoln was superstitious, believed more or less in dreams, consulted Negro oracles, had apparitions and tried to solve them; he said to me once this: "Billy, I fear that I shall meet with some terrible end." You may show my letters on this point to your best physicians, physiologists, histologists, anatomists, etc., but they—my letters—are otherwise private. Please get your learned men to assist us. The idea is worthy of a search and an opinion *from science.* I have a shadow of an opinion. The precise inquiry would be this: "*Was Lincoln's physical organization, as compared with other men, of a low order, and was it of a low order when only Lincoln was looked at by himself and not compared with other men?*" This is a question of much interest to me and will be to the world of science. Lincoln is a kind of an enigma. When your Boston man said: "Lincoln died at the right time, etc.," he did not know what he was talking about, was sputtering in the dark. Lincoln would have led us gloriously, peacefully, to the end; his martyrdom may have increased his fame, through the horror of his taking off, but you and I are not talking about the sympathy of the world but are looking deeper or higher, just as you please to express it. The observations of that man were cruel—your Massachusetts man, I mean. Lincoln rose equal to the emergencies and would have risen to them under all circumstances. He would have seen the reconstruction measures clearly, clearly. I have a decided opinion on this point, but have no time to express it.

In a late letter to you, the one enclosed with the Ann Rutledge lecture, I made a fool of myself, and it was on this I said to you: "How do you like my description, etc., of the old settlers, etc.?" I did not intend that. I meant to draw out of you only an idea of the people and their classes in and about New Salem, etc. I corrected the language

on the outside of the letter.* By the way, just now—Sunday morning
—Mr. Weik has handed me yours of August 4, directed to me at
Springfield, Illinois, and forwarded to me here—cannot answer it
now—too late. The fact that I am writing the Life of Lincoln is now
known to quite all persons. Enclosed I send you a slip, etc., which please
keep till you hear from me.

Your friend,
W. H. HERNDON.

*In re the words organization and organism—about synonyms,
though there is a little scientific difference. Ask the physician the
exact difference and write to me.   H.

Greencastle, Indiana, August 18, 1887.

Friend Whitney:

Will you please give me your opinion, first, as to whether Lincoln
really loved and trusted Judge Davis? Did Davis have any influence
on Lincoln, etc., etc.? *Speak fully.*

Second, what office did Dubois want that Lincoln did not, would
not, give him? You know that Dubois in a letter to you said that
Lincoln threw him away, etc., and was ungrateful, etc. Who got that
office? *Speak fully.*

Third, who was most influential among the big men in getting Judge
Davis appointed one of the judges of Supreme Court? Davis told me
that Lincoln gave him no assistance in the getting of it, etc. *Speak
fully* and I'll not blab. Please write to me on the above questions.

Your friend,
W. H. HERNDON.

Do answer my other letter wherein I ask about the antenatal, etc.
The threats, kicks, knocks, bangs, stops, cuffs, etc. You know what I
mean.   H.

Greencastle, Indiana, August 22, 1887.

Mr. Bartlett.

My dear Friend:

Your three letters of the fourteenth, seventeenth, and eighteenth of
August are before me, and I shall answer them in the order of their

dates. Now, as [to] the first one. I do not think that New Salem scenery and their people had much to do with Lincoln. He had no sense of the beautiful in the physical world but had in the moral world. The people of New Salem had a good deal to do in forming L.'s life, probably not as much as one would suppose. Lincoln in head was above them. The Ann Rutledge story, the facts of it, did affect Lincoln's life, I know, up to '42 and it is quite likely longer, possibly to his death. I fear that the world will damn me for opening things, unknown things, but I am determined to open. Great men have great mothers, and if this nation wants great men, it must build up great women, and in order to do that the nation must open all the avenues of life to her, make her equal to man before the law. She must be thrown on her own resources and thus in the struggle of life develop herself. You speak loudly of my lecture, but I shall have no time to write the Life of Lincoln in such a style. I am exceedingly poor, poor indeed, and would starve if I tried to write a full Life of Lincoln in such a style, as is in the Ann Rutledge lecture. My Life of Lincoln will be a limited one, kind of subjective, inner life, with a mere thread of history running along. This life, if it ever sees the light, will cause a squirm.

As to the second letter, I still adhere to my idea that Lincoln had not arrived, intellectually at least, to the height of his power, and you may answer that, by the tables of facts made by insurance and other companies and ways that it is set down, the average life of man, say at 45–50, but I reply: did not Lincoln grow up to 1865, over the average age; and now will you fix the limit of Lincoln's development, my friend? What authorizes you to do it? Come, be fair. Compare his Gettysburg speech with his speeches, say, from 1840 to 1850. I am firm in my convictions, because founded on facts: if Lincoln grew up from youth to '65—over the average life of man—will you say: "Here is the limit of Lincoln's greatness"? But how do you know it? You have no fact to prove it and so I have the logic of things on my side. As to his physical development, I am not quite certain of my idea on that particular, am not decided on it, am thinking on it.

In your third letter you give me a story about Lincoln's ambition, the Scott story, the Chamberlain story; and to which I say: in part the story is evidently, to me, correct. Lincoln was ambitious, and in that he was selfish. Mr. Lincoln's idea was that he ought to be retained the second term because he knew all the facts of the great Rebellion, and that no man could learn and understand them in two years, and that it was best under all the circumstances to keep him there. Lincoln doubtless did consider his success in his second term of vastly more importance than the advancement of Grant, or all men on the earth. No earthly doubt of it, no doubt of it, none. Lincoln, however, did not intend to be understood that the Rebellion had better succeed than his, L.'s, defeat for the second term. Lincoln would have offered himself up as a sacrifice to squelch the Rebellion and free the slaves, for with him it was the whole matter; the Rebellion was a question of human liberty, white as well as black; see his Philadelphia speech. This is my opinion, good or bad. Lincoln remains unknown and, oh, what a big mysterious man! In one of your letters you ask me this question in substance: "Do you think that Lincoln wished to be known, thoroughly known?" and to which I answer emphatically: "No, he was a hidden man and wished to keep his own secrets." As I trail the man step by step, like a dog trails a fox, I find many new spots, many new holes, much to admire and much to regret. It nearly kills me in my old age to persist in my search. Please pardon allusion to myself.

Your friend,

W. H. HERNDON.

Greencastle, Indiana, August 25, 1887.

Friend Whitney:

I have received your two excellent letters—facts in them which I have dreamed of long since, but didn't *know*. I thank you for them. Davis, at Bloomington, told me, by inference at least, that Lincoln didn't give him the judgeship of his own accord, but that someone else got it for him, etc. How is this? In one of your letters, before these two, you state that Lamon's Life of Lincoln is full of mistakes, especially as to what I did and said—at least infer this much. How is this? If you know of any mistakes in the book, please note them down and write them out for me. Your letters are helping to form history. They are very well written too. Please do not fail to accommodate the world and your friend. Probably I shall go home about September 5–10 for a while.

Your friend,

W. H. HERNDON.

Greencastle, Indiana, September 2, 1887.

Mr. Bartlett.

My dear Sir:

I duly received your two letters, enclosing opinions of two of your very best physicians, etc., and for which I thank you very much. I cannot afford to surrender my facts for theories. The pork theory, the miasmatic theory, is guesswork, and not formed on fact. The Western people lived on the very best food in the world—venison, bear, turkey, fish, etc., etc., including some hog. What I said to you I shall adhere to: as to mind, development, etc., but as to Lincoln's organization, physical, I still think that he had a fine network of nerve under the coarse flesh. You know the crankiness of physicians; they have to seek for life, its sources, its origin, etc., and this makes them insane, i.e., cranky—theoretical above all classes of men. I have seen them examined in court too often not to notice their tending, their trend.

I am going to Springfield in about five days, where you can address me—am worn out, must take rest and recover—am getting along admirably well in my book, as I see it. I shall write to you when I feel able to do so and after getting home.

Your friend,

W. H. HERNDON.

No man had better take up this story unless he mastered Lincoln. I would say to all: Go slow.

Private

Springfield, Ill., September 22, 1887.

Mr. Bartlett:

I have been under the weather for some two weeks or I would have written to you in answer to your last. Nothing new has happened and no new views formed about Lincoln physically or intellectually. I stick to my opinions expressed to you. I will tell you a secret about Lincoln which must be kept private. I tell you the secret because it lets light into Lincoln. Mr. Lincoln's mother, Nancy Hanks, was the illegitimate child of a Virginia planter, and right here it was that Lincoln got his mind; it never came out a Hanks in this world. The Hankses are the lowest people in the world, if we may judge of them by their history of 1790–1814. It is held by some that Abraham Lincoln is the illegitimate child of one Enloe, but I do not think that they are borne out by good and sufficient evidence. I simply state these facts or supposed facts to you in order that you may understand the origin of things and by knowing the origin you may infer much, if you will carry it out. Lincoln knew all these facts or supposed facts and hence in part his sadness; his domestic life was a hell, a burning, scorching hell in the domestic world and hence an increased sadness and gloom. There flitted before this great man an apparition, an idea that he was to meet with some terrible end. Now when you look at these things and know the peculiarities of his physical organization, you will not be surprised at Lincoln's sadness, gloom, and melancholy. This terribly reticent, secretive, shutmouth man never talked much about his history, plans, designs, purposes, intents; and when a man tells you this or that about what Lincoln said, believe what you must and no more. Lincoln had profound policies and never revealed himself to any man or woman, and this his nature caused the devil domestically. Lincoln is unknown and possibly always will be. Some time next month, nothing happening, I will send you your photos. I will be glad to see you in Illinois at any time.

Your friend,
W. H. HERNDON.

Springfield, Ill., September 25, 1887.

Friend Bartlett:

On the 22d *inst.* I wrote to you a private and confidential letter in which I stated to you that Abraham Lincoln's mother, Nancy Hanks, was an illegitimate child of a Virginia planter. I repeat what I said to you in that letter; and there is no doubt of the fact. Mr. Lincoln told me the fact, and the record of the woman bears out her son's statement that she was an illegitimate child of a Virginia planter. Here Mrs. Lincoln got her mind and her blood. She was an intellectual woman beyond a doubt. Her son told me so, and all other persons who knew the woman prove that she was rather a great woman. She cared nothing for forms, etiquette, customs, etc., etc., but burst through them without a care for consequences; she was a social creature, very much so, loved the company of men more than women, and by her peculiar nature she got up a bad reputation; and because she had a bad reputation it was, it is still, charged that Abraham Lincoln is the child of one Enloe. My own opinion, after a searching examination, is that Mrs. Lincoln, Nancy Hanks, was not a bad woman, was by nature a noble woman, free, easy, and unsuspecting. My own opinion after a sweeping and searching examination, investigation, is that Abraham Lincoln was the child and heir of Thomas Lincoln and Nancy Hanks Lincoln. I admit that all things are not perfectly clear to me; and yet I think that the weight of the testimony is in my favor on both of these grounds. Old Thomas Lincoln, Abraham's father, was castrated, fixed, cut, but no one can fix the exact time of the loss of his manhood. That event being uncertain, lets in the presumptions of chastity, virtue, and heirship, and on these hangs the weight of testimony alone. This is pretty close rubbing, is it not? I will write to you again and close up this subject forever, I hope. Now I want to ask you a question and it is this: Shall I tell out the whole story and argue things out as I see it?

Your friend,
W. H. HERNDON.

It will take an exhaustive argument.

Private

Springfield, Ill., September 30, 1887.

Friend Bartlett:

I wrote to you two letters dated about the 22d and 26th *inst.* and [in] the first of which I tried to explain Mrs. Nancy Hanks Lincoln's parentage, etc. In the one of the 26th I tried to explain the paternity of Abraham Lincoln. Now I wish to explain the facts somewhat of Lincoln's origin, the doubt of it, etc. It is said to me that Thomas Lincoln, Abraham's father, was castrated and there is not much doubt of it, but the material question is: When was he castrated? Nancy Hanks, Abraham's mother, married Thomas Lincoln when she was about twenty-two years of age. She had three children by Thomas Lincoln—at least the three children were born when or after Thomas and Nancy were married. If she had been a bad woman, why did she not have children before marriage? The first child, Sarah, was born in eight months less two days after the marriage and lived and married. Abraham was born in two years thereafter, after Sarah, and Thomas two years thereafter . . . making six years from the marriage. She, Nancy, ceased to have children in, say, 1812. (There is no proof of the exact time.) She, Nancy, was in the vigor and prime of life when she ceased to breed, and why did she cease thus to bear children? Because Thomas was castrated. Mrs. Nancy Hanks Lincoln, Abraham's mother, died in 1816; she had no children from 1812 to 1816, and why? Because her husband lost his manhood and because she was a virtuous woman. Had she bred right along, Thomas being castrated, then she would have let a stray bull in the pasture. Thomas Lincoln married a Mrs. Johnston. She had three children by her first husband Johnston. Her first husband died about 1817 and then [she], too, in the vigor and the prime of life, had no more children by Thomas Lincoln, because he was cut, fixed, castrated. If the time of Lincoln's castration was before marriage, then Abraham is the illegitimate child of someone, but, if after Thomas, her youngest son, then Abraham was got in lawful wedlock. Under this state of facts, do you not see the importance of presumptions? The law conclusively presumes that all persons born in lawful wedlock shall be presumed to be the lawful child and heir of the husband and the wife unless it should be conclusively proved that the marriage was incapable of procreation by nature or accident. No one now living can fix the time when Thomas Lincoln was castrated. The presumption of law saves Abraham's paternity. This is close shaving on so important a subject.

In addition to the above there appear to have been two Nancy Hankses—one the mother of Abraham and the other the mother of Dennis Hanks, a bastard, and illegitimate. Now at this late date, when men say that they had connection with Abraham's mother, can there not be a mistake in the identity of persons? It appears in evidence before me that a Mr. Haycraft wrote, in 1860 or 1861, to Mr. Lincoln asking him some question about himself, Abraham. It appears, it is a fact, because I have copies of Mr. Lincoln's letters to Haycraft, that Abraham Lincoln replied, in answer to a question about his own mother and himself: "In the main you are right about my history. My father was Thomas Lincoln and Mrs. Sally Johnston was his second wife. You are mistaken about my mother; her maiden name was Nancy Hanks." This is all that Lincoln said in the Haycraft letter. Intelligent men do say that they did know the difference between the two Nancys and so the matter stands. It, however, gets back to the question of castration. If Thomas Lincoln was castrated before he married Nancy, then the fact is or was that Nancy Hanks, Abraham's mother, was a bad woman, but no one fixes the exact date of the sad fact. Now you must presume that every grown man has the power of procreation and you shall presume that all children born in lawful wedlock are legitimate, unless you can prove that the pair had no earthly opportunity of access, or that the man was by nature or by accident deprived of his manhood.

I promised you, near the beginning of our correspondence, that I would reveal to you some things. I have done as I promised and so you will have to judge for yourself. I am satisfied that Abraham Lincoln was the lawful child of Thomas Lincoln and Nancy Hanks and that she was a virtuous woman. I hope that you can read my letters, hastily written as you must know.

Your friend,
W. H. HERNDON.

Please keep these three letters till you go hence and then hand them down as drafts of legitimacy and virtue.   H.

Springfield, Ill., October 1887.

Friend Bartlett:

Your letter, dated the 30th *ult.*, was handed to me a day or so since. Yes, Mr. Butler is correct in saying that Mr. Lincoln was East in 1849, not '40. On the adjournment of Congress, the 30th, he passed through some of the New England States, making some speeches for Taylor as I remember it. I do not think that Lincoln was in New England in 1840, have no recollection of it, do recollect the one in 1849. . . .

My book will be ready for the press, say in December or January next. I am bothered a great deal how to act in the matter. I thank you for your suggestions. You are correct in saying that the whole truth should be told of most men and yet it would not do for Lincoln. Lincoln is still going up, the growing great ideal man. I know a good deal about Lincoln—more than I dare state in a book. I watched the man closely for thirty years, twenty of which were just across the table 10 x 3 feet. I was his friend, a fast one, an unswerving one, and he knew it. I was from '34 to 1865 for Lincoln against the world, saw in him a great man, a man of destiny, took notes, etc., etc. Lincoln to the world is a profound mystery, an enigma, a sphinx, a riddle, and yet I think that I knew the man. He was uncommunicative, silent, reticent, secretive, having profound policies, and well-laid, deeply studied plans. He moved men at pleasure and for his own ends. He was a remorseless trimmer with men. They were his tools, and when they were used up, he threw them aside as old iron and took up new tools. On principles he was as true as steel, and while I say all this, his ends were his country's and man's.

You are correct again when you say that the noblest of women can lose their character quickly in a little village or in a new and sparsely settled country. Everybody knows everybody, and any man's business is the business of the whole community. Such people love to tattle and to lie about one another. They have nothing to do but to tattle and to lie in small things. In cities no man's business is his neighbor's, and so each man and woman attends to his or her business and goes on unnoticed and uncriticized, but woe to the woman in a little village if she makes a false step. One more word about Thomas Lincoln, Nancy Hanks, and Abraham Enloe. Thomas Lincoln caught Enloe at his house under suspicious circumstances, etc. Lincoln and Enloe had a fight about it, and Lincoln bit off Enloe's nose. Possibly Thomas Lincoln left Kentucky to get rid of the devil. Nancy Hanks was as far above Thomas Lincoln as an angel is above mud. It is said that she didn't care anything for Thomas, and now let me conclude this revealing letter by saying to you that Nancy Hanks was a great noble woman; a woman of a very fine cast of mind; was a broad-minded, liberal, generous-hearted, quickly sympathetic woman; a woman far above her surroundings, meditative, introspective, sad, daring, fearless, and in some cases indiscreet. Lincoln himself told me much of this description of his mother. I know it by what her neighbors say of her and with which neighbors I have talked.

Your friend,

W. H. HERNDON.

Enloe was a kind of genius, a rogue, a rake, a libertine, a man of force and of mind, a brokendown genius.

Since writing the above I received your kind letter dated the 22d *inst.* and for which I sincerely thank you. I wish greatly to be understood by all men. I have often said that Mr. Lincoln was an infidel and I say it now. In 1835–36 Mr. Lincoln in the village of New Salem wrote a little book on *Infidelity*. In that little work, burnt up by a friend, Mr. Hill, Lincoln denied the miraculous conception of Christ, ridiculed the Trinity, and denied that the Bible was the divine special revelation of God. Here are facts, well-settled facts. Now what is an infidel? As the infidels use the word, it means those who deny that the Bible is the divine special revelation of God. If you will turn to Worcester's dictionary, you will find that that is the meaning of the word. Whether this is so or not, the infidel has the right to define himself and the terms which he uses. Lincoln was a deist if that word suits, fits, the case better. I well know that all this is no evidence of a want of religion in Mr. Lincoln. It is rather an evidence that he had his own religion. I have said for more than twenty years that Mr. Lincoln was a thoroughly religious man, a man of exalted notions of right, justice, duty, etc., etc. Lincoln's religion was of the grandest and noblest type, kind. But when Mr. Bowditch says that Mr. Lincoln was not an infidel, I am at a loss to know what an infidel is. Lincoln was a strong believer in an overruling Providence, no man more so. He had a grand belief here. Am I understood, friend? Rest assured, Mr. Bartlett, that no theories go in my book; fact, science, if I can catch it, only will be mentioned in the Life. Facts, facts, facts, shall be my guide. The Eastern people, bless 'em too, must give us poor devils of the great West some little credit for common sense and the practical. We pride ourselves on the useful and the practical. We are a people who have not a great pride in mental speculation nor in theories. Write us down "practicals."

Your friend,
W. H. Herndon.

I judge that Mr. B. uses the word infidel as synonymous with atheism, which he is not warranted in doing. Excuse me.   H.

Friend Weik:

On last Saturday I received your good long letter, dated the 10th *inst.*, giving me much information, "much ideas." I guess that we had better bow to the semi-omnipotence of public opinion and bend to the inevitable with grace and as much dignity as we can reserve. I do not see the use of fighting the unavoidable and losing what we have a chance of getting. We can tell all necessary truths, all those truths which are necessary to show Lincoln's nature, etc., characteristics, etc. We need not, *nor must we, lie.* Let us be true as far as we do go, but by all means let us with grace bow to the inevitable. If the people will not take the truth—"God's naked truth"—let the crime rest on them and not on our heads. Talk to me of the progress of this age! Sugarcoat a lie and it goes down sweetly. The mass of men vomit at the truth unless it is sweetened with the lie. Falsehood is worshiped and the truth crucified: it always has been so and always will be so. *I say bow down to the inevitable.*

I am glad to know that you were in Chicago feeling your way, glad that Whitney was kind to you and did all he could for us. I agree with him that New York or Boston is the place for our contemplated book. I think Swett can do us good with Griggs, etc. When the MSS are done, I'll go to Chicago if I can. You and I will have to meet here, say for a month, and fix up things, understand one another as to what things shall be said and how and when said. When and where shall we meet? I have written nothing as yet except a little on Lincoln's civil policy and will not till you and I see each other and well understand things. To write anything now would be folly. Bow to the inevitable with grace.

I received the Preface and first chapter—have read them—are very good, but the first chapter will have to be changed, rewritten, modified, gutted. "Make things straight and rosy." Success is what we want. We want no failures. Do what is necessary to gain that end, short of lying, or fraud. Please Lincoln's friends, the publishers, and all mankind, past, present, and the future. Go to any necessary expense in getting a typewriter. Now you have my views in full.

I have tried to see Doctor Jayne, but he has been in Chicago; saw

Matheny, but failed to get his photo, promised it; will send J. C. Conkling's photo and Ben Edwards's if I can get it.

I saw Susan Talbott, Lincoln's sweetheart as said; she says that Lincoln never courted her to the end of a proposal; have written two letters to Sarah, but I fear that she will not blab. Mrs. Talbott intimated to me that Sarah would not blab, if L. courted her. It is evident that Lincoln and the girls were warm friends, if nothing more. I saw Brown; he says that Melvin has Lincoln's lectures; saw Mr. Grimsley, the son of Mrs. Brown, who says that his mother never had a lecture of Lincoln's. I have written to Melvin twice, but he has not answered. I am doing all I can to further things along and will to the end, am trying to please the world and all mankind and womankind too, bless 'em. By all means bow to the inevitable and do the best that you can under all circumstances.

Your friend,
W. H. HERNDON.

Springfield, Ill., January 27, 1888.

Friend Weik:

Mr. Lincoln was a conscientious conservative; he believed in Law and Order. See his speech before the Springfield Lyceum in 1838; the essence of that speech was obedience to and respect for law. The burning of a Negro by a mob in St. Louis was the cause, the text rather, of that speech, the occasion of it, etc. Lincoln too was absolutely conservative. See his speech in Congress made June 1848. The talk in part of that speech was suggested by some remarks of someone about amendments to the Constitution; he says: "No slight occasion should tempt us to touch it (the Constitution). Better not take the first step, which may lead to a habit of altering it. Better rather habituate ourselves to think of it as unalterable. It can scarcely be made better than it is. New provisions would introduce new difficulties and thus *create and increase* appetites for further change." Here is a kind of blind worship of old things, etc., by Lincoln, and this is in conformity as I know of his general nature. (See Barrett's Life of Lincoln, page 98.) If you wish to talk of L.'s conservatism, here is a splendid chance. Make a note and write a page on L.'s staid and absolute conservatism.

Again, if you write a chapter on the war and the *lost cause* and Jeff

Davis, trying to arouse his fellow-conspirators to a further struggle, etc., etc., quote Milton's speech put in the mouth of the superior fiend, Satan, "he called so loud that all the hollow deep of Hell resounded." It, the speech, runs thus: "Princes, potentates, warriors, the flower of heaven once yours, etc." This is a fine thing to insert in our book. First draw a picture of the rebellion, the conspirators, Confederate army, the warring cause, the lost cause, etc., etc., then quote the whole speech, etc. Draw it out finely. Put the speech in Jeff Davis's mouth. Here then are two good ideas which you can elaborate and make a fine paragraph or two. . . .

While Mr. Lincoln and I were partners, we kept no books as to our partnership, though we did, for a while, as to others. Mr. Lincoln did most of the circuit court business while I stayed at the office. Sometimes I went on the circuit and, if I were with Lincoln around in the counties, all the money collected by us was instantly divided. If I were not on the circuit, was at the office attending to our affairs at home, Lincoln would collect monies due us and our fees on the circuit and divide it, putting his half in his pocketbook and using it as he wanted to; he would wrap my half up in a roll, putting my name on a slip of paper and then wrapping it, the slip, around the roll of money and then putting it in his pocketbook and when he came home he would come to the office and hand me my money; he did this always and at last it so excited my curiosity that I asked him this question: "Why, Lincoln, are you so particular in this matter?" and to which he instantly replied: "Well, Billy, I do it for various reasons: first, unless I did as I do I might forget that I collected money or had money belonging to you; secondly, I explain to you how and from whom I got it so that you have not to dun the men who paid; thirdly, if I were to die you would have no evidence that I had your money and you could not prove that I had it. By marking the money it becomes yours and I have not in law or morality a right to use it. I make it a practice never to use any man's money without his consent first obtained. So you see why I pursue this course and now what do you think of this method with reasons?" and to which I replied: "It is all right, Mr. Lincoln, but so far as I am concerned, you need not be so particular. I know it's all right anyway with you."

Your friend,
W. H. HERNDON.

Springfield, Ill., June 13, 1888.

Friend Weik:

When you were here reading over the Lincoln MS my mind was exclusively engaged on the thread of the Lincoln story, on facts *asserted* and not on what was *omitted*. I was watching the story of L.'s life, and I now say that it was, is, admirably told. But there are some things *omitted* that I think should go in. In the chapter on the war I once gave you Jeff Davis's idea of this Union. I quoted a book in your office, Davis's works. I at the same time gave you Lincoln's idea of this Union and secession. I referred to Lincoln's first inaugural, first part of it, for his idea and to Davis's works for his idea. The issue in the two books is stated sharply, between Lincoln and Davis. See my piece and the works referred to. Now I humbly think that this issue should be fully stated. Slavery was at the bottom, I know, and yet could any State voluntarily go out of the Union and dissolve its relation to all the States, the National Union? Was the Union made by the whole *people* of the United States or by the *States* AS STATES? *Was it a National Union perpetual or a partnership* between the States subject to be dissolved lawfully, as it were a commercial firm? I think that this should be stated and explained. Secondly, I regret that my description of the pioneer was not inserted in the MS. Thirdly, I would suggest that Lincoln's ideas of filling up the mouth of the Sangamon River be explained truly and more fully. In speaking of Mr. Lincoln as lawyer I sent you some time since a conversation between Colonel King and Lincoln on *how* to decide a law case when one was brought before King, who was a justice of the peace. See MS how Lincoln acted when he tried a case, etc. This story is a good one and explains that Lincoln struck for what he thought was positive and gained his cases mostly that way. By no means call the pioneers around New Salem ruffians, because it would be a lie. No better people ever lived than they; they were brave, generous, hospitable, a wild and an uncultured people. Radford, whose store was sacked, was a vile slanderer and I suppose he slandered the men or women. Radford was a vile, blustering, crazy fool. I knew Radford and his wife, and good Lord deliver me from such a couple. If we could get at the bottom of the story, I guess that the people were more than half right. Possibly the people did not want such a couple with attendants, etc., in the neighborhood. The sons and daughters of these old pioneers are some of the best people in Menard County.

If my lectures on Lincoln are to form an addendum, a note at the end of the book, why not let them go in as I have written them, you correcting any and all mistakes of language, etc.? The printed slip pinned to the piece and written by me in your city was a part of the two lectures and delivered at the same time, including what Holland said of Lincoln.

What is herein said is good-naturedly and suggestively said. I will write more as my ideas come up one after another. Possibly we had better see one another again before you go East with our book, etc.

Your friend,
W. H. HERNDON.

P.S.   Am busy replanting corn, got no good ink, hand trembles, etc.   H.

Springfield, Ill., July 10, 1888.

Friend Weik:

First Mr. Lincoln would come down to the office about 8 a.m., sometimes in a good-natured, cheerful mood, speak pleasantly, tell a good story, and thus he would continue till twelve o'clock; about 2 p.m. he would return to the office, on the same day, in a sad, terribly gloomy state, pick up a pen, sit down by the table, and write a moment or two, and then become abstracted and wholly absorbed on some question; he would often put his left elbow on the table in his abstracted moods, resting his chin in the palm of his left hand. I have often watched Mr. Lincoln in this state while he was lost in the world of his thoughts, gazing in the distance. In this condition of things neither he nor I would speak. Occasionally I did ask him a question in his moods but he would not answer, probably for thirty minutes. In the meantime, I would quite forget that I had asked a question. To my surprise, say in thirty minutes, he would answer my question freely and accurately. He had pushed my question aside for the time being. Mr. Lincoln, in his abstractions or in his misery, *seemed* to me to be a little off, so odd was he, and yet I know that for the time being he was in the lone land of his greatest thoughts. It has been said of Mr. Lincoln that he was a many-sided man and, if he was, he certainly was a many-mooded man. I can see Lincoln now in my mind looking sad and grim, sitting at our table, pen in hand, while his chin rested in the palm of his left hand, his elbow resting on the table, he gazing in the distance all the while. There is a sad picture for you truly, and you can write it out to suit yourself. It is a correct and a true picture.

Secondly, I was deputy clerk of the Supreme Court of the State of Illinois and had some peculiar advantages to hear and to see. Mr. Lincoln would come down from his home to the Supreme Courtroom about seven or eight o'clock in the evening. The lawyers—Browning, Logan, Bushnell, and other lawyers—were studying their cases and making abstracts and briefs, etc. Lincoln would come into the room in a good humor, in one of his best moods, speak kindly and pleasantly to all, and say: "You men sitting here so mum puts me in mind of a story." The lawyers would say: "What is the story, Lincoln? Come, tell it," and tell it he would, and that story would suggest another, and so he would break up all reading, abstract, and brief business; he would keep on till twelve or one o'clock in the night.

Thirdly, I have seen him break up, as it were, social parties, gatherings, etc., at dances, etc., etc., as I have often told you; he would annoy the women dancers, because the men dancers would stop in the dance to hear the story. Bear all these little incidents in your mind; it is these things that please the reader. Just think of a merry dance going on with music, women, and wine, and "Old Abe" in the corner of the dancing hall with his eight or ten chums around him telling one of his best, *just loud* enough for the ladies to hear, and you have a picture of the reality which I have seen more than once. "Old Abe" would enjoy to the ends of his toenails his social cruelty. You could see that it did him good all over. Lincoln would have his fun, cost what it might. . . .

Your friend,
W. H. HERNDON.

These little things are the charm of the life of the great.

I have told you some of these things before this, but I want you to be sure and remember 'em.

Springfield, Ill., August 13, 1888.

Friend Weik:

Your letters about the contract, etc., are at hand. I sent you the new power of attorney and hope it is broad enough to cover our purposes. You state, Jesse, your case admirably well, "lawyer like." I have no statement to make, deeming it wise to say nothing on what I have done for over twenty-five years. It has always been my purpose to give you the Lincoln records, letters, evidences, etc., under conditions. Jesse, after our book is out and when I hear a statement of your case, accounts, etc., I will do what is fair, honest, just, between man and man. I think I am a reasonable creature and easy to deal with. I think you can risk my word on the question of justice, right, and equity. So let the thing rest till the book, which we are writing, is out and we know the facts throughout and thoroughly. I admit that you have been kind and clever to me, and this I willingly and gladly confess to you. You have done much work and spent much money in and about our endeavor, book. I hope that our book will compensate both of us when out and some or all sold. I regret to hear that you are "sorter blue," but glad to hear that you are *desperate,* i.e., determined, to push things to the end. I sincerely regret to hear about so many obstacles thrown in our way and which have to be removed. Every enterprise in this world has its obstacles and greatness comes to men out of the struggle. You will find competition and opposition to all worthy endeavors, but to beat down competition and crush opposition is the province [?] of a persistent and determined man. You have my best wishes for your success, entire and complete success. I shall continue to send you well-authenticated Lincoln facts when I hear of them. I am making inquiries every day almost for new facts about Lincoln, and when good and true I'll send to you. How do you like Sarah's letter? That letter opens a field for speculation; therefore will you *please* look up Speed's letter to Lincoln, or Lincoln's to Speed, in which Speed or Lincoln use the word *Sarah?*—Speed told me to erase the word *Sarah,* if he had not, in Speed's communications to me—and when found please give me the *exact date* of that letter. Did not Speed say to Lincoln something like this: "Have you seen *Sarah?*"? When you get the date of the above, will you please give me the *exact time* when Sarah says that Lincoln courted her? I kept no copies of either of the letters. I think Sarah said that the time of which she speaks was in 1840–41. Please look, in the third place, in one of the early numbers of the *Century* and find a letter from Lincoln to Stuart in which he uses the words, "that fatal night." I think it was on the first day of January 1841, the night when he was to have married Mary Todd but got crazy and didn't marry her. Give me the exact date. It is quite likely that Lincoln was courting both women at once or it may be that Sarah refused Lincoln and that he jumped into hell in mere desperation, etc. I want the *exact time* when Lincoln says that he was to have married Mary Todd and had so much gloom, sadness, sorrow, etc., etc. Now, as part of the story, steps in Mrs. Francis and her conspiracy in '42. You and I can unriddle the facts, the story, and make a good chapter. I say, how do you like the Sarah letter?

In one of your letters you state to me that our MS is in New York, and in your recent letters you state that you have 'em and are rewriting, etc. Has the MS been returned with objections? If so, what are the objections? Please keep me well informed about our business and I'll pray for you. If you can't succeed in our enterprise in New York, can you not go to "Bosting" or other city?

Have you accepted any of my suggestions? Please write to me a good long letter stating what is what—all about things in general.

I am just done digging "taters" and am going to the city on business.

Hastily,
Your friend,
W. H. HERNDON.

I saw Judge Matheny and J. B. Hines, prosecuting attorney who lived in the neighborhood of Miss Wilson, now Mrs. Drennan, and both say that the story about Lincoln courting Miss Wilson is false in every particular.

Springfield, Ill., September 27, 1888.

Friend Weik:

I received your two letters and lost one on the streets, the one containing the envelopes. I read the first and second pages of our book and they read well. I hope today on going to the city to find my letter which I somehow lost in my hurry to get home.

Enclosed you will find Governor Palmer's photo, marked No. 1 on the back of the card. . . . Judge B. S. Edwards is marked No. 2. . . . Butterfield was never a member of the Sangamon bar and never appeared in it. Probably C. C. Brown's, John E. Rosette's, E. B. Herndon's, *et al.*, ought to go in the group. Some may feel offended in passing them over unnoticed. We want friends and not enemies. What say you?

The Democrats here are mad at Nicolay and Hay for saying that Douglas was a "shyster." Douglas at the bar was a broad liberal-minded gentleman, a good lawyer, courteous, was not very well read in the law but his great good common sense carried him along with the best of the bar. In law Douglas was generous, courteous, fair, and as I remember it, he never stooped to gain his case. Douglas was anything but a "shyster." In politics Douglas did stoop a little to conquer much, but in law never. I did not worship Douglas but am willing to do him justice; he was naturally a great man, a good lawyer, a gentleman, and a patriot. I have known Douglas since 1837. We want friends, and let us speak ill of no one.

Hastily,
Your friend,
W. H. HERNDON.

P.S.   When I get proof sheets, shall I send back to you or shall I make notes stating page and line to be corrected? I prefer this latter course.   H.

Springfield, Ill., October 10, 1888.

Friend Weik:

. . . Today for the first time I carefully read pages 1, 2, 3 of our book, the pages you sent me. I make such suggestions as strike me: first, erase the word *last* as noted on the paper or insert after the word *scarce, through his mother,* and this will bring out what Lincoln said; he claimed that he got his mind from his mother as his own declaration in the slip shows. Lincoln said that his mother was by nature a great woman, great-hearted and great-headed; will write you about her, etc., etc., soon according to my impressions; give it now on third and fourth pages. Secondly, I have used the word *then* for *it,* because we are speaking of ancestry and origin; thirdly, I have used the word *he* in place of *they.* Please send the slip back to me. This is the only proof sheet that I have seen. . . .   Do you want my photo taken in 1871, to go among the members of the Sangamon bar? Put Lincoln himself in that group too.

In Arnold's Life of Lincoln he makes Abraham's mother a *tanner* of coon skins, etc. This is all nonsense. Write to Chapman and get Dennis Hanks's recollection of the facts asserted. Women in this section never did any coon skin tanning, nor tanning of any kind. Arnold makes Lincoln's table groan with wild game, such as venison, turkey, quail, duck, fish, squirrel, etc., etc. This is all nonsense. Mrs. Lincoln was too avaricious for such things. She kept, as a general thing, a stingy table. Sometimes she would give parties and then it was that she flamed out in some splendor. Mrs. Lincoln kept or set a poor table. Lincoln never invited his friends to his general tables. Mrs. Lincoln would give him hell if L. did and pay it down "right off" with tongue and broomstick.

Jesse, in one of my letters to you I stated that we wanted friends, defenders, etc., and to that end let us speak illy of no one. I said some hard things of Logan; wipe 'em out. So I said that Stuart pursued us, L. and myself; wipe that out too. This is the prudent course, is it not?

While I am about it, let me state to you the impressions which Mr. Lincoln's conversations made on me about his mother. I took no note at the time of what he said, could not. I include the impressions left on me by conversations with David Turnham, old man Wood, Dennis Hanks, the Grigsbys, and some Kentuckians. Turnham and Mr. Wood were well acquainted with Mrs. Lincoln. In the first place, Mr. Lincoln told me that his mother was a kind of genius, a great-hearted and a big-headed woman. He further stated to me that she was over-souled with goodness, tenderness, and sympathy. Mr. Wood verifies part of this, so does Turnham. Dennis Hanks and others say that she was a careless woman, careless of dress, show, or glitter. Dennis Hanks says that Abraham and Sarah did not know what cleanliness, civilization, etc., were till Thomas Lincoln married Mrs. Johnston. Abraham's mother despised forms, ceremonies, etiquette, loved the company of men more than women, because more like herself *in mind*. Mrs. Lincoln was a rather sad woman, especially at times in Indiana where she was high above her surroundings, including all the Hankses, and I may say the same thing in Kentucky; and when she broke out, it was like the sunshine in a cloudy and stormy day, giving warmth and cheer to the world. In many things Mr. Lincoln and his mother were alike, especially in self-reliance, hate of forms, love of substance, in sadness, carelessness of dress, looks, sensitiveness, and secretiveness. You now have my ideas of Mrs. Lincoln. I told you in one of our private conversations that one cause of Mrs. Lincoln's bad reputation among women was because of her bold steps with men. Mrs. Lincoln was a good thinker rather than a good house- and child-cleaner; she was a rather gloomy woman in Indiana, so says Mr. Wood. Mr. Wood takes his idea of gloom from the fact of a meditative mind, a mind with an idea. Mrs. Lincoln pushed aside all forms, ceremonies, and what fashion builds, was sensitive and secretive; she acted from within and not from the without. You know that Mrs. Lincoln is charged with unchastity and the like. Do not these charges come from the fact, among the women, her neighbors, that she was a bold, reckless, courageous, daring, self-reflecting, and self-reliant woman, one with an idea of her own? I read a description of Mrs. Lincoln in some Kentucky paper some years since which in part confirms my impression long since made. One or two words the author in the Kentucky paper changed after the first issue. Mrs. Lincoln was Mrs. Lincoln and no one else.

Your friend,
W. H. HERNDON.

Springfield, Ill., November 10, 1888.

Friend Weik:

Some proof sheets received and read—read well. *Corrections* . . . Erase the word "ruffians." You promised me at the Revere to do it. You would set loose ten thousand hornets on my head. Put in the words wild men, untamed men, or some such words. The leading characteristics of these men were integrity, generosity, hospitality, and courage; had great good horse sense, and some were quite cultured for time and place. You will never see the like of these men. The children, grand, and great-grandchildren of these people are some of the best people in Menard and it would not do to say *Ruffians.* . . . There are three claimants for the poetry: Doctor Merryman, old man Handcock— our local Scotch or English poet—and Oliphant, but the better idea is that Handcock was the man. Oliphant was not a man of any value on earth, except to drink whisky and run with bad women, as I remember it. Matheny, I think, says it was Merryman who wrote the poetry; Lightfoot says Handcock, and that is what I heard on the street at the time, but it makes not much difference.

Be sure that Lincoln comes all the way up to Bogue's Mill. It *seems* to me that he did and that I, at that time, saw Lincoln, but be sure that I am right. The records will fix it; it has now been fifty-six years since I saw what now seems to be the truth to me. Try and get me right. If L. came up to Bogue's Mill, I saw Lincoln, and if he did not, then I did not see him at Bogue's Mill.

I will see Matheny about Oliphant again and that fine-dressed man. Was not O. that man? I see two grammatical errors, which you will correct. I'll see to *facts*, doing the very best I can in that field. I am not certain about Oliphant and the young well-dressed rake.

It has been thrown up to me recently that Butler did board Lincoln free from 1836 to 1843. I have written to Will Butler, asking him to see his sister too and get his and his sister's opinion on the facts. I think the charge is a lie. Butler was poor from '36 to 1843 and couldn't afford it, nor would L. accept of such long continued gratuity. Will send you Butler's letter in answer to mine, if he writes me.

Please send me a certified copy of the contract between us and Belford, Clarke & Co., publishers, etc., and oblige greatly.

Your friend,

W. H. HERNDON.

P.S. If you will get a copy of a letter from Lincoln to Haycraft now in your possession, you will see that Lincoln called his mother *Nancy Hanks* out and out. This will help you in the first or second chapters to correct doubts.

Springfield, Ill., November 10, 1888.

Mr. Bartlett.
My dear Sir:

I owe you about one hundred apologies, but can at this moment give you three: first, I am a very poor man and have to work today for tomorrow's bread and butter; secondly, I am a farmer and have to attend to its duties; thirdly, I am hurried with my book, now in the hands of the publishers, Messrs. Belford, Clarke & Co.—proof sheets corrected up to chapter five. These are the reasons why I have not written to you before. I might say that I had nothing to write about interesting to you. When you come back to Boston, I will write to you and will then send you some important notes which I drew up solely for my own satisfaction. I hope that they will assist you; when they come to hand, copy and send back to me. Give any person copies of the notes with the understanding that they, nor the facts in them, are to be published for years. You may do the same with any or all of my letters. Robert Lincoln is living and the publication of them or the facts of them would offend "Bob," who religiously hates me for telling naked truths about his noble father. "Bob" came from Chicago once raging to be somehow satisfied. He had some extra fool advisers in Chicago, nice, dainty, finical, kid-gloved asses who loved smooth literature with no admixture of truth in it, no robust truth. You know that this is not my method of thinking or writing, speaking or acting. My poor book will, I guess, suit no one, but that I cannot help. The Life is mostly an analysis of Lincoln, an attempt to let people peep into the inner man, a thread of his history running through the book at the same time. The time is not yet to correctly and accurately estimate and weigh Lincoln. We are too close to him and the times in which he lived and out of which, with conditions, he wrought his great glory; he is the ideal man of America and probably will be an ideal man of all English-speaking people. Everything about Lincoln should be known correctly and you will help to preserve important facts in relation to him. You will get in the book truths, facts, opinions, where I give only truth, no admixture of falsehood, if I can avoid it. I have been writing on facts, to get them, twenty-five years or more. The book treats of Mr. Lincoln as an individual, domestically, socially, as friend, lawyer, statesman, politician, his religion and philosophy, his philosophy, etc., etc.—don't go much into war matters; only a kind of a one-eye glimpse of it. How does this ring, how does it suit, my friend? . . .

Can't tell you anything more about my Life of Lincoln, hope it will be out by the middle of January or first of February next. I send my highest regards to all, wife and children.

Your friend,
W. H. HERNDON.

Springfield, Ill., November 22, 1888.

Friend Jesse:

Your letter of the 15th was duly received and in answer to it let me say that the Introduction which we agreed to was written by us while I was in Greencastle and is the one which I referred to by me in my letters and the one to which you referred was not as it stands agreed to. In my great hurry to comply with your wish to hurry up things, I neglected to erase the words to which you refer. My neglect probably led to the misunderstanding. Charge it to me.

I went and saw Matheny on Tuesday and he and I had a long conversation about Bogue, Oliphant, *et al.* The truth is as follows: Bogue had goods on the *Talisman* and to that extent was captain. Oliphant was the captain of the boat, etc., hands, etc., measurably. Oliphant was the man to whom the grand supper was given. He and the woman with him were the persons who acted so badly. Oliphant was no poet that M. and I knew of. My idea of Oliphant you have in one of my letters. Matheny says emphatically that Doctor Merryman wrote the poetry. At the time that the poetry came out, it was understood on the streets that Handcock, our local Scotch poet, wrote it. However, it makes no difference who wrote it. Unless you have some better evidence, follow the above.

I saw a gentleman in M.'s office, during the above conversation, whose name is John M. Pierson, who married Miss Wilson, daughter of Judge Wilson of the Supreme Court. Mr. Pierson is a gentleman; he told me that on traveling up the Ohio or somewhere that he met a well-dressed gentlemanly Kentuckian who told him that Nancy Hanks was kept, as it were, by Enloe. The Kentuckian spoke as if he knew the facts somehow. This Mr. Pierson is a Kentuckian, and his father lived near Thomas Lincoln, say in the same county in Kentucky. I send this to you to go with the rest of things. . . .

Enclosed with this is a piece which I am desirous to have go in our book at some appropriate place which will be found as we go along. Correct it and let her slide in. Again I wish that the piece on Lincoln's power over men should go in; *he was the King ruler of men by divine right.* I can better the one which I wrote you in much haste. This continual *much haste* frets me. Can the pieces go in before it is too late? Won't bother you any more if I can hold off—a hard thing to do. Can they go in? Please answer. In the enclosed piece you will see that I do not quote the whole of the poetry, namely, "There is a tide, etc." Please quote it all just as in Shakespeare. I couldn't find it—hurried then and now—have been for weeks and am now putting away apples, turnips, etc., etc. Will get through soon, I hope, and then I can help you more.

You can, if you wish, strike out those words which you refer to in your last and then all things will stand fairly and as evidently intended; am for the city.

Your friend,
W. H. HERNDON.

P.S.   I am glad that the election is over, though I am whipped badly. The election, the result of it, surprises all here. There is one consolation, and it is this. Harrison will make a good President, as I verily believe. What do you think, Jesse?   W. H. H.

Springfield, Ill., November 22, 1888.

Friend Weik:

Some few days since I sent you a piece on Lincoln's love of law and order, etc., which I wish to go in our book. However, if it changes that expression, that idea, that language, in the other parts of the book and causes repetition, erasures, and trouble, or too many changes and alterations, then discard it, using if possible that little speech which I made L. make. Law and order, liberty and union, were Lincoln's inspirations during his whole political life—*a fact, a great fact.* Possibly the changes had better be made and insert the piece. That little speech can be inserted anywhere when a proper place is found. I will send, probably with this, a piece on L.'s power over men which can go in my lecture at the end of the book just between the last paragraph and the one above it. I do not think that will bother you or the publishers much. Please correct grammatical errors only. It is a good analysis of Lincoln's power over men. If you conclude to insert Lincoln's love of law and order above-mentioned, please correct grammatical errors only. Touch both pieces lightly.

I saw Littler on Saturday last; he says that Lincoln did not make nor attempt to make a speech at that moment of time spoken of when Ben Edwards said: "I would rather shake hands with the devil than to shake hands with Douglas on this question," or as some put it: "I would shake hands with the devil on this question." Littler said that Lincoln made a speech, a glorious, grand one on the same evening in the hall of the House of Representatives eclipsing *all* others—Trumbull's, Lovejoy's, *et al.* The speeches, except Lincoln's, were made in Wright's Grove west of the city about one mile, and near the fair grounds. The speeches, etc., were made in the fall of 1858. Littler says that Lincoln wept like a child at that moment of time, scene, etc.

I saw Keys, who was my informant about Nicolay and Hay's charging Douglas with being a shyster. Keys now says that they used substantially that word, not the very word shyster. I will get things all right, correct, if I have to interrogate men a hundred times and investigate things often and often. I desire greatly to get at the exact truth.

Jesse, would it not be well to insert in our preface the fact that our book was not designed to supersede any other Life of Lincoln, only to supplement them? Remember what we said at the beginning of things. Again, would it not be right and eminently proper for us to acknowledge our obligations *in the preface* to all persons who have given us honest opinions and well-established truths in relation to the attributes, qualities, or characteristics of L. and the facts of his life? You can insert these ideas without sending them back to me to adapt, etc. Again I want, wish, you to be gratefully and honorably mentioned in the preface. I said this once and I say it to you earnestly again. If anything of this kind is put in a new and corrected preface, send to me to see, etc., etc., if you please. These ideas are, or some of them are, in our agreed preface dated September 1, 1887, and a copy of which you sent to me; see original. . . .

If you ever see any notice of our forthcoming book made by Belford, Clarke & Co., please send to me and I'll send back to you, and if you ever see any criticisms or notice of our book by anyone in the distant future, please send to me and I'll return to you. Here in the country I see nothing and hear nothing. Please at all times remember the above requests, do.

Dave Littler tells me this additional story. During some of the political canvasses, the people in Logan County, Illinois, just north of this county and adjoining it, had determined to have a large meeting, a grand rally, and had appointed the day and the hour. When the day and hour arrived, the heavens opened with a terrific storm; it blew in hurricanes and rained in torrents. Only about twenty persons appeared. Lincoln had felt this sting of disappointment and therefore he did not wish others to be disappointed. After some reflection he said: "Boys, the day is bad, too bad for many people to appear here to hear me speak, but as you have dared the storm to hear a speech, you shall not be disappointed. Come, let's us go over to Armington's Hall and I'll give you a talk, such as I have." The twenty went over to the hall in Atlanta, and Littler said to me: "For a calm, cool, profound speech I never heard so great, so learned, in the liberty line, so dispassionate a speech in my life. I learned," said Littler to me, "more of the ideas, in the two hours' speech, of Republicanism then and there than I ever knew before. Why, the speeches of other men sounded dull and dead to me after that." Lincoln must have done his best on this occasion, because Littler felt what he said and did not seem to color his story.

Excuse your friend,

W. H. HERNDON.

I am in much haste for the city loaded with the products of the farm. H.

The place, village, at which the speech was made was Atlanta, Logan County, Illinois. H.

Springfield, Ill., December 1, 1888.

Friend Jesse:

Your good long letter, dated the 25th *ult.*, was duly received. The letter is a good and a satisfying one; and now (1) as to *Nancy Hanks*. We promised in our preface to suppress nothing true and to suggest nothing false in the *characteristics* and *history* of *Lincoln*. If we strike out *her* acts—and doings—it is suppressing nothing true nor suggesting anything false as to *Lincoln's characteristics* and facts of his life. We did not start out to write the life of Nancy Hanks, but of Lincoln, the man in a special line, namely, his characteristics and the facts of his life. We violate no promise to the world if we suppress Nancy's unchastity, if a fact. The reason why we wanted Nancy's character and acts was to show by contrast how a great man can rise out of the ashes. That's all. There is a plenty of contrast material without Nancy's illegitimacy. Men would charge me with revealing a sacred private matter which Lincoln in his good nature gave to me. Lincoln said to me: "Don't tell this while I live," and I have kept my word. The world is not ready for the truth, the whole truth yet. I am decidedly in favor of striking out all mention of her illegitimacy and unchastity if such is the fact. I, so far I am concerned, wish to escape severe and angry criticism *on this delicate point.* I want the book to be a success, a complete success, and I am in favor of putting the book on the safe side. No one will get mad because we suppress Nancy Hanks's illegitimacy or unchastity, if true, but thousands will go crazy, wrathy, furious, wild, etc., if we insert such suggestion. Jesse, get on the safe side and be prudent. Now you have my candid opinion, and if you do not agree with me, do what you think best, most proper, most wise, and I'll stand square up to you, you keeping to the record and to the truth.

Now (2) about that good little dog story, and as you may not get it exactly right, let me restate it. Thomas Lincoln with his family started to go from Indiana to Illinois in March 1830. The weather was rough and cold. When Lincoln got somewhere near the line that divides Indiana from Illinois, after traveling several days, the family came to one of those long loggy corduroy bridges laid over a wide swamp. The water was over the logs and a thin sheet of ice bridged the water. Now and then there were posts along the bridge to direct the traveler. The family came to the edge of the swamp. Abraham drove the oxen, two yoke, but when he attempted to go into the swamp and on the bridge, he could not make the oxen break the ice, without apparent cruelty. Abraham coaxed and threatened by turns, but the oxen would not go on the ice, and at last Abraham saw that force must be applied, so he swung his long ox lash around and around over the oxen, high in the air, and brought the lash down, cutting open the hide. The oxen at last went on the thin ice, broke their way, etc. When about half-way over, Abe heard his poor dog bring a kind of despairing howl; he stopped the oxen, pulled off his shoes, rolled up his pants, got out of the wagon, jumped into the cold water, the sheets of ice hitting his shins. He got to the dog, took him, frightened nearly to death, in his long and strong arms, carried him to the wagon, put him in it, the dog crouching close to Mrs. Lincoln's feet, scared half out of his wits. The oxen were soon told to go on, and *on* they went through the ice. After the family had crossed and got on dry land, Abe found difficulty in getting the dog out of the wagon; at last he had to haul him out by force. When the dog was out and on dry land, he cut up such antics as no dog ever did before; he ran round and round Abe and laid down at his feet, got up and ran round and round again and again; he seemed, was, grateful to Abe, his benefactor. Lincoln said to Dubois after telling him the story: "Well, Jesse, I guess that I felt about as glad as the dog." This story I got from Dubois, he getting it from L. many, many years ago when the two were young men. In writing what you do write, if you wish to know my authority, when, where, etc., etc., I can tell you quickly. In fact, Jesse, I have in my memory a thousand unwritten facts about our good man, Abe, that were told me by good and truthful people, but this is not to be wondered at when you think that I have been gathering facts of L.'s life for nearly a quarter of a century, in addition to what I learned from 1834 to 1865 of him by actual contact.

Being in a hurry when I wrote the first part of this letter, I forgot to say to you that you can safely say that, *in law*, Abraham Lincoln was the son and heir of Thomas Lincoln and Nancy Hanks Lincoln and be safe in the saying of it. The general reader will not notice the sharp point, *in law*. This may help us; L. was born in lawful wedlock and that is enough for us. Couch the idea somehow in general words. I cannot think.

As to Lincoln's courtship with Ann Rutledge, let me say that L. is not to be censured. The facts are that Hill, McNamar, and Lincoln courted the girl at one and the same time; she preferred McNamar and L. ceased to pay much attention to her, if any. McNamar after his engagement with Ann went to New York and was gone about two years. The relatives of the girl convinced her that McN. had deserted her and at last, through the Rutledges, Greens, *et. al.*, the girl consented to receive the visits of Lincoln. Evidently somehow she let L. know of her determination to cease expecting McNamar. Lincoln *then* and *not before* plunged in the second time, and won. The poor girl unfortunately died a short time before L. and her were to be married. I see nothing wrong in all this. Lincoln acted the man in this matter as he always did in all matters. Publishers of books know too much and would gut things of all pith and point if they could. You and I ought to know something after studying Lincoln for thirty years or more.

What shall I say to General McClernand about a new photo? He gave me the one I sent you. I guess McC. is poor and cannot well give a new one. . . . Hope you will get some [photos] in Indiana near Gentryville, and if you go to New York, my good fellow, don't run off with some pretty "gal." . . .

Send on the proofs and I'll correct as to *facts* alone. You attend to grammar and other matters. I will return the proof slips as you request. Can any corrections be made in our book after "the advance sheets are sent me and when the plates are cast"?

I saw a gentleman on Tuesday last in Hay's office who said he saw an advertisement or notice of our book, but by whom it was issued he did not say ; have heard of no circular as yet from the publishers ; hope to see one soon, etc.

One more word about our bar group. You say in your letter that to mention, put in our book, too many photos of persons, little and unimportant fellows, having no connection with Lincoln in politics and at the bar, would, if not in the text, injure the book. However that may be, the photos which I send you are not little unimportant fellows, having no connection, etc. Many of these men were Lincoln's bosom friends, political, personal, etc., dear and near. They practiced at the bar with him for years and I think, humbly think, that outside of the matter of the book, its composition, etc., the group of the Sangamon bar is the most important phase of our book, the most interesting, the best thing to study, etc. This group will be looked at and studied for generations. If there are too many photos to group, the engravings can be put on consecutive pages or any way to suit, etc. You are a little mistaken when you say that when Lincoln was admitted to the bar of the circuit and Supreme Court there were Logan, Shields, *et al.* First come Stuart, Logan, Baker, etc., and Matheny *et al.* come in about '43. Lincoln was admitted, I think, in '37. Stuart, Logan, Baker, were before Lincoln. All of these men came along successfully, some before and some after Lincoln. All that I have just mentioned came here say from 1832 to '46. However, I suppose this makes no difference in your general idea.

As to your proposition made to me at the Revere House in this city at present I shall neither accept nor reject. I do not like to make a contract about things when I am in the dark as to facts about it. I am determined when I know all the facts of the case to do you justice in the end, if our written contract does not do so, under all circumstances. You may infer from this that your proposition is rejected and am now obliged to you for the past.

Give my best respects to father, brother, and sister if you please.

Your friend,

W. H. HERNDON.

P.S.   Please file all my letters good, bad, and indifferent. They will be useful sometime.   H.

LINCOLN'S NATURE—ONE SIDE

Springfield, Ill., December 22, 1888.

Friend Jesse:

I guess that you will dislike this letter about as heartily as you *dislike* anything. Nevertheless, I shall send it and ask it to be filed away. I suppose that you will agree with me that Lincoln had a low and feeble circulation. It follows physiologically, does it not, that he had a slow, but a somewhat healthful irritability; that is, his whole organism moved slowly to the influences of all kinds of stimuli—he thought slowly and acted slowly and, as I said in one of my lectures on Mr. Lincoln in '66, his body and mind seemed as if they needed oiling? A man thus conditioned has his spells of sadness—gloom and melancholy —if not his spells of despair. This state of Mr. Lincoln made him, as it were, at periods, unconscious of his surroundings, and to arouse that somewhat dormant consciousness he needed a stimulant, and that was found in a story, and tell it he would. The human mind is active and cheerful or sad and gloomy according to the quantity and quality of the blood sent from the heart through the brain. This story telling, this stimulant, sending more blood to the brain, aroused the whole man to an active consciousness, sense of his surroundings. Grave men in grave times, sometimes his ministers, would approach him in order to state the urgency of some matter that needed his immediate attention. Mr. Lincoln would look up to his minister half sleepily, dreamily, saying: "Mr. Secretary, take a chair." He would, in a moment or two, after the secretary had stated his errand, tell some story, much to the disgust of his minister, who would censuringly say: "Mr. President, this is no time for story telling; the times are grave and full of war, and the country is fast drifting to ruin." Mr. Lincoln would good-naturedly reply: "Come, Mr. Secretary, sit down, sit down, I have a perfect and a profound respect for you and, were it not for these stories, I should die, they are vents through which my sadness, my gloom and melancholy, escape." Mr. Lincoln would thus arouse his half-dormant consciousness into activity, into full play and power; and after he had been thus aroused he would listen to what the secretary or minister eagerly told him, like a philosopher, and in a short moment he would make his answer, his reply, so wisely and so earnestly as to convince the man that that point or that subject had been thoroughly and maturely considered before, long, long before, this moment of meeting. This state of Mr. Lincoln, particularly so if it was accompanied by mental and nervous exhaustion, produced by long and intense study, caused him to have delusions—saw apparitions, specters, and the like. This man was, as a general rule, a sad—a gloomy and melancholy—man, but at exceptional times a momentarily happy one, and it was a curious thing to see him sink quickly back into his usual state of sadness and gloom and become, as it were, oblivious of his surroundings, man and the world. Let no man blame Mr. Lincoln for being sad or seeing apparitions; his sadness and his gloom came naturally out of his organism and his apparitions from the same source somewhat and from nervous and mental exhaustion. Let no man rudely censure Mr. Lincoln for his story telling, because the telling of them aroused him and made him happy for a time. Had this great man been of an ardent temperament, with swift and strong volumes of rich blood pouring through his brain, had he been impulsive—quick to think and quick to act—rashly running before the complete development of the individual ideas into national ideas and of facts, marching with banners hastily before his people, blindly grasping at the trend and drift of things, hungry and longing for a quick end of the national quarrel, groping his way before ideas and facts, this great nation would have been two governments this day. This feeble and low circulation, this slow irritability which slowly responded to stimuli, this organism with herculean strength not having much wear and tear about it, by nature conserving its forces—this great man with a great heart and greater head, with a sublime patience and an endless endurance, saved the nation from division and consequent ruin. Was not Mr. Lincoln the right man, in the right time, and in the right place? Surely, surely there is a Providence in the affairs of men, has been, now is, and forever will be, as we poor mortals see it.

Your friend,
W. H. HERNDON.

P.S. I know that this does not suit you; you dislike such stuff terribly, and yet some persons may like it. You dislike all speculation, including my piece on L.'s power over men and the piece on L.'s love of law and order.   H.

Publish if you can and think worthy.   H.

Springfield, Ill., January 4, 1889.

Friend Weik:

Mr. Lincoln and I had various and diverse conversations in relation to the spirit of the times and about slavery from '53 to '61. I was an out-and-out abolitionist, radically so. Mr. Lincoln was a very conservative man and a cautious one; he thought slowly and moved slowly in the matter of his opposition to slavery. I declared often and often in his presence and *to him* that the Fugitive Slave Law was a *thing* engendered in hell. I said to Mr. Lincoln repeatedly from '53 to '61 that this continent was not broad enough nor long enough to contain the principles of Liberty and the despotism of Slavery for any great length of time together, and that one or the other must go to the wall and die there, not only cease to be a factor of power in the political world, but that one or the other, Liberty or Slavery, must die. I said to Mr. Lincoln often and often that ill-gotten gain did no man any good and that this applied to nations as well as individuals, that God would [right] wrong and establish justice. "This," said Mr. Lincoln, "is my idea, my prediction, and note it."

Little did I know how great our people are as a mass of men; how little did I know of the vast number of great men in the country who were wise leaders and brave ones in the terrible war; and how much less did I know that the great big man was touching my shoulder at the moment.

This figure Mr. Lincoln actually used just as I have told it to you. I remember the conversation well, just as well as if it had happened on yesterday. Occasionally I remember some of our conversations on philosophy, science, art, law, etc., etc., which have never been made public. I would send them to you, but what's the use? The Book is fixed, like the law of the Medes and Persians, cast-ironed.

Your friend,
W. H. HERNDON.

Springfield, Ill., January 5, 1889.

Friend Weik:

Mr. Speed told me this story of Lincoln. Speed about 1839–40 was keeping a pretty woman in this city, and Lincoln, desirous to have *a little*, said to Speed: "Speed, do you know where I can get *some?*" and in reply Speed said: "Yes, I do, and if you will wait a moment or so I'll send you to the place with a note. You can't get *it* without a note or by my appearance." Speed wrote the note, and Lincoln took it and went to see the girl; handed her the note after a short "how do you do, etc.," Lincoln told his business, and the girl, after some protestations, agreed to satisfy him. Things went on right; Lincoln and the girl stripped off and went to bed. Before anything was done, Lincoln said to the girl: "How much do you charge?" "Five dollars, Mr. Lincoln." Mr. Lincoln said: "I've only got three dollars." "Well," said the girl, "I'll trust you, Mr. Lincoln, for two dollars." Lincoln thought a moment or so and said: "I do not wish to go on credit. I'm poor and don't know where my next dollar will come from and I cannot afford to cheat you." Lincoln, after some words of encouragement from the girl, got out of bed, buttoned up his pants, and offered the girl the three dollars, which she would not take, saying: "Mr. Lincoln, you are the most conscientious man I ever saw." Lincoln went out of the house, bidding the girl good-evening, and went to the store of Speed, saying nothing. Speed asked no questions and so the matter rested a day or so. Speed had occasion to go and see the girl in a few days, and she told him just what was said and done between herself and Lincoln, and Speed told me the story, and I have no doubt of its truthfulness.

Again Mr. Lincoln told the following story of himself to Judge Matheny, Milton Hay, and myself, all of us recollecting the story alike. Mr. Lincoln went up to Bloomington Court, and was gone from home some two weeks and was desirous to get home to attend to our own court. This was about 1850–51. Lincoln started home from Bloomington late on Saturday evening, got to Salt Creek, about twenty miles north of this city, and put up for the night with a Mr. Cottenbarger, an old friend of Lincoln. The house was a log one and had but one room in it, Cottenbarger having just settled in a wild place. There were three beds in the room and some curtains between the beds. The bedsteads were arranged so that the foot of one bed was close up against the head of the other—the old man in the southeast corner, the grown daughter in the middle, and Lincoln's north. The people all went to bed, and way in the night the girl's feet, by accident and when asleep, fell on Lincoln's pillow. Occasionally in her sleep she moved her feet about. This put the *devil* into Lincoln at once, thinking that the girl did this of a purpose. Lincoln reached up his hand and put it where it ought not to be. The girl awoke, got up, and went to her mother's bed and told what had happened. Possibly Lincoln had tried to repeat what he had done just before. The mother said to the girl to pacify [her]: "For God's sake, say no more and go to bed, the man means nothing. If the old man hears of this, the deuce will be to pay." Lincoln heard the conversation between mother and daughter and thought that it might be possible that the old man was awake and not asleep. Lincoln knew Cottenbarger's physical power—a great big burly strong man with great courage—and he therefore fixed his eye on a large heavy hickory chair in the room with which to defend himself if Cottenbarger should attack him. However, all things settled down calmly and all went to sleep again, except Lincoln, now mortified to death at what he or *the devil in him* had done. Early in the morning Cottenbarger got up, got a long keen butcher knife and whetted it in the rocky jamb, reached up the chimney and cut down a piece of dried venison, took a piece of bread, and went off into the woods. Lincoln in the meanwhile, shivering, kept his eye on the old man and on the chair. Lincoln heard some whispering between the old man and his wife and was convinced that the old man had heard all, and Lincoln really expected the devil was to pay. As soon as the old man had gone, the old woman got up, made the fire, and in a hurry got breakfast and hustled Lincoln off as quick as possible. Lincoln, glad to get off, jumped quickly in his buggy and was off for home, a deeply and thoroughly mortified man. Cottenbarger had great discretion and hurried off to avoid a terrible fight with Lincoln. This hurt L. so badly that he had to tell it to his friends for relief.

Your friend,

W. H. Herndon.

P.S.   You are a very modest young man and how does this suit you? Would the stories do to "point a moral or adorn a tale"? Would they not do for riders?

Springfield, Ill., January 11, 1889.

Friend Jesse:

You remember, in the last proofs you speak about the *Richmond* article going into the *Conservative* by a kind of *trick* and that Lincoln knew it, by inference or impliedly, etc. So far all right. You then make Lincoln make much of it, take advantage of it, when he knew how it was got in, etc. Please insert this: "It is probable that he used it with effect." Again in my correction I say substantially that the *Conservative* was a Democratic paper with pro-slavery tendencies; add or insert: "looking out of Republican eyes," or "was so by Republican construction." Then the whole in this particular will be exactly correct. Erase the words: "Lincoln told me" in the long-armed ape Stanton story. I intended to erase or modify it, but when it was too late; was in a hurry to get the proofs to you. Lincoln *may* have told me the story. *Please* see to it and have it corrected. I want no errors if I can help it. You do not give me enough time to get things correct. I intend to keep on the safe side. If you have sent on the proofs, can you not write a note to the publishers to insert the qualifications above or to send you the slip and you correct? Please do this. Someone will come back at us for the errors unless corrected. I want to be right and do right to all men everywhere and at all times. In the last proofs you, in speaking of Stuart *et al.*, say that *envy* is a *degrading* passion. I wish to say a word in order to put you right in your views of human nature. Every organ of the body and every faculty of the mind is for some good purpose in the providence of God. Envy is a feeling and, whether it springs from the mind or body, it is inwrought in human nature and runs down through all the animal world. Envy has its divine purposes and *what* is it, for example? If I see a man in some high position, has wealth, has a pretty woman, and I envy the man's possessions, it is an evidence that I want the position, want the wealth, want the pretty creature; and this *want* makes me struggle to get what I want. Envy is a spur, a whip, a nettle, a stimulant, driving my ambition to get what I do want. Envy to fret at another's success is a degrading passion when abused, or rather it is the abuse of envy, the over-fret, that makes the *abuse* degrading. Jealousy is a good thing unless abused, so is appetite, so is the divine passion for woman, and so let no man say that God has given to nature, embodied in men, a degrading passion. It is poor, imperfect man that abuses the divine in him. Lincoln was *envious* and he manifested it in many of his speeches; he wanted Douglas's position, and his envy, free from hate, made him struggle for it, and that struggle gave him not only Douglas's position, but a higher one, and satisfied his *wants* and gratified his *ambition*. Lincoln did not abuse that divine quality of his nature to get what he wanted. Lincoln in his speeches, various ones, tells on himself, proclaims it to the world, unwittingly, unconsciously. You do not like this kind of stuff, and yet it is necessary to think and get right. Your friend likes to get at the bottom of things by analysis and induction, by synthesis and deduction, and to pardon his follies and his weaknesses. You, I think, are a worshiper of the pure narrative style, a good thing by the way, and I forgive you for the worship of it. Will you be as generous to your friend? I gave you my ideas of envy once before in a piece on Lincoln which you have in your possession. Good friend, pardon me for this repetition of ideas.

The more I think of Mrs. Francis, Mary Todd, and Mr. Lincoln, the more am I convinced that Mary Todd helped Mrs. Francis in the conspiracy to yoke Lincoln. Miss Todd wanted L. terribly and worked, played her cards, through Mrs. Francis's hands. By the way I now think that Speed told me a part if not the whole of the conspiracy. Speed and [undeciphered] about Lincoln and it [undeciphered] he told me the story at a day long before I commenced thoroughly taking notes in 1865.

Again, the more I think of the Ann Rutledge story, the more do I think that the girl had two engagements, i.e., that she was engaged to two men at one and the same [time]. I do not recollect that she ever got a release from McNamar, though she tried to get one. Lincoln jumped in when Ann was ready to receive his jump. I do not think that Abraham acted badly. I shall change my opinion of events and things on the coming of new facts and in more mature reflection in all cases, and so excuse me for "sorter" wabbling around. I reserve the right to change when I am wrong in fact or opinion. I do not by this wish that the text of the book be changed, because it is substantially correct anyhow. I have no suggestions to make and no pieces now to put in the book further than you know of, etc. Ugly weather here. How is it in Indiana?

[W. H. HERNDON.]

Springfield, Ill., January 15, 1889.

Friend Weik:

Your letter, dated the 11th *inst.*, was received, and I shall do by you as I would wish to be done by. I shall answer all your questions directly or indirectly put. First, if you know that it will be for our best interests to go on to New York, go; secondly, if you know that you need help about the index, employ that help. I received some photos and will distribute them when I get able to go out and to the city. I am sorry that the index bothers you so much. It seems to me that our book ought to be got in two volumes. The three volumes will make it cost so much that it cannot be bought by the mass of readers. It seems so to me, but I suppose that you and the publishers know what is best. You speak again about the distribution of profits, etc., of our book. I said to you once that when I know the facts of the case I would, as I saw it, do you justice, and so I will. Thirdly, the second or new contract with B., C. & Co. does not give them the power or authority to *give* away our books to pay for the ads. In your letter to me, dated December 22, 1888, you state that both contracts are alike, identical except in a few things. I think that you err in this opinion woefully. The old contract required B., C. & Co. to pay all expenses, etc., and to reimburse them for the costs, etc., they had 1500 copies of our book. The second contract is silent on that question, but the silence on that question *is no authority*, even implied, to give away 416 copies. Why not charge us with the costs of the agents and all other expenses? It appears from the said account that 1061 new copies of our book were issued and only 415 copies accounted for. You may stand and sanction all this, but I shall not. I will hold someone responsible for the loss, wrong, call it what you will. There is a day after tomorrow. I shall struggle against all swindles. There has been from 1887 to this day a kind of mystery hanging and hovering over this whole book affair. You do not answer my letters nor the questions put to you in them. Human nature would teach you that your silence breeds suspicion. You should be prompt and explicit in your business with me. You should willingly and fully explain to me all things in relation to this book business. I repeat to you that you are a d——d bad correspondent. You ought to take it for granted that, when I ask questions of you, those questions are interesting, important to me, and rest on my mind, vexing me if not answered. Again I say that there was and is a perpetual mystery hanging over this book business. Why were the contracts with B., C. & Co. made in your *name alone* and not in the name of H. and W.? Why throw up the old contract by which we were to receive 40¢ per set and take a new one at 25¢ per set? What was the consideration given us for the abandonment of the 40¢ clause and take 25¢? Why did you not bounce the report sent me from B., C. & Co.?

Now as to changing the three volumes into one, I, as a matter of course, object. You know that I objected in the first place to the three-volume idea, wanted a cheaper book for the *People*. White's idea of the stream of literature was and is correct. Inventions follow the same law and so do taste, learning, ideas, fashion, etc. Do not spend any more money than you can help at the Western Literary Association. Would be glad to hear from you while at the association; send along the papers if any should speak of us and our book. One volume will do if the matter, new and old, is not cut down; want all in the new edition. The royalties to remain the same as in the three volumes.

What do you think of Bob's acts? I'll tell you what I think, I think he's a d——d fool. He has the insane rage of his mother without the sense of his father. Robert Lincoln is "a wretch" of a man. Will you tell B., C. & Co. what he has done?

I keep getting good complimentary letters from different quarters. I think the book is selling faster than B., C. & Co. are at present aware of. It so seems to me from the letters which I receive and from newspaper notices, etc., etc. There are two things about the book that strike me: first, no one doubts its truth; and, secondly, no one says that it, in any way, is prejudiced against Mr. Lincoln. All say it is truthful and will shape Lincoln's character for all coming time. When nice, dainty, over-sensitive men, mere hero worshipers, get cooled down, the Life will be (ours) the leading Life of L. for many, many years. This is my opinion. By the way, send me a few of your circulars, those written by yourself as soon as you get them, please.

Your friend,
W. H. HERNDON.

Springfield, Ill., January 23, 1889.
Friend Jesse:
You are not the very best correspondent I ever saw, but I suppose

that I will have to put up with it. I sent you the last proofs as soon as I could; have been under the weather all winter, only going to the city twice this winter, my son going in my place and doing my business. By the way, I see that our friend Whitney in Chicago is to be handled pretty roughly in the woman-shooting case—Mrs. Rawson's case. I expect it will be proved that Whitney went too far, went way beyond the duties and privileges of an attorney and did unprofessional things, possibly corrupt things; am sorry for it on two grounds: first, on Whitney's account, and, secondly, on our book's account. . . .

I am extremely anxious to have three corrections made in our proofs, book: first, the *Conservative* newspaper story wherein Matheny and Stuart indirectly cut a figure; secondly, the story of Lincoln and Stanton, the long-armed ape story; and, thirdly, the Parker sermon story wherein Lincoln is made *to mark* a sentence. In the second case, if I distinctly remembered that Lincoln said *to me* he heard Stanton say what he is made to say, I would not dodge, but I cannot state it so sharply, so distinctly. I heard the story often and from many men in this city, Chicago, and other places.Hence I cannot fix the man who first told me the story. In the third place, I loaned Lincoln the Parker sermon *unmarked* and, when it was returned to me, it was marked, and that is all that I can truthfully state. In the *Conservative* newspaper story as told by you in the proofs I cannot help you much. The records in your possession will explain the history fully. In reading the Matheny letter you will see what Lincoln thought of the Fillmore move and the *Conservative* newspaper, and by my letters to you what he thought of Matheny, Stuart, etc. You see that it all corresponds with what I told you. What Lincoln said about M. and S. is private, sacredly so. Lincoln scorned the whole move with all his soul. This I do know. Do you want any more facts about Lincoln to complete your record for the present or the future? State your wish, for it is a bother to me and costs me money, only a little it is true, but that little is *much* to me.

I hope that the inundated state of the proofs has gone down by this time, hope that you are done trembling and free from all distress. Jesse, this is a bad state of literary affairs, is it not? Pray, Jesse, for better times. Here is a place and now the time that faith, with works and prayers, will do good. What do you think? Seriously, I judge from what you say about the many proofs recalled that you are struggling to correct errors, make amendments, and to have things correct, true, etc., according to the facts, opinions, etc., of the records. I thank you for all this many times, many times, Jesse.

Will you *please* send me the new title page and the new preface or introduction to our book before the plates are cast, soldered together somehow? Copies, any kind, will do just as well.

Your friend,
W. H. HERNDON.

P.S.   Lincoln came out of the great Douglas race in 1858, after speaking probably fifty or sixty times, a new man, vigorous, healthy, fresh as a young man, better-colored, more elastic, more cheerful, less sad, stronger, and improved every way. Douglas was worn out, voice gone, broken down, a wreck, as it were. Saw both men during and just before and just after the race and state what I saw and know. Lincoln's voice was less husky, broken, wheezy; it improved all the time.

Springfield, Ill., February 9, 1889.

Friend Jesse:

I desire to leave my ideas on Mr. Lincoln's sadness, gloom, and melancholy on the record. I have studied Mr. Lincoln from 1834 to the year 1889, and I have come to the conclusion long since that his sadness, etc., were caused by three things principally: first, his organization; secondly, his knowledge of the low condition of his family and his descent, not including any idea of his illegitimacy resting on his own mind; and, thirdly, his domestic relations, the hell of his domesticity or his domestic life. In this opinion I waive any idea of prenatalism, the influence of his mother's mind on him during her pregnancy, and hereditary influence. I would risk my chances in heaven on this long-settled opinion, founded on long years of observation, experience, and reason. You may reply: "Do not the letters from Boston from Bartlett, the artist, and from physicians—able, distinguished, and learned, from Boston—settle that question, rather unsettle it?" and to which I reply: "Neither Mr. Bartlett nor any physician from Boston gave his opinion on the precise question. Their letters and opinions were on Mr. Lincoln's low organization, not on the causes of Lincoln's sadness, gloom, and melancholy." Now you have my distinct, definite, and clean-cut ideas. Generally I write to you loosely, carelessly, and rapidly, not caring what I said as to manner or method of expression, but sticking to the precise or substantial truth. This was all I cared for, knowing that you would polish up things to suit yourself. I once talked about miasmatic influences on Lincoln in answer, as it were, to Nicolay and Hay's opinion on miasma. You have the letters and I stick to them in substance, but they are not on the precise questions in this letter, though they bear on them somewhat. I need not say to you that I have studied the sciences somewhat relating to these questions, and think that I am fully supported by them. In conclusion let me say to you this: The world will never rest till it knows all about Lincoln, inside and outside.

Your friend,
W. H. HERNDON.

Springfield, Ill., October 5, 1889.

Friend Bartlett:

I received your kind letter from France, dated July 22, for which I thank you. Your letter should have been answered long since but I had two reasons for not answering: first, I have some hard work to do on my farm; and, secondly, I had nothing to say and this last is a good reason. I am glad to know that your son has, at the great Paris Exposition, won a medal of honor. As you well say, for a young man just out of his "teens" to take the high honor which he did is glory enough. Success in Paris means much in his field. Every American feels proud of American success; I do not care whether this success is in science or art. Tell your son for me to put his eye on his high ideal and keep it there with hope and chisel in hand till his highest piece shall walk out a perfect thing before admiring men. This masterpiece I do candidly wish he may execute. I love the youth of our land and pray for their success in all the walks of life. Their honor is America's honor. In fact, as I see it, America is the hope of the world.

We out West feel the pressure of hard times, the armies of trusts, the power of monopolies, rings, and the like, but we are rich in all the necessaries of life. We have never in the West, in certain lines of latitude and longitude, raised such crops as we have this year. The trusts begin to shake, because they are scared over threatened State and national legislation, and well they be, for the people are being aroused.

I do not like, as a general rule, to interfere with commerce, but robbery I have no respect for and trusts are robbers.

You were informed at the time you wrote your letter that my poor book was out, and I somewhat fear that you do not like it. The Life of Lincoln is having a good run, as I am told. In your letter you state a big fact, and it is this: "Truth is not, so far as I ever learned, in any general demand." The criticisms generally are favorable and yet some of them are savage, but I guess I can stand it quite bravely. Give my best love to all your family.

Your friend,
W. H. Herndon.

I'll send you those Lincoln notes just as soon as Senator Fowler [1] is done with them. He lost his lovely daughter, and I do not wish to say anything to him just now about the notes.   H.

Springfield, Ill., December 12, 1889.

Friend Jesse:

Your letter dated the 3d *inst.* is at hand. I do not see how I can ratify and confirm an act not already done. I can do this: I can consent that you make the contract spoken of in yours of the third with Belford, Clarke & Co., as long as you confine the contract to the terms of yours of the 3d *inst.*, including the idea that B., C. & Co. account to us every three months, as in the old contract, or you can write out the contract and send it to me and I'll sign it. . . . I trust you, Jesse, for I know nothing about book making and the sale of the books, am totally green in this business. I hope that the royalty plan spoken of by you will be the best thing that we can do in the matter. They— B., C. & Co.—will get some advantage or they would not make the new contract. I am quite intuitive about men as well as coming events. Lincoln used to pay great attention, or had respect rather, to that peculiarity of my nature, and in coming to the office of a morning, during the exciting years from '54 to '60, he would always say: "Billy, how is your bones philosophy this morning?" He said this because I frequently told him that this or that would inevitably take place be-

---

[1] See Herndon's letter of February 18, 1886.

cause I felt it *in my bones.* This I told him often. Lincoln was entirely logical, had no intuition at all. You will see this better told in the Everyday Life of Lincoln. . . .

I am glad to know that you will soon go at work in collecting new materials and in writing up the pith and marrow of our new matter. I promised Mr. Pierce that he should see our note on his matter sent to us. The Lincoln Locofoco skunk story [1] is in two of my letters now in your hands, hunt 'em up if you use the story. What I have sent you as new matter, you can use or not at your pleasure. Much of what I say to you about the new matter, notes, etc., etc., for the book, will send you all things worthy of your attention and the world's, glad that you want to make the book perfect as it can be, a great historical monument for Lincoln especially. Mr. White [2] thinks that the story, etc., of the chronicles of Reuben or the Grigsby episode ought to be stricken out in the third edition, as it cannot be in the second edition. If it had never gone in the first edition, *possibly* I would say, don't put it in, but as it has gone before the world, I am, as I now feel, opposed to modifying, changing, or wholly omitting it in the third edition. The whole story only goes to show the condition of society in Indiana, Lincoln's home from 1816 to 1831, that Lincoln was affected by his environments, but that in after life he was strong and great enough, through his struggles, to cast it off and rise above his early environments, which not one man in a million can do. The episode is a part of his history, explains the *germs of his wit and his humor.* I admire the good tastes of life as well as any man or woman and cannot be made to defend the nasty, obscene, or vulgar under any circumstances, but I do fail to see why the episode causes a blush on any man's or woman's cheek. Some people are too nice for this material sphere, this muddy globe of ours. I'll think about this matter further. You know that I am easily managed, want our book to be a glorious success.

Your friend,

W. H. HERNDON.

Make no kind of a reply to what Nicolay and Hay say of our book.

---

[1] See pp. 397–398.
[2] An editor at Belford, Clarke & Co.

Springfield, Ill., December 20, 1889.

Friend Bartlett:

Your letter, dated the 17th *ult.*, was duly received, for which I thank you. I fear that what you say about Robert Lincoln is true; he has his mother's insane temper without his father's discretion. I have a tender feeling for the man, first, because of the "boy," and, secondly, on account of his father; and yet I must say that Bob is a "little wee bit of a man." I am sorry that he did as you were informed he did. It is just like Bob, however. A book cannot be put down by such methods. Such acts will, if known, add to the sale of the Life of Lincoln, the sale of any book. I am told that the Life of L. can be had in Paris, Brentano's, Rue de l'Opéra.

I owe you an explanation and I'll give it here. When I finished the Life of Lincoln, I was as poor as a church mouse and even so yet. To get it published I had to *bend to terms.* I was compelled to wait for books or money till the publishers were paid in full. They have not as yet been paid, as I am informed. Consequently, I have received up to this day no books, no money, neither of them. I am compelled to work on my farm today for my tomorrow's bread and butter. This explains to you why I have not sent you a copy, but I will some time, if I live. You must not think, my friend, that I am stingy or ungrateful.

I think that you are correct when you say that truth, in no quarter of the globe, is in much demand, and never has been, and never will be. Men love old truths, never new ones, as a general rule; they handle truths gingerly, but there are souls that do love the truth for its own sake, and sooner or later the Life of L. will find them. I drew the picture of Mr. Lincoln as I saw and knew him. I told the naked God's truth, and I'll stand by it, let the consequences be what they may be. I think that the great majority of the critics look at the book favorably. I get a great many private letters congratulating me on the book. It is a curious and a wonderful fact that no critic and no other man doubts the facts, the truths, stated by me in the Life of L. I have seen some savage attacks on the book. One editor says it is vulgar, obscene, etc., the article, as supposed, was inspired by Bob. Pardon me for talking so much about this subject.

Now let me talk some about other things. The Democracy was in the late elections victorious. The depleting in the Republican ranks

STEPHEN A. DOUGLAS

Lincoln's Compilation on Slavery

LEDGER

LINCOLN'S
NOTEBOOKS

Prepared by
Lincoln for
His Debates
with Douglas

was mostly caused by the high tariff and consequent high taxation on the necessaries of life, caused by it. Trusts, rings, corners, and the like methods of swindling have caused some suffering and much "cussing." President Harrison seems up to this date a weak brother and an obstinate one. If he does not improve soon, he will make President Pierce's administration quite respectable. The great fight in Congress this winter will be over two subjects: first, the tariff, and second, over the distribution of the excess of money, the surplus in the Treasury put there by the high tariff. I am not shooting politics at you at all, only giving you, in this line, what is, has been, and will be.

In one of my letters I said something to you about crops. In Kansas the people are burning corn in place of coal, finding it the cheaper fuel of the two. We can send to Europe somewhere near two hundred millions of bushels of wheat, and other farm products in proportion. We are rich in things to eat but suffer somewhat for money, the great surplus in the Treasury causing a contraction in the money market. You say that America will have to go through her troubles and if it is not one thing it is another—correct, but do not all general human troubles keep us from stagnating and going backward? Progress is slow but sure.

I see that the Knights of Labor and the Farmers' Alliance have united, and if they can agree, they will soon be victorious, because they are in the majority. But the question is: Can they agree and stick? I see that the W.C.T.U. has swallowed up the Women's Rights party and that it—the Woman's Christian Temperance Union—has split wide open. So reformers can't somehow agree and stick. I see that the idea of single tax is growing and so is communism; anarchism and other wild *isms* are struggling for life. The devil seems to be in hand all around everywhere.

Respects to all.

Your friend,
W. H. HERNDON.

Springfield, Ill., January 23, 1890.

Friend Weik:

Yours of the 12th *inst.* is at hand and is the most satisfactory letter yet received from you. Today I send you by express a bundle of letters, etc., by express, not having money to pay postage. The letters you can read and burn up, unless there is some other *valuable* matter in them. There are some important letters and other matter from Hon. Ed. L. Pierce of Milton, Massachusetts. I have received two or four letters stating that the period or time from 1844 to '50 was not sufficiently elaborated. Mr. Pierce explains Lincoln's first Eastern trip through New England to see Bob, etc. There is likewise a newspaper— three articles by Mr. Pierce—which is good. Please read carefully all that Mr. Pierce says and write out a good long piece and insert in our book and give him credit for it in the note. This I promised Mr. Pierce. What he says is important and on a point that none of the Lives of Lincoln has touched upon. Lincoln said, during this trip East, his first trip, that (to some city in Massachusetts) "I understand you have some abolitionists out here. We killed one out West a few months ago." This was saying the wrong thing at the wrong place. Note what Pierce says and quote it. In fact, read all that Pierce says carefully and write out a good piece and insert in our book and do not fail to give our authority. There are some papers from Charles Friend [1] of Kentucky about Nancy Hanks, Thomas Lincoln. From this man's testimony it appears that there was but one Nancy Hanks and, if that is so, then Thomas Lincoln married Dennis Hanks's mother. Read what Charles Friend says. Probably no attention need be paid to it, though file away the papers as evidence.

You wish me to read over our book and note mistakes. Jesse, when I sent you the corrections, I told you to put the corrections on a separate piece of paper so that you could refer to them easily in mass, but it seems "the gal" was uppermost in your mind, and so the devil is to pay. It is possible that I can do you no good, because I have no time to reread and correct. You know my pecuniary conditions and have to toil all the time in some way, in mind or body, to get my bread and butter. I owe the bank here $21, and it bothers me terribly. If I had that sum, I could do you good. This frets and annoys me so that I cannot read or think.

I wish you would write out a short eulogy on Lincoln's virtue during his married life. Lincoln, I know, as well as I know anything, was true to his wife, to his marriage vow. His idea was that a woman had the same right to play with her tail that a man had, and no more nor less,

[1] See pp. 340–343.

and that he had no moral or other right to violate the sacred marriage vow. I have heard him say it a dozen or more times. "Lincoln's honor," as Judge Davis said, "saved many a woman." This is true to my own knowledge. I have seen women make advances and I have seen Lincoln reject or refuse them. Lincoln had terribly strong passions for woman, could scarcely keep his hands off them, and yet he had honor and a strong will, and these enabled him to put out the fires of his terrible passion. It is a physiological truth that most male consumptives have goatish passions. This eulogistic piece should have gone in the first edition of our book but was somehow overlooked. Don't fail to put it in the second edition. It would have done us good then and will now.

Your request to search our book over and make notes of errors, etc., for the second edition comes like a clap of lightning from a clear sky. I cannot do as you request, do what you wish, as quick as lightning "*at once.*" Had I known it in time, I could have done as you wish, but I cannot now "*at once*" do it quicker than lightning. You will have to run over my letters and pick out what corrections I have made to you heretofore—sorry for it, but can't help it now. . . .

Your friend,

W. H. HERNDON.

Springfield, Ill., February 8, 1890.

Friend Jesse:

Your letter of the 31st *ult.* is at hand. I am much obliged to you for it and especially for the twenty-one dollars' accommodation. When I wrote to you my letter about money I was gloomy, but did not intend to ask you for it, was only stating, as it were to myself, the *Sheol* I was in and as an excuse to you why I could do nothing to assist in the correction of the book. However, I am more obliged to you than ever because the advance was voluntary and of your own good free will. The loan puts my feet on solid ground once more. You must believe me when I say I thank you a thousand times for the money. . . .

I am glad to know that the letters from others which I have sent you please Jesse. I want Jesse pleased and his hopes lifted up, glad he is out of his blues, out of his *quasi*-despair, and in full blooming hope. Why, Jesse, if you could know all the compliments which I receive by letter and in the city from all classes, strangers too, you would feel good all over. If I can find some more letters like those which I have sent you, and I have them, I'll send to you. You know that I am careless with my letters, as a general thing, but I'll save good ones and send to you. Do not despair of our book. You once said to me substantially this: that the popularity of our book would not depend on what critics, good and bad, said, but would depend on what was said by word and what went from mouth to mouth, and that is true and ever will be. You may write to Mrs. Curtis and others if you think prudent, but let Providence be your guide. By the way, Nicolay and Hay, *I think*, have given us a back-handed lick, a malicious hit, it may be. See *Century* page 574, second column at the top. Keep cool and say nothing. As to the man Powers, he is a poor devil who keeps the monument affair and who has been accused of extortion from visitors to the monument. This has been said publicly. This man is a fool and so let him pass as unworthy of notice. I know the man and I say he is an ass and a poor ass at that. I guess that N. and H. are envious, that's what's the matter. . . .

You know that I have never said anything to you, or to anyone else for that matter, that was not true, not the fact, and so I promise you to be as vigilant as I can be under all circumstances. You know that a man who has to struggle today for his tomorrow's bread is rather a poor hand in mental work or in literature. Don't know what stirred up Powers except natural "cussedness."

You ask me to make some notes of my life and send to you for publication. I'll do so, but they will be few and of no value to anyone. Do you want them for Appleton's *Biographical Dictionary?* That firm has likewise written to me for some facts of my life.

Enclosed you will find a good letter from ex-Senator Fowler, once Senator from Tennessee. He speaks fairly and is a personal friend of mine. He and I became acquainted in this city *about* 1865, possibly before this. I've a good letter from General James Grant Wilson. . . . Grant Wilson says it is, our Life, an admirable work.

What I said to you about B., C. & Co. was said to arouse you to watchfulness, no more. Keep your eyes wide open on B., C. & Co. Do you never doubt?

Your friend,
W. H. HERNDON.

P.S. The Lord be praised for your loan. H.

Springfield, Ill., March 7, 1890.

Friend Weik:

. . . What you state about the English edition of our book is more or less satisfactory, and yet I would suggest that you find out the all, the whole of the thing. What Mr. Bartlett says about *"Bob"* he thinks is true, doubtless has been so informed. I have faith in Bartlett. I hope that the second edition of our book will soon be issued and quickly sold, want to see the third edition badly, as it will contain many new and important facts; glad that you begin to *hope*, for you say that the book is on the upgrade; glad that you have got some new and good letters on your own account, doing justice to our book; yes, I'll send all the good letters which come to me. I am glad that Horace White proposes to write us out his ideas on L.'s campaign in '58, it will be good; glad that you have personally got much and good new matter when you know that I have been corresponding for some years. His letter is dated November 17, 1889 and is from France. If Robert is able and willing to buy up whole editions of our book, we can supply him to his heart's content, can do so I suppose every month or so. If no one in London will sell the books, we can land them on the wharf and notify the minister of the fact. Weik, I always thought Bob a weak brother, but never thought that he was such a d——d fool. Why, his acts in this matter are little, mean, malicious. He is a Todd and not a Lincoln, is a little bitter fellow of the pig-headed kind, silly and cold and selfish. I do not think that he will suppress the book in this way. The book will live and be read when he is dead and forgotten, or only remembered by his name being in the book. This is my judgment. I suppose that Bob will cremate the Life of his father and scatter the ashes in the Thames or over the sea. If this will satisfy his little soul, let him alone in his glory. Success to him in his efforts to suppress the truth. Can he stop the sun from shining? If you think prudent, you can copy the above quotation, the foregoing one, and send it to Belford, Clarke & Co. It may be an act of justice to notify them of what my correspondent says, but in no case is my name nor my correspondent's name to be made public. I want no controversy with Robert on his father's account. I respect him so much, worship him, if you please, that I do not want any words with Bob. I cannot help but feel kindly toward the little fellow. Tell B., C. & Co. that my name as well as my correspondent's must in no case be made public if they use it in any way. I see no impropriety in sending to B., C. & Co. the quotations, but you think about it.

Occasionally I get letters highly complimentary of our book. One man from Pennsylvania says: "I see by the papers that your book has been well received; it does not surprise me, as such a grand work will have a large sale." Others say substantially: "Thank heavens that we have at last a true Life of Lincoln, one that we can swear by." It is a curious fact, Jesse, that no man, no critic, no reader, ever doubts the truth, fullness, of our book. I have never heard or read that any person doubts *the facts or opinions* in the Life of Lincoln. The book must sell and sell well as long as men love the truth more than false-hood. All the good people want is a good chance to get the book, and you are the man to hustle it along, push it vigorously so that the world can get it easily and cheaply. The reason the folks do not write to you is because they do not know where you live. A Mr. Wilson from Maryland says: "The book is as interesting as a novel, etc.," and so it runs. I know that some of our books have gone to Germany and France, because men of veracity have told me that they have sent them themselves.

Jesse, do not now come here till the weather is settled, say December 20, or better January 1. You know that I am tolerably old and do not wish to wade or swim to the city, mud, mud, mud, and nothing but mud.

Your friend,
W. H. HERNDON.

I'll come anyhow on three or four days' notice, mud or no mud, but would prefer about January 1.   H.

Springfield, Ill., April 4, 1890.

Friend Weik:

Enclosed you will find a letter of mine written to C. O. Poole, my old friend, which was published in the New York *Sun* of March 24, 1890. The little slip accompanying the letter will explain why it was written. It was a hasty letter, not written for publication, but I suppose it struck Poole and possibly the editor of the *Sun*. Please read the letter over and over and get the spirit of it. Jesse, there is a good chance for you to write out an eloquent note. In the first place Lincoln placed his administrative abilities in his power to rule men; he said this to Swett; see our Life of L., page 533. Read carefully from the words, "In his conduct of the war," down to and including, "I have kept these discordant elements together as well as anyone could." When this is done, read his farewell Springfield speech, wherein he, Lincoln, appeals to the Christians, invokes their power, and winds them around his finger. . . . Then think a little. When this is done, look at his Cabinet, etc., etc., and why they, the members of it, were so appointed, men who opposed him in the Chicago convention. Lincoln was a shrewd, sagacious, long-headed man, a cunning fox. From the time of his farewell Springfield speech he was at long-headwork reconciling antagonistic elements, discordant elements, with which he had to deal; he used all just as he wished. I say he used all and made all his tools; he was the superior of all and governed all by his intellectual superiority. Now read Swett's letter as above referred to, and you will catch the idea of the note or piece which I want you to write out fully and eloquently. Read my letter to Poole over and over; it will help you. Can't such a piece go in the text of the book? Lincoln was a long-headed old fox, a shrewd manipulator of men, a man full of practical political sagacities. As Swett says, he was the great American trimmer when men had to be used. What I have said in the Poole letter and in this letter is true of Lincoln, true to the letter and the spirit.

Jesse, why don't you write to me more frequently? I am half dead for a letter from you.

Your old friend,
W. H. HERNDON.

P.S.   The note can best come in on page 541, after the words, "bargained for."

Lincoln's idea was, how to make the North *one*, a solid and united *one*.

By appointing these Cabinet men he made the friends of each his friends.

Springfield, Ill., July 6, 1890.

Friend Jesse:

Your letter, dated the 28th *ult.*, inclosing B., C. & Co.'s report or statement of their account with us, was duly received, for both of which I am much obliged. The statement, the report, is all wrong. First, the last contract with B., C. & Co. and ourselves requires the binders and printers to make a statement of the number of books bound and the number of books printed, etc. No such statements are made accompanying B., C. & Co.'s report. Secondly, it seems that, from the account furnished us by B., C. & Co., we are charged with 416 copies of our book sent to *editors*, possibly you as editor. Now what right has B., C. & Co. to give away 416 copies of our book? B., C. & Co. agree to give us a royalty 25¢ for every book sold or set of books sold. If they, B., C. & Co., thus paid their advertisement account with the papers, then so many sets of the book are *sold* and we are entitled to pay for the 416 thus sold. Where is this army of editors? Who are they and where do they live? 416 Eds.! 416 lies, eh? These 416 copies were given away, if any were given away, since the new edition was issued.

Now, Jesse, drop the woman right off or take one for good right off, "*at once*," and sharply attend to our business in a quick sharp business way and all will yet go right. I am determined not to be swindled. I have been warned of this by different men at different places and times. A screw is loose somewhere and the thing to be done is to find it and put it in its place.

I have kept B., C. & Co.'s statement. Write to them for another and hereafter require duplicate statements in order to save trouble. *Please* read the two contracts over and over carefully, study them and stand square on them and enforce them. Look sharply into things, keeping your eyes open, and while thus acting hunt up my last three letters and answer the various questions—*do, please.*

Jesse, I speak to you in a friendly way, but am firm in my determinations not to be swindled.

Your friend,
W. H. Herndon.

Springfield, Ill., July 25, 1890.

Friend Jesse:

Your good letter, not to say excellent, dated the 20th *inst.*, was duly received. . . . I have always thought that something was wrong and am glad to know that *part* of the wrong going and wrongdoing is to be attributed to bad agency and other crooked management of the firm. . . .

You ask me to write out the story of *how I did it*, etc. I will send you a note of it soon; am busy as a bee in selling my vegetables, fruits, etc., in order to live. Jesse, it's a bad thing to be poor, ain't it?

. . . By the way, Jesse, there is a healthy change going on about our book. Men who cursed it when it first appeared now say upon the whole it is a good book. The second sober thought will bring men around to the truth or the love of it at last. Whether the book pays right now or not, one thing is certain, and that is: that the book will live. As the race of man progresses, the more the race loves truth. Men in this particular get braver every day. I can feel that *in my bones*.

Your friend,
W. H. HERNDON.

Springfield, Ill., September 24, 1890.

Friend Weik:

Enclosed is a letter from McArthur which you may wish to see. . . . I send you likewise a letter from Mr. King, an old abolitionist, friend of mine, is truthful. He says that Alsop, another old abolitionist and friend of mine, and himself got the anti-slavery men *generally* to vote for Lincoln in '46 in this, then Lincoln's, district. I have no doubt of the truth of this, none at all. This will account for Lincoln's overwhelming majority over Peter Cartwright. I think Erastus Wright, the pension man, opposed Lincoln. You can make a note of these facts, or fact. . . . King's letter I have answered, giving him and Alsop great credit for what they and friends did in the matter. They increased Lincoln's majority greatly. This I know of my own knowledge. King and Alsop were strong leaders of the anti-slavery cause in Lincoln's district in '46.

About the year '56 a gentleman from Chicago by the name of Z. Eastman, editor of an anti-slavery paper in Chicago, came into my office and introduced himself to me. After some general and running conversation on *this* subject and *that*, Mr. Eastman said to me: "Herndon, I know you as a firm and true anti-slavery man, but we anti-slavery men North don't know Mr. Lincoln so well. What are his ideas on slavery and can we trust him?" I said to Mr. Eastman in reply: "Mr. Lincoln is a natural-born anti-slavery man, and now you go home and use the influence of your paper for Lincoln." (This paper was the predecessor of the Chicago *Tribune* or the *Press and Tribune*, I forget exactly which, think it was the *Tribune*.) "Can you trust yourself?" I said further to Mr. Eastman. "And if you can, then you can trust Lincoln, for God will keep him right. Now you keep the people right and, as to Lincoln, you can trust [him]. Tell our friends in Chicago and elsewhere to *trust*." Mr. Eastman was a committee man from Chicago who was appointed to investigate, etc. He went home to Chicago and opened his paper, as far as he could, for Lincoln. This is how the anti-slavery men in Illinois were such strong friends of Mr. Lincoln. Eastman was appointed, by Mr. Lincoln, United States Consul to Great Britain as I remember it. Mr. Eastman and myself have written to each other since this matter transpired. In this conversation Mr. Eastman asked me if it would not be wise for the anti-slavery men to go into the Know-Nothing lodges and rule them. I said to him: "No, never do this wrong to our cause. We are for the broadest liberty for all men." I have cut things short. Our conversation in '56 was probably two or three hours long and much was said of Lincoln, slavery, the anti-slavery cause, the progress of it, hopes, etc., etc. I have forgotten the name of Eastman's paper, have once or twice called or said it was the *Star*, but I think I was wrong in this. The *Tribune* men can tell you.

Let me tell you something else which I distinctly remember; see our Life of Lincoln, pages 367–8, and read what I said as editorial in the *Journal*. You will perceive in the piece that Douglas frequently interrupted Lincoln, and now as to the why of it. Lincoln in opening his speech said this: "I willingly give Senator Douglas, who now sits in front of me, the privilege of correcting me where I am wrong in the facts about the whole matter of the Kansas-Nebraska Bill, which was introduced by the Senator himself and which is the offspring of the ambition and goal of slavery; I say that I extend to him the privilege of correcting me in my facts and not in my inferences, as they are subject of dispute among men and would cause too many collateral issues to be raised and of no value to the main subject." Mr. Douglas was irritated and thoroughly aroused; he made statements often, and irrelevant ones, under the privilege of correcting facts. This was about to interrupt and break the thread of it, Mr. Lincoln's speech, as a whole and set speech, when Mr. Lincoln said: "I revoke, I withdraw, what I have said to the Honorable Senator as to privilege and shall assert what I do assert on my own responsibility." This ended the annoyance to Lincoln and to the vast crowd in the hall. Douglas saw and took a mean advantage of the privilege granted to him by Lincoln; he made statements about things not in dispute nor bearing on the issues in dispute nor debate. In my opinion he did so to interrupt Lincoln and fret him and thus destroy the effect of L.'s speech. All this I saw and heard and distinctly remember it.

Your friend,
W. H. HERNDON.

Springfield, Ill., October 2, 1890.

Friend Jesse:

I take it for granted that you are not of this world just now, nor will you be for some time; but when you do come to earth, you can read this letter at your leisure or throw it away. . . .

I wish to relate to you an important fact. Soon after the assassination of Mr. Lincoln, I interviewed Mr. Judd, two or three times, in relation to his knowledge of Lincoln *generally* and particularly about what L. said in reference to the questions he intended to ask Douglas at Freeport. Turn to our Life of L., 410. Douglas put seven questions to L. at Ottawa. Lincoln went to Chicago and had a meeting of his friends and told them that he intended to put four questions to Douglas at Freeport and among those questions was the second one which was substantially this: "Can a territory exclude slavery from its limits while in a territorial condition or state?" At the meeting of Lincoln's friends at Dixon or Chicago were Peck, Judd, Ray, *et al.* All of them, after Lincoln had read the four questions to be put to Douglas at Freeport, objected to them and said in substance that Douglas would not positively answer the question directly and that, if he did, it would be in the affirmative and that would elect him to the Senate again. "It is none of your business, Mr. Lincoln, particularly to put the question because you are the candidate for the United States Senate, and that is your particular business," said Lincoln's friends. Lincoln replied: "Douglas will answer the question as soon as asked and, if he does not, I will push him to the wall at every joint debate or wherever I shall speak, otherwise than in joint debate, and the sooner Douglas answers, the better for him. The people demand a direct answer." "Douglas will answer in some glittering generalities and evade the question," said Peck, Ray, *et al.* "Yes, he will answer directly," said Lincoln; and to which Lincoln's friends said: "To put the question is none of your business, Mr. Lincoln," and to which Mr. Lincoln said: "Yes, it is my business, and if Douglas answers the question, which he will, either way he is a dead cock in the pit." Mr. Lincoln here went into a kind of argument to convince his friends that he was right and concluded by saying: "I am after larger game. The battle of 1860 is worth a hundred of this." . . . Lincoln evidently wanted to kill Douglas politically and did it effectively. I say that Judd told me what Lincoln said in the meeting of friends at Dixon or Chicago, I think Chicago, though White says that the meeting was at Dixon. Probably he is correct. Though Peck, Ray, Judd, *et al.*, say that Lincoln uttered the above words, still I doubt the *exact words*, because, as you well know, Mr. Lincoln was one of the most secretive men that ever lived. The expression means that "I am a candidate for the Presidency of the United States of America. That is what I am fighting for." I do not think that Mr. Lincoln ever uttered the words as stated, though he looked at the time for the office. I think at most that the words as above are inferences, legitimate ones. Lincoln never told mortal man his purposes and plans—never. Evidently L. beat around the bush. As I think of things, I'll write you.

Your friend,
W. H. HERNDON.

P.S.   When you come to this sphere of man and mud, you will please write to me.

Springfield, Ill., December 4, 1890.

Friend Weik:

In my last letter to you I stated that I had something to tell you about Lincoln which took place in '54, October, I think. I will now state it and, as you were present, you may remember it, and if you do not, this may refresh your memory. If you will turn to my Life of Lincoln and read a short piece of editorial for our *Journal* written by me, page 368, on the evening of the speech, you will see that I stated that

Douglas frequently interrupted Mr. Lincoln during his speech. In reading your excellent letter to me of February 27, 1890, and at the beginning of it you speak to me at least, feelingly and eloquently, of Lincoln and his speech in '54. Your remarks in that letter to me, the one which constitutes a chapter in the Life of Lincoln and spoken of above, caused me to be put in the same state, condition, consciousness, that I was in on the moment of the debate, and I saw everything, heard everything, as on the moment of the speech, after reading your remarks in the letter spoken of. We are curious creatures and the mind and its laws are a riddle to me. Is it not true that we remember things once supposed to be lost forever by being put in the same *state* as we were when we saw or heard the thing?

Mr. Lincoln, after opening his speech and clearing away the underbrush so that he might have a clear and open view of things, said substantially this: "I give Senator Douglas the privilege of correcting me in any facts which I shall state, but not the inferences which I shall draw from them, as they are the nib of the whole question and would open too broad a field of debate now and here." Douglas sat right under Lincoln and was a little "cocked" at the time. For some time Douglas made no corrections nor suggestions but, as Lincoln proceeded, Douglas got hot and a little vexed, if not angry. Lincoln began to get warmer and struck harder and heavier blows, and then it was that Douglas quite every moment made some sideshow, so-called corrections of unimportant things, collateral ones not in issue at all in any way. The large audience saw and felt that Douglas was taking a mean advantage of Lincoln's granted privilege to him. The crowd at last got angry and showed its feelings in different ways though not inappropriately, not boisterously, generally. Lincoln himself began to *feel*, and I could see in his eyes a little ill feeling. You know that I understood Lincoln, I think, inside and outside. The crowd got madder and madder at the foolish corrections so called made by Douglas. Men were uneasy and restless and the women, God bless 'em, said by their acts: "Sit down, Mr. Douglas." Lincoln got more angry every moment and at last in self-defense, rising to his full height coolly, calmly, said: "Senator Douglas, I withdraw the privilege of correcting me which I gave you a moment ago, and now, friends, the facts which I shall hereafter state I shall state on my own responsibility." When this was said, I could see smiles of approbation run over the faces of the crowd and all was calm, peaceful, and pleasant after that. Before this, things looked a little "scary," "fighty," in one corner of the hall. I took notes of his, L.'s, speech and loaned them to Governor Yates, who made in '56 and '58 many good speeches from them. I was up in the gallery on the little elevation near the speaker. My piece in the *Journal* shows my honest opinion of Lincoln's speech and of the appearance and actions of Douglas. The reason why I have written this to you is that you may wish to make a *note* of it some time for your letter to me.

I wish now to make another statement. If you remember, you once asked me if the text in Lamon's Life of Lincoln was correct, page 396, as I remember it, and in answer to which question I said: "It was substantially correct," and I say so now. Our Judge J. H. Matheny said to me, only a month or so before he died, which was some two months since, that he heard Lincoln say in substance: "If Douglas can draw off such and such men from the cause of Republicanism and be made to support him, who says he does not care whether slavery is voted up or voted down, if he can get strong and influential leading Republican papers to laud him, and if he can attack and partly crush Buchanan's administration and can get in Illinois so many votes to Buchanan's none, then he will play the devil at Charleston." From a letter of yours written to me a good while ago I infer that you did not get mine fully explaining, or confirming, Lamon. Excuse a friend, won't you?

Your friend,
W. H. HERNDON.

Springfield, Ill., January 6, 1891.

So far as a knowledge of the inner life and characteristics of Abraham Lincoln are concerned, I consider JESSE W. WEIK the best-equipped man of his day and generation. He was my associate in writing the *Life of Lincoln*, recently given to the world, and is the most enthusiastic student of *Lincoln's marvelous growth* I have ever met. His zeal and indefatigable search for facts never allows him to stop short of the naked truth, and he therefore knows his great subject inside and outside, mentally, morally, and physically. Realizing that I am now too old and infirm . . . I have turned over to him all the letters, manuscripts, and other material pertaining to Lincoln which I have been steadily gathering together since *that memorable day in April 1865, when the bullet of Booth did its fatal work.* . . . I know that his heart is in his work *and that his love for the immortal railsplitter will* . . . *be his greatest inspiration* . . . etc.

[W. H. HERNDON.]

Springfield, Ill., January 1891.

Friend Weik:

When I was in Greencastle in 1887 I said to you that Lincoln had, *when a mere boy*, the syphilis, and now let me explain the matter in full, which I have never done before. About the year 1835–36 Mr. Lincoln went to Beardstown and during a devilish passion had connection with a girl and caught the disease. Lincoln told me this and in a moment of folly I made a note of it in my mind and afterwards I transferred it, as it were, to a little memorandum book which I loaned to Lamon, not, as I should have done, erasing that note. About the year 1836–37 Lincoln moved to Springfield and took up his quarters with Speed; they became very intimate. At this time I suppose that the disease hung to him and, not wishing to trust our physicians, wrote a note to Doctor Drake, the latter part of which he would not let Speed see, not wishing Speed to know it. Speed said to me that Lincoln would not let him see a part of the note. Speed wrote to me a letter saying that he supposed L.'s letter to Doctor Drake had reference to his, L.'s, crazy spell about the Ann Rutledge love affair, etc., and her death. You will find Speed's letter to me in our Life of Lincoln. The note to Doctor Drake in part had reference to his disease and not to his crazy spell, as Speed supposes. The note spoken of in the memorandum book was a loose affair, and I never intended that the world should see or hear of it. I now wish and for years have wished that the note was blotted out or burned to ashes. I write this to you, fearing that at some future time the note—a loose thing as to date, place, and circumstances—will come to light and be misunderstood. Lincoln was a man of terribly strong passions, but was true as steel to his wife during his whole marriage life; his honor, as Judge Davis has said, saved many a woman, and it is most emphatically true, as I know. I write this to you to explain the whole matter for the future if it should become necessary to do so. I deeply regret my part of the affair in every particular.

Your friend,
W. H. HERNDON.

P.S. Mrs. Dale was my guest for several days, say in '71, and she saw that memorandum book and took some notes of its contents, and it may some time come to light from that quarter, and so you have this as my defense. H.

Springfield, Ill., February 5, 1891.

Friend Jesse:

I want to give you a kind of bribery story about Mr. and Mrs. Lincoln which took place soon after Lincoln was elected President. The story comes through Hermann Kreismann, who was appointed by Lincoln secretary of legation, when Judd was appointed Minister to Germany. Krcismann is a gentleman and can be relied on. The story is as follows. One Henderson of New York wished to be appointed to some office in the Custom House of New York. To get the office he sent to Mrs. Lincoln, in care of some jewelry house in this city, a diamond brooch to be given to her upon the condition that he could get the promise of the office from Mrs. L. Kreismann and Judd come to Springfield on some important business and were to meet Lincoln at some place by appointment, but he did not come as agreed, Mrs. Lincoln having cornered him and he could not get away. Mrs. Lincoln got the diamond brooch, having promised Henderson to get the office for him. Kreismann was dispatched to hunt up Lincoln. He went to Lincoln's house and was ushered in, in a hurry and probably by the servant, she not telling Mr. and Mrs. Kreismann found Mrs. L. in a hysterical fit, cutting up like a crazy woman. She was begging Lincoln to appoint Henderson. Lincoln refused several times but Mrs. L. kept up her yells, her hysterical fit, till Lincoln, in order to get rid of the woman and quiet the fit, did promise Mrs. L. that Henderson should have the office, and Henderson got it according to promise. Henderson was subsequently indicted in the United States court for defrauding the government but was acquitted on some technical point. Henderson knew how to reach Mrs. L. and did reach her in Henderson's way. Lincoln, to keep quiet in his house and to get the woman's fingers out

POLITICAL CARTOONS BY L. H. STEPHENS, 1864
Courtesy of the Henry E. Huntington Library

POLITICAL CARTOONS BY L. H. STEPHENS, 1864

Courtesy of the Henry E. Huntington Library

of his hair, did a wrong thing, if he knew why Mrs. Lincoln was so anxious for Henderson's appointment. Such is woman and such is man the world over, weak creatures indeed. Lincoln must have had an idea of the motives and the cause of them that prompted Mrs. Lincoln to want Henderson appointed. By the way, Lincoln had no true notions of the propriety of things, as a general rule. I suppose that in this case Lincoln did not know what to do. The devil was after him and he stumbled. Poor bedeviled fellow, unfortunate man!

Bob Lincoln was in this city about six weeks since, came here to bury his son, and while here someone, probably a friend of mine, asked Bob if he had seen Herndon's Life of Lincoln, and to which question he replied: "No, nor do I wish to see it." In this I rather think that "our minister to England" was a little mistaken, if I have heard the truth. You must remember that Bob is not his "daddy" nor like him in any respect whatever. Bob is little, proud, aristocratic, and haughty, is his mother's "baby" all through. He will never be President, though ambitious for it.

How is your *clerk* and is she helping you? When I was younger than I am now and wished to say something smart, I took a toddy as *exciter*, but your pretty wife will be your stimulant and tonic. Give her my warmest regards, and if you will let me, I will say give her my love.

Your friend,
W. H. HERNDON.

Springfield, Ill., February 13, 1891.

Mr. Bartlett.
My dear Friend:

Your note, dated the 5th *inst.*, is now before me, stating that you are back to America again and intend to stay at home where men are free. I am glad to hear you say that and am pleased to know that you are at home, am very glad to hear from you at all times, and especially now. I thank you for your opinion of my book, but regret to say that it has not paid me anything as yet. The publishers, Belford, Clarke & Co. of New York, "busted" some years or so since, are men of no capital or brains. Privately I had to take the business out of their hands and give it to the house of Scribner's, which have the capital and the brains and will push the thing. The edition of the book which they will publish will have much new, good, and excellent matter in it. I have been for years collecting new facts about Lincoln and intend to keep at it till I can hear no more facts to gather, and then the world can have the MSS. . . .

There was quite a political revolution here in November last—cause, the McKinley tariff bill, principally, though other things helped. Since you went to Paris, a third party has risen up and threatens to disturb the old parties. We have in this State a "deadlock" now in our legislatures over the election of a United States Senator. I think that the deadlock will break this week, but politics do not interest you and I shall say no more of them.

If your wife is with you, give her, and any of the children in Quincy, my highest regards.

Your friend,
W. H. HERNDON.

Springfield, Ill., February 21, 1891.

Friend Jesse:

In your letter of the 8th *inst.* you ask me if I remember Mr. Lincoln's lecture here in 1858–59, and in answer to your question, let me say *I do distinctly remember it.* It was delivered here in Myer's Hall on the north side of the square, nearly midway between Fifth and Sixth Streets and some time, I think, in February—probably January '59. I heard the lecture and remember the subject of it very well. The title of it was substantially "The Time of the Different Inventions," mostly those mentioned in the Bible. Probably the word "discoveries" would suit the title as well. Knowing Mr. L. as well as I did, I was anxious to hear him, and did listen to him well, thoroughly, attentively, and curiously too. I know that Mr. L. was not fitted, qualified, in any way to deliver a lecture to our people, who were intelligent, well read, and well educated. I was not mistaken in the lecture which Mr. L. read; it was a lifeless thing, a dull dead thing, "died aborning." It fell on the ears of the audience a cold flat thing. There was no life, imagination, or fancy in it, no spirit and no life. The whole thing was a kind of farce and injured Mr. L.'s reputation as a man of sense among his friends and enemies.

Mr. Lincoln was a peculiar, mysterious man. I wrote to you once that Mr. L. had *a double consciousness*, a double life. The two states, never in the normal man, co-exist in equal and vigorous activities though they succeed each other quickly. One state predominates and, while it so rules, the other state is somewhat quiescent, shadowy, yet living, a real thing. This is the sole reason why L. so quickly passed from one state of consciousness to another and a different state. In one moment he was in a state of abstraction and then quickly in another state when he was a social, talkative, and a communicative fellow. In our office on the west side of the square we had a long office table running north and south. Mr. L. always took his seat on the east side of the table, looking westward, and I sat on the west side of the table looking eastward, and thus we sat face [to face]. About one o'clock in the daytime the sun, especially in the summer, streamed through the western windows of our office and flooded Lincoln's face, so that I could see to the very back part of his eyes. When thus situated and in one of his abstract moods I studied the man and think that I could read his thoughts clearly, distinctly, certainly *in a general way*. You know my love of reading men, mind, moods, characteristics, etc. You are aware that I love the science of the mind quite over all studies and I had the very best of opportunities to do so. On looking at the man under the above conditions speculatively, critically, he would to the observer's surprise without warning burst out in a loud laugh or quickly spring up and run downstairs as if his house were on fire, saying nothing. Sometimes it took a strong effort on his part to awake, arouse himself from one condition on purpose or with intent to live in another state of consciousness. To do this he would tell a story or read a chapter in such a book as Jack Downing, Nasby, Bill Nye, or Josh Billings. The sharp points of one state of consciousness touched the other state, and it was therefore easy for him to pass from one state to another and a different state. Such was the man always. This law of the man may spring out of the double brain, each part lying close together side by side and touch to touch, one life in one hemisphere of the brain and the other life in the other. Jesse, you don't like this kind of stuff, I know, and will quit it, cutting it short for your sake, yes, for your sake.

I was sorry that your lecturing tour was a failure. Jesse, do not try to lecture in the West till you first go East and create a big name and then it will wave and ring out West. I tried to make a little money here years ago by lecturing in the West but it was a dead flat failure as to money, so I learned that I should have gone North first and then traveled West, so the world wags. "Westward the star of Empire," goes, and so do all business, inventions, discoveries, literature, etc., etc., etc., etc.

I must get back to Lincoln. Lincoln's little offhand speeches made on his trip to Washington were wise things, i.e., they showed that Lincoln was determined to keep his own secrets and make no blunders, excite no hate, arouse no bad feelings, say nothing that would bind him till the development of the last fact in the great drama in which he was to take part. These speeches were called "Lincoln's last jokes," by way of contempt for the man and his cause. Let us defend Lincoln in this matter by stating the facts, ideas, purposes, etc., of the little things. I stated this to you before, but I repeat it because you may forget the facts and what I said. You know that you have been in love's purgatory for about two years, a most glorious purgatory too, when we know that some sweet priestess can slip us out by her love and her gracious ointments. God bless the woman.

Can you not pick out the suppressed parts of Mr. Swett's letter and publish them in notes under the Swett letter, stating the facts that Swett suppressed them because he thought that no one would believe him in such radical views? I know that they are true and correct opinions of Lincoln in every particular. I hope that you recollect the facts of our writing to him and his letter of reply.

I said to you while I was in Greencastle that Lincoln told me that John T. Stuart, Matheny, and the leading Fillmore men in this section were bribed by the Buchanan corruption fund, said that he believed that the Fillmore party, i.e., leaders of it through the State, were bought and sold like hogs are sold in the market. That induced me to kill the *Conservative* published here. I had two ideas in getting in the Richmond *Enquirer* article: first, I wanted it published in the *Conservative* so as to show the rank and file of the Fillmore boys the course they were expected to move—vote and act and in the end shout for slavery; and, in the second place, I wanted to kill the *Conservative* out and out. It did soon die, possibly for want of funds or because of the Richmond *Enquirer* piece. The Richmond *Enquirer's* article maintained that slavery was right in principle and that it covered the white race as well as the black. It was a long piece and a well-written one. Here then is a full explanation of what I told you when I was in your city. I remember too of writing to you some general words about this matter, but I repeat in order to make the matter full and plain. Lincoln *knew* what he was talking about, let me assure you. This cannot now go in print, but it can go to the world if needed, in the great future.

Jesse, in the last two years I have written to you many letters sending you enough facts, good and true ones, to fill a volume the size of our book. The consequence is that all cannot go in our book and a selection must be made, leaving out much for some future biographer to use, if we cannot use the matter in some future edition of the Life of L. Looking at it in this light, I have selected three pieces which I prefer to all others, and they are:

First, what was the war about, nullification, secession.

Secondly, Lincoln's double consciousness—in two letters one a long time since and the other this week.

Thirdly . . . The third I have forgotten, will remember it and write you to fill the blank.

Your friend,
W. H. HERNDON.

P.S. Am glad that you are on a high horse about the Scribners. I guess that they will push things ahead vigorously.   H.

Springfield, Ill., February 26, 1891.

Friend Jesse:

I wish to say a word or two about Mr. Lincoln's fatalism. First, he believed that both matter and mind are governed by certain irrefragable and irresistible laws, and that no prayers of ours could arrest their operation in the least. Secondly, that what was to be would be inevitably. Thirdly, that the laws of human nature are persistent and permanent and could not be reversed; he said this in his printed speech in '42; and, fourthly, he said, while he was President, that he did not rule events, during any time in his administration, but that events ruled him. All these things are of record and there is no mistake about it. It follows that Mr. Lincoln was a fatalist, as he himself has said, though his fatalism was not of the extreme order like the Mahometan idea of fate, because he believed firmly in the power of human effort to modify the environments which surround us. He made efforts at all times to modify and change public opinion and to climb to the Presidential heights; he toiled and struggled in this line as scarcely any man ever did. As to free will, he said that that which was governed by a force outside of itself was not self-governed and that which was not self-governed was not free, though he admitted that the will to a very limited extent, in some fields of operation, was somewhat free. The laws of the universe were, except as to human nature, *outside* of the will and governed it. The will, in addition, had to act along the lines of human nature, including the laws of motive, thus giving the will only a small field of action for the exercise of its freedom, so called.

I wish to use the above statement of facts for an end, namely, to show that Mr. Lincoln believed that men are the children of conditions, of circumstances, and of their environments which surround them, including a hundred thousand years or more of education with acquired habits and the tendency to heredity molding them as they are and will forever be. His whole philosophy made him free from hate, free from love, intense and free from malice. No man was responsible for what he was, thought, or did, because he was a child of conditions. No man was censured by him or ought to be by others; he was, by his philosophy, full of charity for his fellow-man. No man was to be eulogized for what he did or censured for what he did not do or did do. Hence Lincoln could well exclaim: "With malice toward none and charity for all." I never heard him censure anyone but slightly, nor eulogize any, probably with two milk and cider efforts, one of which was on Thomas Jefferson and the other on Henry Clay. He himself said: "I am not accustomed to deal in eulogies." I have often thought that he did not care anything for men, thought that he looked through them for, or at, the principle behind them, and of which they were the representative. He worshiped principle, laws.

You once sent me a bitter invective said to be spoken by Lincoln to one Duff Green, a Southern nullifier and free trader, who had spoken to L. harshly about the war and its cruelties. The invective will be found, as you told me, in Belford's magazine. Now from the above, my friend Jesse, do you not see that the Belford piece is an absurdity, "a bald lie made out of whole cloth"? So are such invectives said to be from Lincoln. Another invective said to be pronounced by L. against an African slave-driver will be found in Holland's *romantic* Life of L.

at pages 433–34. This is all mere "bosh, a lie." Again there is another piece, though not of the same kind as the above, to be found the *Independent*, year 1859–60, New York. The article was written by a Mr. *Gulliver* for the New York *Independent*. Gulliver, eh! I counted nine or more barefaced errors in the article. Gulliver said that Lincoln opened to him his methods of education in a free and easy style. Jesse, I could pick out a hundred, if not a thousand, such things as the above now and then floating around in the newspapers. See, I have purposely written to you this, so that, if you need it, which I do not think you do, you can be on your guard as to the correctness of what you hear and read.

If Lincoln's limited fatalism leads to the banishment of malice, causes freedom from malice and vindictiveness, to his broad and living charity for the foibles of his fellow-man, and to his general love for all men of all races and all religions, and to his nobility of *thought and deed*, then the race had better adopt a limited fatalism as theory and practice of its daily life, rather than the so-called Christianity.

Jesse, I should like to know what you are doing about our Life of L. and what you intend to do about it in the future, as well as what you have done since the first edition of the Life published by B., C. & Co., but I know that you will not answer. I shall not ask any questions, but shut my eyes and say: "Good Lord, help me to see."

FRIEND HERNDON.

Springfield, Ill., February 27, 1891 [1]

Friend Bartlett:

Your very kind letter of the 18th *inst.* was duly received and is now in my hand. I thank you for your good wishes. Pay or no pay, as to my book, I shall give to the world the facts of Lincoln's life, truly, faithfully, and honestly. The great future can then write its own book and be paid therefor. The world moves in its own way and in its own time. . . .

Today I have written to Mr. Weik at Greencastle, Indiana, my partner in the book business, requesting him to send you the photos which you speak of. The others, including the portfolio, I have and

---

[1] A notation at the head reads: "Last letter from Mr. Herndon. He died March 1, 1891."

will send you in a short time. I live in the country six miles north of the city and do not feel well enough right now to get out and attend to your business—rough and muddy roads too, to crawl over. I do not wish to risk the business in other hands.

To help you somewhat, I hope, in your conceptions, ideas, about Mr. Lincoln, let me say to you that he had a double consciousness, if not a treble consciousness. First, he was a terribly gloomy, sad man at times. Secondly, he was at times full of humor, "jokey," witty, happy. Gloom and sadness were his predominant state. Thirdly, at times he was neither sad nor humorous, but was simply in a pleasant mood, i.e., he was not in a gloomy nor a mirthful fit, was kindly, thoughtful, not serious even—a state of thought and good feelings united for the moment. This state appeared in him when in a pleasant conversation with friends. This last state was not of long duration. Lincoln was a curious, mysterious, quite an incomprehensible man. Do not think that I exaggerate. These states, double or treble, are the causes why the photos are different a little as to likeness. The moment Lincoln took his seat at the photo machine and looked down the barrel of it, he became sad, rather serious, as all business with him was serious, life included. . . . You may show this short and hasty note to those who visit you when you get the photos, if you wish and think it will keep them.

Your friend,
W. H. HERNDON.

Part Two

EVIDENCES

1. *Letters to Herndon*

FROM HORACE WHITE

Tribune Office, Chicago, Ill., May 17, 1865.

Dear Sir:

Your letter of the 15th *instant* is received. The apostrophe to the Declaration of Independence, to which you refer, was written by myself from a mind recollection of Mr. Lincoln's speech at Beardstown, August 12, 1858. On the day following the delivery of the speech, as Mr. Lincoln and myself were proceeding by steamer from Beardstown to Havana, I said to him that I had been greatly impressed by his concluding remarks of the day previous, and that, if he would write them out for me, I felt confident their publication would be highly beneficial to our cause as well as honorable to his own fame. He replied that he had but a faint recollection of any portion of the speech, that, like all his campaign speeches, it was necessarily extemporaneous, and that its good or bad effect depended upon the inspiration of the moment. He added that I had probably overestimated the value of the remarks referred to. In reply to my question whether he had any objection to my writing them out from memory and putting them in form of a verbatim report, he said: "None at all." I accordingly did so. I felt confident—then, and I feel equally assured now—that I transcribed the peroration with absolute fidelity as to ideas, and with commendable fidelity as to language. I certainly aimed to reproduce his exact words, and my recollection of the passage as spoken was very clear. After I had finished writing, I read it to Mr. Lincoln. When I had finished the reading, he said: "Well, those are my views, and if I said anything on the subject, I must have said substantially that, but not nearly so well as that is said." I remember this remark quite distinctly, and if the old steamer *Editor* is still in existence, I could show the place where we were sitting. Having secured his assent to the publication I forwarded it to our paper, but inasmuch as my report of the Beardstown meeting had been already mailed, I incorporated the remarks on the Declaration of Independence into my letter from Lewistown two or three days subsequently.

Although a matter of little moment, I have given you the facts thus in detail because you seem specially interested in it. Looking at the passage now, I discover that it is not exactly in Mr. Lincoln's style, which I deem unfortunate, as it fails to convey the tremendous *directness* which

271

he always gave to his utterances on those occasions when he rose to impassioned eloquence. And I will say here that, in such moments, I have never heard his equal, and I believe I have listened at times to nearly all the public speakers of considerable reputation in this country. I cannot conceive that Patrick Henry, Mirabeau, or Vergniaud ever surpassed him on those occasions when his great soul was inspired with the thought of human rights and Divine justice. I presume that your suspicions in regard to the passage on the Declaration of Independence have been aroused by noticing a slight aberration from his style, as I do not remember ever having related these facts before, although they have often recurred to me as I have seen the peroration resuscitated again and again, and published (with good effect, I trust) in the newspapers of this country and England.

In regard to the other topic in your letter I can only say that I accompanied Mr. Lincoln almost constantly during the memorable campaign of 1858, that I had the pleasure of hearing nearly all his speeches —those which were published and those which were not—and I am sure that I never heard him say anything of the sort attributed to him by Bishop Simpson. I might add that it seems totally unlike him. My acquaintance with Mr. Lincoln commenced in 1854, and continued, with frequent meeting, until his death, and I certainly should not hesitate to pronounce Bishop Simpson's citation an entire mistake.

Very sincerely your friend & obedient servant,

HORACE WHITE.

FROM HORACE WHITE

Office of Daily Tribune, Chicago, Ill., May 22, 1865.

Dear Sir:

Yours of the 20th is received. You can act upon your own discretion as to using the matter which I communicated to you, or my name in connection with it. I care nothing about it.

I think you are peculiarly qualified, by long and intimate association with Mr. Lincoln, by knowledge and appreciation of his character, and sympathy with his personal, professional, and political aims in life, to be his biographer. You were perhaps more nearly *en rapport* with him than any other. I trust you will not put off the task which you have proposed to yourself until others less informed, or not informed at all, shall have distorted him. I would not recommend undue haste, but, considering the uncertainty of life, I would remark that you cannot employ your time more profitably to others (however it may be to yourself), than in pushing your task to completion with reasonable diligence.

This reminds me that I was applied to the other day by Dr. Holland of Springfield, Massachusetts, to write something for a biography of Mr. L. which he is preparing. His proposition to me was that I should send him as much as I could prepare in two or three hours concerning the campaign of 1858. I remarked to him that I thought you were preparing a biography and recommended him to go and see you, and he promised to do so.

Yours truly,
HORACE WHITE.

FROM JOHN HILL

Petersburg, Ill., June 6, 1865.

Dear Sir:

Yours of yesterday is at hand. I will be more prompt this time.

Miss Ann Rutledge died within a few days of September 1, 1835, *certain.* Lincoln bore up under it very well until some days afterwards a heavy rain fell, which unnerved him and—(the balance you know). As to the Lincoln and Smoot story, I know it to be true as it was told me by Mr. Lincoln himself, and I afterwards told Mr. Smoot of it and he remembered it. I remember Lincoln's words, but will see Smoot, and then give it to you. Whatever he says is as true as the word of man. Enclosed I send the printed slip, I published it in 1862. Every item in it I believe to have been true except in relation to keeping a stallion. I made good inquiry before writing and think I arrived at the truth. The order of succession may not be technically true.

As to keeping a stallion, the origin of this was that old Joe Walkins (now dead) kept a horse at Salem, and Lincoln requested him that, whenever a mare came, he would be sure to let him know it as he wanted to *see it.* Walkins did so, and Lincoln always attended, etc.—I have this from W. G. Greene and others as the truth. Mother informs me that when James Short arrives she will be able to give you more information than any or all the men in the county if his memory serves him well.

Should I have anything of interest I will advise you. I will hunt up the books Lincoln kept for Father, etc. He (L.) was Postmaster at Salem a short time.

Yours truly,
JOHN HILL.

FROM DENNIS F. HANKS

Sanitary Fair, Chicago, Ill., June 13, 1865.

Dear Sir:

I received your letter dated the [undeciphered], asking eight or ten interrogatories. I take great pleasure in answering it, question by question as each is put and in the order asked. The ancestors of Mr. Lincoln came from England about the year 1650. They first settled in Buckingham County in the State of Virginia and not in Pennsylvania as stated in Abraham Lincoln's biographies. The ancestors of the Lincoln family were Scotch English. Two men came over from England about 1650— one of these brothers was named Mordecai Lincoln and the other Thomas Lincoln, from whom the descendants derived their nature and their name. All died in Virginia. These two men were ironside Baptists. There was one of the children of these men who was named Mordecai—the son of Thomas—I know none of the children of Mordecai. I think that this Mordecai was the great-great-grandfather of President Lincoln. He was born in Virginia and died about 1700. Mordecai Lincoln was the grandfather of Abraham Lincoln, Mordecai Lincoln was the great-grandfather of Abraham Lincoln. He was born in the State of Virginia. Abraham Lincoln, the son of Mordecai, came with his family from Virginia to Kentucky in about 1780 among the pioneers of Daniel Boone. He, Mordecai, died in Virginia. Mordecai was the father of Abraham's grandfather. Mordecai had six children, four boys and two girls. The only one of his, Mordecai's, sons I now remember was Abraham Lincoln, who was the grandfather of Abraham and the father of Thomas. He was killed by the Indians near Booneville, Kentucky, in ―― County. . . . Abraham Lincoln, the grandfather of Abraham the President, had three sons—Mordecai and Abraham and Thomas Lincoln, the last being the father of Abraham. All these sons and daughters scattered and went, some to Kentucky, some to North Carolina, Tennessee, Indiana, and Illinois. The Hanks family, of which I am one, was not connected with the Lincoln family till about 1808. Thomas Lincoln, Abraham's father, was born in the State of Virginia on the Roanoke. About 1775. Thomas Lincoln was six years old when his father was killed by the Indians. I wish to state one fact here about the killing of Thomas Lincoln, Abraham's grandfather. In Kentucky all men had to clear out their own fields, cut down the trees, split them into rails, etc., and in putting on the last rail, the eighth on the fence, one Indian who had secreted himself shot Thomas Lincoln. Then the

Indian ran out from his hiding place and caught Thomas, the father of
Abraham; Mordecai, the oldest brother of Thomas and uncle of Abraham,
jumped over the fence, ran to the post, shot the Indian through the pivot
holes of the post, the Indian dropped Thomas, ran, and was followed by
the blood the next day and found dead. In the flight he threw his gun in
a tree top which was found. Mordecai said the Indian had a silver half-
moon trinket on his breast at the time he drew his "bead" on the Indian,
that silver being the mark he shot at. He said it was the prettiest mark
he held a rifle on. So remains now of old Thomas Lincoln's children, boys,
three—Mordecai, Thomas, and Silas. The children of Mordecai came to
Sangamon; the children of Silas scattered—some in Kentucky, some in
Tennessee, some in North Carolina—and Thomas Lincoln came to Indiana.
There is Thomas Lincoln, Abraham's father, a young man; he, Thomas,
at the age of twenty-five was married to Nancy Sparrow, not Hanks as
stated in the biographies of the day. Nancy Sparrow, Abraham's mother,
was the child of Henry Sparrow. Henry Sparrow's wife was Lucy Hanks,
Abraham's [mother's] mother. The stories going about, charging wrong
or indecency, prostitution, in any of the above families is false and only
got up by base political enemies and traitors to injure A. Lincoln's reputation, name, and fame. Thomas Lincoln, Abraham's [father], was married to Nancy Sparrow about the year 1808 in Hardin County and State
of Kentucky. Nancy Sparrow, the child of Henry Sparrow, married
Thomas Lincoln when she was about twenty years of age; she was born
in Mercer County, Kentucky. Thomas Lincoln was born in Virginia.
Thomas Lincoln, the father of Abraham, owned about thirty acres in
Hardin County, on a little creek called Knob Creek which empties into
the Rolling Fork. He owned the land in fee simple. After the marriage of
Thomas Lincoln and Nancy Sparrow, say in three or four years, Abraham
was born at that place. The cabin was a double one, with a passage or
entry between. About the year 1813 or '14, as the volunteers of the War
of 1812 were returning home, they came by Lincoln's house and he fed
and cared for them by companies, by strings of them. I was a little boy
at that time, Abraham was a little child, and Sarah, his sister and senior
by two or three years, was then likewise living and a little girl. They had
no other children—cause, a private matter. It is said in the biographies
that Mr. Lincoln left the State of Kentucky because and only because
slavery was there. This is untrue. He moved off to better his condition,
to a place where he could buy land for his children and others at $1.25
per acre; slavery did not operate on him. I know too well this whole
matter. Mrs. Lincoln, Abraham's mother, was five feet eight inches high,

spare made, affectionate—the most affectionate I ever saw—never knew her to be out of temper, and thought strong of it. She seemed to be immovably calm; she was keen, shrewd, smart, and I do say highly intellectual by nature. Her memory was strong, her perception was quick, her judgment was acute almost. She was spiritually and ideally inclined, not dull, not material, not heavy in thought, feeling, or action. Her hair was dark hair, eyes bluish green—keen and loving. Her weight was one hundred thirty. Thomas Lincoln, Abraham's father, was five feet ten inches high, very stoutly built, and weighed 196 pounds; his hair dark, his eyes hazel. He was a man of great strength and courage, not one bit of cowardice about him. He could carry fatigue for any length of time, was a man of uncommon endurance. Mr. Lincoln's friends thought him the best man in Kentucky, and others thought that a man by the name of Hardin was a better man—so the two men through the influence of their friends met at a tavern in Harrodsburg, Kentucky. There the two men had a long and tedious fight and Lincoln whipped Hardin without a scratch. They did not fight from anger or malice but to try who was the strongest man, to try manhood. These two men were great good friends ever after. Thomas Lincoln, the father of Abraham, could beat his son telling a story, cracking a joke. Mr. Thomas Lincoln was a good, clean, social, truthful, and honest man, loving like his wife everything and everybody. He was a man who took the world easy, did not possess much envy. He never thought that gold was God and the same idea runs through his family. One day when Lincoln's mother was weaving in a little shed, Abe came in and quizzically asked his good mother who was the father of Zebedee's children; she saw the drift and laughed, saying: "Get out of here, you nasty little pup, you"; he saw he had got his mother and ran off laughing. About Abe's early education and his sister's education, let me say this: Their mother first learned them ABC's. . . . She learned them out of Webster's old spelling book; it belonged to me and cost in those days 75¢, it being covered with calfskin or suchlike covering. I taught Abe his first lesson in spelling, reading, and writing. I taught Abe to write with a buzzard's quill which I killed with a rifle and, having made a pen, put Abe's hand in mine and moving his fingers by my hand to give him the idea of how to write. We had no geese then, for the country was a forest. I tried to kill an eagle but it was too smart; wanted to learn Abe to write with that. Lincoln's mother learned him to read the Bible, study it and the stories in it and all that was moral and affectionate in it, repeating it to Abe and his sister when very young. Lincoln was often and much moved by the stories. This Bible was bought in Philadelphia about 1801 by my father and mother and was mine when Abe was taught to read in it. It is now burned together with all property, deeds, family and other records. This fire took place in Charleston, Coles County, Illinois, December 5, 1864; lost all I have; my wife died December 18, 1864. I was born in Hardin County, Kentucky, in 1799, May 15, on Nolan Creek near Elizabethtown. I was ten years older than Abraham and knew him intimately and well from the day of his birth to 1830; I was the second man who touched Lincoln after his birth, a custom in Kentucky then of running to greet the newborn babe. A man by the name of Hazel helped to teach Abraham his ABC, spelling, reading, and writing, etc. Lincoln went to school about three months with his sister, all the education he had in Kentucky. Parson Elkin, a preacher of the old Baptist religion, came to Mr. Thomas Lincoln and frequently preached in that neighborhood.

At about the year 1818 Thomas Lincoln, the father of Abraham, had a notion in his head: formed a determination to sell out his place and move to Indiana, then a new State, where he could buy land as said before at $1.25 per. He sold out to [undeciphered]. Mr. Lincoln got $300 and took it, the $300, in whisky. The thirty-acre farm in Kentucky was as knotty, knobby as a piece of land could be, with deep hollows, ravines, cedar trees covering the parts, knolls, knobs as thick as trees could grow. Lincoln's house was in a hollow of a high, tall, and peaky hill and boarded with cedar. Stood up against the sky all around. Mr. Lincoln as stated before sold his farm for whisky. He cut down trees, made a kind of flatboat out of yellow poplar. He made the boat on the Rolling Fork at the mouth of Knob Creek, Hardin County, Kentucky, loaded his household furniture, his tools, whisky, and other effects, including pots, vessels, rifles, etc., etc., on the boat. He took no dogs, chickens, cats, geese, or other domestic animals. He floated on awhile down the Rolling Fork and upset and lost the most of the tools, etc., and some of his whisky. He went along by himself, not taking his family. From the Rolling Fork he ran into the Beach Fork and thence into the great Ohio. He landed at Thompson's Ferry at Posey's house or farm. He started out from the ferry in search of a place and found one and located it by making blazes, brush heaps, etc., to make a location, which he afterwards bought at $2.00 per acre, purchased it under the $2.00 act. This was an eighty-acre tract, and Mr. Lincoln, not being able to pay for it, lost his $80, which he paid to the government and which the government kept and has today. When he had cornered the land, blazed it off, marked the boundaries, he proceeded on horseback, with his own food and his horse's fodder behind him, to Vincennes, where he paid the $2.00 per acre as stated before. Mr. Lincoln never owned the land, more than a kind of pre-emption right, and sold it when he moved to Illinois. I fared like him in all these particulars. He then returned to the State of Kentucky from Spencer County, Indiana, then Perry County, since divided as Hardin County, Kentucky, was, as Sangamon County. From the old homestead in Kentucky, Hardin, now LaRue County, Thomas Lincoln, Nancy—father and mother of Sarah and Abe—the two children, and two feather beds, clothing, etc., mounted two horses and went back to Spencer County, then Perry County, Indiana, where said land was located on a little creek called Pigeon Creek, about north of the Ohio and about seventy miles northwest of Hardin County, Kentucky, and across and north of the Ohio. They had no wagons, no dogs, cats, hogs, cows, chickens, or suchlike domestic animals. Abe was at this time seven years of age. Abe read no books in Kentucky. Abe was a good boy, an affectionate one, a boy who loved his father and mother dearly and well, always minding them well. Sometimes Abe was a little rude. When strangers would ride along and up to his father's fence, Abe always, through pride and to tease his father, would be sure to ask the stranger the first question, for which his father would sometimes knock him a rod. Abe was then a rude and forward boy. Abe, when whipped by his father, never balked, but dropped a kind of silent unwelcome tear, as evidence of his sensations or other feelings. The family landed at Thompson's Ferry on the Ohio and over the Kentucky side, crossed the Ohio, and landed at Posey's farm on the Indiana side. Hence seventeen miles northwest of the ferry. I went myself with them backwards and forwards to Indiana and back to Kentucky and back to Indiana, and know the story and all the facts well. We all started from Kentucky in September 1818 and was three or four days to the ferry and one day from the ferry out to the place of location. Here they stopped, camped, erected a little two-face camp open in front, serving a momentary purpose. Lincoln saw a wild turkey near the camp on the second day after landing, and Mrs. Lincoln, Abe's good mother, loaded the gun. Abe poked the gun through the crack of the camp and accidentally killed one, which he brought to the camp house. Thomas Lincoln then went on getting trees for the logs of his house, cutting down the brush and underwood, Indiana then being a wilderness and wholly a timberous country. I assisted him to do this, to cut timber, haul logs, etc., and helped him erect his log cabin, a camp, one story high, just high enough to stand under, no higher. This took only one day. Abe could do little jobs, such as carry water, go to the springs, branches, etc., by digging for water which was got by hills. This was a temporary affair. This was in 1818. We, Lincoln's family, including Sally and Abe and myself, slept and lodged in this cabin all winter and till next spring. We in the winter and spring cut down brush, underwood, trees, cleared ground, made a field of about six acres, on which we raised our crops. We all hunted pretty much all the time, especially so when we got tired of work, which was very often, I will assure you. We did not have to go more than four or five hundred yards to kill deer, turkeys, and other wild game. We found bee trees all over the forests. Wild game and meat were our food. We ate no wild locust, like John the Baptist. We had to go to the Ohio River seventeen miles to mill, and when we got there the mill was a poor concern; it was a little bit of hand horse mill, the ground meal of which a hand could eat as fast as it was ground. Yet this was a Godsend. The mill was close to Posey's. The country was wild, full of game, dense with vegetation, swampy. We could track a bear, deer, wolf, or Indian for miles through the wild matted pea vines. Indians, wild bears, wolves, deers, were plenty. We had no trouble with the Indians in Indiana; they soon left westward. In the fall and winter of 1819–20 we commenced to cut the trees, clear out the brush and underwoods and forest for our new grand old log cabin, which we erected that winter; it was one story, eighteen by twenty feet, no passage, one window, no glass in it. The lights were made from the leaf coming off from the hog's fat. This was good and mellow light and lasted well. The house was sufficiently high to make a kind of bedroom overhead, a loft. This was approached by a kind of ladder made by boring holes in the logs forming [undeciphered] one side of the house, and this peg over peg we climbed aloft, the pegs creaking and screeching as we went. Here were the beds; the floor of the loft was clapboards, and the beds lay on this. Here I and Abe slept, and I was married there to Abe's stepsister, Miss Elizabeth Johnston, not Johnson. During this fall Mrs. Lincoln was taken sick with what is known as the milk sickness; she struggled on day by day, a good Christian woman, and died on the seventh day after she was taken sick. Abe and his sister did some work, little jobs, errands, and light work. There was no physician nearer than thirty-five miles. She knew she was going to die and called the children to her dying side and told them to be good and kind to their father, to one another, and to the world, expressing a hope that they might live as they had been taught by her to love men, love, reverence, and worship God. Here in this rude house, of the milk sickness, died one of the very best women in the whole race, known for kindness, tenderness, charity, and love to the world. Mrs. Lincoln always taught Abe goodness, kindness, read the good Bible to him, taught him to read and to spell, taught him sweetness and benevolence as well. From this up to 1821 Mr. Lincoln lived single, Sarah cooking for us, she then being about fourteen years of age. We still kept up hunting and farming it. Mr. Lincoln, Abe's father, was a cabinet-maker and house-joiner, etc.; he worked at this trade in the winter at odd times, farming it in the summer. We always hunted; it made no difference what came, for we more or less depended on it for a living, nay for life. We had not been long at the log cabin before we got the usual domestic animals, known to civilization. These were driven out from near the Ohio River or hauled in a cart pulled by one yoke of oxen. Mrs. Lincoln was buried about one-fourth of a mile from the log cabin and the Baptist Church; the pastor was Lamon. Abraham learned to write so that we could understand it in 1821. David Elkin of Hardin County, Kentucky, called Parson Elkin, whose name has been mentioned before, paid a visit. I do not think Elkin came at the solicitation and letter writing of Abe, but came of his own accord or through the solicitation of the church to which Mr. Lincoln belonged. Abe was now twelve years old. Elkin came over to Indiana in about one year after the death of Mrs. Elkin, and preached a funeral sermon on the death of Mrs. Lincoln. Parson Elkin was a good, true man and the best preacher and finest orator I ever heard. I have heard his words distinctly and clearly one-fourth of a mile. Some little time before this funeral service he, Thomas Lincoln, went to Kentucky and married Johnston, whose maiden name was Bush. When Thomas Lincoln married her, she had three children, two daughters and one son. The family came to Indiana with their stepfather and their mother. There was now five children in the family, Sarah and Abe Lincoln, Elizabeth, John D., and Mathilda Johnston. I married Elizabeth. I was just twenty-one; she was fifteen. Thomas Lincoln now hurried his farming, his calling and business, always remember hunting. Now at this time Abe was getting hungry for books, reading everything he could lay his hands on. The marriage of Thomas Lincoln and the widow Johnston was in 1821, Abraham being now twelve years old. Webster's old spelling book, the Life of Henry Clay, *Robinson Crusoe,* Weems's Life of Washington, Æsop's fables, Bunyan's *Pilgrim's Progress*—I do not say that Lincoln read these books just then, but he did between this time and 1825. He was a constant and I may say stubborn reader, his father having sometimes to slash him for neglecting his work by reading. Mr. Lincoln, Abe's father, often said: "I had to pull the old sow up to the trough," when speaking of Abe's reading and how he got to it then; and now he had to pull her away. From the time of the marriage of Thomas Lincoln and Mrs. Johnston, Mrs. Lincoln proved an excellent stepmother. When she came into Indiana, Abe and his sister was wild, ragged, and dirty. Mrs. Lincoln had been raised in Elizabethtown in somewhat a high life; she soaped, rubbed, and washed the children clean, so that they looked pretty, neat, well, and clean. She sewed and mended their clothes, and the children once more looked human as their own good mother left them. Thomas Lincoln and Mrs. Lincoln never had any children, accident and nature stopping things short. From 1820 to 1825 Mr. Lincoln and Mrs. Lincoln each worked ahead at their own business: Thomas at farming, cabinet-making, hunting; she at cooking, washing, sewing, weaving, etc., etc. About the year 1825 or 1826 Abe borrowed, of Josiah Crawford, Ramsey's Life of Washington, which got spoiled as specified generally in the President's life and paid as therein described: he pulled fodder at 25¢ per day to pay for it. He worked three or four days. Abe was then growing to be a man and about fifteen or sixteen years of age. He was then just the same boy in every particular that he subsequently exhibited to the world from 1831 to the time of his death. At this early age he was more humorous than in after life, full of fun, wit, humor, and if he ever got a new story, new book, a new fact or idea, he never forgot it. He was honest, faithful, loving truth, speaking it at all times, and never flinching therefrom. Physically he was a stout, powerful boy, fat, round, plump, and well made as well as proportioned. This continued to be so up to the time he landed in Salem, Sangamon County. In 1825 or 1826 he then exhibited a love for poetry and wrote a piece of humorous rhyme on his friend Josiah Crawford that made all the neighbors, Crawford included, burst their sides with laughter. I had it; was lost in the fire. He was humorous, funny, witty, and good-humored at all times. Sarah married a man Aaron Grigsby; she married him in 1822 and died in about twelve months in childbirth. About 1826 and 7, myself and Abe went down to the Ohio and cut cordwood at 25¢ per cord and bought stuff to make each a shirt. We were proud of this. It must have been about this time that Abe got kicked by a horse in the mill, and who did not speak for several hours and when he did speak, he ended the sentence which he commenced to the horse, as I am well informed and believe. From the last period 1825–26 and 7, Lincoln was constantly reading, writing, cipher[ing] a little in Pike's Arithmetic. He excelled any boy I ever saw, putting his opportunities into conversation. He then some[how] had or got Barclay's English Dictionary, a part of which I have now and which can be seen now at my house and which I am to give to W. H. Herndon of the city of Springfield. During these years the sports of Mr. Lincoln were hunting, shooting squirrels, jumping, wrestling, playing ball, throwing the mall overhead. The story about his carrying home a drunken man is not true as I think or recollect. He was good enough and tender enough and kind enough to have saved any man from evil, wrong, difficulties, or damnation. Let him claim nothing but what is true. Truth and justice and mankind will make him the great of the world; he needs no fictions to back him. Lincoln sometimes attempted to sing but always failed, but while this is true he was harmony and time and sound. He loved such music as he knew the words of. He was a tricky man and sometimes when he went to log-house raising, corn shucking, and suchlike things he would say to himself and sometimes to others: "I don't want these fellows to work any more," and instantly he would commence his pranks, tricks, jokes, stories, and sure enough all would stop, gather around Abe, and listen, sometimes crying and sometimes bursting their sides with laughter. He sometimes would mount a stump, chair, or box and make speeches— stories and stories, anecdotes and suchlike things; he never failed here. At this time Abe was somewhat [undeciphered] he was now as well as before a kind of forward boy and sometimes forward too when he got stubborn; his nature went an entire revolution. One thing is true of him—always was up to 1830 when our intimacy ended, because he went to Sangamon and I went to Coles County—he was ambitious and determined, and when he attempted to excel man or boy his whole soul and his energies were bent on doing it, and he in this generally almost always accomplished his ends. From these years 1826 and '27 what has been said of other years is applicable up to 1830—working, chopping, toiling, woman, child, and man. The plays and sports were the same. In 1829 (March) Thomas Lincoln moved from Spencer County, Indiana, and landed in Macon County, Illinois, ten miles west of Decatur. In that spring and summer the log cabin which I now have on exhibition at the Sanitary Fair in Chicago was erected. Lincoln helped cut the logs; so did John Hanks. Abe hauled them and I hewed them all and raised it the next day we raised the cabin. Abraham and his neighbors had a mall railing party 1830, and he and they then split the rails to fence the ten acres of land which was done. In the spring and summer of 1830 the ten acres of land were broken up into the place. This was on the north fork of Sangamon River in Mercer County, Illinois. Lincoln was twenty years of [age] when he left Indiana, not twenty-one—as said in the books. In the fall of 1830 he went down the Sangamon, he then being twenty-one years of age, with John Hanks in a boat of some kind.

I now have told you all I recollect and think worthy of being told. I hope this will put history right, as I have taken time to reflect and to refresh my memory by conversations, times of well-authenticated date, by records, friends, and papers. All of which I do hereby certify to be true in substance, time, and fact, knowing what is said to be true personally as I was an actor pretty much all my life in the scene.

Your friend,

D. F. HANKS.

FROM JOHN HILL

Petersburg, Ill., June 27, 1865.

Dear Sir:

Yours of 21st came duly to hand. Have awaited an opportunity to see Capt. Wright in relation to Matheny's speech before replying.

The article in the *Missouri Republican* in relation to Mr. Matheny's speech at this place in 1856 was written by Capt. Wright. Also an article in the *Index* of corresponding date. The articles excited considerable sensation at the time. They were not verbatim but substantially correct. I think I remember that before the publication of the article in the *Index* it was submitted to Matheny, and he endorsed the report of his remarks. The reports in the two papers very nearly correspond, and, I think, aside from party coloring, are correct in every particular.

As to Mr. Lincoln's book on Infidelity, I gave you all my knowledge verbally. Since my early childhood I remember to have heard it alluded to hundreds of times by different old settlers. Of late years I have heard less of it, as these old men have many of them passed away. I have a bitter remembrance of it by my father's connection with it. You know that there are always some few things that strike into the mind of a child at early age which time will never eradicate. This is one of the circumstances from which I date my earliest remembrance. It could not have been on account of Lincoln's position, as at the time I knew no more as to who he was than I did of the inhabitants of the Fiji Islands. When I heard of my father having morally compelled Mr. Lincoln to burn the book, on account of its infamy, etc., pointing to Voltaire, Paine, etc., the circumstance struck me so forcibly that I have never heard the words infidelity, Paine, or Voltaire since without thinking of it. My mother was strictly religious, and before hearing of this I had always thought my father to be averse to religion. I was so surprised that I suppose it made the deeper impression. As to date I do not know. It was in the winter time, as tradition says it was done in father's store, while there was fire in the stove, that there it was burned.

Your friend,

JOHN HILL.

FROM N. W. BRANDON

Petersburg, Ill., August 3, 1865.

Dear Sir:

On conversing with Mr. Short I have elicited the following additional facts in reference to Mr. Lincoln.

Mr. L. used to tell Mr. S. the following anecdote of himself. Once, when Mr. L. was surveying, he was put to bed, in the same room with two girls, the head of his bed being next to the foot of the girls' bed. In the night he commenced tickling the feet of one of the girls with his fingers. As she seemed to enjoy it as much as he did, he then tickled a little higher up, and as he would tickle higher, the girl would shove down lower, and the higher he tickled the lower she moved. Mr. L. would tell the story with evident enjoyment. He never told how the thing ended.

You can have the benefit of the above, even if your readers cannot.

Mr. S. says Mr. L. was, in Salem times, an habitual reader of the St. Louis *Republican* and the Sangamon *Journal*. He used to read a great deal, improving every opportunity, by day and by night. I never knew of his reading a novel. History and poetry and the newspapers constituted the most of his reading. Burns seemed to be his favorite. L. had a copy of *The American Military Biography,* which he read a great deal. He read aloud very often, and frequently assumed a lounging position when reading. He read very thoroughly, and had a most wonderful memory. Would distinctly remember almost everything he read. Used to sit up late of nights reading, and would recommence in the morning when he got up. He was not an unusually early riser, at least it was not considered early for country habits, though for the city it would be very early.

Mr. L. was very fond of honey. Whenever he went to S.'s house he invariably asked his wife for some bread and honey. And he liked a great deal of bee bread in it. He never touched liquor of any kind.

There was nothing of the joke about him. Whenever he went at anything he went at it to do it. Whenever he walked with me, he would keep me in a trot all the time. Always put things through in a hurry. Was a fast eater, though not a very hearty one. Didn't sleep very much as he always sat up late.

He didn't go to see the girls much. He didn't appear bashful, but it seemed as if he cared but little for them. Wasn't apt to take liberties with them, but would sometimes. He always liked lively, jovial company, where there was plenty of fun and no drunkenness, and would just as lief the company were all men as to have it a mixture of the sexes. He was very agreeable in company and everybody liked him. Was always full of life and of fun, always cheerful, always had a story to tell. Was very sociable and fond of visiting. Knew every man, woman, and child for miles around. Was very fond of children. Was fond of cats, would take and turn it on its back and talk to it for half an hour at a time. I never in my life saw him out of humor. He never got angry. Once when Major Hill was wrongly informed that Mr. L. had said something against his, H.'s, wife, the Major abused him a great deal for it, talking to Mr. L. very roughly and insultingly. Mr. L. kept his temper, denied having said anything against her, told the Major that he had a very high opinion of her, and that if he knew anything in the world against her, it was the fact of her being his wife.

Mr. L. was fond of wrestling, in which he excelled.

Renewing the offer of my poor services,

Yours truly,

N. W. BRANDON.

FROM S. A. CRAWFORD

January 4, 1866.

Dear Sir:

I received your letter of September 28, and also another of December 15.

I beg leave to be excused for not answering your first letter as I was very busy a-getting ready to start to Nelson County, Kentucky, to see about my father's estate, and as you did not say anything about us writing to you, we neglected, as we concluded that you had got all the information that you wanted. There was one thing that I did not think of telling you, when you were here; that was: the place you were sitting on when you were here was a plank that Abraham Lincoln whipsawed about the year 1830.

We moved to this county in 1824, and soon after became acquainted with the Lincoln family. When Abraham was a strap of a boy and his playmates would fall out with him, he would laugh and make rhymes and sing them, and tell the boys that he intended to be President yet. While other boys would quarrel, he would appear to be a peacemaker; and while others would romp and laugh, he would be engaged in the Arithmetic, or asking questions about some history, heard or read of.

First Chronicles of Reuben. (*Now there was a man in those days whose name was Reuben, and the same was very great in substance in horses and cattle and swine, and a very great household, and it came to pass that when the sons of Reuben grew up, that they were desirous of taking to themselves wives, and being too well known as to honor, in their own country, so they took to themselves a journey into a far country; and procured to themselves wives. And it came to pass that when they were about to make the return home, that they sent a messenger before them to bear the tidings to their parents; so, they inquired of the messengers, what their sons and their wives would come. So, they made a great feast and called all their kinsmen and neighbors in, and made great preparations; so, when the time drew near, they sent out two men to meet the grooms and their wives with a treat to welcome them and to accompany them; so, when they came near to the house of Reuben, their father, the messengers came on before them and gave a shout, and the whole multitude ran out with shouts of joy, and music playing on all kinds of instruments of music, some playing on harps, and some on viols, and some blowing on rams' horns, some casting dust and ashes toward Heaven; and amongst the rest Josiah blowing his bugle, making sound so great that it made the neighboring hills and valleys echo with the resounding acclamation; so when they had played and harped, sounded, till the grooms and brides approached the gate, the father, Reuben, met them and welcomed them in to his house, and the wedding dinner being now ready, they were all invited to sit down to dinner. Placing the bridegrooms and their wives at each end of the table, waiters were then appointed to carve and wait on the guests; so, when they had all eaten, and were full and merry, they went out and sang and played till evening, and when they had made an end of feasting and rejoicing, the multitude dispersed, each to his own home; the family then took seats with their waiters to converse awhile, at which time preparations were being made in an upper chamber for the brides to be first conveyed by the waiters to their beds; this being done, the waiters took the two brides upstairs to their beds, placing one in a bed at the right hand of the stairs and the other on the left. The waiters came down, and Nancy the mother inquired of the waiters, which of the brides was placed on the right hand and they told her. So, she gave directions to the waiters of the bridegrooms, and then they took the bridegrooms and placed them in the wrong beds, and came downstairs; but the mother being fearful that there might be a mistake, inquired again of the waiters and learning the fact, took the light and sprang upstairs, and running to one of the beds exclaimed: Reuben! you are in bed with Charles's wife! The young men, both being alarmed, sprang out of bed and ran with such violence against each other, that they came very near knocking each other down, which gave evidence to those below that the mistake was certain. They all came down and had a conversation about who had made the mistake, but it could not be decided.) So ended the chapter.*

I will tell you a joke about Joel and Mary; it is neither a joke or a story, for Reuben and Charles had married two girls, but Billy has married a boy.

> *The girls he had tried on every side*
> *But none could he get to agree;*
> *All was in vain, he went home again*
> *And since that, he is married to Natty.*
>
> *So Billy and Natty agreed very well;*
> *And mamma's well pleased at the match.*
> *The egg it is laid but Natty's afraid,*
> *The shell is so soft that it never will hatch.*
> *But Betsey, she said: "You cursed baldhead,*
> *My suitor you never can be;*
> *Besides, your low crotch proclaims you a botch*
> *And that never can answer for me."*

This memorized by Mrs. Elizabeth Crawford, an old blind lady, that can hardly see; written by her son and forwarded.

S. A. CRAWFORD.

FROM S. A. CRAWFORD

January 8, 1866.

Dear Sir:

I have done as you requested me to do. I have written all of the Chronicles of Reuben, and poetry that my old mother could memorize of Mr. Lincoln writing at the time he worked with her and father. At the time Mr. Lincoln wrote this, it appears that there was a little coolness existing between the two families. Mr. Lincoln not being invited to the great wedding feast, made use of a little of his novelty, in stating facts that did occur.

Reuben did go to bed with Charles's wife, and Charles to bed with Reuben's wife. I took the Reuben's Chronicles to Gentryville and read them in public, R. D. Grigsby, being present, got very mad over it, but Natty, who married Billy, being present, affirmed the same to be false.

I am very anxious for one of the books of your great intended work.

Yours truly,
S. A. CRAWFORD.

FROM J. GILLESPIE

Edwardsville, January 31, 1866.

Dear Sir:

Yours enclosing a sketch of your lecture on the character of Mr. Lincoln is received and I must say that I think you have delineated him with great truth and force. You wish me to give you my views and recollections respecting him. Ever since his death I have been endeavoring to recall to mind his prominent twists of character and I must confess that the task is no easy one. Mr. Lincoln had but few peculiarities and hardly an eccentricity. His mind was made up of the traits which belong to mankind generally. He was a remarkably temperate man, eschewing every indulgence, not so much, as it seemed to me, from principle as from a want of appetites. I never heard him declaim against the use of tobacco or other stimulants although he never indulged in them. He was genial but not very sociable. He did not seek company, but when he was in it, he was the most entertaining person I ever knew. He was once pressed into service to entertain Mr. Van Buren at Rochester in your county and he succeeded to admiration. Mr. Lincoln was ambitious but not very aspiring. He was anxious to be in Congress, but I think he never aspired to anything higher until the prospect for the Presidency burst upon him. I am very sure that Mr. Lincoln was not aware of his own abilities or standing and that he never expected to attain a very marked distinction. In 1858 he made a speech in this place and had an appointment for one next day at Greenville. I took him out in my buggy. On the way the principal subject of conversation was the canvass he was conducting with Mr. Douglas. Knowing Lincoln's power of using anecdotes, I asked why he did not employ them in the discussion. He replied that he thought the occasion was too grave and serious. He said that the principal complaint he had to make against Mr. Douglas was his continual assumption of superiority on account of his elevated position. Mr. Lincoln's idea was that in the discussion of great questions nothing adventitious should be lugged in as a makeweight. That was contrary to his notions of fairness. His love of wealth was very weak. I asked him on the trip above spoken of how much land he owned. He said that the house and lot he lived on and one forty-acre tract was all the real estate he owned and that he got the forty for his services in the Black Hawk War. I inquired why he never speculated in land, and pointed to a tract that I had located with a land warrant which cost me ninety cents an acre. He said he had no capacity whatever for speculation and never attempted it. All the use Mr. Lincoln had for wealth was to enable him to appear respectable. He never hoarded nor wasted but used money as he needed it and gave himself little or no concern about laying up. He was the most indulgent parent I ever knew. His children literally ran over him and he was powerless to withstand their importunities. He was remarkably tender of the feelings of others and never wantonly offended even the most despicable, although he was a man of great nerve when aroused. I have seen him on several occasions display great heroism when the circumstances seemed to demand it. He was very sensitive where he thought he had failed to come up to the expectations of his friends. I remember a case. He was pitted by the Whigs in 1840 to debate with Mr. Douglas, the Democratic champion. Lincoln did not come up to the requirements of the occasion. He was conscious of his failure and I never saw any man so much distressed. He begged to be permitted to try it again and was reluctantly indulged, and in the next effort he transcended our highest expectations. I never heard and never expect to hear such a triumphant vindication as he then gave of Whig measures on policy. He never often to my knowledge fell below himself. In religious matters Mr. Lincoln was *theoretically* a predestinarian. His stern logic and perhaps early bias led him to that result. He was never ashamed of the poverty and obscurity of his early life. He was thoroughly master of all the phases of frontier life and woodscraft, and his most amusing stories consisted of incidents in his boyish days amongst his country playfellows. He had a marvelous relish for everything of that sort and the happiest faculty of turning his numerous reminiscences to good account in illustration in after life. No man could tell a story as well as he could. He never missed the nib of an anecdote. He always maintained stoutly that the best stories originated with country boys and in the rural districts. He had great faith in the strong sense of country people and he gave them credit for greater intelligence than most men do. If he found an idea prevailing generally amongst them, he believed there was something in it, although it might not harmonize with science. He had great faith in the virtues of the *mad stone,* although he could give no reason for it and confessed that it looked like a superstition, but he said he found the people in the neighborhood of these stones fully impressed with a belief in their virtues from actual experiment and that was about as much as we could ever know of the properties of medicine. Mr. Lincoln had more respect for and confidence in the masses than any statesman this country has ever produced. He told me in the spring of 1864 that the people were greatly ahead of the politicians in their effort for and confidence in putting down the rebellion. He said the government had been driven by the public voice into the employment of means and the adoption of measures for carrying on the war which they would not have dared to put into practice without such backing. He prized the suggestions of the unsophisticated people more than what was called statecraft or political wisdom. He really believed that the voice of the People in our emergency was next thing to the voice of God. He said he had no doubt whatever of our success in overthrowing the rebellion at the right time. God, he said, was with us and the people were behaving so nobly that all doubt had been removed from his mind as to our ultimate success. The army and the navy, he said, were in the right trim and in the right hands. He firmly believed that no people in ancient or modern times had evinced as much patriotism or such a self-sacrificing spirit as the loyal people of the United States. But Mr. Lincoln's love of justice and fair play was his predominating trait. I have often listened to him when I thought he would certainly state his case out of court. It was not in his nature to assume or attempt to bolster up a false position. He would abandon his case first. He did so in the case of Buckmaster for the use of Denham *vs.* Burns and Arthur in our Supreme Court in which I happened to be opposed to him. Another gentleman less fastidious took Mr. Lincoln's place and joined the case. In 1856 Mr. Lincoln had set his heart upon the United States Senate. There was a majority for the first time in the history of Illinois against the Democratic party in the Legislature. This result was mainly attributable to his efforts, and he was the first choice of all but five of the opposition members. I was a member and enthusiastically for Lincoln. We, his friends, regarded this as perhaps his last chance for that high position. There was danger, if we did not succeed in electing our man soon, that some of the members who had been elected as free-soilers would go over to Matteson and elect him. When the voting commenced to our amazement five of our men steadily refused to vote for Mr. Lincoln and threw their votes upon Judge Trumbull. After several ballots I went to Mr. Lincoln and asked him what he thought we ought to do. He said unhesitatingly: "You ought to drop me and go for Trumbull. That is the only way you can defeat Matteson." Judge Logan came up about that time and insisted on running Lincoln still, but the latter said: "If you do, you will lose both Trumbull and myself, and I think the cause in this case is to be preferred to men." We adopted his suggestion and turned upon Trumbull and elected him. Although it grieved us to the heart to give up Mr. Lincoln, this, I think, shows that Mr. Lincoln was capable of sinking himself for the cause in which he was engaged. Mr. Lincoln's sense of justice was intensely strong. It was to this mainly that his hatred of slavery may be attributed. He abhorred the institution. It was about the only public question on which he would become excited. I recall a meeting with him once at Shelbyville when he remarked that something must be done or slavery would overrun the whole country. He said there were about 600,000 non-slaveholding whites in Kentucky to about 33,000 slaveholders; that in the convention there recently held it was expected that the delegates would represent these classes about in proportion to their respective numbers, but when the convention assembled there was not a single representative of the non-slaveholding class. Everyone was in the interest of the slaveholders and, said he: "This thing is spreading like wildfire over the country. In a few years we will be ready to accept the institution in Illinois, and the whole country will adopt it." I asked him to what he attributed the change that was going on in public opinion. He said he had put that question to a Kentuckian shortly before, who answered by saying: "You might have any amount of land, money in your pocket, or bank stock, and while traveling around nobody would be any the wiser; but if you had a donkey trudging at your heels, everybody would see him and know that you owned slaves. It is the most glittering, ostentatious, and displaying property in the world; and now," says he, "if a young man goes courting, the only inquiry is how many Negroes he or she owns and not what other property they may have." The love for slave property was swallowing up every other mercenary passion. Its ownership betokened not only the possession of wealth but indicated the gentleman of leisure who was above and scorned labor. These things Mr. Lincoln regarded as highly seductive to the thoughtless and giddy-headed young men who looked upon work as vulgar and ungentlemanly. Mr. Lincoln was really excited and said with great earnestness that this spirit ought to be met and if possible checked. That slavery was a great and crying injustice, an enormous national crime, and that we could not expect to escape punishment for it. I asked him how he would proceed in his efforts to check the speed of slavery. He confessed that he did not see his way clearly. I think he made up his mind from that time that he would oppose slavery actively. I know that Mr. Lincoln always contended that no man had any right, other than mere brute force gave him, to a slave. He used to say that it was singular that the courts would hold that a man never lost his right to his property that had been stolen from him but that he instantly lost his right to himself if he was stolen. Mr. Lincoln always contended that the cheapest way of getting rid of slavery was for the nation to buy the slaves and set them free. As you say, Mr. Lincoln could hardly be considered a genius, a poet, or an inventor, but he had the qualities of a reformer. He endeavored to bring back things to the old landmarks but he never would have attempted to invent and compose new systems. He had boldness enough, when he found the building rocked and going to decay, to restore it to its original design, but not to contrive a new and distinct edifice. He believed that the framers of our government expected slavery to die out and adapted the system to that end but that their views were being frustrated by adventitious circumstances by which we were surrounded and the political ideas which had begun to take root just before the Revolution than to any superior intelligence or liberality on our part. He contended that we were more indebted to our government than it was to us, and that we were not entitled to greater credit for our liberality of sentiment on political questions than others equally liberal who were born and raised under less favorable auspices. Mr. Lincoln never, I think, studied history except in connection with politics; with the exception of the history of the Netherlands and of the revolutions of 1640 and 1688 in England and of our revolutionary struggle, he regarded it as of trifling value as teaching by example. Indeed he thought that history as generally written was altogether too unreliable. In this connection he alluded to the fact that General I. D. Henry, the most prominent figure in the Black Hawk War of 1832, was completely ignored by the historians. He also referred to the almost universal belief that a spirited passage at arms took place in Congress between Tristram Burgess and John Randolph when, as Mr. Lincoln said, he never believed they had been in Congress together.

The above is about all I can scrape up relating to Mr. Lincoln. If it is of any use to you, you are welcome to it.

Your friend,
J. GILLESPIE.

FROM ELIZABETH CRAWFORD

February 21, 1866.

Dear Sir:

Your letter of the 5th came to hand in due time, and we should have answered it sooner, but our business has been so that we could not conveniently have time. You wished me to tell you whether Abraham Lincoln ever made any pretensions of religion during his stay in this country. I never heard of his ever making any such pretensions. I don't think he ever did; though he seemed to be a well-wisher, he went to meeting sometimes, and was well behaved. You also wished to know what songs he used to sing. I can't remember many of them. He used to sing one that was called "John Anderson's Lamentation," and one that was called "William Riley," and one that was made about General Jackson and John Adams, at the time they were nominated for the Presidency; though I can't memorize but very little of any of them. He sang but very little when he was about the house; he was not noisy. As to his jests or jokes, I can't recollect, though he had a good many. I will give you as much of his favorite songs as I can memorize, as follows:

John Anderson's Lamentation

O sinners! poor sinners! take warning by me;
The fruits of transgressing, behold now and see;
My soul is tormented, my body confined;
My friends and dear children left weeping behind.

Much intoxication, my ruin has been;
And my dear companions have barbarously slain,
In yonder cold graveyard, her body doth lie,
Whilst I am condemned, and shortly must die.

Remember John Anderson's death and reform
Before Death overtakes you and vengeance comes on.
My grief's overwhelming, in God I must trust;
I am justly condemned, my sentence is just.

I am waiting the summons, in eternity to be hurled;
Whilst my poor little orphans are cast on the world.
I hope my kind neighbors their guardians will be;
And Heaven, kind Heaven, protect them and me.

Mr. Herndon, I have given you as much of the above song as I could memorize.

This was a favorite song of Abraham Lincoln's.

Now I will give you a line or two of the Jackson song, that he used to sing, and then I will have to close as my eyes are so weak that I can't see the lines on the paper.

Let auld acquaintance be forgot,
And never brought to mind,
And Jackson, he, our President;
And Adams, left behind.

Excuse bad writing,
ELIZABETH CRAWFORD.

From Elizabeth Crawford

May 3, 1866.

Dear Sir:

Your letter of April 19 has come to hand and I was glad to hear that you were well pleased with what I had written. You wish me to tell you the names of some of our wild woods flowers. There is the wild sweet william, wild pink, lady slipper, wild roses, butterfly weed, wild honeysuckle, blue flag, yellow flag, and there is a great many other kinds, that I can't recollect the names of at this time.

Now I will give you the names of some of the garden flowers that were cultivated in this country by the first settlers or nearly so, say in 1824–26 and on for several years, and some of them till this time. The sweet pink, the poppy, the marigold, the larkspur, the touch-me-not, the pretty-by-night, the lady-in-the-green, the sword lily, the flower bean, the holly-hock, the bachelor's button—these buttons the girls used to string and hang them up in their houses for an ornament; they were very pretty, as there were white ones and red ones. The roses, the sweet or damask rose, the pinny, the old maid's eyes, the velvet pink, the mullen pink, the garden sweet williams, the carolina pink.

You wish me to tell you the names of some of the trees that grew in Spencer County. The black oak, the white oak, the poplar, the dogwood, the hickory, the sweet gum, the maple, the redbud, ash, and many other kinds. I will give you a few more of the names: the willow, box elder, the plum, the crab apple, the elm, the catalpa—this is a beautiful tree when in full bloom; the wild plum is plentiful in places in this country.

Well, now I will give you a part or all of a song that Abraham Lincoln used to sing, called it "Adam and Eve's Wedding Song." This song was sung at Abraham's sister's wedding. I do not know [whether] A. Lincoln composed this song or not. The first that I ever heard of it was, the Lincoln family sung it. I rather think that A. L. composed it himself, but I am not certain.

I know that he was in the habit of making songs, and singing of them. I do not wish to write anything but the truth; I have aimed at that all the time. I wish he had a true history, and hope to read a true one, when yours is done.

"Adam and Eve's Wedding Song" as follows:

> *When Adam was created, he dwelt in Eden's shade,*
> *As Moses has recorded; and soon an Eve was made.*
> *Ten thousand times ten thousand*

Of creatures swarmed around
Before a bride was formed
And yet no mate was found.

The Lord then was not willing
The man should be alone
But caused a sleep upon him
And took from him a bone.

And closed the flesh in that place
And then he took the same
And of it made a woman
And brought her to the man.

Then Adam he rejoiced
To see his loving bride,
A part of his own body,
The product of his side.

This woman was not taken
From Adam's feet we see,
So he must not abuse her,
The meaning seems to be.

This woman was not taken
From Adam's head, we know,
To show she must not rule him;
'Tis evidently so.

This woman she was taken
From under Adam's arm,
So she must be protected
From injuries and harm.

Mr. Herndon, please excuse bad writing and mistakes as I am so blind that I can't see the lines on the paper.

ELIZABETH CRAWFORD.

FROM LEONARD SWETT

Chicago, July 17, 1866.

Dear Sir:

I received your letter today, asking me to write you by Friday. Fearing, if I delay, you will not get it done in time, I will give you such hasty thoughts as may occur to me tonight. I have mislaid your second lecture, so that I have not read it at all, and have not read your first one since about the time it was published. What I shall say therefore will be based upon my own ideas rather than a review of the lectures. Lincoln's whole life was a calculation of the law of forces and ultimate results. The world to him was a question of cause and effect. He believed the results to which certain causes tended would surely follow. He did not believe that these results could be materially hastened or impeded. His whole political history, especially since the agitation of the slavery question, has been based upon this theory. He believed from the first, I think, that the agitation of slavery would produce its overthrow, and he acted upon the result as though it was present from the beginning. His tactics were to get himself in the right place and remain there still until events would find him in that place. This course of action led him to say and do things which could not be understood when considered in reference to the immediate surroundings in which they were done or said. You will remember in his campaign against Douglas in 1858 the first ten lines of the first speech he made defeated him. The sentiment of the "house divided against itself" seemed wholly inappropriate. It was a speech made at the commencement of a campaign and apparently made for the campaign. Viewing it in this light alone, nothing could have been more unfortunate or inappropriate. It was saying just the wrong thing, yet he saw it was an abstract truth, and standing by the speech would ultimately find him in the right place. I was inclined at the time to believe these words were hastily and inconsiderately uttered, but subsequent facts have convinced me they were deliberate and had been matured. Judge T. L. Dickey says that at Bloomington at the first Republican Convention in 1856 he uttered the same sentences in a speech delivered there, and that after the meeting was over, he—Dickey—called his attention to these remarks. Lincoln justified himself in making them by stating they were true, but finally at Dickey's urgent request he promised that for his sake or upon his advice he would not repeat them. In the summer of 1859, when he was driving with a party of his intimate friends at Bloomington, the subject of his Springfield speech was discussed. We all insisted it was a great mistake, but he justified himself and finally said: "Well, gentlemen, you may think that speech was a mistake, but I never have believed it was, and you will see the day when you will consider it was the wisest thing I ever said." He never believed in political combinations, he never believed any class of men could accomplish in politics any particular given purpose, and consequently whether an individual man or class of men supported or opposed him—never made any difference in his feelings or his opinions of his own success. If he was elected, he seemed to believe that no person or class of persons could ever have defeated him, and if defeated, he believed nothing could ever have elected him. Hence when he was a candidate he never wanted anything done for him. He seemed to want to let the whole question alone, and for everybody else to do the same. I remember after the Chicago Convention, when a great portion of the East were known to be dissatisfied at his nomination, when fierce conflicts were going on in New York and Pennsylvania, and when great exertions seemed requisite to harmonize and mold in concert the action of our friends, Lincoln always seemed to oppose all efforts made in that direction. I arranged with Mr. Thurlow Weed after the Chicago Convention to meet him at Springfield. I was present at the interview, but he said nothing. It was proposed that Judge Davis should go to New York and Pennsylvania to survey the field and see what was necessary to be done. Lincoln consented, but it was always my opinion that he consented reluctantly. He said that the pressure of a campaign was an external force coercing the party into unity. If it failed to produce that result, he believed any individual effort would also fail. If the desired result followed, he considered it attributable to the great cause and not aided by the lesser ones. He sat down in his chair at Springfield and made himself the Mecca to which all politicians made pilgrimages. He told them all a story, said nothing, and sent them away. All his efforts to procure a second nomination were in the same direction. I believe he earnestly desired that nomination. He was much more eager for it than he was for the first one, and yet from the first he discouraged all efforts on the part of his friends to obtain it. From the middle of his first term all his adversaries were busy at and for themselves. Chase had then a few secret societies and an immense patronage extending all over the country, Frémont was constantly at work, yet Lincoln would never do anything either to hinder them or to help himself. He was considered too conservative and his adversaries were trying to outstrip him in satisfying the radical element. I had a conversation with him upon this subject in October 1863 and tried to induce him to recommend in his annual message the constitutional amendment abolishing slavery. I told him I was not very radical but I believed the results of this war would be the extermination of slavery; that Congress would pass the resolution and that it was proper at that time to be done. I told him, if he took that stand, it was an outside position and no one could maintain himself upon any measure more radical, and if he failed to take the position, his rivals would. Turning to me suddenly he said: "Is not that question doing well enough now?" I replied that it was. "Well," said he, "I have never done an official act with a view to promote my own personal aggrandizement and I don't like to begin now. I can see that time coming—whoever can wait for it will see it—whoever stands in its way will be run over by it." His rivals were using money profusely. Journals and influences were being subsidized against him. I accidentally learned that a Washington newspaper through a purchase of the establishment was to be turned against him, and consulted him about taking steps to prevent it. The only thing I could get him to say was that he would regret to see the paper turned against him. Whatever was done had to be done without his knowledge. Bennett with his paper, you know, is a power. The old fellow wanted to be noticed by Lincoln and he wanted to support him. A friend of his who was certainly in his secrets . . . came over to Washington and intimated, if Lincoln would invite Bennett to come over and chat with him, his paper would be all right. Bennett wanted nothing. He simply wanted to be noticed. Lincoln in talking about it said: "I understood it. Bennett has made a great deal of money—some say not very properly—now he wants me to make him respectable. I have never invited Mr. Bryant or Mr. Greeley here. I shall not therefore especially invite Mr. Bennett." All Lincoln would say was that he was receiving everybody, and he should receive Mr. Bennett if he came. Notwithstanding his entire inaction he never for a moment doubted his second nomination. One time in his room, disputing as to who his real friends were, he told me if I would not show it he would make a list of how the Senate stood when he got through. I pointed out some five or six that I told him I knew he was mistaken in. Said he: "You may think so, but you keep that until the Convention and tell me then whether I was right." He was right to a man. He kept a kind of account book of how things were progressing for a few months, and whenever I would get nervous and think things were going wrong, he would get out his estimates and show how everything in the great scale of action, the resolutions of legislatures, the instructions of delegates, and things of that character, was going exactly as he expected. These facts with many others of a kindred nature have convinced me that he managed his politics upon a plan entirely different from any other man the country has ever produced. It was by ignoring men and ignoring all small causes but by closely calculating the tendencies of events and the great forces which were producing logical results. In his conduct of the war he acted upon the theory that but one thing was necessary, and that was a united North. He had all shades of sentiments and opinions to deal with, and the consideration was always presented to his mind: How can I hold these discordant elements together? Hence in dealing with men he was a trimmer and such a trimmer the world has never seen. Halifax, who was great in his day as a trimmer, would blush by the side of Lincoln, yet Lincoln never trimmed in principles. It was only in his conduct with men. He used the patronage of his office to feed the hunger of these various factions. Weed always declared that he kept a regular account book of his appointments in New York, dividing the various titbits of favor so as to give each faction more than it could get from any other source, yet never enough to satisfy its appetite. They all had access to him, they all received favors from him, and they all complained of ill-treatment, but while unsatisfied they all had "large expectations" and saw in him the chance of getting more than from anyone else they were sure of getting in his place. He used every force to the best possible advantage. He never wasted anything and was always giving more to his enemies than he would to his friends, and the reason was because he never had anything to spare, and in the close calculation of attaching the factions to him he counted upon the abstract affection of his friends as an element to be offset against some gift with which he must appease his enemies. Hence there was always some truth in the charge of his friends that he failed to reciprocate their devotion with his favors. The reason was that he had only just so much to give away. He always had more horses than oats. An adhesion of all forces was indispensable to his success and the success of the country. Hence he husbanded his means with a nicety of calculation. Adhesion was what he wanted. If he got it gratuitously, he never wasted his substance paying for it. His love of the ludicrous was not the least peculiar of his characteristics. His love of fun made him overlook everything else but the point of the joke sought after. If he told a good story that was refined and had a sharp point, he did not like it any the better because it was refined. If it was outrageously low and dirty, he never seemed to see that part of it. If it had the sharp ring of wit, nothing ever reached him but the wit. Almost any man that would tell a very vulgar story has got in a degree a vulgar mind, but it was not so with him. With all his purity of character and exalted morality and sensibility, which no man can doubt, when hunting for wit he had no ability to discriminate between the vulgar and the refined substances from which he extracted it. It was the wit he was after, the pure jewel, and he would pick it up out of the mud or dirt just as readily as he would from a parlor table. He had very great kindness of heart. His mind was full of tender sensibilities. He was extremely humane, yet, while these attributes were fully developed in his character and, unless intercepted by his judgment, controlled him, they never did control him contrary to his judgment. He would strain a point to be kind, but he never strained to breaking. Most men of much kindly feeling are controlled by this sentiment against their judgment, or rather that

sentiment beclouds their judgment. It was never so with him. He would
be just as kind and generous as his judgment would let him be—no more.
If he ever deviated from this rule, it was to save life. He would sometimes, I think, do things he knew to be impolite and wrong to save some
poor fellow's neck. I remember one day being in his room when he was
sitting at his table with a large pile of papers before him. After a pleasant talk, he turned quite abruptly and said: "Get out of the way, Swett;
tomorrow is bulletin day and I must go through these papers and see if
I cannot find some excuse to let this poor fellow off." The pile of papers
he had were the records of courts martial of men who on the following
day were to be shot. He was not examining the records to see whether the
evidence sustained the finding. He was purposely in search of occasions
to evade the law in favor of life. I was one time begging for the life of
a poor [fellow]. It was an outrageously bad case. I confessed I was
simply begging. After sitting with his head down while I was talking,
he interrupted me, saying: "Grant never executed a man, did he?" I have
been watching that thing. Some of Lincoln's friends have insisted that
he lacked the strong attributes of personal affection which he ought to
have exhibited. I think this is a mistake. Lincoln had too much justice to
run a great government for a few favorites, and the complaints against
him in this regard when properly digested amount to this and no more:
that he would not abuse the privileges of his situation. He was certainly
a very poor hater; he never judged men by his like or dislike for them.
If any given act was to be performed, he could understand that his
enemy could do it just as well as anyone. If a man had maligned him or
been guilty of personal ill-treatment and abuse and was the fittest man
for the place, he would put him in his Cabinet as he would his friend.
I do not think he ever removed a man because he was his enemy or because he disliked him. The great secret of his power as an orator, in my
judgment, lay in the clearness and the perspicuity of his statements.
When Lincoln had stated a case, it was always more than half argued
and the point more than half even. The first impression he generally
conveyed was that he had stated the case of his adversary better and
more forcibly than his opponent could state it himself. He then answered
that state of facts fairly and fully, never passing by or skipping over a
bad point. When this was done he presented his own case. There was a
feeling, where he argued a case, in the mind of every man who listened
to him, that nothing had been passed over; yet if he could not answer the
objections he argued in his own mind, and himself arrive at the conclusion to which he was leading others, he had very little power of argu-
mentation. The force of his logic was in conveying to the minds of others

the same clear and thorough analysis he had in his own, and if his own mind failed to be satisfied, he had no power to satisfy anybody else. His mode and force of argument was in stating how he had reasoned upon the subject and how he had come to his conclusion rather than original reasoning to the hearer; and as the mind of the listener followed in the groove of his mind, his conclusions were adopted. He never made a sophistical argument in his life and never could make one. I think he was of less real aid in trying a thoroughly bad case than any man I was ever associated with. If he could not grasp the whole case and master it, he was never inclined to touch it. From the commencement of his life to its close I have sometimes doubted whether he ever asked anybody's advice about anything. He would listen to everybody, he could hear everybody, but he never asked for opinions. I never knew him in trying a lawsuit to ask the advice of any lawyer he was associated with. As a politician and as President he arrived at all his conclusions from his own reflections, and when his opinion was once founded, he never had any doubt but what it was right. You ask me whether he changed his religious opinions toward the close of his life. I think not; as he became involved in matters of the gravest importance, full of great responsibility and great doubt, the feeling of religious reverence and belief in God, His justice and surrounding power, increased upon him. He was full of natural religion. He believed God as the most approved church member, by the same system of great generalizations as of everything else. He had in my judgment very little faith in ceremonials and forms; whether he went to church over a month or over a year troubled him very little. He failed to observe the Sabbath very scrupulously. I think he read Petroleum V. Nasby as much as he did the Bible. He would ridicule the Puritans and swear in a moment of vexation, but yet his heart was full of natural and cultivated religion. He believed in the great laws of truth, the rigid discharge of duty and his accountability to God, the ultimate triumph of right and the overthrow of wrong. If his religion were to be judged by the line and rule of church creeds and unexceptionable language, he would fall far short of the standard, but if by the higher rule of the purity of conduct, of honesty of motive, of unyielding fidelity to the right, and acknowledging God as the Supreme Ruler, then he filled all the requirements of true devotion and love of his neighbor as himself. One great public mistake by his character as generally received and acquiesced in: he is considered by the people of this country as a frank, guileless, unsophisticated man. There never was a greater mistake! Beneath a smooth surface of candor and apparent declaration of all his thoughts and feelings, he exercised the most exalted tact and the wisest discrimination. He handled and moved man remotely as we do pieces upon a chessboard. He retained through life all the friends he ever had, and he made the wrath of his enemies to praise him. This was not by cunning or intrigue in the low acceptation of the term, but by far-seeing reason and discernment. He always told enough only of his plans and purposes to induce the belief that he communicated all, yet he reserved enough to have communicated nothing. He told all that was unimportant with a gushing frankness, yet no man ever kept his real purposes or penetrated the future further with his deep designs. I wish I had time to add some things and in the whole to make this shorter and better, but I have not. I shall try if desirable to give you parts from time to time, but you will please remember they are confidential.

Yours truly,
LEONARD SWETT.

FROM MARY S. VINEYARD

Weston, Mo., July 22, 1866.

Dear Sir:

I do not think you pertinacious in asking the question, relative to old Mrs. Bowling Green, because I wish to set you right on that subject. Your information, no doubt, came through my cousin Mr Gaines Green, who visited us last winter. Whilst here he was laughing at me about Mr. Lincoln, and among other things spoke of the circumstance, in connection with Mrs. Green and child. My impression is now that I tacitly admitted it (for it was a season of *trouble* with me), and I gave but little heed to the whole matter. We never had any hard feelings towards each other that I knew of. On one occasion did I say to Mr. L. that I did not believe he would make a kind husband, because he did not tender his services to Mrs. Green in helping her carry her babe. As I said to you in a former letter, I thought him lacking in smaller attentions.

One circumstance presents itself just now to my mind's eye. There was a company of us going to Uncle Billy Green's; Mr. L. was riding with me, and we had a very bad branch to cross; the other gentlemen were very officious in seeing that their partners got over safely; we were behind, he riding on, never looking back to see how I got along; when I rode up beside him, I remarked: "You are a nice fellow; I suppose you did not care whether my neck was broken or not." He laughingly replied (I suppose by way of compliment) that he knew I was plenty smart to take care of myself. In many things he was sensitive, almost to a fault.

He told me of an incident: that he was crossing a prairie one day, and saw before him a hog mired down, to use his own language; he was rather fixed up and he resolved that he would pass on without looking towards the shoat; after he had gone by, he said, the feeling was irresistible and he had to look back, and the poor thing seemed to say so wistfully: *There, now! my last hope is gone,* that he deliberately got down and relieved it from its difficulty.

In many things we were congenial spirits. In politics we saw eye to eye, though since then we have differed as widely as the South is from the North. But methinks I hear you say: Save me from a *political woman!* *So say I.* The last message I ever received from him was about a year after we parted in Illinois. Mrs. Able visited Kentucky and he said to her in Springfield: "Tell your sister that I think she was a great fool because she did not stay here and marry me."

Characteristic of the man.

Respectfully yours,
MARY S. VINEYARD.

FROM J. HENRY SHAW

Beardstown, Ill., August 22, 1866.

Dear Sir:

In the case of the People *vs.* William Armstrong, I was assistant prosecuting counsel. The prevailing belief at that time (and I may also say at the present) in Cass County was as follows. Mr. Lincoln, previous to trial, handed an almanac of the year previous to the murder, to an officer of court, stating that he might call for one during the trial, and if he did, to send him that one. An important witness for the People had fixed the time of the murder to be in the night near a camp meeting, that "the moon was about in the same place that the sun would be at ten o'clock in the morning and was nearly full"; therefore he could see plainly, etc. At the proper time Mr. Lincoln called to the officer for an almanac, and the one prepared for the occasion was shown by Mr. Lincoln, he reading from it that, at the time referred to by the witness, the moon *had already set.* That, in the roar of laughter following, the jury and opposing counsel neglected to look at the date. Mr. Carter, a lawyer of this city who was present at, but not engaged in, the Armstrong case, says he is satisfied that the almanac was of the year previous, and thinks he examined it at the time. This was the general impression in the courtroom. I have called on the sheriff who officiated at that time, James A. Dick, who says that he saw a Goudy's Almanac laying upon Mr. Lincoln's table during the trial, and that Mr. Lincoln took it out of his own pocket. Mr. Dick does not know the date of it. I have seen several of the petit jurymen who sat upon the case who only recollect that the almanac *floored* the witness. But one of the jury, the foreman, Mr. Milton Logan, says that the almanac was a Jayne's Almanac, that it was the one for the year in which the murder was committed, and that there was no trick about it, that he is willing to make an affidavit that he examined it as to its date and that it was the almanac of the year of the murder. My own opinion is that, when an almanac was called for by Mr. Lincoln, *two* were brought, one of the year of the murder and the other of the year previous; that Mr. Lincoln was entirely innocent of any deception in the matter. I the more think this from the fact that Armstrong was not cleared by any want of testimony against him, but by the irresistible appeal of Mr. Lincoln in his favor. He told the jury of his once being a poor, friendless boy, that Armstrong's father took him into his house, fed and clothed him and gave him a home, etc., the particulars of which were told so pathetically that the jury forgot the guilt of the boy in their admiration of the father.

It was generally admitted that Lincoln's speech and personal appeal to the jury saved Armstrong. Mr. James Taylor (now a resident of Springfield) was clerk of the circuit court of Cass County at that time. By calling upon him, you can probably get his description of the affair.

The murder occurred, I think, in 1857. He was indicted in Mason County, and a change of venue to this county. At the November term, 1857, of Cass Circuit Court, Mr. Lincoln labored hard to get Armstrong admitted to bail, but his motion was overruled. The trial and acquittal occurred at the May term, 1858.

Yours respectfully,
J. Henry Shaw.

From J. Henry Shaw

Beardstown, Ill., September 5, 1866.

Dear Sir:

Six of the seven interrogatories propounded by you in yours of the 1st *inst.* have relation to a motion for a writ of *habeas corpus* in the Armstrong case. In reply, I would say that I have no recollection of there having been an effort made for a *habeas corpus* in that case. I went to the record and also searched *all the papers* in the case, but nothing can be found intimating that such a motion was made. It is not usual, or at least necessary, that the papers connected with such a motion be filed with the indictment, and possibly by writing to Judge Harriott at Pekin you might find the facts in the case. My impression is that no such motion was made. My recollections of that trial are rather good, from the fact that I was with Mr. Lincoln a great deal of the time during both of the terms in which the Armstrong case was pending. My connection with him during those terms was as follows:

Not knowing that he was intending to attend our November term, 1857, I wrote to him that I wished his assistance for defendant in the case of Ruth A. Gill *vs.* Jonathan Gill at that term, which was a suit for custody of child and alimony. He came down, I then supposed, exclusively to attend to that case. The question of divorce was left for a jury, who brought in a verdict for complainant, who also got the custody of the child, but the question of alimony, the most important point in that case, was left open until the next term of court. At this term, November 1857, Mr. Lincoln argued the motion in the Armstrong case to admit to bail, which was overruled. At the May term I expected Mr. Lincoln down to assist in the *alimony* case again, and he came in due time, called at my office, and said I had been suing some of his clients, and he had come down to attend to it. He then had reference to a new chancery case entitled "George Moore *vs.* Christina Moore and the heirs of Peter Moore" for a specific performance, the defendants all living near Springfield. I explained the case to him, and showed him my proofs. He seemed surprised that I should deal so frankly with him and said he should be as frank with me, that my client was justly entitled to a decree, and he should so represent it to the court, that it was against his principles to contest a clear matter of right. So my client got a deed for a farm, which, had another lawyer been in Mr. Lincoln's place, would have been litigated for years, with a big pile of costs, and the result probably the same. Mr. Lincoln's character for professional honor stood very high. He never vexed an opponent, but frequently threw him off his guard by his irresistible good humor. But I digress—I still thought that Mr. Lincoln had come to our court more particularly to attend to the Gill and Moore cases, and was very much surprised afterwards to see the immense interest he took in the Armstrong case. He went into it like a Giant. The evidence bore heavily upon his client. There were many witnesses, and each one seemed to add one more cord that seemed to bind him down, till Mr. Lincoln was something in the situation of Gulliver after his first sleep in Lilliput. But when he came to talk to the jury (that was always his forte) he resembled Gulliver again; he skillfully untied here and there a knot and loosened here and there a peg, until, getting fairly warmed up, he raised himself in his full power and shook the arguments of his opponents from him as though they were cobwebs. He took the jury by storm. There were tears in Mr. Lincoln's eyes while he spoke. But they were genuine. His sympathies were fully enlisted in favor of the young man, and his terrible sincerity could not help but arouse the same passion in the jury. I have said it a hundred times, that it was Lincoln's *speech* that saved that criminal from the gallows, and neither money or fame inspired that speech, but it was incited by gratitude to the young man's father, who, as Mr. Lincoln said, "was his only friend when he was a poor homeless boy." These are the only facts which I now recollect occurring at our court worthy of your notice concerning that case. I might say, however, as part of the previous history of the case, that the indictment was found at the October term, 1857, of the Mason Circuit Court, against James H. Norris and William Armstrong. The indictment charges that on the 29th day of August 1857 they murdered James Preston Metzker—Norris striking him on the back of the head with a club and Armstrong striking him in the right eye with a *slingshot*. Norris was tried at the October term, 1857, Mason Circuit Court, found guilty of manslaughter, and sent up for eight years. Dilworth and Campbell were council for Norris.

At the October term, 1857, Mason County, William Walker appeared as counsel for Armstrong, and made two motions, one to quash the indictment, which was overruled; the other to discharge the prisoner, which was withdrawn.

At the close of the trial of Armstrong in the Cass Circuit Court Mr. Lincoln had possession of the slingshot with which it was shown Armstrong killed Metzker. He, Mr. L., handed it to me, saying: "Here, Henry, I'll give you this to remember me by."

I have that same slingshot now. It was made by Armstrong for the occasion. He took a common bar of pig lead, pounded it round, about the size of a large hickory nut, then cut a piece of leather out of the top of one of his boots, and with a thread and needle he sewed it into the shape of a slingshot, and thus improvised in a few minutes a very fatal weapon. If I can be of any other assistance to you in your worthy undertaking, shall be at your service.

Yours respectfully,
J. HENRY SHAW.

FROM JOHN HAY

Legation of the United States, Paris, September 5, 1866.

My dear Mr. Herndon:

I am so constantly busy that I have had no quiet day in which to write you what you desired in your letter several months ago. I have been chargé d'affaires nearly all summer, my day filled with official business and my night with social engagements equally imperative. Even now, I write because I am ashamed to wait any longer and have a few minutes disposable. I will answer your questions as you put them without any attempt at arrangement.

Lincoln used to go to bed ordinarily from ten to eleven o'clock unless he happened to be kept up by important news, in which case he would frequently remain at the War Department until one or two. He rose early. When he lived in the country at Soldiers' Home, he would be up and dressed, eat his breakfast (which was extremely frugal—an egg, a piece of toast, coffee, etc.), and ride into Washington, all before eight o'clock. In the winter at the White House he was not quite so early. He did not sleep very well but spent a good while in bed. Tad usually slept with him. He would lie around the office until he fell asleep and Lincoln would shoulder him and take him off to bed.

He pretended to begin business at ten o'clock in the morning, but in reality the anterooms and halls were full before that hour—people anxious to get the first ax ground. He was extremely unmethodical: it was a four years' struggle on Nicolay's part and mine to get him to adopt some systematic rules. He would break through every regulation as fast as it was made.

Anything that kept the people themselves away from him he disapproved—although they nearly annoyed the life out of him by unreasonable complaints and requests.

He wrote very few letters. He did not read one in fifty that he received. At first we tried to bring them to his notice, but at last he gave the whole thing over to me, and signed without reading them the letters I wrote in his name. He wrote perhaps half a dozen a week himself, not more.

Nicolay received members of Congress, and other visitors who had business with the Executive Office, communicated to the Senate and House the messages of the President, and exercised a general supervision over the business.

I opened and read the letters, answered them, looked over the newspapers, supervised the clerks who kept the records, and in Nicolay's absence did his work also.

When the President had any rather delicate matter to manage at a distance from Washington, he very rarely wrote, but sent Nicolay or me.

The House remained full of people nearly all day. At noon the President took a little lunch—a biscuit, a glass of milk in winter, some fruit or grapes in summer. He dined at from five to six and we went off to our dinner also.

Before dinner was over, members and Senators would come back and take up the whole evening. Sometimes, though rarely, he shut himself up and would see no one. Sometimes he would run away to a lecture or concert or theater for the sake of a little rest.

He was very abstemious, ate less than anyone I know. Drank nothing but water, not from principle, but because he did not like wine or spirits. Once in rather dark days early in the war, a Temperance Committee came to him and said the reason we did not win was because our army drank so much whisky as to bring down the curse of the Lord upon them. He said dryly that it was rather unfair on the part of the aforesaid curse, as the other side drank more and worse whisky than ours did.

He read very little. Scarcely ever looked into a newspaper unless I called his attention to an article on some special subject. He frequently said: "I know more about that than any of them." It is absurd to call him a modest man. No great man was ever modest. It was his intellectual arrogance and unconscious assumption of superiority that men like Chase and Sumner never could forgive.

I can't write any more today. I may see you before long—I don't know —and so I won't waste time by telling you what you must know as well as I do.

I believe Lincoln is well understood by the people. Miss Nancy Bancroft and the rest of that patent-leather kid-glove set know no more of him than an owl does of a comet blazing into his blinking eyes.

Bancroft's address was a disgraceful exhibition of ignorance and prejudice. His effeminate nature shrinks instinctively from the contact of a great reality like Lincoln's character.

I consider Lincoln Republicanism incarnate, with all its faults and all its virtues. As, in spite of some evidences, Republicanism is the sole hope of a sick world, so Lincoln, with all his foibles, is the greatest character since Christ.

Yours,
JOHN HAY.

From J. Gillespie

Clerk's Office of the Circuit Court of Madison County, Ill.,
Edwardsville, September 19, 1866.

Dear Sir:

Yours of the 10th is received in reply to which I have to say that I only remember the general run of the events connected with the Senatorial election in 1854 in which Mr. Lincoln and Mr. Trumbull were candidates and in which Trumbull succeeded. We held a caucus in which all but five of the opponents of the pro-slavery Democracy were present and at which Lincoln was selected as our candidate when the Houses met in joint convention. Those five, to wit: Judd of Cook, Cook of LaSalle, Palmer of Macoupin, and Allen and Baker of Madison, voted for Trumbull while the rest of us voted for Mr. Lincoln. The reason they gave, according to my recollection, for voting for Trumbull was that, having been elected as Democrats, they could not vote for anyone but a Democrat for United States Senator. I tried hard to persuade them to go with us. They stated that they had no objection to Mr. Lincoln except his political antecedents, but that they could not sustain themselves at home if they were to vote for him, but expressed regret that they were so circumstanced. After a number of ballots I asked Mr. Lincoln what he would advise us to do, when he said promptly: "I would go for Trumbull by all means." We understood the case to be that Shields was to be run by the Democrats at first and was then to be dropped and Joel A. Matteson put up, and it was calculated that certain of our men who had been elected on the free-soil issue would vote for him after they had acted with us long enough to satisfy their consciences and constituents. Our object was to make an election before they got through with their program. We were savagely opposed to Matteson and so was Mr. Lincoln, and he said that if we did not drop in and unite upon Trumbull, those men would go for Matteson and elect him, which would be an everlasting disgrace to the State. We reluctantly complied with Lincoln's suggestions and went up on Trumbull and elected him. Mr. Lincoln did not appear to have any hard feelings towards Trumbull, although he was of course disappointed and mortified at his own want of success. This is the impression left on my memory of the event. I do not remember how many ballots we had, but I should think we had five or six. I do not think there was much ill feeling felt or manifested amongst Lincoln's friends, although we looked upon it as a great misfortune to him personally that he could not succeed on that occasion, but at home there was considerable bitterness displayed by some of the old Whigs who regarded it as an affront put upon men who had belonged to that party. Trumbull was present when the election came off, but I do not believe that he was charged with being instrumental in bringing about the result, nor do I suppose that he took any pains to prevent it or any active part in the matter, one way or another. I know that we, the opponents of the pro-slavery party, harmonized during the rest of the session. I remember that Judge S. T. Logan gave up Mr. Lincoln with great reluctance. He begged hard to try him one or two ballots more, but Mr. Lincoln urged us not to risk it longer. I never saw Mr. Lincoln more earnest and decided. He said he was satisfied that he could not get the support of those five men, and it would be unwise to contend any more and incur the risk of electing Matteson. I know that the friends of Matteson were grievously disappointed at the result. They felt sure that he would be elected in due season and appeared to be taken by surprise when we united on and elected Trumbull. These are my impressions, but owing to the length of time which has elapsed and the vagueness of my recollection, I would not be answerable for anything more than their correctness in general and not in detail. You are at liberty to make such use of them as you may deem proper if their publication can conduce in any way to vindicate the truth of history. If not necessary, I should of course prefer not to have them made public.

Your friend,
J. GILLESPIE.

FROM R. B. RUTLEDGE

[October 1866.]

Dear Sir:

Believing that any authentic statements connected with the early life and history of the beloved Abraham Lincoln should belong to the great American people, I submit the following replies to the interrogatories contained in your recent letter. I trust largely to your courtesy as a gentleman, to your honesty and integrity as a historian, and to your skill in writing for the public, to enlarge wherever my statements seem obscure, and to condense and remove whatever seems superfluous. Above all, I trust to your honor and your sense of right and consistency, to exclude from print anything which in your judgment may injuriously affect the surviving actors in the great drama which you propose to re-enact once more.

Many of my statements are made from memory with the aid of association of events; and should you discover that the date, location, and circumstances of the events here named should be contradictory to those named from other sources, I beg of you to consider well the testimony in each case, and make up your history from those statements which may appear to you best fitted to remove all doubt as to their correctness.

You ask, first: When did you first become acquainted with Lincoln, where was it, and what was he doing? I answer: In the year 1830 or 1831 in the town of New Salem, Illinois. He was at that time a clerk in the store of Denton Offutt, having just returned with Offutt from New Orleans, with whom he had gone on a flatboat as a hand to that city. At that time he boarded with John Cameron, a partner of my father in laying out the town of New Salem, and in building a mill on the Sangamon River. At that period New Salem was a small village of not more than ten or fifteen families, who lived in log cabins, and who were as sociable and familiar as persons are who find themselves thus isolated from the great world outside. The mill was a saw and grist mill, was the first one built on the Sangamon River, and supplied a large section of country with its meal, flour, and lumber. At times when it was necessary to construct a dam to afford the proper water power, word would be sent through the neighborhood, and the people would come ten and fifteen miles *en masse,* and assist gratuitously in the work.

On such occasions Mr. Lincoln was ever ready to work with his stalwart hand, and to assist in constructing or repairing the dams or mill, raising houses in the village, etc., and this too when he had no personal interest in the success of the enterprise.

This is mentioned here as an illustration of the generosity and nobleness of the settlers at that early day. It also shows an element of the character of the people among whom Mr. Lincoln received his first impressions and may assist in proving that he was then, and why he always appeared afterwards, one of the people, and an ardent sympathizer with the masses.

It has been stated that Mr. Offutt owned or had an interest in the mill and that Mr. Lincoln was employed to assist in taking care of the new enterprise. This is a mistake. James Rutledge and John Cameron, partners, first commenced erecting a mill on Concord Creek, about six miles below New Salem, where they owned the land, but large inducements being offered and the proprietors fearing a scarcity of water, removed to New Salem in 1828 and built the mill and laid out the town. Neither Mr. Lincoln or Mr. Offutt had any pecuniary interest in it. It belonged solely to Rutledge and Cameron, and Mr. Lincoln only assisted in repairing it as other neighbors did, gratuitously. He was at this time the clerk of Mr. Offutt, who kept a general country store, including dry goods, groceries, and all the varieties which belong to such an establishment.

You ask, second: Did he board with you—your father and family—how long—when—and all about it? On Mr. Lincoln's arrival at New Salem, he boarded with John Cameron along with Offutt. He afterwards boarded with my father, during the years 1833 and 1834, as appears from papers still in the possession of the family. I am satisfied he boarded with us both prior and subsequent to the years named, but so long a time has intervened that I cannot fix the date with precise certainty.

You ask, third: In regard to my father and the family. My father was born in South Carolina, removed to Kentucky, and from thence to White County, Illinois, in 1816. The first three children, Jane, John, and Ann, were born in Kentucky; the later six were born in Illinois—David, Robert, Nancy, and Margaret born in White County, and William and Sarah in Sangamon County. My father removed to Sangamon County in 1825 and died in Menard County, which was formerly a part of Sangamon County, December 3, 1835.

Fourth: You make some pertinent inquiries concerning my sister and the relations which existed between herself and Mr. Lincoln. My sister Ann was born January 7, 1813, and died August 25, 1835. She was born in Kentucky and died in Menard County, Illinois. In 1830, my sister being then but seventeen years of age, a stranger calling himself John McNeil came to New Salem. He boarded with Mr. Cameron and was keeping a store with a Samuel Hill. A friendship grew up between McNeil and Ann which ripened apace and resulted in an engagement to marry. McNeil's real name was McNamar. It seems that his father had failed in business, and his son, a very young man, had determined to make a fortune, pay off his father's debts, and restore him to his former social and financial standing. With this view he left his home clandestinely, and in order to avoid pursuit by his parents changed his name. His conduct was strictly high-toned, honest, and moral, and his object, whatever any may think of the deception which he practiced in changing his name, entirely praiseworthy.

He prospered in business and, pending his engagement with Ann, he revealed his true name, returned to Ohio to relieve his parents from their embarrassments, and to bring the family with him to Illinois. On his return to Ohio, several years having elapsed, he found his father in declining health or dead, and perhaps the circumstances of the family prevented his immediate return to New Salem. At all events he was absent two or three years.

In the meantime Mr. Lincoln paid his addresses to Ann, continued his visits and attentions regularly, and those resulted in an engagement to marry, conditional to an honorable release from the contract with McNamar. There is no kind of doubt as to the existence of this engagement. David Rutledge urged Ann to consummate it, but she refused until such time as she could see McNamar, inform him of the change in her feelings, and seek an honorable release. Mr. Lincoln lived in the village, McNamar did not return, and in August 1835 Ann sickened and died. The effect upon Mr. Lincoln's mind was terrible; he became plunged in despair, and many of his friends feared that reason would desert her throne. His extraordinary emotions were regarded as strong evidence of the existence of the tenderest relations between himself and the deceased. McNamar, however, returned to Illinois in the fall after Ann's death.

Fifth: Ann was, as before stated, seventeen years old in 1830. My age at the same time was twelve. She went to school to Mentor Graham, who was a successful and popular teacher in 1832 and 1833. My sister was esteemed the brightest mind of the family, was studious, devoted to her duties of whatever character, and possessed a remarkably amiable and lovable disposition. She had light hair and blue eyes.

Sixth question: I have already written you in relation to my acquaintance with Samuel Hill, Offutt, Green, and others. Perhaps too much credit is awarded William Green for Mr. Lincoln's knowledge of grammar. Mr. Lincoln clerked for Offutt in 1831 and 1832. James Rutledge owned an interest in a grocery in New Salem, a remnant of a stock belonging to Rutledge and Sinco. Sinco bought a lot of horses, took them south, and broke up. Rutledge sold out to Lincoln and William Berry. Mr. Lincoln only had possession a very short time and never gave it his personal attention. He soon sold out to Berry, who gave his note to Lincoln for the amount, who paid Rutledge with Berry's note. Soon after, Berry failed, and after a while Lincoln came to Rutledge and made him a tender to pay half the note. This Rutledge utterly refused to accept from Mr. L., alleging that he had taken Berry's note for the debt and, if he could not make it out of him, he would not accept it at all. About this time Mr. Lincoln was employed in surveying, he having learned the science, and being engaged in a good business in the profession.

Seventh: My father moved to and laid out the town of New Salem in the summer of 1829. I moved in 1836 with my mother and elder brother from Menard County to Fulton County, Illinois, and from thence in the fall of 1837 to Van Buren County, Iowa. My father was born in South Carolina, May 11, 1781, and died in Menard County, Illinois, December 3, 1835, being about fifty-four years of age.

Eighth: I cannot give you a satisfactory reply to many items embraced in this inquiry, for the lack of dates or circumstances corroborating them. Many things said of him and done by him are indelibly fixed in my mind, but the absence of the proper surroundings impels me to withhold them. Mr. Lincoln studied Kirkham's Grammar; the valuable copy which he delighted to peruse is now in my possession. He also studied natural philosophy, astronomy, chemistry, etc. He had no regular teacher, but perhaps received more assistance from Mentor Graham than any other person. He could be seen usually when in pursuit of his ordinary avocations with his book under his arm; at a moment of leisure he would open it, study, close it, and recite to himself. When in young company he has been known to excite the most uproarious laughter by singing the tune called "Legacy" in the "Missouri Harmony," substituting the words "Old Gray" for "Red Grape." The effect is very ludicrous as anyone can see by reference to the lines quoted. His enjoyment of a joke was very intense; and all that has been said in truth of his disposition is no exaggeration.

About the year 1832 or 1833 Mr. Lincoln made his first effort at public speaking. A debating club, of which James Rutledge was president, was organized and held regular meetings. As he arose to speak, his tall form towered above the little assembly. Both hands were thrust down deep in the pockets of his pantaloons. A perceptible smile at once lit up the faces of the audience, for all anticipated the relation of some humorous story. But he opened up the discussion in splendid style to the infinite astonishment of his friends. As he warmed with his subject, his hands would forsake his pockets and would enforce his ideas by awkward gestures; but would very soon seek their easy resting place. He pursued the question with reason and argument so pithy and forcible that all were amazed. The president, at his fireside after the meeting, remarked to his wife that there was more in Abe's head than wit and fun, that he was already a fine speaker, that all he lacked was culture to enable him to reach the high destiny which he knew was in store for him. From that time Mr. Rutledge took a deeper interest in him.

Soon after Mr. Rutledge urged him to announce himself as a candidate for the Legislature. This he at first declined to do, averring that it was impossible to be elected. It was suggested that a canvass of the county would bring him prominently before the people and in time would do him good. He reluctantly yielded to the solicitations of his friends and made a partial canvass. The result, though he was defeated, was highly gratifying to him and astonished even his most ardent admirers.

At the next election he was placed as a candidate for Assembly on the regular Whig ticket, and was triumphantly elected in a district profoundly Democratic.

In illustration of his goodness and nobleness of heart, the following incident is related. Ab Trout, a poor bare-footed boy, was engaged one cold winter day in chopping a pile of logs from an old house or stable which had been pulled down. The wood was dry and hard and the boy was hard at work, when Lincoln came up and asked what he got for the job, and what he would do with the money. "Ab" said $1.00 and, pointing to his naked feet, said: "A pair of shoes." Abe told him to go in and warm and he would chop awhile for him. The boy delayed a little, but Lincoln finished the work, threw down his ax, and told him to go and buy the shoes. "Ab" remembered this act with the liveliest gratitude. Once he, being a cast-iron Democrat, determined to vote against his party and for Mr. Lincoln; but the friends, as he afterwards said with tears in eyes, made him drunk and he had voted against Abe. Thus he did not even have an opportunity to return the noble conduct of Mr. Lincoln by this small measure of thanks.

In the early times of which we write an appeal was often made to physical strength to settle controversies. To illustrate this feature of the society in which Mr. Lincoln was mingling, it may be well to relate an incident.

Two neighbors, Henry Clark and Ben Wilcox, had had a law-suit. The defeated declared that although he was beaten in the suit, he could whip his opponent. This was a formal challenge and was at once carried to the ears of the victor, Wilcox—and as promptly accepted. The time, place, and seconds were chosen with due regularity—Mr. Lincoln being Clark's and John Brewer Wilcox's second. The parties met, stripped themselves all but their breeches, went in, and Mr. Lincoln's principal was beautifully whipped. These combats were conducted with as much ceremony and punctiliousness as ever graced the dueling ground. After the conflict the seconds conducted their respective principals to the river, washed off the blood, and assisted them to dress. During this performance, the second of the party opposed to Mr. Lincoln remarked: "Well, Abe, my man has whipped yours, and I can whip you." Now this challenge came from a man who was very small in size. Mr. Lincoln agreed to fight provided he would "chalk out his size on Mr. Lincoln's person, and every blow struck outside of that mark should be counted foul." After this sally there was the best possible humor and all parties were as orderly as if they had been engaged in the most harmless amusement. In all matters of dispute about horse-racing or any of the popular pastimes of the day, Mr. Lincoln's judgment was final to all that region of country. People relied implicitly upon his honesty, integrity, and impartiality.

Very soon after Mr. Lincoln's coming to New Salem and while clerking for Offutt, Offutt made a bet with William Clary that Abe could throw down in a wrestle any man in the county. This bet was taken, and Jack Armstrong, a rough, and the best fighter in Sangamon, was pitted against him. The match took place in front of Offutt's store. All the men of the village and quite a number from the surrounding country were assembled. Armstrong was a man in the prime of life, square-built, muscular, and strong as an ox. The contest began, and Jack soon found so worthy an antagonist that he "broke his holt," caught Abe by the leg, and would have brought him to the ground, had not Mr. Lincoln seized him by the throat and thrust him at arm's length from him. Jack having played foul, there was every prospect of a general fight. At this time James Rutledge, having heard of the difficulty, ran into the crowd and, through the influence which he exerted over all parties, succeeded in quieting the disturbance and preventing a fight.

His physical strength proved of vast utility to him in his many arduous labors, up to the time he became President, and a man of less iron frame would have sunk under the enormous burdens laid upon him during four years marked by executive cares that have no parallel in history.

After this wrestling match Jack Armstrong and his crowd became the warmest friends and stanchest supporters of Mr. Lincoln. This Jack Armstrong was father of the boy who was some years afterwards arrested and tried for the murder of young Metzker, and who was voluntarily defended and cleared by Mr. Lincoln. The account of this remarkable trial is already before the public and it is not necessary that I should repeat it here. Mr. Lincoln never forgot the friends with whom he was associated in early life. Soon after his nomination for the Presidency, some grandchildren of James Rutledge circulated the report that Mr. Lincoln had left their grandfather's house without paying his board bill. These boys were reared under Copperhead influences and continued in the faith during the war. This slanderous report reached the ears of Mrs. Rutledge, widow of James Rutledge, and whom he always called "Aunt Polly." She took immediate steps to correct the infamous libel and caused a letter to be written Mr. Lincoln. Mr. Lincoln at once wrote Mrs. Rutledge, expressing his thanks for her kindness and the interest manifested in his behalf, recurring with warm expressions of remembrance to the many happy days spent under her roof.

While Mr. Lincoln was engaged in surveying, he wore jeans, pantaloons, "foxed," or covered on the forepart and below the knees behind, with buckskin. This added to the warmth, protected against rain, and rendered them more durable in performing the labor necessary to his calling. His other clothing was such as worn by all the inhabitants of the village.

Trials of strength were very common among the pioneers. Lifting weights, as heavy timbers piled one upon another, was a favorite pastime, and no workman in the neighborhood could at all cope with Mr. Lincoln in this direction. I have seen him frequently take a barrel of whisky by the chimes and lift it up to his face as if to drink out of the bunghole. This feat he could accomplish with the greatest ease. I never saw him taste or drink a drop of any kind of spirituous liquors.

I am very respectfully yours, etc.,

R. B. RUTLEDGE.

I have omitted an incident in the early life of Mr. Lincoln which I will here relate. The only man who was ever successful in bringing Lincoln to the ground in a wrestle was Lorenzo D. Thompson, a very large and powerful man. This match took place at Bearstown, Illinois, the general rendezvous while waiting for orders to march against Black Hawk and his warriors. In this match Lincoln was taken by surprise, and in the first trial Thompson brought him to the ground, but in two successive matches Lincoln came off victorious. R.B.R.

From John Jones

Winterset, Iowa, October 22, 1866.

Having seen the statements made by R. B. Rutledge in reference to the early life of Abraham Lincoln and having known Mr. Lincoln and been an eye-witness to the events as narrated, from my boyhood, I take pleasure in saying they are literally true.

As to the relation existing between Mr. Lincoln and Ann Rutledge, I have every reason to believe that it was of the tenderest character, as I know of my own knowledge that he made regular visits to her. During her last illness he visited her sick chamber and on his return stopped at my house. It was very evident that he was much distressed, and I was not surprised when it was rumored subsequently that his reason was in danger. It was generally understood that Mr. Lincoln and Ann Rutledge were engaged to be married. She was a very amiable and lovable woman and it was deemed a very suitable match—one in which the parties were in every way worthy of each other.

(Signed) JOHN JONES.

From R. B. Rutledge

Oskaloosa, November 18, 1866.

My dear Friend:

I some time since received your very kind letter of 3d *inst.* and owe you an apology for not answering sooner, but know you will pardon my seeming indifference, when I tell you I have been moving from Burlington to this place.

You suggest that the probable cause of Ann's sickness was her conflicts, emotions, etc.; as to this I cannot say. I, however, have my own private convictions; the character of her sickness was brain fever.

I am glad to know that you feel as I do, that injustice is done Mentor

Graham, and trust largely to your sense of justice to place him in his true light, before the reading world, and award to him that meed of praise that is due the man who assisted in laying the foundation of Mr. Lincoln's greatness. I know of my own knowledge that Mr. Graham contributed more to Mr. Lincoln's education while in New Salem than any other man. If Mr. Graham is living and you should meet him, tell him I remember my old teacher with gratitude.

I received a copy of your lecture, a day or two since, which is bold, manly, and substantially true. I will take the liberty to throw a little light on one point for your future use; to wit, Samuel Hill first courted Ann. She declined his proposition to marry, after which McNamar paid his addresses, resulting in an engagement to marry; after McNamar left Menard County to visit his parents and during his prolonged absence, Mr. Lincoln courted Ann, resulting in a second engagement, not conditional, as my language would seem to indicate, but absolute. She, however, in the conversation referred to by me, between her and David, urged the propriety of seeing Mr. McNamar, inform him of the change in her feelings, and seek an honorable release, before consummating the engagement with Mr. Lincoln by marriage.

I hope to be able to visit you this winter, as I assure you nothing would give me more pleasure than to see and talk with the man who appreciates the virtues and character of Abraham Lincoln.

I am, my dear friend,
Very truly yours,
R. B. Rutledge.

From R. B. Rutledge

Oskaloosa, November 21, 1866.

Dear Sir:

I have just received your two letters of 18th and 19th *inst.* and hasten to answer.

You ask, first: Do I truthfully paint the old pioneers, with classes—the oldest class and our fathers? I answer: You do. You ask, secondly: Do I get the condition of Mr. Lincoln's mental suffering and condition truthfully? I cannot answer this question from personal knowledge, but from what I have learned from others at the time you are substantially correct. You ask, thirdly: Do I truthfully describe New Salem, her surroundings, from 1825 to 1837? I answer: Your picture is well and truthfully drawn, as it appeared to me from 1828 to 1836, the time in which I was familiar with the place. You ask, fourthly: Do I get the facts all correctly, and tell them truthfully? I answer: Subtantially you do, but probably a little in error in detail in one or two particulars; to wit, in your lecture you say three men fell in love with Ann Rutledge simultaneously. The facts are William Berry first courted Ann and was rejected; afterwards Samuel Hill; then John McNamar, which resulted in an engagement to marry at some future time. He, McNamar, left the county on business, was gone some years; in the meantime and during McNamar's absence, Mr. Lincoln courted Ann and engaged to marry her, on the completion of the study of law. In this I am corroborated by James McRutledge, a cousin about her age, and who was in her confidence. He says in a letter to me just received: "Ann told me once in coming from a camp meeting on Rock Creek, that engagements made too far ahead sometimes failed, that one had failed (meaning her engagement with McNamar), and gave me to understand that as soon as certain studies were completed she and Lincoln would be married." He says you and Mr. Cogsdell talked with him on this subject, but he did not tell you as much, as he thought you had a design in it; you can correspond with him and say to him that this is no longer a delicate question, inasmuch as it must of necessity become a matter of history, that I desire the whole truth to be recorded. I think you are in error as to the cause of Ann's sickness; you will pardon me for my frankness, as I wish to assist you in developing the truth, the whole truth, and nothing but the truth.

I have no doubt but Ann had fully determined to break off the engagement with McNamar, but presume she had never notified him of the fact, as he did not return until after her death.

You are also in error in relating the conversation had with McNamar on October 14, 1836; you will bear in mind, McNamar left the county in 1832 or 1833 to fetch his father's family to Menard County, and did not return with them until the fall of 1835, after Ann's death. His mother died some years after he brought her to Menard County and was buried in the same graveyard. McNamar had purchased the farm on which we lived at the time of Ann's and father's death, prior to his leaving the county in 1832.

You ask me how I like your lecture. I answer I like it very much; the great wonder with me is, how you have unearthed, developed, and brought to light and life so much dead matter, and made so few mistakes.

I am, dear sir, truly your friend,

R. B. RUTLEDGE.

P.S. In folding this, Mrs. Rutledge suggests that she would be pleased to *desire* your photograph for her new album, as she desires to fill it up with new as well as old friends.

Yours,
RUTLEDGE.

From J. D. Wickizer

Chicago, Ill., November 25, 1866.

My dear Sir:

Some time ago you asked me to relate any anecdote or incident I might know connected with the late lamented President Lincoln. The following "pig story," No. 2, is literally true.

In 1855 Mr. Lincoln and myself were traveling by buggy from Woodford County Court to Bloomington, Ill., and in passing through a little grove, we suddenly heard the terrific squealing of a little pig near by us. Quick as thought Mr. L. leaped out of the buggy, seized a club, and pounced upon an old sow, and beat her lustily, that was in the act of eating one of her young ones, and thus he saved the pig and then remarked: "By jingo! the unnatural old brute shall not devour her own progeny." This, I think was his first proclamation of freedom. The following shows his ready wit. In 1858 in the court at Bloomington, Ill., Mr. Lincoln was engaged in a case, of not very great importance, but the attorney on the other side, Mr. Scott, a young lawyer of fine abilities (now a judge), was always very sensitive about being beaten, and in this case manifested unusual zeal and interest. The case lasted till late at night, when it was finally submitted to the jury. Mr. S. spent a sleepless night in anxiety, and early next morning learned to his great chagrin he had lost the case. Mr. Lincoln met him at the court house and asked him what had become of his case, with lugubrious countenance and melancholy tone. Mr. S. said: "It's gone to h——l." "Oh, well," said Mr. L., "then you'll see it again."

When do you expect to finish the Life of Mr. Lincoln? I opine it would be a very readable book, from what I have seen of it.

I think your portraiture of him is most excellent. But I think, take him in all, we shall never look upon his like again. I have a little word in his own handwriting he gave me at Washington, August 22, 1864, the last time I ever saw him, which I intend to keep most sacredly and hand down to *"posterity yet unborn."*

Let me hear from you, God and Liberty; answer.

J. D. Wickizer.

Hon. Sec. of War, please see & hear my particular friend Capt. Wickizer.

A. Lincoln.

Aug. 22, 1864

From R. B. Rutledge

Oskaloosa, December 4, 1866.

Dear Sir:

Your letter of 1st *inst.* is before me, and I answer: first, I think Mr. Lincoln read law in 1834 and 1835, read surveying probably in 1833 and '34; second, I cannot say whether Mr. Lincoln was radically a changed man, after the event of which you speak or not, as I saw little of him after that time; third, when he first came to New Salem and up to the time of which we write, Mr. Lincoln was all life and animation, seemed to see the bright side of every picture; fourth, cannot say as to his habit of learning eloquent pieces by heart, he was ever ready with an appropriate response to any vein of humor or eloquence when occasion required, have frequently heard him repeat pieces of prose and poetry, his practice was, when he wished to indelibly fix anything he was reading or studying on his mind, to write it down, have known him to write whole pages of books he was reading; fifth, cannot tell you how he read in the woods, as I never intruded on his retirement, simply know he read in the woods by seeing him return and having heard him say he had been reading in the brush, have seen him reading, walking the streets, occasionally become absorbed with his book, would stop and stand for a few moments, then walk on, or pass from one house in the town to another, or from one crowd or squad of men to another, apparently seeking amusement, with his book under his arm, when the company or amusement became dry or irksome he would open his book and commune with it for a time, then return it to its usual resting place, and entertain his audience; sixth, as well as I remember he was not what is usually termed a quick-minded man, although he usually would arrive at his conclusions very readily, seemed invariably to reflect and deliberate, never acted from impulse so far as to arrive at a wrong conclusion on a subject of any moment.

I desire you to learn all you can from James McRutledge as to the breaking off the engagement between Ann and McNamar.

Very truly yours,
R. B. Rutledge.

From J. Gillespie

Edwardsville, December 8, 1866.

Dear Friend:

Yours of yesterday is received in which you ask if I remember whether

Mr. Lincoln was given to abstract speculation or not. My impression is that he was less given to pure abstraction than most of thoughtful and investigating minds. I should say that he was contemplative rather than speculative. He wanted something solid to rest upon and hence his bias for mathematics and the physical sciences. I think he bestowed more attention to them than upon metaphysical speculations. I have heard him discourse upon the problem whether a ball discharged from a gun in a horizontal position would be longer in reaching the ground than one dropped at the instant of discharge from the muzzle of the gun, and he said it always appeared to him that they would both reach the ground at the same time even before he had read the philosophical explanation. He was fond of astronomy, but I can't call to mind any reference of his to geology. He doubtless had read and thought of the subject but it did not engage his attention to the degree that astronomy and mechanical science did. He invited me one day at Washington city to call upon him in the evening when he said we would go to the observatory and take a look at the moon through the large telescope. It proved to be cloudy and I did not go. I have no recollection of ever hearing Mr. Lincoln express himself in reference to the infinities; sometimes his mind ranged beyond the solid grounds on which it delighted to dwell. He exercised himself in endeavoring to trace out the source and development of language and he told me that on one occasion he prepared, or perhaps delivered, a lecture in Springfield on that subject and that he was surprised to find his investigations in that direction so interesting and instructive to himself. He used to say [of] the attempt to ascertain wherein wit baffled him more than any other undertaking of the kind that the first impression would be that the thing was of easy solution but the varieties of wit were so great that what would explain one case would be wholly inapplicable to another. I am of opinion that there was a slight tinge of fatalism in Mr. Lincoln's composition which would or might have led him to believe somewhat in destiny. Mr. Lincoln told me once that he could not avoid believing in predestination although he considered it a very unprofitable field of speculation because it was hard to reconcile that belief with responsibility for one's acts. After he became President he gave unmistakable indications of being a believer in destiny. I feel quite sure that there was not a moment when he despaired of success in putting down the rebellion, and he trusted more in Divine power than in human instrumentality. Mr. Lincoln had as strong a faith that it was in the purposes of the Almighty to save this country as ever Moses had that God would deliver the Israelites from bondage, and he came to believe that he himself was an instrument foreordained to aid in the accomplishment of this purpose as well as to emancipate the slaves. I do not think that he was what I would term a blind believer in fate or destiny but that he considered the means foreordained as well as the end and therefore he was extremely diligent in the use of the means. Mr. Lincoln had a remarkably inquiring mind, and I have no doubt he roamed over the whole field of knowledge. There were departments, however, upon which he fixed his attention with special interest. Those which were of a practical character and having a solid and indisputable basis he made himself master of so far as time and opportunity would allow, and this will account for his bringing out certain branches in conversation and being silent in regard to others about which he must have read as much as persons ordinarily do. He did not seem to think that to be of much value which could not be proven or rather demonstrated. His love of and capacity for analysis was wonderful. He analyzed every proposition with startling clearness and only discussed those branches of his case upon which it hinged, leaving the others clear out of view. He was a marvel of fairness in debate both in the courts and the political arena and he never desired to obtain an unfair advantage. From this I should infer that the sense of right and wrong was extremely acute in his nature. Mr. Lincoln was undemonstrative and consequently his character had to be studied to be understood. One would not comprehend his salient traits at first acquaintance and so he was sometimes misunderstood. He was by some considered cold-hearted or at least indifferent towards his friends. This was the result of his extreme fairness. He would rather disoblige a friend than do an act of injustice to a political opponent. His strong sense of justice made him hate slavery intensely, but he was so undemonstrative that he seldom gave utterance to his feelings even on that question. He never talked feelingly on the subject to me but once, although he knew that I agreed with him about the wrongs of that institution. To sum up his character I should say that he had greater natural mental caliber than any man I ever knew. He was extremely just and fair-minded. He was gentle as a girl and yet as firm for the right as adamant. He was tender-hearted without much show of sensibility. His manners were kind without ostentation. He was unquestionably ambitious for official distinction but he only desired place to enable him to do good and serve his country and his kind. It was somewhat strange how Mr. Lincoln, constituted as he was, could be a radical. But radical he was so far as *ends* were concerned, while he was conservative as to the *means* to be employed to bring about the ends. I think he had it in his mind for a long time to war upon slavery until its destruction was effected, but he always indicated a preference for getting rid of slavery by purchase rather than the war power. He was an artful man and yet his art had all the appearance of simple-mindedness. For instance, he would not begin the work of emancipation when proposed by Frémont nor would he proclaim the freedom of the slave until he had given the masters one hundred days' notice to lay down their arms. This was done to place them obviously in the wrong and strengthen his justification for the act. Mr. Lincoln knew that it was not in the power of the masters to lay down their arms, but they being in the wrong, he had no scruples about making that wrong appear monstrous. He was grave and gay alternately. He was the most rigidly logical in debate and yet he illustrated every point by a humorous anecdote. Study with Mr. Lincoln was a business, not a pleasure. He was extremely diligent when he had anything to do in preparing himself, but when his task was done, he betook himself to recreation. The information he gathered up was in reference to special questions and not with a view of laying in a general store of knowledge, expecting that he would have occasion to use it, and yet his natural tastes and aptitudes led him to explore most of those departments of study which bore mainly on the practical affairs of life. He had not a particle of envy in his nature. He always admitted that Douglas was a wonderfully great political leader, and with a good cause to advocate he thought he would be invincible. Mr. Lincoln appeared to be either extremely mirthful or extremely sad although if he had griefs he never spoke of them in general conversation. It was as a humorist that he towered above all other men it was ever my lot to meet. In early times Illinois was conspicuous for the number of its story tellers. The prevailing taste at that time took that direction. When Mr. Lincoln was about, I never knew a man who would pretend to vie with him in entertaining a crowd. He had an unfailing budget of genuinely witty and humorous anecdotes with which he illustrated every topic which could arise. The application was always perfect and his manner of telling a story was inimitable, although there was no *acting* in his manner, for he was not in the least degree histrionic. He never invented any of his stories but simply retailed them, but how he could gather up such a boundless supply and have them ever ready at command was the wonder of all his acquaintances. It might seem that this faculty would detract from his dignity, but it did not. No man ever commanded greater respect from or inspired more confidence in an audience than Mr. Lincoln did. He used his stories as much for producing conviction in the minds of his hearers as for creating merriment. If Mr. Lincoln studied any one thing more than another and for effect, it was to make himself understood by all classes. He had great natural clearness and simplicity of statement, and this faculty he cultivated with marked assiduity. He despised everything like ornament or display and confined himself to a dry bold statement of his point and then worked away with sledge-hammer logic at making out his case. I believe Mr. Lincoln succeeded in his purpose, for I think the great body of our people understood and appreciated him better than any man this country has ever produced.

In religious matters I think Mr. Lincoln cared but little for tenets or sects but had strong and pervading ideas of the infinite power, wisdom, and goodness of Deity and of man's obligations to his Maker and to his fellow-beings. He was economical without being parsimonious. He never attempted a speculation in his life but always displayed a commendable zeal and alacrity to obtain business. He was brave without being rash and never refrained from giving utterance to his views because they were unpopular or likely to bring him into danger; at the same time he abstained from needlessly giving offense. Mr. Lincoln never idolized particular men but had wonderful faith in the honesty and good sense of the masses. In politics he was an old-line Whig, a devout believer in a national currency, the development of American industry, and internal improvements by the general government. He always deprecated the removal of men from office for opinion's sake. Although Mr. Lincoln was eminently national in his feelings he looked with disfavor upon the American party and contended that a love of liberty and free government was not confined to this country; he ascribed our beneficent institutions rather to circumstances, and his aim was to restrict it to its original design. Mr. Lincoln had the appearance of being a slow thinker. My impression is that he was not so slow as he was careful. He never liked to put forth a proposition without revolving it over in his own mind, but when he was compelled to act promptly, as in debate, he was quick enough. Douglas, who was a very skillful controversialist, never obtained any advantage over him. I never could discover anything in Mr. Lincoln's mental composition remarkably singular. His qualities were those ordinarily given to mankind, but he had them in remarkable degree. He was wonderfully kind, careful, and just. He had an immense stock of common sense and he had faith enough in it to trust it in every emergency. He had passed through all the grades of society when he reached the Presidency, and he had found common sense a sure reliance and he put it into practice. He acted all through his career upon just such principles as every man of good common sense would approve and say: that is just as I would have done myself. There was nothing of the Napoleonic in his style of doing things. If he had been in Napoleon's place, he never would have gone off to Egypt to strike a blow at England, and he would have been equally careful not to send an army to Moscow. Lincoln had no superhuman qualities, which we call genius, but he had those which belong to mankind generally in an astonishing degree. If I may be allowed the expression, Mr. Lincoln was a great common man. He was a giant, but formed and fashioned like other men. He only differed from most men in degree. He had only their qualities, but there he had them in larger measure than any man of modern times. He loved the masses but was not strikingly partial to any particular individual. Mr. Lincoln cared but little for minor elections but entered very zealously into important and general ones. Hence he was not generally successful at home and was not considered a good political organizer because he allowed the subordinate offices to be filled by those opposed to him. When he had a larger theater to operate upon, however, it cannot be denied that he acted with great boldness and skill. He succeeded in breaking down the best organized party that ever existed in this or any other country and that under the lead of the most consummate chieftain we have ever had. Douglas was bold, original, and energetic. Politics with him was a trade. It was only an episode in Mr. Lincoln's life. Douglas was idolized by his followers. Lincoln was loved by his. Douglas was the representative of his partisans. Lincoln was the representative man of the unsophisticated people. Douglas was great in the estimation of his followers. Lincoln was good in the opinion of his supporters. Douglas headed a party. Lincoln stood upon a principle. Lincoln did not begin his operations for the Presidency at the head of a party. He had the tact and good fortune to combine much of the old Whig and Democratic parties as rebelled against Southern dictation, with the free-soilers proper, and thus secured a majority of the free States. At the time of his death he had, however, succeeded in organizing a party. He had gained the confidence of a majority of the whole people in his fitness for the place. All but the old political hacks had settled down in the belief that he was master of the situation and was the right man in the right place. The amazing popularity he obtained was attributable to two things. He had been successful under the most trying circumstances and then he was most emphatically one of the people. He said and did things in a way that commended itself to the public taste and so that all could understand it. The masses are naturally delighted at seeing one of their own class elevated, if he proves competent and particularly if he succeeds by doing things in their way. The idea that the affairs of state cannot be carried on in a plain common sense way is as old as the time of the Egyptian priesthood. Statesmen have generally given countenance to this absurdity and inculcated the idea that statecraft was beyond the comprehension of ordinary mortals. When we found Mr. Lincoln administering the affairs of government with so much vigor and success, we felt proud of him. There was a strong tinge of sadness in Mr. Lincoln's composition. He was not naturally disposed to look on the bright side of the picture. He felt very strongly that there was more of discomfort than real happiness in human existence under the most favorable circumstances, and the general current of his reflections was in that channel. He never obtruded those views upon others but on the contrary strove as much as possible to be gay and lively. There was a slight dash of what is generally called superstition in Mr. Lincoln's mind. He evidently believed that the perceptions were sometimes more unerring than reason and outstripped it. I can't say that he fully believed in presentiments, but he undoubtedly had gloomy forebodings as to himself. He told me after his election that he did not count confidentially on living to get through with the task set before him, and I did not think that he apprehended death in the natural way; still I do not believe that he took any precautions to guard against danger. I met him once, coming alone from the War Office to the White House, and remarked to him that I thought he was exposing himself to danger of assassination. He replied that no precautions he could take would be availing if they were determined to kill him. I rode out with him that evening to the Soldiers' House, when he was accompanied by an escort of cavalry; on the way he said that the escort was rather forced upon him by the military men, that he could see no certain protection against assassination if it was determined to take away his life. He said it seemed to him like putting up the gaps in only one place when the fence was down all along. Mr. Lincoln was pre-eminently humane. He said to me once that Ould, the rebel commissioner for exchanges, had just notified them that he had put 16,000 of the men paroled at Vicksburg into the field without exchanging. "Now," said he, "these men are liable to be put to death when recaptured, for breach of parole. If we do not do something of that sort, this outrage will be repeated on every occasion. What would you do under such circumstances?" "Well," said I, "that is too big a question for me." "It is indeed a serious question," said Mr. Lincoln, "and I have been more sorely tried by it than any other that has occurred during the war. It will be an act of great injustice to our soldiers to allow the paroled rebels to be put into the field without exchange. Such a practice would demoralize almost any army in the world if played off upon them. It would be nearly impossible to induce them to spare the lives of prisoners they might capture. On the other hand," said he, "these men were no doubt told by their superiors that they had been exchanged and it would be hard to put them to death under such circumstances. On the whole," said he, "my impression is that mercy bears richer fruits than any other attribute." Mr. Lincoln was capable of immense physical and mental labor. His mind and body were in perfect harmony. He was very powerful physically. He was reputed to be one of the best wrestlers in the country. The first time I saw him was in 1832 in the campaign against Black Hawk. He was engaged in wrestling with a man named Dow Thompson from St. Clair County. The latter was the champion of the southern part of the State, while Lincoln was put up as the champion from the north. I never heard Mr. Lincoln complain of being fatigued. I think he was an utter stranger, in the early part of his life at least, to the feeling. I have heard him regret while he was President that it was impossible for him to give audience to all who wished to see him, and I do not think that he was disengaged for an instant, from the time he assumed the Presidential office until his death, from the consideration of public affairs, except when he was asleep. He was not in the habit of idolizing particular men, and you would seldom hear him sounding the praises of anyone. He admired Mr. Clay and Mr. Webster and had great respect for General Taylor. Of all men in the South (of those who differed from him on the slavery question, I mean), Mr. Stephens of Georgia was his favorite. I have frequently heard him speak in very respectful terms of Stephens. On the other hand he never manifested any bitter hatred towards his enemies. It was enough for him in a controversy to get the better of his adversary in argument without descending to personal abuse. He had not a particle of envy in his nature. I recollect his telling me once that he went to Cincinnati to attend to a patent case. He was expected to take the lead in the management of the suit but to be assisted by a young lawyer of that city. He said he prepared himself, as he thought, thoroughly and flattered himself that he knew something of mechanics but said: "When I came to compare notes with my young associate, I found that I knew nothing." Said he: "I told my client that my associate could lose all I knew and not miss it, and I insisted that he should take the lead." It required no effort on his part to admit another man's superiority, and his admission that General Grant was right and he was wrong about operations at Vicksburg was not intended for effect as some suppose but was perfectly in character. I am unable to call to mind any expression from Mr. Lincoln of a preference for one article of diet over another. I should judge that he was totally indifferent on that head. Mr. Lincoln had an astonishing memory. I never found it at fault. He could recall every incident of his life, particularly if anything amusing was connected with it. Mr. Lincoln used anecdotes as labor-saving contrivances. He could convey his ideas on any subject through the form of a simple story or homely illustration with better effect than any man I ever knew. To illustrate: I was talking with him once about State sovereignty. He said the advocates of that theory always reminded him of the fellow who contended that the proper place for the big kettle was inside of the little one. There is one little incident in the political life of Mr. Lincoln which perhaps ought to be explained, as it has been charged by some against him as an act of dereliction of duty; and that was his jumping out of a window, to avoid voting as a member of the Legislature. The facts were these: Governor Carlin convened the Legislature of 1840–41 by proclamation, two weeks earlier than it would have met under the Constitution. At the previous session an act had been passed legalizing the suspension of specie payments by the bank until the end of the next session of the general assembly. On the morning of the last day of the first two weeks of the session, as we supposed, it was ascertained that the Democrats had determined to adjourn *sine die,* make those two weeks a distinct session, at the end of which the bank would be compelled to resume specie payments or forfeit its charter. The Whigs believed that this step would be not only unfair to the bank, which had had no notice of or made any preparation for such a proceeding, and that it would benefit only the banks of other States, which held the paper of our bank, by enabling them to draw its specie for its bills which they held while it could get nothing from them on their bills which it held and that the loss or the depreciation of our bank circulation would fall principally upon our citizens who were holders of small sums. The Whigs determined if possible to prevent the *sine die* adjournment, knowing that the Constitution would convene the Legislature on the following Monday. It required a quorum to adjourn *sine die.* Less than a quorum could adjourn from day to day. As the Constitution then stood, it was necessary to have two members to call the ayes and nays to show that a quorum was not voting. If the Whigs absented themselves, there would not be a quorum left even with the two who should be deputed to call the ayes and nays. The Whigs immediately held a meeting and resolved that they would all stay out except Lincoln and me, who were to call the ayes and nays. We appeared in the afternoon, motion to adjourn *sine die* was made, and we called the ayes and nays. The Democrats discovered the game, and the sergeant-at-arms was sent out to gather up the absentees. There was great excitement in the House, which was then held in a church in Springfield. We soon discovered that several Whigs had been caught and brought in and that the plan had been spoiled, and we, Lincoln and I, determined to leave the hall and, going to the door, found it locked, and then raised a window and jumped out but not until the Democrats had succeeded in adjourning. Mr. Gridley of McLean accompanied us in our exit. The result of this operation was just as we anticipated. The bank resumed and paid out nearly all of its specie to banks and brokers in other States while not a cent could be obtained from them, as the banks everywhere had been authorized to suspend specie payments. In a few weeks the folly of the course of the majority became apparent, and they themselves introduced a bill again legalizing a suspension but it was too late. Our bank had been too much weakened and it went under at the general resumption of specie payments. I think Mr. Lincoln always regretted that he entered into the arrangement, as he deprecated everything that savored of the revolutionary. In politics Mr. Lincoln was before all things in favor of perfect equality. He consequently detested aristocracy in all its forms and loved our government and its founders almost to idolatry. He was for a national currency, internal improvements by the general government, and the encouragement of home manufactures. On this latter subject I have heard him make arguments greatly more powerful and convincing than anything I have ever heard or read.

This is a hasty sketch of what I remember concerning Mr. Lincoln. If my attention should be directed to any particulars, I might be able to recall other things and shall take great pleasure in answering any calls you may make on me. Let me hear from you often. If I can be the means of imparting any information touching the life of a truly good and great man, I shall be supremely gratified. I feel proud of his fame as I have ever regarded him as the genuine product of American institutions.

Yours truly,

J. GILLESPIE.

FROM GRANT GOODRICH

Chicago, December 9, 1866.

Dear Sir:

Your favor of the 5th is received. In reply I have to say, Mr. Lincoln was my associate first in the trial of three cases *vs.* Grace Lawson in 1845 for fraud and misrepresentations, in the sale of land. The cases were severely contested. Messrs. Butterfield and Collins and Edw. Baker, Esqs., being counsel for defendant. Mr. Lincoln in closing the case made the best jury argument I ever heard him make. Judge Pope said it was one of the best he ever heard.

The case of Parker *vs.* Hoyt was for infringement of a patent waterwheel. My recollection is it was commenced in 1846 or '47; Mr. Lincoln was employed for the defendant. It was for trial in June 1848. There was some technical error in the notices of the matter in dispute and on motion of the plaintiff most of the defendant's evidence was excluded and defeat seemed inevitable. At that time a term of the United States District Court was held at Chicago on the first Monday of July. The only way of saving the case was to get it over to the term at Chicago, by which time would be

secured to correct the error in the notices. Motions were made on both
sides which involved numerous questions new to the counsel and court, as
very few patent cases had then been tried in that court. The time occupied
in this discussion was so extended that the case had to be transferred to
Chicago for trial.

The testimony was procured, but under the rulings of the Court was
excluded for the main purpose for which it was offered, but was admitted
for another purpose. We placed great reliance on an elder patent to
establish the want of novelty in the invention of the plaintiff. The case
was prosecuted with great zeal and ability, and the trial lasted for several
days. Mr. Lincoln took a great interest in the case. He had tended a saw-
mill for some time and was able in his argument to explain the action of
the water upon the wheel, in a manner so clear and intelligible that the
jury was enabled to comprehend the points and the line of defense. It was
evident he had carried the jury with him, in a most masterly argument
the force of which could not be broken by the reply of the opposing counsel. But the Court was evidently impressed with the conviction that the
plaintiff should recover, and charged on every material point for the
plaintiff and in effect told the jury that the prior patent on which we so
much relied was no defense.

After the jury had retired, Mr. Lincoln became very anxious and uneasy. The jury was in another building, the windows of which opened on
the street. They had been out for some two hours. In passing along the
street, one of the jury on whom we had very much relied, he being a very
intelligent man and firm in his convictions, held up to him one finger. Mr.
Lincoln became very much excited, fearing it indicated that eleven of the
jury were against him. He was assured that if this man was for him, he
would never yield his opinion. He replied, if he was like a juryman he
had in Tazewell County, the defendant was safe. That he was there employed to prosecute a suit for a divorce. His client was a very pretty, refined, interesting woman in court. The defendant was a rotten, gross,
morose, garrulous, fault-finding, cross, and uncomfortable person, entirely unfitted for the husband of such a woman. And though he was able
to prove the use of very offensive and vulgar epithets applied by him to
his wife, and all sorts of annoyances, but no such acts of personal violence
assigned by the statute to justify a divorce. He did the best he could and
appealed to the jury to have compassion on the woman and not bind her
to such a man and such a life as awaited her as the wife of such a man. The
jury took about the same view of it in their deliberations. They desired to
find for her but could find no evidence which would really justify a verdict
for her, and drew up a verdict for the defendant and all signed but one,

who, when asked to do so, said: "Gentlemen, I am going to lie down to sleep and when you get ready to give a verdict for that woman, wake me up, for before I will give a verdict against her, I will be here until I rot and the pismires carry me out of the keyhole." "Now," said Mr. Lincoln, "if that juryman will stick like that man, we are safe."

In a short time the jury came in with a verdict for the defendant. He always regarded this as one of the most gratifying triumphs of his professional life. He was afterwards employed in one or two other patent suits, but they never came to a final trial. He had a great deal of mechanical genius, could understand readily the principles and mechanical action of machinery, and had the power in his clear simple illustrations and style to make the jury comprehend them.

The most important case he ever had and the one in which his powers were exhibited with most advantage, was the Rock Island Bridge case. Hon. N. B. Judd was attorney in that case.

And now, friend Herndon, I have complied with your request, imperfectly it is true, but as well as I could. You will admit that, while I say I have none but the tenderest feelings for you, you have never given me occasion to entertain any others. I therefore, as your friend, and the friend of Mr. Lincoln, propose to say a few things, prompted by that friendship, but which I know the vanity of all men rebel against.

First, in my opinion you are the last man who ought to attempt to write a Life of Abraham Lincoln. Your long and intimate association with him unfits you for the task. No one holding the intimate relations to another which you did to him ever has succeeded. There may be exceptions, but I cannot now remember one. They are mere eulogists, or having known him, in other conditions than on those fields, those departments, where his fame was won, he regards and exhibits him in those humble and different aspects and characteristics in which the public have no taste, and which bring him down from the high [point?] of his triumphs, [undeciphered] him down everyday affairs of life which are stale and insipid to the public. To enter into the private everyday life of ordinary or extraordinary men can only be made endurable to readers, or safe to the fame of the subject, with the most discriminating taste and art; and no one is safe to undertake it, without much practice, and knowledge of the public taste. Again, contact with great men always dispels something of the awe with which they are contemplated at a distance. In intimate association, we fix upon some characteristic or peculiarity and fail to catch other lineaments. We can only regard them as the kind friend, amusing companion, and generous mind. In the distance we see the bold outline of the mountain; its summits wrapped in sunshine, or swathed in cloud; when we approach it, we catch a view of the deep, it may be dark gorges, the rugged cliffs, the lean rocks, and distorted outlines. So in the characters of our dearest friends. See how Boswell with all his literary abilities failed in his Life of Johnson. No blow so severe was ever struck at Johnson. Think of these things.

If I am to judge of what your production will be by the publication of a portion of your Salem lectures, I am more solicitous still. I fear you did not realize what an injury and injustice you did to the memory of your dear friend and mortification you caused his friends, but especially his widow and children. Ask yourself, if he was living, whether he would not have revolted at the uncovering to the public gaze that drama of his life? And shall his friends exhibit what we know he would have preserved in sacred privacy? If the facts are truly stated, I should as soon think of exposing his dead body, uncoffined, to the vulgar gaze of the public eye. It should never have been dug up from the grave, when time had buried it.

Besides, your style is not well adapted to such an undertaking. The want of practice is palpable. Your style is purely legal, such an one as is acquired by drawing legal documents and pleadings, and is decidedly different from our form by familiarity with the best writers. It is rugged, abounding in adjectives and explications, full of climaxes and hard dry words. It reads as if it had been jerked out word by word; it gives one the sense you have in riding in a lumber wagon over a frozen road, or the noise made in machinery when a cog has been broken.

Now, my friend, I have spoken plainly, but sincerely. I may do you injustice, but it is not intentional. I may lose your friendship by it, but I have only done what I would wish one to do to me under the same circumstances. And I have observed, in myself and others, that the very points in which strength is supposed, are the very points of weakness.

I am yours, etc.,
GRANT GOODRICH.

Springfield, Ill., December 10, 1866.

Mr. Goodrich.
Sir:

I thank you for the first part of your letter giving me an account of the patent case which Mr. Lincoln "tended" to. I say I thank you for it. As to the second part of your letter, I guess I shall have to treat you as Lincoln always did treat you, as an exceedingly weak-headed brother. The more he kicked you, the closer you clung to him. Do you remember? Analyze yourself.

Yours truly,
W. H. HERNDON.

FROM J. H. LITTLEFIELD

Washington, December 11, 1866.

Respected Friend:

I have been trying very hard to obtain a file of papers for you but I fear I shall have to give it up. (I had hoped to get files owned by private individuals.) The Washington *Star* contains the fullest account of the entry of Mr. Lincoln in the city of Washington in 1861. The gentleman that reported for it is a friend of mine and is entirely reliable and he says that he had an interview with Mr. Lincoln when he first arrived here in '61. It will be necessary to employ a person to copy such parts of the *Star* and other papers as may seem required for your work. I would copy them myself but I cannot possibly find time, besides Mrs. L. is very sick with pneumonia. If it is your wish, I will employ a person to copy such parts of the *Star* and other papers as you may require at once. I will state an anecdote that came under my observation. In 1862 there was considerable said about the Yazoo River expedition. Mr. Lincoln one evening at the White House was suffering with pain caused by the extraction of a "raging tooth." Pete Halstead, several others, and myself called on Mr. Lincoln and found him out of the room which he generally occupied. We sat down in the private Secretary's room and remained there some minutes when Mr. Lincoln, hearing our voices, came in and sat down (just as he used to in the office in Springfield), and notwithstanding the pain that afflicted him, chatted humorously with here and there a flash of real logic that showed that he comprehended the situation. The Yazoo River expedition received his attention; he said by the way of preamble that he found it necessary to yield here a little and there a little in order to keep peace in the family and that if he interfered in a plan that was not essential, vital, the West Pointers, i.e., the regular officers who had the execution of all plans, would in some way or other obstruct or defeat the execution of his scheme; therefore, inasmuch as they had to be depended upon at *last,* he found it best to trust them at *first* and rely on events and the power of persuasion to rectify errors. In regard to the Yazoo River expedition, he said (pointing to the map; this was a large map which hung in his room which he often referred to): "How can a force go down a river that is only a few rods wide when it cannot get down a river that is a mile wide? And if it could, it would only wind about and come out into the same river that it is contended by the military officers you cannot pursue—the Mississippi—and for this reason you wish to leave the Mississippi about Vicksburg. This expedition proposes to follow the Yazoo and come out in the Mississippi. What have you accomplished? You have gained nothing. I can't better make this clear than by relating an incident that came under my own observation. There was a man in Illinois a good many years since that was troubled with an old sow and her pigs; again and again the old man and his sons drove her out and repeatedly found her in the lot. One day he and his boys searched about and found that she got into the lot through a certain hollow log that had been placed in the fence; they took out this log and built up the fence by placing the log a little differently than before, and the next day, what was the astonishment of the old lady to find that she and her *litter* came out of the log *outside* of the field instead of *inside*. It is just so with the Yazoo River expedition," said Mr. L. "It comes out of the same side of the log."

This little story, it seems to me, illustrates the fact that Mr. L. comprehended military problems far better than was generally supposed. I will endeavor from time to time to arrange little incidents that I was an eye-witness of, or collect such anecdotes that have not yet been published as may seem to be of some service to you. If you should desire to have a faithful likeness engraved of Mr. Lincoln, I may be of some service. I am now painting General Grant in oil and expect to publish his picture in *pure line* engraving, the head of which will be six inches long. I expect also to paint a life-size head of Mr. Lincoln which I will have engraved if I can bring it about. It is quite doubtful if there is a living artist that has such varied and serviceable remembrances of the good man as your humble servant. When your book is ready for publication, I may put you on track of good houses in New York or elsewhere. Please write me at your earliest convenience, and if you desire it, I will set a man to copying the points you require at once. I should esteem it a great favor if you would favor me with a copy of your lecture on the courtship, etc., of Mr. Lincoln.

Affectionately yours,
J. H. LITTLEFIELD.

FROM HENRY WILSON

Natick, Mass., May 30, 1867.

My dear Sir:

In looking over my papers, I find a letter of yours of the 20th of August last requesting me to give you my ideas of Mr. Lincoln's character as a man and a public officer. With this letter, I find another letter of yours dated December 21, 1860, in answer to a letter of mine asking you to give me your opinion of the President just elected. In this letter to me you say of Mr. Lincoln what more than four years of observation confirmed. After stating that you had been his law partner for sixteen years, and his most intimate and bosom friend all that time, you say: "I know him better than he does himself. I know this seems a 'lie,' but I will risk the assertion. Mr. Lincoln is a man of *heart,* was as gentle as a woman's and as tender, but he has a will as strong as iron. He therefore loves all mankind, hates slavery, every form of despotism. Put these together—love for the slave and a determination, a *will,* that justice, strong and unyielding, shall be done, where he has got a right to act—and you can form your own conclusion. Lincoln will fail *here;* namely, if a question of political economy, if any question, comes up which is doubtful, questionable, which no man can demonstrate, then his friends can rule him; but when on justice, right, liberty, the government and Constitution, Union, humanity, *then you may all stand aside;* he will rule them and no man can move him, no set of men can. There is no fail *here.* This is Lincoln, and you mark what I say. You and I must keep the people right; God will keep Lincoln right. Don't you fear, Mr. Wilson; I have conversations with him, but am not authorized to speak."

These words of yours made a deep impression upon my mind, and I came to love and trust him even before I saw him. After an acquaintance of more than four years, I found that your idea of him was in all respects correct, that he was the loving, tender, firm, and just man you represented him to be, while upon some questions in which moral elements did not so clearly enter he was, perhaps, too easily influenced by others. As Chairman of the Military Committee, I had nearly fifteen thousand nominations of his to act upon and was often consulted by him in regard to nominations, and also the legislation for the army, and I had the best opportunity to see him under all circumstances. I saw him often under the most trying circumstances at the War Department by day, and by night too, and I had the best possible opportunities to study and judge him, and I can truly say that your description of this loving, tender, true, just man was a correct one.

Mr. Lincoln was a genuine democrat in feeling, sentiment, and action. How patiently and considerately he listened, amid the terrible pressure of public affairs, to the people that thronged his ante-room. I remember calling upon him one day during the war on pressing business. The ante-room was crowded with men and women seeking admission. He seemed oppressed, care-worn, weary. I said to him: "Mr. President, you are too exhausted to see this throng waiting to see you, you will wear yourself out, and you ought not to see these people today." He replied with one of those smiles in which sadness seemed to mingle: "They don't want much and they don't get but little, and I must see them."

During the war his heart was oppressed and his life burdened with the conflict between the tenderness of his nature and what seemed to be the imperative demands of duty. In the darkest hours of the conflict desertions were frequent, and army officers urgently pressed the execution of the sentence of the law, but it was with the greatest effort he would bring himself to consent to the execution of the judgments of the military tribunals. I remember walking early one Sabbath morning with a wounded Irish officer who came to Washington to say that a soldier who had been sentenced to be shot in a day or two for desertion had fought bravely by his side in battle. I told him that we had come to ask him to pardon the poor soldier. After a few moments' reflection he said: "My officers tell me the good of the service demands the enforcement of the law, but it makes my heart ache to have this poor boy shot. I will pardon him, and then you will join in blaming me for it. You all censure me for granting pardons, and yet you all ask me to do so." No man ever had a more loving and tender nature than Mr. Lincoln.

He was, as you say, a firm man where he clearly saw duty, but most earnest, devoted, and ablest friends in and out of Congress pressed him for months to issue a declaration of emancipation, but he could not be coaxed nor driven into action till he saw the time had come to do it. His firmness was again tried after he wrote the letter to Mr. Clay and other rebels in Canada, the time of Mr. Greeley's mission. Our timid politicians were alarmed. The Democratic Convention at Chicago was about to meet. Some of our most active men hurried on to Washington to induce him to write another letter modifying the other. Learning this, I hurried to Washington, saw these timid leaders about the White House, and made an appointment in the evening with Mr. Lincoln. When the time came, I said to him that I had come to Washington to say to him that I believed it would be fatal to us if he qualified his letter, that the letter would be great strength in the canvass, that it had given great confidence to the anti-slavery men, and they would determine the result. He spoke of the pressure upon him, of the condition of the country, of the possible action of the coming Democratic Convention, and of the uncertainty of the election, in tones of sadness. After discussing for a long time these matters, he said with great calmness and firmness: "I do not know what the result may be, we may be defeated, we may fail, but we will go down with our principles. I will not modify, qualify, nor retract my proclamation, nor my letter." I can never forget his measured tones, nor words, nor cease to feel that his firmness, amid the pressure of active friends, saved our cause in 1864.

Yours truly,
HENRY WILSON.

FROM LEONARD SWETT

Chicago, Ill., August 29, 1887.

My dear Sir:

Your inquiry in reference to the circumstances of the appointment of David Davis, as one of the Justices of the Supreme Court, reached me last evening. In reply I beg leave to recall the fact that, in 1860, the politicians of Illinois were divided into three divisions, which were represented in the Decatur Convention by the votes on the nomination for Governor. The largest vote was for Norman B. Judd, of Chicago, his strength in the main being the northern part of the State. I was next in order of strength, and Yates the third, but the divisions were not materially unequal. The result was, Yates was nominated, Yates's strength being about Springfield and Jacksonville, extending to Quincy on the west, and mine was at Bloomington and vicinity, and south and southeast.

These divisions were kept up awhile after Mr. Lincoln's election and were considered in the distribution of Federal patronage. A vacancy in the United States Senate occurred early in 1861 by the death of Stephen A. Douglas, and Governor Yates appointed O. H. Browning of Quincy to fill the vacancy. There was also a vacancy upon the Supreme bench of the United States to be filled from this general vicinity by Mr. Lincoln in the early part of his administration, and Judge Davis of Bloomington, and Mr. Browning of Quincy, were both aspirants for the position. Mr. Browning had the advantage that Lincoln was new in his seat, and Senators were august personages, and, being in the Senate, and a most courteous and able gentleman, Mr. Browning succeeded in securing nearly all the Senatorial strength, and Mr. Lincoln was nearly swept off his feet by the current of influence. Davis's supporters were the circuit court lawyers, mainly in the eastern and central part of the State. These lawyers were at home, and their presence was not a living force felt constantly by the President at Washington.

I was then living at Bloomington and met Judge Davis every day. As months elapsed, we used to get word from Washington in reference to the condition of things; finally one day the word came that Mr. Lincoln had said: "I do not know what I may do when the time comes, but there has never been a day when, if I had to act then, I should not have appointed Mr. Browning."

Judge Davis, General Orme, and myself held a consultation in my law office at Bloomington; we decided that the remark was too Lincolnian to be mistaken, and no man but he could have put the situation so quaintly. We decided also that the appointment was gone and sat there glum over the situation. I finally broke the silence, saying in substance: "The appointment is gone; I am going home to pack my carpet-sacks for Washington." "No, you are not," said Davis. "Yes, I am," was my reply, "Lincoln is being swept off his feet by the influence of these Senators and I will have the luxury of one talk with him before he acts."

I did go home, and two days thereafter, in the morning about seven o'clock, for I knew Mr. Lincoln's habits well, was at the door of his room at the White House and spent most of the forenoon with him. I tried to impress upon him that he had been brought into prominence by the circuit court lawyers of the old Eighth Circuit, headed by Judge Davis. "If Judge Davis with his tact and his force had not lived, and all other things had been as they were, I believe you would not be sitting now where you are sitting." He replied: "I guess that is so." "Now," I said, "it is the common law of mankind that one raised into prominence is expected to recognize the force that lifts him, or, if from a pinch, the force that lets him out. The Czar Nicholas was once attacked by an assassin, a kindly hand warded off the blow and saved his life. The Czar hunted out the owner of that hand and strewed his pathway with flowers through life. The Emperor Napoleon III has hunted out everybody who even tossed him a biscuit in his prison at Ham, and has made him rich. Here is Judge Davis, whom you know to be in every respect qualified for this position, and you ought in justice to yourself and public expectation to give him this place." We had an earnest pleasant forenoon, and I thought I had the best of the argument and I think he thought so too.

I left him and went to Willard's Hotel to think over the interview, and there a new thought struck me. I therefore wrote a letter to Mr. Lincoln and returned to the White House. Getting in, I read it to him and left it with him. It was in substance that he might think, if he gave Davis this place, he, when *he* got to Washington, would not give him any peace until he gave me a place equally good. That I recognized the fact that he could not give this place to Davis, which would be charged to the Bloomington faction in our State politics, and then give me anything—I would have [to] be just to the party there; that this appointment, if made, should "kill two birds with one stone"; that I would accept it as one-half for me, and one-half for the judge; and after that, if I or any of my friends ever troubled him, he could draw that letter as a plea in bar, on that subject. As I read it, Lincoln said: "If you mean that among friends, as it reads, I will take it and make the appointment."

He then made a request of the judge after his appointment, in reference to continuance of a clerk in his circuit, and wrote to him a notice of the appointment which he received the same afternoon I returned to Blooming-ton. Judge Davis was about fifteen years my senior. I had come to his circuit at the age of twenty-four, and between him and Lincoln I had grown up, leaning in hours of weakness on their own great arms for support. I was glad of the opportunity to put in the mite of my claims upon Lincoln and give it to Davis and have been glad I did it every day since.

An unknown number of people have almost every week since, speaking perhaps extravagantly, asked me in a quasi-confidential manner, how was it that you and Lincoln were so intimate and he never gave you anything? I have generally said: "It seems to me that is my question, and so long as I don't complain I do not see why you should." I may be pardoned also for saying that I have not considered every man not holding an office out of place in life. I got my eyes open on this subject before I got an office, and as in Washington I saw the Congressman in decline, I prayed that my lat-ter end might not be like his.

Yours truly,
LEONARD SWETT.

FROM CHARLES FRIEND

Sonora, Ky., July 31, 1889.

Dear Sir:

While living in Hodgenville there came a man from Illinois who said that it was reported in that State that Abe Enloe was Abe Lincoln's father. I heard the question put to old Uncle Abe Enloe by my brother-in-law Mr. A. H. Redman. There was another gentleman present, Dr. W. H. Holt. Redman asked if it was true that he, Abe Enloe, was Abe's father. The old man drew himself up to his full height—some six feet three inches—and stroked his long white beard and remarked that it was an honor to be proud of to even to be thought to be the father of a President and one that had risen by his own merits to hold the proud position of President of these United States. "But," said he, "I was only fifteen years old when Abe was born." "Then," said Redman, "you could not have been, being at that time only fourteen years old when he was begotten." "Now," said Uncle Abe, "not too fast, for I passed into puberty at fourteen years and could have been his father at that age as easily as at any time from that until the present moment. Now to set the matter forever at rest, I will say I never put my hand on her naked flesh on any part of her body save her hands, and never in my life had carnal intercourse with her. And further, I believe that he was the son of Thomas Lincoln. I think all this grew out of his name being the same as mine, but I can account for that name; his grandfather was named Abraham Lincoln. The grandfather was killed by the Indians on Salt River not far from where now stands Shepherdsville at an old salt works. I will further say that, if he is not Thomas Lincoln's son, he was the son of Charles Friend, this boy's grandfather"—pointing at your correspondent—"or William Cessna or George Brownfield; his long bony body seems to point to the Brownfields more strongly as they were all long, bony people often over six and a half feet in height." The reason I think he might be a son of Charles Friend is that Nancy Hanks's, Abe's mother's, first child, Dennis F., was by Charles Friend but his shape does not point to that family, as they were a short thick heavy-set people and the Cessnas are of the same shape, being closely related to the Friends. You ask me a question, was he, Thomas Lincoln, castrated? I heard a cousin of my father, Judge Jonathan Friend Cessna, say that his father William Cessna said that Thomas Lincoln could not have been Abe's father for one of Thomas's testicles was not larger than a pea or perhaps both of them were no larger than peas; and "Uncle Fillie Cessna" said he believed that Abe was my uncle and he based this reason on the fact that Nancy Hanks's first child, Dennis Hanks, was Charles Friend's boy. Be that as it may, let it go. Now whose son was Dennis Friend Hanks? There never was but one Hanks family in this county (Hardin), and they were all sisters. Mary or Polly who married Thomas Sparrow, Elizabeth or Betsey who married Jesse Friend, Nancy who married Thomas Lincoln. When Charles Friend married my grandmother Sallie Huss, he told her that he had a son by Nancy Hanks and she told him to get the boy away [?] so and Dennis stayed with his father until Sparrow and the other families left here for Indiana and Illinois. Uncle Dennis asked grandfather if he might go with him, and Thomas Sparrow and the old people gave their consent. My grandmother told me the facts.

CHARLES FRIEND.

FROM CHARLES FRIEND

Sonora, Hardin County, Ky., August 20, 1889.

Dear Sir:

Yours of the 10th *inst.* received ten o'clock this morning. Where could have been? There never were but one family of Hanks in this county that

I ever heard of and they were all women; I never heard anything against the women except Nancy. Judge J. F. Cessna, cousin of my father, told me that Uncle Isaac Friend was once in love with her and at a party at night after a log rolling in the day he (Isaac) was laying with his head in her lap and swore that he felt the child kick in her belly when talking to the boys about the matter. Later he learned that his brother Charles Friend had done the work for her, Dennis Friend Hanks was the boy that did the kicking which kicked Uncle Isaac out of marrying her. I have written Uncle Dennis several times and asked him what relation he had to President Lincoln, and he will never answer it. The first letter he ever wrote me, he said: "My mother was a Hanks; she says your grandfather was my father; this don't doubt." Every old person that I ever talked to on the subject agree by saying that Nancy Hanks, Dennis's mother, was A. Lincoln's mother.

Nancy Hanks married Thomas Lincoln
Betsey   "   "   Thomas Sparrow
Polly   "   "   Jesse Friend
"   "   "   Levi Hall

These women were all sisters. Uncle Jesse Friend moved from here to Paris, Illinois, and died there. One of his daughters married a Mr. Hatfield and returned to Kentucky. Thomas Sparrow raised Uncle Dennis. A. Lincoln calling Dennis cousin can be accounted for easy enough. In this county all bastard children are taught to call their mothers "aunt," and of course he would naturally call Lincoln cousin. I have asked Dennis if his mother was not a sister to Betsey Sparrow. If they were, there would have to be two Nancys, sisters in one family, which I cannot believe. I know I am right. . . .

I will say here I saw the remains of President Lincoln "in state" at Indianapolis, and if anyone had taken me to the coffin and said: "There lies your friend George Brownfield, Jr.," I would have sworn before any jury that it was he, if I had not known better, the resemblance was that close. Judge Jonathan Friend Cessna told that his father William Cessna told him that one if not both of Thomas Lincoln's testicles were not larger than a pea; he, William Cessna, also said that Charles Friend was father of Dennis, a half, if not a whole, brother of A. Lincoln. He did not believe it possible that Thomas could have been his father. During the war LaRue County sent Dr. J. H. Rodman to Washington to see the President to have the number of men corrected that was called for from the county under the draft. He sent up his card and Mr. Lincoln sent word to Dr. Rodman that he would see him. Rodman said that there was men there waiting to see the President that had been there for weeks but could not get a glance. In course of the conversation Dr. Rodman told him that the county had sent him a nice cane from near where he was born and that he would send it up as soon as the silversmith put a gold head on it. Lincoln said: "How will I know who gave it to me?" Doctor said: "The names of the donors will be engraved on it to the President A. Lincoln." Abe said: "What a fool. I am like the Irishman that went to the Post Office; when the Postmaster asked his name, said: 'Faith aint my name on the lither?' Of course my name will be on the cane." President asked Dr. Rodman about the Cessnas, Brownfields, Friends, Ashcrafts, Kirkpatricks, and at last said: "Where is my old friend and playmate Austin Golliher? . . ."

Dr. J. H. Ródman said he seemed to know more about the general topography of the county than any person he ever saw, described any house and farm, hill, creek, and family that lived here when he was a boy. He, Lincoln, asked about an old storm house that stands on Nolan Creek about one and a half miles east of Hodgenville near a fine spring where the young people used to hold their dances. Reverend John Duncan, a Baptist preacher, told me that he and Abe used to go hunting both night and day and at one time they worked all one day trying to dig some kind of a "varmint" out of the ground. I guess the man you allude to is Abe's old friend Austin Golliher of LaRue County. He lives about twenty miles from here. He is the only person now living that knows anything about Lincoln or the Hankses. I could go and see him some day if it was not for the expense of going. I would visit him and get all he knows. He is very old and what is done must be done quickly as his days are few.

Yours truly,

CHARLES FRIEND.

Could you send me any of A. Lincoln's writing or his signature?   C. F.

If you write a history, don't you think you ought to give me a copy? Lucy Hanks, Nancy's mother, married Henry Sparrow as said; who did Levi Hall marry?

FROM HORACE WHITE

51 East 55th Street, New York, January 26, 1891.

Dear Mr. Herndon:

Your letter of the 25th is received. Mr. Villard has returned from Europe. His address at present is: Plaza Hotel, New York City.

Mr. Hermann Kreismann, whom you will undoubtedly remember, came to this country with Mr. V. but he has gone back to Berlin, where he now resides. He has a fund of Lincoln reminiscences which it would be worth your while to tap. One of them is to this effect: That after L.'s election as President, but before he had left Springfield, Judd and Kreismann went to Springfield on an important political errand and made an appointment to meet L., but he did not come and Kreismann dispatched to his house in quest of him. Arrived at the house he was ushered into a room where both Mr. and Mrs. L. were. The latter was on the floor in a sort of hysterical fit, caused by L.'s refusal to promise the position of naval officer of New York Custom House to Isaac Henderson, who had sent a diamond brooch to a Springfield jeweler to be given to Mrs. L. in case she could secure the promise of this office. The fit continued until the promise had been obtained. Henderson was, in fact, appointed. He was afterwards indicted by the grand jury for defrauding the government, and tried before Judge Nelson, but was saved from conviction by some technicality.

You must not use this on my narration. Indeed, it would be best not to use it at all. Kreismann has other reminiscences, but I don't know whether he could be prevailed on to write them out. Mr. Villard can give you his address. You remember he (K.) was appointed Secretary of Legation at Berlin when Judd was appointed Minister.

Mr. Villard accompanied L. in his journey from Springfield to Washington in the spring of 1861; i.e., in February, when he went to assume the office of President. He had also seen a good deal of L. in the campaign of 1858.

With cordial good wishes,

Ever your friend,
HORACE WHITE.

2. Statements Collected by Herndon

JOHN HANKS'S STATEMENT

I was born in Kentucky on the ninth day of February 1802 in Nelson County in four miles of Beardstown. My father moved to Hardin County in 1806. I knew Abraham Lincoln in Kentucky. Abraham was known among the boys as a bashful, somewhat dull, but peaceable boy; he was not a brilliant boy, but *worked* his way by toil; to learn was hard for him, but he walked slowly, but surely. He went to school to a man by the name of Hazel; the school was but a short distance. Lincoln lived on the bank of Knob Creek, about a half-mile above the Rolling Fork, which empties into Salt River, which empties into Ohio River. Abraham Lincoln's mother and I were cousins. Abraham and I are second cousins. I knew Mrs. Nancy Lincoln, or Nancy Sparrow before marriage. She was a tall slender woman, dark-skinned, black hair and eyes, her face was sharp and angular, forehead big. She was beyond all doubts an intellectual woman, rather extraordinary if anything. She was born in Mercer County, Kentucky, about 1780; her nature was kindness, mildness, tenderness, obedience to her husband. Abraham was like his mother very much. She was a Baptist by profession.

My recollection—in fact Abraham's father told me so—that his great-grandfather was an Englishman, came from England and settled in Virginia. This is the family reputation. When I was in Kentucky in 1864, I was shown a house in Mercer County which was said to be the house that Abraham's grandfather had built. I doubt the house, but I don't the farm, about ten miles from the mouth of Kubick River, about ten or twelve miles from Harrisburg, southeast from Harrodsburg.

I knew Thomas Lincoln in Kentucky, knew him well. He was cabinet and house carpenter, farmed after he got married, still working at his trade. He was a man about five feet ten inches high, weighed about 180, eyes dark gray, hair black, a little stoop-shouldered, a good-humored man, a strong brave man, a very stout man, loved fun, jokes, and equaled Abe in telling stories. Happiness was the end of life with him. He, Thomas, was older than his wife, say about five years, being born about 1775. Thomas was born in Virginia; so was his wife. Thomas was six years of age when he came to Kentucky. His father was killed by the Indians, as Dennis Hanks has said. The Indian story of Dennis Hanks is generally correct as told you by Dennis, so is Chapman's story generally correct. Thomas

345

told me so. My father and Lincoln's were born in old Virginia in what is called the Rappahannock River. We knew each other in Virginia; that is, the founders did. Abraham's mother was my first cousin. Abraham's grandmother was my father's sister. Abraham's grandfather and mother on his mother's side lived in Mercer County, Kentucky, about twenty miles south of Abraham's grandfather on his father's side, the one killed by the Indians. Dennis Hanks and I are cousins. Mr. Sparrow and Mrs. Sparrow never came to Illinois. They lived in Kentucky in Mercer County. Sparrow married my father's sister. Henry Sparrow was his name, lived and died in Mercer County, never came to Indiana. They came from old Virginia. All these families came from about the same county, can't say what county.

Thomas Lincoln moved to Indiana in 1818, probably 1816, and settled in Spencer County, near what is now called Gentryville, Indiana. I stayed in Kentucky, did not come out when Dennis Hanks did. Dennis Hanks came out in about 1818. Mrs. Lincoln died, say in 1818, I think, and lies buried southeast of the Lincoln farm about a half-mile in a rise, knoll, or knob. She was buried by the side of Mr. Hall and his wife, as I understand it. I came out to Indiana in 1822 after Thomas Lincoln had married his second wife, and stayed in Indiana near to and with Thomas Lincoln for four years. I remember Abraham well in Indiana. He was then ten years of age, and fourteen years when I left Indiana and went back to Kentucky. I was, in 1822, twenty years.

Abraham was farming when I got there and when I left and went to Kentucky, he went to school but little. He went to school to Dorsey or Swaney, I can't now say which. Old man Lincoln's house was a rough, rough log one, not a hewed one; his second one was sorter hewed, but is gone—never standing in 1860. The third one was hewed logs—that one was never occupied by Lincoln; it was up but not inhabited; the house stood east and west and faced the south, chimney on east end. It was, is, about four miles to Gentryville from the Lincoln farm, west of east a little. The house stood on a round hill, knoll, or knob. Lincoln's farm was on the forks of Big Pigeon and Little Pigeon. The Big Pigeon is north and the Little one south.

When Lincoln, Abe, and I returned to the house from work, he would go to the cupboard, snatch a piece of corn bread, take down a book, sit down in a chair, cock his legs up as high as his head, and read. He and I worked bare-footed, grubbed it, plowed, mowed, and cradled together, plowed corn, gathered it, and shucked corn. Abraham read constantly when he had an opportunity; no newspapers then; had monthly meetings at church, sometimes at private houses. Abe went to church generally—not always. I know he read Weems's Washington when I was there, got it wet—it was on a kind of bookshelf close to the window—the bookshelf was made by two pins in the wall and a clapboard on them, books on that. Lincoln got it of Crawford, told Crawford and paid it in pulling fodder by two or three days' work. He frequently read the Bible. He read *Robinson Crusoe,* Bunyan's *Pilgrim's Progress.* Lincoln devoured all the books he could get or lay hands on; he was a constant and voracious reader. I never could get him in company with woman; he was not a timid man in this particular, but did not seek such company. He was always full of his stories, as much so in Indiana as Illinois. He would go out in the woods and gather hickory bark, bring it home, and keep a light by it and read by it, when no lamp was to be had—grease lamp—handle to it which stuck in the crack of the wall. Tallow was scarce. Abraham was a good hearty eater, loved good eating. His own mother and stepmother were good cooks for their day and time. In the summer he wore tan linen pants and flax shirt and in the winter he wore linsey-woolsey, that is, during the time I was there. I have seen Lincoln—Abraham—make speeches to his stepbrothers, stepsisters, and youngsters that would come to see the family.

I moved from Kentucky to Illinois in the fall of 1828 and settled where I now live—four miles northwest of Decatur—and built the first house in Decatur. I wrote to Thomas Lincoln what kind of a country it was; he came to this State the first day of March 1830—to my house. He then built ten miles west of Decatur, and about a hundred steps from the N.F. of Sangamon River and on the north side of it on a kind of bluff. The house, the logs of it, I cut myself in 1829 and gave them to old man Lincoln. The house set east and west, fronted south, chimney at west end, the same house which was shown in Chicago. Lincoln broke up fifteen acres of land. Abraham and myself split the rails; he owned four yoke of oxen; broke prairie in the summer; broke thirty acres for my brother; he broke prairie for others. Two yoke belonged to Thomas Lincoln and two to my brother. Dennis Hanks came out at the summer time. Mr. and Mrs. Hall—Dennis Hanks married Abraham's stepsister, so did Hall. Abraham during the winter of 1830–31 walked three miles and made a thousand rails for Major Warnick.

I knew Abraham's own sister Sarah; she was a short-built woman, eyes dark gray, hair dark brown; she was a good woman, kind, tender, and good-natured, and is said to have been a smart woman. That is my opinion.

After Abraham got to Decatur, rather to Mercer, my county—a man by the name of Posey came into our neighborhood and made a speech; it was a bad one, and I said Abe could beat it. I turned down a box or keg, and Abe made his speech. The other man was a candidate; Abe wasn't. Abe beat him to death, his subject being the navigation of the Sangamon River. The man, after the speech was through, took Abe aside and asked him where he had learned so much and what he did so well. Abe explained, stating his manner and method of reading and what he had read; the man encouraged Lincoln to persevere.

Offutt came to my house in February 1831 and wanted to hire me to run a flatboat for him, saying that he had heard that I was quite a flatboat man in Kentucky; he wanted me to go badly. I went and saw Abe and John Johnston, Abe's stepbrother; introduced Offutt to them. We made an engagement with Offutt at 50¢ per day and $60 to make the trip to New Orleans. Abe and I came down the Sangamon River in a canoe on March 1831, landed at what is now called and known as Jamestown—five miles east of Springfield—once called Judy's Ferry. We left our canoe in charge of Mr. Mann, walked afoot to Springfield, and found Offutt. He was at a tavern in Oldtown, probably Elliott's; it was Elliott's. He, Offutt, expected to find his boat according to contract at the mouth of Spring Creek, five miles north of Springfield, got disappointed. Abe, Johnston, and myself went down to the mouth of Spring Creek and there cut the timbers to make the boat; we were about two weeks cutting our timber—suppose it was on Congress land. Abe walked afoot to Springfield, thence to Judy's Ferry, got the canoe, and floated it down to the mouth of Spring Creek, where the timber was cut; we then rafted the logs down to Sangamon River to what is called Sangamontown, seven miles northwest of Springfield. We boarded where we were working at the mouth of Spring Creek, walked one mile, eat two meals a day. When we got to Sangamontown we made a shanty, shed. Abe was elected cook. We sawed our lumber at Kirkpatrick's mill on Prairie Creek about one and a half miles southwest of Sangamontown. We hewed and sawed the timber at the mouth of Spring Creek. We finished making and launching the boat in about four weeks. We loaded the boat with barrel pork, corn, and live hogs, and left Sangamontown. I remember a juggler's show at Sangamontown. Abe went to it. Abe was full of jokes during all this time, kept us all alive. Offutt was a Whig, so was Lincoln, but he could not hear Jackson wrongfully abused—especially where a lie and malice did the abuse. I can say that Abe never was a Democrat; he was always a Whig; so was his father before him.

We landed at the New Salem mill about April 19 and got fast on Rutledge's mill dam, now called Bill's mill dam. We unloaded the boat, that is, we changed goods from one boat to a borrowed one, rolled the barrels forward, bored a hole in the end of the boat over the dam—water ran out and thus we got over; on the dam part of a day and one night. We then went on down to the Yellow Bank or the Blue Banks on the Sangamon River near Squire Godby's about one mile above the mouth of Salt Creek.

We purchased some hogs of, I think, Squire Godby—am not sure—tried to drive them, couldn't, ran them back in the pen, caught them, Abe held the head of them, I the tail, and Offutt sewed up their eyes, wouldn't drive, couldn't put them in a cart, carried them to the boat about one mile to the river. Abe received the hogs, cut open them. Johnston and I hauled them to Abe. We then proceeded, Offutt, John Johnston, Abe Lincoln, and myself, down the Sangamon River, thence into Illinois. We kept our victuals and in fact slept down in the boat, at one end; went down by a kind of ladder through a scatter hole. We used plank as sails and cloth, sometimes, rushed through Beardstown in a hurry—people came out and laughed at us— passed Alton, Cairo, and stopped at Memphis, Vicksburg, Natchez, etc. There is nothing worthy of being known going down the river.

I can say we soon—say in May—we landed in New Orleans. There it was we saw Negroes chained, maltreated, whipped, and scourged. Lincoln saw it, his heart bled, said nothing much, was silent from feeling, was sad, looked bad, felt bad, was thoughtful and abstracted. I can say knowingly that it was on this trip that he formed his opinions of slavery; it ran its iron in him then and there—May 1831. I have heard him say often and often. Offutt, Johnston, Abe, and myself left New Orleans in June 1831. We came to St. Louis on the steamboat together, walked to Edwardsville twenty-five miles northeast of St. Louis, Abe, Johnston, and myself. Abe and Johnston went to Coles County and I to Springfield, Sangamon County. Thomas Lincoln had moved to Coles County in 1831 in, say, June.

I came near forgetting some facts. I was in the Black Hawk War, was in Sherman's defeat, which was on the fourteenth day of May 1832. Lincoln was out on that war. I went in March 1832; Lincoln started as captain of the New Salem company about the same time. Lincoln was at Dixon's Ferry at the time of Sherman's defeat. I did not go to the Battle of the Bad Axe. Lincoln, I think, was there, though not in the action, as I understand it. I was out about four or six months; so was Lincoln. Lincoln went with Major Henry, I know. I was discharged at Ottawa and Lincoln at Rock Island or near that; met at Dixon's Ferry, after the Sherman defeat. Lincoln went on with Henry. We were ordered to build a fort at Ottawa to protect the people. The Sherman defeat affair grew out of the drunkenness, folly, cowardice. The fight with Black Hawk was about sundown, one hour by sun at or near Sycamore Creek. About 700 Indians and about 200 whites.

Saw Abe in Springfield in 1833, summer; he was in town on business and so was I. I saw him frequently from this time, every year from this time till he was elected President. He practiced law in Decatur. He came out to my house frequently, leaving court in the evening and after court was over, ended. I ate dinner with him after he was elected President. He wrote me a letter that he was going to see his mother, came by Decatur, I went with him, saw his father's grave. He stayed with his mother once. We ate dinner at, in, Farmington. Pretty woman there that took Abe's eyes, I assure you. We then went back to Charleston and came to Springfield. I saw him in Washington when he was inaugurated, was in his rooms several times. Never saw him again till I saw his dead form in the city of Springfield.

I served in the army of the U.S.A. in 1861 and toiled those three years to preserve and defend what he loved.

I can say that this testimony can be implicitly relied on. Mr. Lincoln loved this man, thought him beautiful, honest, and noble. Lincoln has stated this to me over and over again.

HERNDON.

MRS. THOMAS LINCOLN'S STATEMENT

Old Mrs. Lincoln's home, 8 miles south of Charleston,
Friday, September 8, 1865.

Mrs. Thomas Lincoln says:

I knew Mr. Lincoln in Kentucky. I married Mr. Johnston, he died about 1817 or '18. Mr. Lincoln came back to Kentucky, having lost his wife. We, Thomas Lincoln and myself, were married in 1819, left Kentucky, went to Indiana, moved there in a train, think Kramer moved us. Here is our old Bible dated 1819; it has Abe's name in it. Here is Barclay's Dictionary dated 1799; it has Abe's name in it, though in a better handwriting; both are boyish scrawls. When we landed in Indiana, Mr. Lincoln had erected a good log cabin, tolerably comfortable. This is the bureau I took to Indiana in 1819, cost $45 in Kentucky. Abe was then young, so was his sister. I dressed Abe and his sister up, looked more human. Abe slept upstairs, went up on pins stuck in the logs, like a ladder; our bedsteads were original creations, none such now, made of poles and clapboards. Abe was about nine years of age when I landed in Indiana. The country was wild, and desolate. Abe was a good boy; he didn't like physical labor, was diligent for knowledge, wished to know, and if pains and labor would get it, he was sure to get it. He was the best boy I ever saw. He read all the books he could lay his hands on. I can't remember dates nor names, am about seventy-five years of age; Abe read the Bible some, though not as much as said; he sought more congenial books suitable for his age. I think newspapers were had in Indiana as early as 1824 and up to 1830 when we moved to Illinois.

Abe was a constant reader of them. I am sure of this for the years of 1827–28–29–30. The name of the Louisville *Journal* seems to sound like one. Abe read history papers and other books, can't name any one, have forgotten. Abe had no particular religion, didn't think of that question at that time, if he ever did. He never talked about it. He read diligently, studied in the daytime, didn't after night much, went to bed early, got up early, and then read, eat his breakfast, got to work in the field with the men. Abe read all the books he could lay his hands on, and when he came across a passage that struck him, he would write it down on boards if he had no paper and keep it there till he did get paper, then he would rewrite it, look at it, repeat it. He had a copybook, a kind of scrapbook, in which he put down all things and then preserved them. He ciphered on boards when he had no paper or no slate, and when the board would get too black, he would shave it off with a drawing knife and go on again. When he had paper, he put his lines down on it. His copybook is here now or was lately. (Here it was shown to me by Mrs. Thomas Lincoln.) Abe, when old folks were at our house, was a silent and attentive observer, never speaking or asking questions till they were gone, and then he must understand everything, even to the smallest thing, minutely and exactly; he would then repeat it over to himself again and again, sometimes in one form and then in another, and when it was fixed in his mind to suit him, he became easy and he never lost that fact or his understanding of it. Sometimes he seemed perturbed to give expression to his ideas and got mad, almost, at one who couldn't explain plainly what he wanted to convey. He would hear sermons [by the] preacher, come home, take the children out, get on a stump or log, and almost repeat it word for word. He made other speeches, such as interested him and the children. His father had to make him quit sometimes, as he quit his own work to speak and made the other children as well as the men quit their work. As a usual thing Mr. Lincoln never made Abe quit reading to do anything if he could avoid it. He would do it himself first. Mr. Lincoln could read a little and could scarcely write his name; hence he wanted, as he himself felt the uses and necessities of educating, his boy Abraham to learn, and he encouraged him to do it in all ways he could. Abe was a good boy, and I can say what scarcely one woman, a mother, can say in a thousand and it is this: Abe never gave me a cross word or look and never refused in fact, or even in appearance, to do anything I requested him. I never gave him a cross word in all my life. He was kind to everybody and to everything and always accommodated others if he could, would do so willingly if he could. His mind and mine, what little I had, seemed to run together, more in the same channel. Abe could easily learn and long remember, and when he did learn anything he learned it well and thoroughly.

What he thus learned he stored away in his memory, which was extremely good. What he learned and stored away was well defined in his own mind, repeated over and over again and again, till it was so defined and fixed firmly and permanently in his memory. He rose early, went to bed early, not reading much after night. Abe was a moderate eater, and I now have no remembrance of his special dish; he sat down and ate what was set before him, making no complaint; he seemed careless about this. I cooked his meals for nearly fifteen years. He always had good health, never was sick, was very careful of his person, was tolerably neat and clean only, cared nothing for clothes, so that they were clean and neat, further cut no figure with him, nor color, new stuff, nor material; was careless about these things. He was more fleshy in Indiana than ever in Illinois. I saw him every year or two. He was here after he was elected President of the United States. (Here the old lady stopped, turned around and cried, wiped her eyes, and proceeded.) As company would come to our house Abe was a silent listener, wouldn't speak, would sometimes take a book and retire aloft, go to the stable or field or woods, and read. Abe was always fond of fun, sport, wit, and jokes. He was sometimes very witty indeed. He never drank whisky or other strong drink, was temperate in all things, too much so, I thought sometimes. He never told me a lie in his life, never evaded, never quarreled, never dodged nor turned a corner to avoid any chastisement or other responsibility. He never swore or used profane language in my presence nor in others' that I now remember of. He duly reverenced old age, loved those best about his own age, played with those under his age; he listened to the aged, argued with his equals, but played with the children. He loved animals generally and treated them kindly; he loved children well, very well. There seemed to be nothing unusual in his love for animals or his own kind, though he treated everybody and everything kindly, humanely. Abe didn't care much for crowds of people; he chose his own company, which was always good. He was not very fond of girls, as he seemed to me. He sometimes attended church. He would repeat the sermon over again to the children. The sight of such a thing amused all and did especially tickle the children. When Abe was reading, my husband took particular care not to disturb him, would let him read on and on till Abe quit of his own accord. He was dutiful to me always; he loved me truly, I think. I had a son John who was raised with Abe. Both were good boys, but I must say, both now being dead, that Abe was the best boy I ever saw or ever expect to see. I wish I had died when my husband did. I did not want Abe to run for President, did not want him elected, was afraid somehow or other, felt it in my heart that something would happen to him, and when he came down to see me after he was elected President, I still felt that something told me that something would befall Abe and that I should see him no more. Abe and his father are in Heaven, I have no doubt, and I want to go to them, go where they are. God bless Abraham.

When I first reached the home of Mrs. Lincoln and was introduced to her by Colonel A. H. Chapman, her grandson by marriage, I did not expect to get much out of her. She seemed so old and feeble; she asked me my name two or three times and where I lived as often, and would say: "Where Mr. Lincoln lived once, his friend too." She breathed badly at first but she seemed to be struggling at last to arouse herself, or to fix her mind on the subject. Gradually by introducing simple questions to her, about her age, marriage, Kentucky, Thomas Lincoln, her former husband, her children, grandchildren, Johnston, she awoke as it were a new being, her eyes were clear and calm; her flesh is white and pure, not coarse or material; is tall, has bluish large gray eyes; ate dinner with her, sat on my west side, left arm, ate a good hearty dinner, she did.

When I was about to leave, she arose, took me by the hand, wept, and bade me good-by, saying: "I shall never see you again, and if you see Mrs. Abraham Lincoln and family, tell them I send them my best and tenderest love. Good-by, my good son's friend, farewell."

I then went to Thomas Lincoln's grave.

[HERNDON.]

NAT GRIGSBY'S STATEMENT

Gentryville, Ind., September 12, 1865.

My name is N. Grigsby, am fifty-four years of age, knew Abraham Lincoln well. My father came from Kentucky in the fall of 1815 and settled in what is called now Spencer County, once a part and portion of Perry. Thomas Lincoln moved to this State in the year 1816 or 1817. He came in the fall of the year and crossed the Ohio River at what is called Ephraim Thompson's Ferry, about two and a half miles west of Troy. The country was a wilderness and there were no roads from Troy to the place he settled, which place is about one and a half miles east of Gentryville, the town in which I now live and you are visiting. Thomas Lincoln was a large man, say six feet or a little less, strong and muscular, not nervous. Thomas Lincoln was a man of good morals, good habits, and exceedingly good-humored, he could read and sign his name, write but little. Mrs. Lincoln, the mother of Abraham, was a woman about five feet seven inches high; she had dark hair, light hazel eyes, complexion light and exceedingly fair. Thomas Lincoln and his wife had two children, one Sally and one Abraham. Sally was about ten years when she landed in Indiana. Abe was about eight or nine years of age. Thomas Lincoln, when he landed in Indiana, cut his way to his farm with the ax, felling the forest as he went, which was thick and dense—no prairies from the Ohio to his place. I am informed that he came in a horse wagon to his farm; don't know but have heard this said in the family. Abraham Lincoln and Sally and myself all went to school. We first went to school to Andy Crawford in the year 1818 in the winter, the same year that Mrs. Lincoln died, she having died in October. Abe went to school nearly a year, say nine months. I was going to school all this time and saw Lincoln there most, if not all, the time. The second schoolmaster we went to was a Mr. Azel Dorsey. Abraham Lincoln went to school to Azel about six months; I went to school all the time, saw Lincoln there all or at least most of the time. We had to go about two miles to school. The third time we went to school was to a Mr. Sweeney, who taught six months. Lincoln did not go to school to him all the time. Lincoln had to walk about four miles. Lincoln was, about the first school, nine or ten years of age. The second school, he was about fourteen or fifteen, and the third school, he was about sixteen or eighteen. Lincoln was large of his age, say at seventeen; he was six feet and two inches tall, weighed about 160 pounds or a little more; he was stout, withy, wiry. When we went to school, we had Dillworth's speaking book and the American spelling book —not Webster's, I think—Lincoln ciphered at Crawford's school, Dorsey's, and Sweeney's. He used Pike's Arithmetic. Ray's was sometimes used. We only wrote, spelled, and ciphered. We had spelling matches frequently, Abe always ahead of all the classes he ever was in. When we went to Crawford's, he tried to learn us manners, etc. He would ask the scholars to retire from the schoolroom, come in, and then some scholar would go around and introduce him to all the scholars, male and female. Lincoln was studious. Lincoln, while going to school to Crawford, would write short sentences against cruelty to animals. We were in the habit of catching terrapins, a kind of turtle, and put fire on their back, and Lincoln would chide us and tell us it was wrong, would write against it. Lincoln wrote poetry while he was going to school to Dorsey. Essays and poetry were not taught in the school—Abe took it up of his own accord. He wrote a good composition against cruelty to animals whilst going to Dorsey and Sweeney. He wrote poetry when going to these men. These things I remember and know. Cannot remember of his reading any book or books, excepting Æsop's Fables, Bunyan's *Pilgrim's Progress,* the Bible, *Robinson Crusoe.* Our libraries consisted of spelling books, Bibles, arithmetics, songbooks. Lincoln was kindly disposed toward everybody and everything. He scarcely ever quarreled, was prompt and honorable. He never was an intemperate lad; he did drink his dram as all others did, preachers and Christians included. *Lincoln was a temperate drinker.* When he went out to work anywhere would carry his books with him and would always read whilst resting.

We wore buckskin pants, and linsey-woolsey hunting coats to school. This was our school dress—our Sunday dress and everyday dress. Mr. Lincoln was long and tall and, like the balance of us, he wore low shoes, short socks; wool being scarce between the shoe and sock and his britches, made of buckskin, there was bare and naked six or more inches of Abe Lincoln's shin bone. He would always come to school thus, good-humoredly and laughing. He was always in good health, never was sick, had an excellent constitution, and took care of it.

Lincoln did not do much hunting; sometimes went coon hunting and turkey hunting of nights. Whilst other boys were idling away their time, Lincoln was at home studying hard, would cipher on the boards, wooden fire shovels, etc., by the light of the fire that burnt in the hearth; had a slate sometimes, but if not handy would use boards. He would shave boards bright and cipher on them, dirty them, reshave them. Abe would sit up late reading and rise early doing the same.

Mrs. Lincoln, Abe's mother, was born —— and died in the fall, October 1818, leaving her two children. Sally Lincoln was older than Abe—Sally married Aaron Grigsby, my brother, in August 1826. She died in about two years in 1828.

Mrs. Lincoln, the mother of Abe Lincoln, was a woman known for the extraordinary strength of her mind among the family and all who knew her; she was superior to her husband in every way. She was a brilliant woman, a woman of great good sense and morality. Those who knew her best, with whom I have talked, say she was a woman of pale complexion, dark hair, sharp features, high forehead, bright keen gray or hazel eyes. Thomas Lincoln and his wife were really happy in each other's presence, loved one another. Thomas Lincoln was not a lazy man, but a [undeciphered], a piddler, always doing but doing nothing great, was happy, lived easy and contented. Had but few wants and supplied these. He wanted few things and supplied them easily. His wants were limited by wanting few things. Sally was a quick-minded woman and of extraordinary mind. She was industrious, more so than Abraham. Abe worked almost alone from the head, whilst she labored both. Her good-humored laugh I can see now, is as fresh in my mind as if it were yesterday. She could, like her brother Abe, meet and greet a person with the very kindest greeting in the world, make you easy at the touch and word. Her mind, though my brother's wife, was an intellectual and intelligent woman. However, not so much as her mother. My brother William Grigsby and John D. Johnston, a stepbrother of Abe, had a severe fight; it was tended from all around the neighborhood, coming eighteen miles; strong men came, bullies came. Abe was there. Abe and my brother first had the quarrel; Abe, being larger and stronger than my brother, turned over his stepbrother to do the fighting; so they met, fought, fought a half-mile from Gentryville. There was a store there and probably a grocery, and a blacksmith's shop. This was the town then of Gentryville. Johnston was badly hurt, but not whipped. My brother was unhurt, seriously so; Johnston and my brother were brave strong men.

A. Lincoln came here in 1844 and made a speech for Clay. It was a Clay election in Illinois for the race between Polk and Clay. Lincoln spoke here, once, once at Rockport, and once at Carlin township about three-quarters of a mile from the home farm. Lincoln in early years—say from 1820 to '25—was tending towards Democracy. He afterwards changed. Parties at this time Jackson, Adams, and others. What changed Lincoln I don't remember. We were all Jackson boys and men at this time in Indiana.

Lincoln did go to New Orleans; he went to New Orleans about 1828, with a man by the name of Allen Gentry, who took as well as owned the supercargo to New Orleans. The goods were sold down on the river. Abe went as a bow hand, working the foremost oars, getting $8.00 per month, from the time of the starting to the returning home. Gentry paid his way back on a boat. This I know. He made rails for Crawford, took jobs of work sometimes, would go to the river, the Ohio thirteen or sixteen miles distant, and there work. It is sixty miles to the Wabash, he did work on the Wabash, but on the Ohio. Lincoln did not work on the Louisville [undeciphered], but he may have done it nevertheless.

Lincoln did write what is called the Book of Chronicles, a satire on the Grigsbys and Josiah Crawford, not the schoolmaster, but the man who loaned Lincoln the Life of Washington. The satire was good, sharp, cutting, and showed the genius of the boy; it hurt us then, but it's all over now. There is now no family in the broad land who after this loved Lincoln so well and who now look upon him as so great a man. We all voted for him. All that could, children and grown children. I was for Lincoln and Hamlin first, last, and always. Second election I was at Decatur, Alabama, in the service of the United States.

We had political discussions from 1825 to 1830, the year Lincoln left for Illinois. We attended them, heard questions discussed, talked everything over and over, and in fact wore it out. We learned much in this way.

I said heretofore that Abraham made his mark of manhood even while

JOHN HANKS
Collection of
Harry MacNeill Bland

DENNIS HANKS
Collection of
Harry MacNeill Bland

ABRAHAM LINCOLN

*This Portrait Is Reproduced from a Brady Photograph (1864) in the
War Department Collection; Courtesy of the Signal Corps, U. S. Army*

in Indiana. His mind and the ambition of the man soared above us. He naturally assumed the leadership of the boys. He read and thoroughly read his books whilst we played. Hence he rose above us and became our guide and leader, and in this position he never failed to be the leader. He was kind, jocular, witty, wise, honest, just, human, full of integrity, energy, and activity. When he appeared in company the boys would gather and cluster around him to hear his talk. He made fun and cracked his jokes, making all happy, but the jokes and fun were at no man's expense. He wounded no man's feelings.

Mr. Lincoln was figurative in his speeches, talks, and conversations. He argued much from analogy and explained things hard for us to understand by stories, maxims, tales, and figures. He would almost always point his lesson or idea by some story that was plain and near us, that we might instantly see the force and bearing of what he said.

Never heard in the family or out of it that the Lincolns were Quakers coming from Pennsylvania. The history is that they came from Virginia.

A Visit to the Lincoln Farm

September 14, 1865.

I started from Nat Grigsby's house, with him as my guide and friend throughout the trip, except at Rockport on the Ohio River. Grigsby lives in Gentryville, population about three hundred; laid off in 1824, runs north and south mostly, mainly. Started at 8 a.m. Went to the Lincoln farm about one and a half miles east of Gentryville, and a little north. The house is a one-story hewed log one, porch in front; it is not the house that L. lived in, though he built it. The old house—the first and second are gone—fronts south, chimney at east end, has two rooms, the east one and west one, stands on a knoll or knob about 50 feet above the road and about 150 yards north of the road. On the Gentryville road leading to the Hoffman Mills. The country is a heavy timbered one, farms are cleared and cut out of the forests. The woods, the timber, is hickory, white oak, called buckeye, and backlands. The old farm now belongs to James Gentry, son of James Gentry for whom—the old man, the brother of Allen—Lincoln went to New Orleans in 1828 or 1829. John Hearen or Hearner now lives as tenant on the land; it has an orchard on it, part of which Abraham Lincoln planted with his own hands. Allen Gentry got drunk and fell off the boat going to Louisville and was drowned. Abe Lincoln hewed the logs of this new house for his father, one door north and one south, two rooms, plank partitions, one window, two rooms; it has been moved from its original position, placed further south than the old one; it is not as Lincoln left it; it was not completed by Thomas Lincoln. The farm was sold to —— by Thomas Lincoln in 1829, went to the place of the old spring northwest of the house, about 300 yards; it was dry, saw the place, saw various old wells all caved in; it is said water could not be had on that hill, pity; saw five or six old, old apple trees; the old house and shelter are gone, I say again and again; started to find Mrs. Lincoln's grave; it is on a knob, hill, or knoll about a half-mile southeast of the Lincoln house; passed out of the lane going east, landed at the grave, tied my horse; the grave was, is, on the very top or crown of the hill. The knob or knoll is a heavy timbered one. A space is cut out of the forest by piling the trees somewhat as crossbars. In the center of this small cleared place, about fifteen feet from a large white oak tree, rather somewhat between two of these, lies buried Mrs. Lincoln. God bless her; if I could breathe life into her again, I would do it. Could I only whisper in her ear: "Your son was President of the United States from 1861 to 1865," I would be satisfied. I have heard much of this blessed good woman. I stood bareheaded in reverence at her grave. I can't say why, yet I felt in the presence of the living woman translated to another world. "God bless her," said her son to me once, and I repeat that which echoes audibly in my soul: "God bless her." The grave is almost indistinguishable; it has sunk down, leaving a kind of hollow. There is no fence around the graveyard and no tomb, no headboard to mark where she lies. At her head, close to it, I pulled a dogwood bush and cut or marked my name on it. Mrs. Lincoln is buried between two or more persons, said to be Hall and his wife, on the one hand and some children on her left hand. There are two hollows or sinks. Nat Grigsby and Richardson were with me at the time; they said this was *the* grave. Mrs. Richardson saw Mrs. Lincoln buried and says it is not the grave. One of these sinks, graves crumbled in, lies a few feet, ten feet, south of the other; Mrs. Lincoln's is the southern one as I think from [what] Dennis Hanks and A. Lincoln told me. Mrs. Lincoln's body, her ashes, lie just fifteen feet west of a hollow hickory stump and just eighteen feet northeast from a large white oak tree. After looking at the grave and contemplating in silence the mutations of things, death, immortality, God, I left, I hope, the grave a better man, at least if but for one moment.

Went to Dennis Hanks's old place, northeast from the graveyard about three-quarters of a mile, just east of the old Lincoln farm about the same distance. Got Silas Richardson, an old friend of Abe's; he came to Indiana in 1816; so did Lincoln. His mother saw Mrs. Lincoln buried; he went to the graveyard with us, Nat and myself, and made certain what was before doubtful; he agrees with Dennis Hanks and A. Lincoln. Richardson says old man and Mrs. Sparrow, Abe's grandfather and mother, lie on one side of Mrs. Lincoln. Two Banners, probably children, lie on the other side, or an old lady and a child. Mrs. Lincoln lies in the middle. The grave is six feet from said shaved dogwood bush. Mrs. Richardson is eighty-two years of age. Says that Mrs. Lincoln's grave lies four and a half feet south of the one I say is the correct one. Dennis Hanks, A. Lincoln, Silas Richardson, the old lady's son, and myself agree to the place. I only go by recollection and what others say. Mrs. Richardson and her son go by what they saw and know. One John Richardson was the husband of old Mrs. Richardson, and father of Silas Richardson. There is no fence around the grave, no palings, enclosures, of any kind, no headboard, no footboard, to mark the spot where Abraham Lincoln's mother lies; curious and unaccountable, is it not? All is a dense forest, wild and grand.

I then proceeded to old Samuel Howell's house, south of the graveyard about a half-mile, drank out of a good spring near the Little Pigeon Meeting House out of which Abe had kneeled and drunk a thousand times. Spring close to the corner of the old Howell farm, part of which is turned out wild again. I passed the spring, a little east, southeast, up a small rise or swell in the ground, and landed at the famous meeting house, called the Little Pigeon Meeting House. It is a Baptist church now and probably was then, but free to all comers of all and every denomination. The house is a two-story one outside, but one inside; it was intended to let the choir and people sit up there when crowded, but remains unfinished. This house is about one and a half miles from Lincoln's house, south and east. Went through the church, stealing in at the windows. The pulpit was made by Thomas Lincoln. I cut a small piece therefrom as memento. Passed east about fifty yards into the large graveyard, saw the grave of Sarah Lincoln,

Mrs. Grigsby, Abe's sister, God bless her ashes. Mrs. Grigsby and her husband Aaron lie side by side. God bless 'em. They lie ten feet south of Nat Grigsby's wife, first, and mother. Graveyard slopes east and north, is in the forest, fenced in, quite a pretty place. Crawford's schoolhouse lies east of the church, east of the graveyard, and about two hundred yards; it is about two miles from the Lincoln farm, southeast; is near the place enclosed in a field, schoolhouse long since rotted away and gone.

I then started for John Romine's, southwest; met Romine in the road meeting us; his age is sixty years. Says:

I saw Mr. Lincoln hundreds of times; have been in Spencer County since 1815. Lincoln went to New Orleans about '28 or '29, hauled some of the bacon to the river, not for Lincoln but for Gentry. Thomas Lincoln was a carpenter by trade, relied on it for a living, not on farming. Abe didn't like to work it, didn't raise more than was enough for family and stock. Boat started out of the Ohio in the spring—Abe about twenty years of age—started from Rockport, a short distance below, rather at the Gentry landing. Gone about two months. Lincoln was attacked by the Negroes, no doubt of this. Abe told me so, saw the scar myself. Suppose at the Washington farm or near by, probably below at a widow's farm. Abe was awful lazy; he worked for me, was always reading and thinking; used to get mad at him. He worked for me in 1829 pulling fodder. I say Abe was awful lazy; he would laugh and talk and crack jokes and tell stories all the time, didn't ever work but did dearly love his pay. He worked for me frequently, a few days only at a time. His breeches and socks didn't meet by twelve inches, shin bones sharp, blue, and narrow. Lincoln said to me one day that his father taught him to work but never learned him to love it.

Saw old man Gordon's mill, rather the ruins of it. This is the mill where Abe got kicked by a horse. Hunted for Lincoln's name written in tar and black lead and piece on a shaft of the mill, couldn't find it; got a cog or two of the mill. Romine tells me one verse of the Book of Chronicles, it runs thus:

> Reuben and Charley have married two girls,
> But Billy has married a boy.
> Billy and Natty agree very well,
> Mamma is pleased with the match,
> The egg is laid but didn't hatch.

S. T. JOHNSTON'S STATEMENT

Indiana, September 14, 1865.

S. T. Johnston says:

I am aged thirty-four years, resided in the county twenty-five years, from the year 1831 to 1856. The county seat of Warnick County was Booneville, about fifteen miles from Gentryville, northwest. Lincoln used to attend court in that place. He became acquainted with a Mr. Breckenridge there, heard [cases] in which Breckenridge was counsel. He was a fine lawyer. Lincoln attended a murder case, trial and proceedings; was young, aged about eighteen or nineteen years. B. noticed the calm intelligent attention that L. paid to the trial. B. moved to Texas in 1852; Lincoln had not seen B. from 1828 to 1862. B. went to Washington. L. saw Breckenridge. L. instantly recognized B. Lincoln told Breckenridge that he at that time, the trial, formed a fixed determination to study the law and make that his profession. Lincoln referred to the trial, said to Breckenridge that he had listened to his, B.'s, speech at the trial, and said: "Breckenridge, it was the best speech that I, up to that time, ever heard. If I could, as I then thought, make as good a speech as that, my soul would be satisfied." Summers used to attend court there and frequently saw Mr. Lincoln there, knew he always attended court and paid strict attention to what was said and done. The murder case took place in 1828. L. complimented Breckenridge at that trial, saying it was a clear, logical, and powerful effort, etc. Breckenridge looked at the shabby boy.

JOS. C. RICHARDSON'S STATEMENT

Jos. C. Richardson says:

My father came to Spencer County, Indiana, in 1828. Lincoln was tall and rawboned at eighteen. When sixteen years of age, he was six feet high; he was somewhat bony and raw, dark-skinned; he was quick and moved with energy; he never idled away his time. When out of regular work, he would help and assist the neighbors; he was exceedingly studious. I knew him well; he wrote me a copy in my writing copybook which ran thus:

> Good boys who to their books apply
> Will make great men by and by.

This copy was written in 1829. The Weems Washington, the book story, took place in 1829, one year before Abe went to Illinois. Crawford was a close, penurious man, probably did not treat Lincoln generously, but Lincoln did not object to what Crawford required. The book story is correct.

Once Lincoln and Squire Hall raised some watermelons; some of us boys lit into the melon patch accidentally. We got the melons, went through the corn to the fence, got over. All at once to our surprise and mortification Lincoln came among us, on us, good-naturedly said: "Boys, now I've got you"; sat down with us, cracked jokes, told stories, helped to eat the melons.

One day Abe's grandmother wanted him to read some chapters in the Bible for her. L. did not want to do it. At last he took up the Bible and read and rattled away so fast that his poor old grandmother could not understand it. She good-naturedly ran him out of the house with the broom-stick, who, being out, the thing he wanted, he kept shy that day—all done in sport and fun.

Lincoln did keep ferry for James Taylor for about nine months at the mouth of Anderson River on the Ohio, between Troy and Maxville. The Lincoln and Grigsby family had a kind of quarrel and hence for some time did not like each other. Aaron Grigsby had some years before this married Miss Sarah Lincoln, the good and kind sister of Abe. Two other Grigsby boys, men rather, got married on the same night at the same house, though they did not marry sisters; they had an infair at old man Grigsby's, and all the neighbors, except the Lincoln family, were invited. Josiah Crawford, the book man, helped to get up the infair; he had a long huge blue nose. Abe Lincoln undoubtedly felt miffed, insulted, pride wounded, etc. Lincoln, I know, felt wronged about the book transaction. After the infair was ended, the two women were put to bed. The candles were blown out, up-stairs. The gentlemen, the two husbands, were invited and shown to bed. Charles Grigsby got into bed with, by *accident* as it were, Reuben Grigsby's wife, and Reuben got into bed with Charles's wife, by accident as it were. Lincoln, I say, was mortified, and he declared that he would have revenge. Lincoln was by nature witty, and here was his chance. So he got up a witty *poem,* called the Book of Chronicles, in which the infair, the mistake in partners, Crawford and his blue nose, came in each for its share, and this poem is remembered here in Indiana in scraps better than the Bible, better than Wake's hymns. This was in 1829, and the first production that I know of that made us feel that Abe was truly and really *game.* This called the attention of the people to Abe intellectually. Abe dropped the poem in the road carelessly, lost it as it were; it was found by one of the Grigsby boys, who had the good manly sense to read it, keep it, preserve it for years—if it is *not in existence now.*

Grigsby challenged Lincoln to fight. Abe refused, said he was too big. Johnston, Abe's stepbrother, took Abe's part, shoes, met at the old schoolhouse. Johnston got whipped—worsted rather. Richardson says that Lincoln was a powerful man in 1830, could carry what three ordinary men would grunt and swear at; saw him carry a chicken house made of poles pinned together and carried that weight at least six hundred if not much more. Abe was notoriously good-natured, kind, and honest. Men would swear on his simple word; had a high and manly sense of honor; was tender, gentle, etc., etc., never seemed to care for the girls; was witty and sad and thoughtful by turns, as it seemed to me. God bless Abe's memory forever.

WILLIAM WOOD'S STATEMENT

September 15, 1865.

William Wood says:

My name is William Wood; came from Kentucky in 1809, March, and settled in Indiana, New Spencer County. Settled on the hill yonder about one and a half miles north of the Lincoln farm; am now eighty-two years of age. Knew Thomas and Abraham Lincoln and family well. Thomas Lincoln and family came from Kentucky, Hardin County, in 1816, according to my recollection. Mrs. Thomas Lincoln, Abe's mother, was sick about one and a half years after she came. I sat up with her all one night. Mrs. Lincoln, her mother, and father were sick with what is called the milk sickness. Sparrow and wife—Mrs. Lincoln's father and mother—as well as Mrs. L. all died with that sickness, the milk sickness. Thomas Lincoln often and at various times worked for me, made cupboards, etc., other household furniture for me; he built my house, made floors, ran up the stairs, did all the inside work for my house. Abe would come to my house with his father and play and romp with my children.

Abe wrote a piece entitled the Book of Chronicles, a satire on a marriage, infair, and putting the pairs to bed, etc.; it showed the boy—this was in 1829. A. wrote a piece on national politics, saying that the American government was the best form of government in the world for an intelligent people; that it ought to be kept sacred and preserved forever; that general education should [undeciphered] and carried all over the country; that the Constitution should be sacred, the Union perpetuated, and the laws revered, respected, and enforced, etc. (Mr. Wood said much more which I can recollect.) This was in 1827 or '28. Abe once drank, as all people did here at that time. I took newspapers, some from Ohio, Cincinnati, the names of which I have now forgotten. One of these papers was a temperance paper. Abe used to borrow it, take it home and read it, and talk it over with me; he was an intelligent boy, a sensible lad, I assure you. One day Abe wrote a piece on temperance and brought it to my house. I read it carefully over and over, and the piece excelled for sound sense anything that my papers contained. I gave the article to one Aaron Farmer, a Baptist preacher; he read it, it struck him; he said he wanted it to send to a temperance paper in Ohio, for publication; it was sent and published. I saw the printed piece, read it with pleasure over and over again. This was in 1827 or '28. The political article I showed to John Pitcher, an attorney of Posey County, Indiana, who was traveling on the circuit, on law business, and stopped at my house overnight; he read it carefully and asked me where I got it. I told him that one of my neighbors' boys wrote it; he couldn't believe it till I told him that Abe did write it. Pitcher lived in Mount Vernon, Indiana. Pitcher in fact was struck with the article and said to me this: "The world can't beat it." He begged for it. I gave it to him and it was published; can't say what paper it got into, know it was published. Abe was always a man though a boy. I never knew him to swear; he would say to his playfellows and other boys: "Swear off your boyish ways and be more like men." Abe got his mind and fixed morals from his good mother. Mrs. Lincoln was a very smart, intelligent, and intellectual woman; she was naturally strong-minded; was a gentle, kind, and tender woman, a Christian of the Baptist persuasion, she was a remarkable woman truly and indeed. I do not think she absolutely died of the milk sickness entirely. Probably this helped to seal her fate.

Abraham came to my house one day and stood round about, timid and shy. I knew he wanted something. I said to him: "Abe, what is your case?" Abe replied: "Uncle, I want you to go to the river (the Ohio) and give me some recommendation to some boat." I remarked: "Abe, your age is against you, you are not twenty-one yet." "I know that, but I want a start," said Abe. I concluded not to go, for the boy's good; did not go. I saw merchants in Rockport and mentioned the subject to them. In 1829, this was.

Abe read the newspapers of the day, at least such as I took. I took the *Telescope*. Abe frequently borrowed it. I remember the paper now. I took it from about 1825 to 1830, if not longer. Abe worked for me on this ridge (on this road leading from Gentryville to Elizabeth-Dale Post Office place). Abe whipsawed, saw him cutting down a large tree one day; I asked him what he was going to do with it; he said he was going to saw it into planks for his father's new house. The year was 1828 or '29. Abe could sink an ax deeper in wood than any man I ever saw. Abe cut the tree down, and he and one Levi Mills whipsawed it into planks. As I said, the plank was for Lincoln's new house; the house was not completed till after Lincoln left for Illinois. The house that Lincoln lived in is gone. Abe sold his planks to Crawford, the book man. The book story is substantially correct. Josiah Crawford put the plank in his house, where it is now to be seen, i.e., in the southeast room. (I sat on the plank myself—ate a good dinner at Mrs. Crawford's; Mrs. C. is a lady, is a good woman, quite intelligent.[1]) Abe wrote poetry a good deal, but I can't recollect what about except one piece which was entitled "The Neighborhood Broil." Abe always brought his pieces, prose or poetry, to me straight. I thought more of Abe than any boy I ever saw; he was a strong man, physically powerful; he could strike with a mall a heavier blow than any man; he was long, tall, and strong.

Mr. Wood told me an ox story about Abe's bravery which I can recollect. *Tell it.*

Elizabeth Crawford's Statement

September 16, 1865.

I went to Josiah Crawford's, the book man, not the schoolteacher as represented, the schoolteacher was a different man. Landed there about 11 a.m., hitched my horse, Nat Grigsby with me, as he went all the rounds with me and to all places and was present at all interviews and conversations. Mrs. Crawford was absent, at a son's house, distant about three-quarters of a mile, attending to her sick grandchild. I called for dinner. Mrs. Crawford's daughter got us a good dinner, sent for Mrs. Crawford, her daughter rather would send for her. Before Mrs. Crawford came, I looked over the "library," counted the volumes. There were two Bibles, four hymnbooks, Graham's *History of the United States* abridged, *Great Events of America, Pioneers of the New World*, a Testament, *Grace Truman*, Webster's Dictionary, a small one, some newspapers, mostly religious. There were twelve or fifteen books in all. Mrs. Crawford came, is aged about fifty-nine years. She is good-looking, is a lady at first blush, is easily approached, quite talkative, free and generous. She knew Abe Lincoln well.

My husband is dead, died May 1865. Abraham was nearly grown when he left Indiana. Abe worked for my husband, daubed our cabin in 1824 or '25 in which we lived. The second work he did for us was work done for the injured book, Weems's Life of Washington. Lincoln in 1829 bor-

---

[1] Herndon's note.

rowed this book and by accident got it wet. L. came and told honestly and exactly how it was done, the story of which is often told. My husband said: "Abe, as long as it is you, you may finish the book and keep it." Abe pulled fodder a day or two for it. We brought the book from Kentucky. Abe worked on the field yonder, north of the house. Our house was then the same little log cabin which Abe had *"daubed"*; it was made of round logs "unhewn and unbarked." The old cabin, which stood here by this cotton tree, was pulled down and this new one erected there. We had cleared about eighteen acres of land when Abe first worked for us. Abe made rails for us. Our first house was about fifteen square, one room, low. Thomas Lincoln made my furniture; some of it was sold at my husband's administrors' sale. Thomas Lincoln was at my house frequently, almost every week. Sarah Lincoln, Abe's sister, worked for me; she was a good, kind, amicable girl, resembling Abe. The Lincoln family were good people, good neighbors; they were honest and hospitable and very, very sociable. We moved to Indiana in 1824, came from Kentucky. I know as a matter of course Sarah and Sally Lincoln very well, and I say to you that she was a gentle, kind, smart, shrewd, social, intelligent woman. She was quick and strong-minded; she had no education, except what she gathered up herself. I speak more of what she was by nature than by culture. I never was a politician in all my life, but when such men as Abe Lincoln, as in 1860 [ran for office], I, as it were, took the stump; he was the noblest specimen of man I ever saw. Gentryville lies four miles from here northwest. Abe worked for us at various times at 25¢ per day, worked hard and faithful, and when he missed time, would not charge for it. I took some of the rails which Abe cut and split for us and had canes made from them; they were white oak, cut from this stump here; someone got into my house and stole my cane.

Can't say what books Abe read, but I have a book called *The Kentucky Preceptor,* which we brought from Kentucky and in which and from which Abe learned his school orations, speeches, and pieces to recite. School exhibitions used to be the order of the day, not as now, however. Abe attended them, spoke, and acted his part always well, free from rant and swell; he was a modest and sensitive lad, never coming where he was not wanted; he was gentle, tender, and kind. Abe was a moral and a model boy and, while other boys were out hooking watermelons and drifting away their time, he was studying his books, thinking and reflecting. Abe used to visit the sick boys and girls of his acquaintance. When he worked for us, he read all our books, would sit up late in the night, kindle up the fire, read by it, cipher by it. We had a broad wooden shovel on which Abe would work out his poems, wipe off, and repeat till it got too black for more; then he would scrape and wash off, and repeat again and again; rose early, went to work, came to dinner, sat down and read, joked, told stories, etc., etc. Here is my husband's likeness; you need not look at mine. My husband was a substantial man (and I say a cruel hard husband judging from his looks [1]). Sarah Lincoln was a strong, healthy woman, was cool, not excitable, truthful, do to tie to, shy, shrinking. Thomas Lincoln was blind in one eye, and the other was weak, so he felt his way on the work much of the time; his sense of touch was keen. Abe did wear buckskin pants, coonskin, opossum skin caps. Abe ciphered with a coal or with red keel got from the branches; he smoothed and planed boards, wrote on them, ciphered on them. I have seen this over and over again. Abe was sometimes sad, not often; he was reflective, was witty and humorous.

Abe Lincoln was one day bothering the girls, his sister and others playing yonder, and his sister scolded him, saying: "Abe, you ought to be ashamed of yourself. What do you expect will become of you?" "Be President of the United States," promptly responded Abe. Abe wrote a good composition, wrote prose and poetry. He wrote three or four satires; one was called the Book of Chronicles. He said that he would be President of the United States, told my husband so often, said it jokingly, yet with a smacking of deep earnestness in his eye and tone; he evidently had an idea, a feeling, in 1828 that he was bound to be a great man. No doubt that in his boyish days he dreamed it would be so. Abe was ambitious, sought to outstrip and override others. This I confess.

One of Abe's pieces, the Book of Chronicles, ran about this:

> *I will tell you a joke about Josiah and Mary,*
> *'Tis neither a joke nor a try,*
> *For Reuben and Charles have married two girls*
> *But Billy has married a boy.*
> *He tried ——* (Mrs. Crawford blushed)
> *The girls on every side*
> He had well tried.
> *None could he get to agree,*
> All was in vain,
> He went home again,
> *And said that he's married to Natty.*

I don't pretend to give the exact words, nor its rhyme, nor meter now, will think it over, recall it, and write to you in Illinois. The poem is smutty

---

[1] Herndon's note.

and I can't tell it to you, will tell it to my daughter-in-law; she will tell her husband, and he shall send it to you.

I left Mrs. Crawford's about 3 p.m.

Before leaving, she gave me *The Kentucky Preceptor* and a cane made from one of Abe's rails, for both of which I thanked her. I really felt proud of the gift and felt a gratitude for them. Mrs. Crawford is a lady of the Kentucky stamp.

NAT GRIGSBY'S STATEMENT

Gentryville, Ind., September 16, 1865.

After taking the records in Spencer County, Indiana, I went with my old guide and companion Nat Grigsby down to William Thompson, who lived where Colonel Jones had resided—a half-mile west of Gentryville. Colonel Jones was Lincoln's guide and teacher in politics. Colonel J. was killed at Atlanta. Grigsby showed me where Lincoln spoke in 1844. When Lincoln was speaking, Grigsby went into the house where the speech was being made; Lincoln saw G. enter; he stopped short, said: "There is Nat." Lincoln then walked over the benches and over the heads of his hearers, came rolling, took G. by the hand, shook it most cordially, said a few words, went back, commenced his remarks where he had stopped, finished his speech, told G. that he must stay with him all night, slept at Col. Jones's.

When we had gone to bed and way in the night, a cat commenced mewing and scratching, making a fuss generally. Lincoln got up in the dark and said: "Kitty, Kitty, Pussy, Pussy." The cat knew the voice and manner kind, went to Lincoln. L. rubbed it down, saw the sparkling. L. took up the cat, carried it to the door, and gently rubbed it again and again, saying: "Kitty, Kitty, etc.," then gently put it down, closed the doors, commenced telling stories and talking over old times.

As we were going down to Thompson's G. told me this story, which I had heard before.

A man by the name of Charles Harper was going to mill, had an extremely long wheat bag on the horse, and was met by Sister Gordon, who said to Brother Harper: "Brother Harper, your bag is too long." "No," said Brother Harper, "it is only too long in the [undeciphered]." They were brother and sister in the Church. Mrs. Gordon told her husband of the vulgar [words]; Gordon made a fuss, had a church trial. Lincoln got the secret, wrote a witty piece of poetry on the scenes and conversations. The poetry of Abe was good, witty, etc., as said by all who read it.

Mrs. Jack Armstrong's Statement

Mrs. Jack Armstrong says:

Am the wife of Jack Armstrong, was so, knew Abraham Lincoln in July or August 1831, knew this by the birth of one of my children. Lincoln was clerking for Offutt at that time. I was living four miles from New Salem. Our acquaintance began then. Abraham would come out to our house, drink milk and mush, corn bread, butter, bring the children candy, would rock the cradle of my baby, the boy that was put on trial and whom Abe cleared, while I got him, Abe, something to eat. Abe is one year older than I am, am now fifty-five years. My husband Jack Armstrong died, about 1857. I fixed his pants, made his shirts, didn't make any buckskin pants, only fixed his surveyor's pants. He has gone with us to parties, he would tell stories, joke people, girls and boys at the parties. He would nurse babies, do anything to accommodate anybody. I never saw him drink a drop of liquor. Jack Armstrong and Lincoln never had a word; they did wrestle, no foul play, all in a good humor, commenced in fun and ended in sport. I had no books about my house, loaned him none. We didn't think about books, papers, we worked, had to live. Lincoln has stayed at our house two or three weeks at a time.

In reference to the trial of my son, I wrote to Lincoln first, he then wrote to me, have lost the letter, went to see Lincoln at Springfield, saw him in his office; he promised to come down to defend my son, did so, cleared him, told the stories about our first acquaintance, what I did for him and how I did it, etc., was truly eloquent. After the trial was over, L. came down to where I was in Beardstown. I asked him what he charged me, told him I was poor; he said: "Why, Hannah, I shan't charge you a cent, never. Anything I can do for you I will do for you willingly and freely without charges." He wrote to me about some land which some men were trying to get for me. Mr. Lincoln said: "Hannah, they can't get your land, let them try it in the circuit court and then you appeal it, bring it to Supreme Court, and I and Herndon will attend to it for nothing."

In 1863 I wanted to get one of my sons, William, the boy whom Lincoln cleared in Beardstown, out of the army, needed him, all I had, wrote to Lincoln at Washington; he telegraphed to me as follows:

September 1863.

Mrs. Hannah Armstrong:
  I have just ordered the discharge of your boy, William, as you say now at Louisville, Kentucky.

A. Lincoln.

As to the trial, Lincoln said to me: "Hannah, your son will be cleared before sundown." He and the other lawyers addressed the jury and closed the case. I went down to Thompson's parlor. Stanton came and told me soon that my son was cleared, and a free man. I went up to the court house, the jury shook hands with me, so did the Court, so did Lincoln. We were all affected and tears streamed down Lincoln's eyes. He then remarked to me: "Hannah, what did I tell you? I pray to God that William may be a good boy hereafter, that this lesson may prove in the end a good lesson to him and to all."

Mr. Lincoln lectured in the evening after the trial on discoveries and inventions; it was a funny production and, if I can judge, a very good, that is, a solid and good one.

A few days before Mr. Lincoln left for Washington, I went to see him, was a widow; the boys got up a story on me that I went to get to sleep with Abe, etc. I replied to the joke that it was not every woman who had the good fortune and high honor of sleeping with a President. This stopped the sport, cut it short. Well, I talked to him some time and was about to bid him good-by, had told him that it was the last time that I should ever see him, something told me that I should never see him, that they would kill him. He smiled and said jokingly: "Hannah, if they kill me, I shall never die another death." I then bade him good-by.

I never was in Springfield till 1859. The stories going the rounds about jumping. I was in Springfield after my son was cleared, saw him, shook hands with him, saw his wife. Abraham never spoke to me about his wife, never introduced me to her, thought something was the matter with him and her. The first time I went to his house knocked at the door, heard no answer, went to the back door, roused the girl, saw Lincoln come upstairs. . . .

You understand the customs and habits of the people of Menard in 1831 to 1837 as well and better than I do and can write them out, am sick, want to go home, will see you in Springfield sometimes, will then tell you more. Good-by, etc.

JAMES H. MATHENY'S STATEMENT

November 29, 1866.

James H. Matheny says:

That about 1837, 8, and 9 a parcel of young men in this city formed a kind of political society, association, or what not. Lincoln once or twice wrote short poems for the book. None of the poems are recollected in full. One verse of one, on "Seduction," by Lincoln, runs thus:

> *Whatever spiteful fools may say,*
> *Each jealous, ranting yelper,*
> *No woman ever played the whore*
> *Unless she had a man to help her.*

Newton Francis
Evan Butler
Noah Rickard
J. H. Matheny } Some of the members.

DR. FLOYD'S STATEMENT

Dr. Floyd, dentist, says:

Just before Lincoln left for Washington, I met him on the street, and knowing that he had received many threatening letters of assassination, etc., I suggested to him the propriety of care, caution, told him he had better take a cook from his own true and tried female acquaintances here. Mr. Lincoln said: "I will be cautious, but God's will be done. I am in His hands, and will be during my administration, and what He does I must bow to. God rules, and we should submit, etc." This was earnestly said.

(This is correct. H.)

MARY OWENS [1]

Mary S. Owens, daughter of Nathaniel Owens, was born in Green County, Kentucky, on the twenty-ninth day of September 1808. She was

---

[1] In a letter to Jesse Weik, dated March 14, 1887, B. R. Vineyard, the son of Mary Owens, writes: "I have written (also enclosed) a short account of my mother and Mr. Lincoln's courtship of her. I do not wish it published over my signature, but send it to you as my idea of what is probably true, that it may serve you as the basis of what you may wish to write on the subject."

married to Jesse Vineyard on the twenty-seventh day of March 1841. Of this union there were born five children, of whom only two survive. Jesse Vineyard died December 27, 1862, and Mary, his widow, on July 4, 1877.

Mary received a good education, her father being a leading and wealthy citizen of his time and locality. A part of her schooling was obtained in a Catholic convent, though in religious faith she was a Baptist, and in after years united with that denomination, and continued a member thereof until the time of her death. She was good-looking when a girl, by many esteemed handsome, but growing fleshier as she grew older. She was polished in her manners, pleasing in her address, and attractive in society. She had a little dash of coquetry in her intercourse with that class of young men who arrogated to themselves claims of superiority. But she never yielded to this disposition to an extent that would willingly lend encouragement to an honest suitor, sincerely desirous of securing her hand, where she felt she could not in the end yield to a proposal of marriage if he should make the offer. She was a good conversationalist and a splendid reader—but very few persons being found to equal her in this accomplishment. She was light-hearted and cheery in her disposition. She was kind and considerate for those with whom she was thrown in contact.

She first became acquainted with Mr. Lincoln while visiting a sister of hers who had married Bennett Able, and who was an early settler of the country about New Salem. Young Lincoln was a frequent visitor at the house of Able and a warm friend of the family, and during the first visit of Mary Owens, which did not continue a great while, he learned to admire her very much. Later she made a second visit to her sister, Mrs. Able, returning with her from Kentucky. Lincoln had boasted, so it has been said, that he would marry Miss Owens if she came a second time to Illinois, a report of which had come to her hearing. She left her Kentucky home with a predetermination to show him, if she met him, that she was not to be caught simply by the asking. On this second visit Lincoln paid her more marked attention than ever before, and his affections became more and more enlisted in her behalf. During the early part of their acquaintance, following the natural vent of her temperament, she was pleasing and entertaining to him. Later on, he discovered himself seriously interested in the blue-eyed Kentuckian, whom he had really underestimated in his preconceived opinions of her. In the meantime, Mary, too, had discovered the sterling qualities of the young man who was paying her such devoted attention. But while she admired, she did not love him. He was ungainly and angular in his physical make-up, and to her seemed deficient in the nicer and more delicate attentions, which she felt to be

MARY TODD LINCOLN

From a Photograph by Brady (1862)

ABRAHAM LINCOLN

From a Photograph by A. Gardner in Washington Two Weeks before the President's Assassination; Courtesy of Mrs. N. Taylor Phillips

due from the man whom she had pictured as an ideal husband. He had given her to understand that she had greatly charmed him. But he was not himself certain that he could make her the husband he thought she would be most happy with. Later on, by word and in letter, he told her so. His honesty of purpose showed itself in all his efforts to win her hand. He told her of his poverty, and while advising her that life with him meant to her, who had been reared in comfort and plenty, great privation and sacrifice, yet he wished to secure her as a wife. But she felt that she did not entertain for him the same feeling that he professed for her, and that she ought to entertain before accepting him, and so declined his offer. Judging alone from some of his letters, it has been supposed by some that she, remembering the murmur she had heard of his determination to marry her, and not being fully certain of the sincerity of his purposes, may have purposely left him, in the earlier stages of his courtship, somewhat in uncertainty. But later on, when, by his manner and his repeated announcements to her that his hand and heart were at her disposal, he demonstrated the honesty and sincerity of his purposes, she declined his offer kindly but with no uncertain meaning. In speaking of him in after years she always referred to him as a man with a heart full of human kindness and a head full of common sense.

Mrs. N. W. Edwards's Statement

I am the wife of the Hon. N. W. Edwards. Mr. Lincoln married my sister Mary. We came to Springfield about 1835; my sister Mrs. Wallace now came to live with us about that time. Doctor Wallace and she were married in 18—. We had a vacancy in our family by that marriage, wrote to Mary to come out and make our home her home; she had a stepmother with whom she did not agree. Mary was born in 1818, well educated, taught at a private school in Lexington, Mrs. —— keeping it. Mary came to Illinois about 1838. Mr. Lincoln commenced seeing Mary about 1839–40, the winter of 1839 and '40, directly after Doctor Wallace was married. I knew Mr. L. well, he was a cold man, had no affection, was not social, was abstracted, thoughtful. I knew he was a great man long years since, knew he was a rising man, and, nothing else modifying this, advised Mary at first to marry L. L. could not hold a lengthy conversation with a lady, was not sufficiently educated and intelligent in the female line to do so. He was charmed with Mary's wit and fascinated with her quick sagacity, her will, her nature, and culture. I have happened in the room where they were sitting often and often, and Mary led the conversation. Lincoln would listen and gaze on her as if drawn by some superior power, irresistibly so; he listened, never scarcely said a word. I did not in a little time think that Mr. L. and Mary were suitable to each other and so said to Mary. Mary was quick, lively, gay, frivolous, it may be, social, and loved glitter, show, and pomp and power. She was an extremely ambitious woman and in Kentucky often and often contended that she was destined to be the wife of some future President, said it in my presence in Springfield and said it in earnest. Mr. Speed came to see Miss Matilda Edwards, left and went to Kentucky, Miss Edwards staying. Mr. Lincoln loved Mary, he went crazy in my own opinion, not because he loved Miss Edwards as said, but because he wanted to marry and doubted his ability and capacity to please and support a wife. Lincoln and Mary were engaged, everything was ready and prepared for the marriage, even to the supper, etc. Mr. L. failed to meet his engagement, cause: insanity. In his lunacy he declared he hated Mary and loved Miss Edwards. This is true, yet it was not his real feelings. A crazy man hates those he loves when not himself, often, often is this the case. The world had it that Mr. L. backed out, and this placed Mary in a peculiar situation, and to set herself right and to free Mr. Lincoln's mind, she wrote a letter to Mr. L. stating that she would release him from his engagement. Mr. Edwards and myself, after the first crush of things, told Mary and Lincoln that they had better not even marry, that their natures, mind, education, raising, etc., were so different they could not live happy as husband and wife, had better never think of the subject again. However, all at once we heard that Mr. L. and Mary had secret meetings at Mr. L. Francis's, editor of the Springfield *Journal*. Mary said the reason this was so, the cause why it was, that the world, woman and man, were uncertain and slippery and that it was best to keep the secret courtship from all eyes and ears. Mrs. L. told Mr. L. that, though she had released him in the letter spoken of, yet she said that she would hold the question an open one, that is, that she had not changed her mind, but felt as always. The whole of the year of the crazy spell Miss Edwards was at our house, say for a year. I asked Miss Edwards, subsequently Mrs. Strong, if Mr. Lincoln ever mentioned the subject of his love to her. Miss Edwards said: "On my word, he never mentioned such a subject to me; he never even stooped to pay me a compliment."

Mr. Douglas used to come to see Mary, probably it is quite likely that his intentions were true and sincere. Mary was asked one day by some of her friends which she intended to have. "Him who has the best prospects of being President," said Miss Todd. The marriage of Mr. L. and Mary was quick and sudden, one or two hours' notice.

Miss Edwards one day was asked why she married such an old dried-up husband, such a withered-up old buck. She replied: "He had lots of houses and gold." Mary was present at this question and answer, and she then remarked: "Is that true? I would rather marry a good man, a man of mind, with a hope and bright prospects ahead for position, fame, and power than to marry all the houses, gold, and bones in the world." Mary Lincoln has had much to bear, though she don't bear it well; she has acted foolishly, unwisely, and made the world hate her; she opened a private letter of mine after I left Washington because in that letter my daughter gave me her opinion of Mrs. L. She became enraged at me. I tried to explain; she would send back my letters with insulting remarks. Mr. Lincoln shed tears when I left Washington, had been solicited to come to Washington by Mr. and Mrs. Lincoln. Mr. Lincoln said to me: "Mrs. Edwards, do stay with me; you have such a power and control, such an influence, over Mary; come, do stay and console me." This was some time after Willie's death.

Once I took Mr. L. to calm his mind, to cheer him, to inspire him, if you please, with hope and confidence, to turn away his attention from business as well as grief, down to and through the rich conservatory, hot-house, cold house, etc., where the flowers are kept and where the world is represented by flowers that speak, and made the remark to Mr. L.: "Oh, how beautiful this is; these roses, etc., are fine; these exotics are grand," and to which Mr. Lincoln said: "I never was in here before; how spring-like it looks! I don't care for flowers, have no natural and educated taste for such things." I made him walk to the park one day north of the White House. He had not been there for a year, and Tad went with us. Tad locked the gate, hid the key. Mrs. L. told Tad to get the key. Tad laughed and L. thought it smart and shrewd. I respect and love Mr. Lincoln, think he was a great man a good man and an honest one. He was a little ungrateful, I think, for the want of [undeciphered].

Mr. Lincoln was kind and good to his domestic and other servants. One day the girl threatened to leave unless she could get $1.50 per week. Mrs. L. could, rather would, not give the extra 25¢; the girl said she would leave. Mrs. L. said leave. Mr. L. heard the conversation, didn't want the girl to leave, told his wife so, asked, begged her to pay the $1.50. Mrs. L. remained incorrigible. Mr. L. slipped around to the back door and said: "Don't leave. Tell Mrs. Lincoln you have concluded to stay at $1.25, and I'll pay the odd 25¢ to you." Mrs. Lincoln overheard the conversation and said to the girl and Mr. L.: "What are you doing? I heard some conversation, couldn't understand it. I'm not going to be deceived. Miss, you can leave, and as for you, Mr. L., I'd be ashamed of myself."

Mr. Lincoln's habits were like himself, odd and wholly irregular. He loved nothing and ate mechanically. I have seen him sit down at the table and never unless recalled to his senses would he think of food. He was a peculiar man.

Mrs. Lincoln insulted Seward one day. Mr. Seward was the power behind the throne. Mrs. L. had heard of this often and often. One day she said to Mr. Seward: "It is said that you are the power behind the throne. I'll show you that Mr. L. is President yet."

Mr. L. and Mary saw each other in that parlor there. This house is about as it was, excepting this porch, which has been added since. . . .

September 27, 1887.

Mrs. N. W. Edwards said:

Mr. Herndon, have no photos of myself, have had some, unwillingly taken, don't know where any of them are now, have a likeness, a portrait, of myself here which you can have photographed if you must have it. When you go to Indiana I will answer your letters asking questions. I have no photos of Mrs. Lincoln; she too was opposed to having her face scattered abroad. Mrs. Lincoln was an ambitious woman, the most ambitious woman I ever saw, spurred up Mr. Lincoln, pushed him along and upward, made him struggle and seize his opportunities. Lincoln's and Mary's engagement, etc., were broken off by her flirtations with Douglas. Mr. Edwards and myself told Lincoln and Mary not to marry, said so more or less directly; they were raised differently and had no congeniality, no feelings, etc., alike. We never opposed Lincoln's marriage with Mary. It is said that Miss Edwards had something to do [with] breaking Mary's engagement with Lincoln; it's not true. Miss Edwards told me that Lincoln never condescended to pay her even a poor compliment; it was the flirtation with Douglas that did the business. Mr. Lincoln and Mr. Speed were frequently at our house, seemed to enjoy themselves in their conversation beneath the dense shade of our forest trees. After the match was broken off between Mary and Lincoln, Mrs. Francis shrewdly got them together. Doctor Henry, who admired and loved Mr. Lincoln, had much to do in getting Mary and Lincoln together again. Speaking about photos, Mr. Herndon, I am too old now to have one taken. At one time in my life I should not have been much ashamed to show my face. (She once was a very, very pretty woman.   H.)

Mr. Edwards was present during this conversation—said that

When Lincoln first came to Springfield, I assisted Lincoln, offered to buy him a good law library and send him to some law school, and these offers he refused; said that he was too poor and did not wish to involve himself.

Said that Lincoln was, during part of the time, in the legislature of 1841, called session.

Both Mr. Edwards and Mrs. Edwards have been willing at all times to answer all proper questions and to make things plain to me. This memorandum was taken down by me quickly after the conversation was had and is in every particular correct substantially.

W. H. H.

It seems to me, infer it, that Mary Todd flirted with Douglas in order to spur up Lincoln to a great love. Miss Todd used Douglas as a mere tool, refused his hand. Miss Todd didn't know her man. Lincoln was somewhat cold and yet exacting, blew up too quickly. From various conversations with Mr. and Mrs. Edwards I infer as above. Mary Todd wanted Lincoln to manifest a tender and a deep love, but, poor woman, she did not know that Lincoln was an undemonstrative man in this line. The devil was to play and did play his part in Mr. Lincoln's and Miss Todd's affairs, nay, during their lives.

H.

CHARLES S. ZANE'S STATEMENT

About nine o'clock on the morning of the eighteenth of May 1860 I was sitting in the law office of Messrs. Lincoln and Herndon, conversing with a student in the office, when Mr. Lincoln came in. On entering, he said: "Well, boys, what do you know?" and sat down in a chair on the north side of the office. I remarked (to him): "Mr. Rosette, who came from Chicago on the morning train, thinks your chances for the nomination are good." He asked me if I knew what Mr. Rosette's reasons for thinking so were. A short conversation then followed, during which Mr. E. L. Baker entered the office with a telegram which said the names of the candidates for nomination had been announced to the convention; that Mr. Lincoln's name was received with greater applause than that of any other candidate. Soon after, he, Lincoln, went to the telegraph office accompanied by those present. After awaiting there some time the telegraph of the first ballot, the first ballot came over the wires. From the manner in which Mr. Lincoln received this dispatch, it was my impression that it was as favorable as he expected. His opinion was or had been that, if Mr. Seward did not get the nomination on the first ballot or come very near to it, he would not be likely to get it at all. After waiting a short time, another telegram of the second ballot came. This I thought from his manner he considered as virtually deciding the nomination. He then went to the office of the *Illinois State Journal*. The local editor, with four others including myself, returned to the telegraph office and remained until the third dispatch came. Upon receiving it, the operator threw down his pencil, evidently excited; then, taking it up, wrote out the dispatch and handed it to the local, who read it to himself. Those present asked how it looked; he said very bad, which lengthened some of our faces considerably. On the way to the *Journal* office he remarked that it looked bad for Mr. Seward and the other defeated candidates. Entering the office where Mr. Lincoln was seated, the local proposed three cheers for the next President, which were given, then read the dispatch. Mr. Lincoln, being seated, rose up, took the telegram, and read it; then said: "When the second ballot came, I knew this must come." He received all with apparent coolness; from the expression playing upon his countenance, however, a close observer could detect strong emotions within. When the result was made known on the streets, it was followed by shouts for Lincoln.

In the remarks which followed the last dispatch someone said: "Mr. Lincoln, I suppose we will soon have a book containing your life now"; to which he replied: "There is not much in my past life about which to write a book as it seems to me." He then came down out of the office (which was on the second floor) onto the sidewalk. His neighbors and friends, gathering around him, commenced shaking his hand and congratulating him; he then said, jesting: "Gentlemen, you had better come up and shake my hand while you can. Honors elevate some men." After spending a few moments in receiving their cordial congratulations, looking in the direction of his home, he said: "Well, gentlemen, there is a little woman at our house who is probably more interested in this dispatch than I am; if you will excuse me, I will take the dispatch up and let her see it."

As he walked up the street, his friends and neighbors looked after him with a feeling of great satisfaction and, as I thought, mingled with considerable of pride. Others coming up the streets would point after him and say: "Yonder goes Lincoln," showing that he had grown in their interest that morning.

Lincoln played ball pretty much all the day before his nomination, played at what is called fives, knocking a ball up against a wall that served as an alley. He loved this game, his only physical game that I knew of. Lincoln said: "This game makes my shoulders feel well."

I heard Lincoln say about 1858, say in October, that the Know Nothings, their ideas and platform, united to circumscribe the election franchise, universal suffrage. That he was opposed to it. That he wanted to lift men up and give them a chance. Lincoln said that he loved Joseph Gillespie, respected him highly, etc., but he (L.) could not endure to talk to Jo on that ground, that he (L.) got excited, so did Jo and the best way was to quit.

I know of a case in the Supreme Court about 1849–50 in which I (Herndon) wanted Lincoln to assist me to argue a question that involved the law of the extension or extraction, lessening and narrowing, the right of suffrage, it being a city case and I being Mr. L.'s partner as well as city attorney, and he would not help me, saying: "I am opposed to the limitation, the lessening, of the right of suffrage; am in favor of its extension, enlargement; want to lift men up and broaden them; don't intend by no act of mine to crush or contract."

Charles S. Zane says that Julian of Indiana, as well as others in Washington, on the last of February or the first day of March 1861, told them that Seward tried his best, brought to bear on Lincoln all his tact, skill, and power, to get Mr. Lincoln to modify or take out that expression in his first Inaugural wherein he, L., said that he would not retake facts, etc. L. did not do it.

Seward's friends tried to make L. not make Chase one of his secretaries and Chase's men tried the same. Much opposition was made against Cameron, all to no purpose.

Lincoln often modified or changed his policy—these policies which acted as means—though he never changed his policy, his purpose, of saving the Union—never dodged that.

C. C. BROWN'S STATEMENT

C. C. Brown says:

That he came down to Lincoln's office early in the morning of the day when Lincoln was nominated. Lincoln was lying on the sofa, said: "Well, Brown, have you heard anything?" Lincoln said: "Let's go to the telegraph office, Brown." They did go over about 10 a.m. Lincoln stopped awhile till the telegraph brought the intelligence of the first ballot, the second ballot, the third, etc. Lincoln then exclaimed: "I've got him!"

Lincoln played ball with me on that day (so he did with Z. Enos, Baker, etc.). L. was nervous, fidgety, intensely excited. Lincoln told stories. . . .

Lincoln came all the way from Coles County eighty or ninety miles to my wedding. Married John T. Stuart, a relation to Lincoln. In the morning after my marriage Lincoln met me and said: "Brown, why is a woman like a barrel?" [C. C. B.] could not answer. "Well," said Lincoln, "you have to raise the hoops before you put the head in."

Lincoln was our relative; the Todd-Stuart-Edwards family, with preacher and priest, dogs, servants, etc., got mad at Mr. L. because he made the house-divided-against-itself speech. We flinched, dodged, Lincoln; he would explain; he did explain. See his speeches with Douglas.

Lincoln was a radical, fanatically so, and yet he never went beyond the people. Kept his ideas and thoughts to himself, i.e., he never told all he felt.

Brown says further that

Some Eastern man, who had something to do in or with a newspaper in New York, came to our office (S. E. and Brown) on some business before L. was generally spoken of as a candidate. The man expressed a wish to see L. I took him to see Lincoln. The man said to Lincoln: "I told our boys to put your name for President or Vice-President on the banner, etc." Mr. Lincoln said: "Well, my friend, I am much obliged to you. I guess either position is big and high enough for me." (Brown says) I never heard Lincoln say anything about his religious views—or religion in any aspect.

JAMES H. MATHENY'S STATEMENT

J. H. Matheny says:

He was present, he thinks, in the market house in 1840 and heard a debate between Douglas and Lincoln—the subject: Martin Van Buren. Lincoln had asserted that Van had voted for Negro suffrage under certain limitations. Douglas denied it. Lincoln then read from Holland's Life of Van Buren. Douglas said it was a forgery. Lincoln drew Fithian's letter from Van Buren on Douglas. Douglas got mad, snatched up the book and slung it into the crowd, saying: "D——n such a book." (Lincoln told me this story too.—HERNDON.)

Further, Lincoln told me that Douglas was always calling the Whigs Federalists, Tories, Aristocrats, etc. That the Whigs were opposed to freedom, justice, and progress. Lincoln told me that he said: "Douglas says the Whigs are opposed to liberty, justice, and progress. This is a loose assertion, I suppose, to catch votes. I don't like to catch votes by cheating men out of their judgments, but in reference to the Whigs being opposed to liberty, etc., let me say that that remains to be seen and demonstrated in the future. The brave don't boast. A barking dog don't bite."

PETER VAN BERGEN'S STATEMENT

Peter Van Bergen says:

That James Smith, the preacher who once lived here, is now in Dundee, Scotland. Smith was in 1850 preacher of the First Presbyterian Church here. Smith once said to Lincoln: "Lincoln, you are a rising man. You will be President yet." "If I am ever President I'll banish you to Scotland," replied Lincoln good-naturedly. After L. was elected, he received a letter from Smith. Lincoln did appoint him consul at Liverpool.

Speed told Van Bergen that once he [Lincoln] called his Cabinet together and requested their individual opinion as to the necessity and policy of hanging the rebels. Each gave his opinion. Speed tarried after the meeting had adjourned. Lincoln said: "Speed, you are quite a hun man." "Yes," said Speed. "I feel this way," said Lincoln. "Once a man and his small son caught several coons, killed all but one, and the old man tied it with a string." Lincoln came along and the boy told him the story. [Lincoln] said: "Let him go." The boy said: "I wish I could, he could get away, but if I let him go, dad will whip me." "I feel as to hanging, etc., like the boy about the coon. If I let them go, I'll get whipped," said Lincoln.

Van B. says Lincoln showed him, Van B., the war maps of Vicksburg, explained, etc., etc., and finally said: "Grant here displayed about Vicksburg more generalship than ever was shown by any general in America."

JAMES GOURLEY'S STATEMENT

I knew Lincoln as early as 1834; he used to come from New Salem afoot and get books at Stuart & Dummer's office; he was Post Master or Deputy P.M. at that time; he used to come to Stuart & Dummer's office and tell his stories; he once helped fix a fellow up at a hogshead and roll him down; Jack Armstrong was the leader. I ran a foot race in 1836 with H. B. Truett—now of California—got Lincoln to be my judge. Truett had a running suit, Indian style. Lincoln felt good and I beat Truett, a boaster. Lincoln loved to let the wind out of the windy fool. Col. E. D. Baker and I and he ran foot races. I know when Lincoln came to this city—in 1837—probably in May 1836. We played the old-fashioned twin ball, jumped, ran, fought, and danced. Lincoln played twin ball, he hopped well; in three hops he would go 41 feet on a dead level. He was a great wrestler, wrestled in the Black Hawk War; his mode, method, or way, his specialty, was side-holds; he threw down all men. Lincoln was a good player, could catch a ball; he would strip and go at it, do it well.

I heard Lincoln make a speech in Mechanicsburg, Sangamon County, in 1836. John Bell had a fight at the time. The roughs got on him and Lincoln jumped in and saw fair play. We stayed for dinner at Green's close to Mr. [undeciphered], drank whisky sweetened with honey.

The questions discussed were internal improvements, Whig principles. . . .

I heard Mr. Lincoln during the same canvass. Early was a candidate. Lincoln skinned Leick Quinton in the court in 1836. I think it was at the court house, where the State House now stands. The Whigs and Democrats had a general quarrel, then and there. N. W. Edwards drew a pistol on Achilles Morris, during the Congressional race between John T. Stuart and S. A. Douglas; they had a fight in Herndon's grocery, the bricklayer; they fought in a grocery; they both fought till exhausted, grocery floor slippery with slop. Stuart ordered out a barrel of whisky and wine. I became acquainted with Douglas in 1836 when he first came here as Register of the Land Office. Douglas and I wrestled many and many a time. When Harrison, White & Co. ran their race, I was a Harrison man, Lincoln was a Clay man. Heard Douglas and Lincoln speak on the questions of the day many times. He and Lincoln and Calhoun in their great tariff debate in the court house, a rented room in Hoffman's Row, northwest corner of public square. This debate lasted three or four nights or more. Lincoln's arguments were profound, Calhoun was an able man, no mistake. One of the ablest men that ever made stump speeches in Illinois. He came nearer of whipping Lincoln in debate than Douglas did. These men—Douglas, Calhoun, and Lincoln—I have often heard from 1834 to 1840.

Lincoln was a great temperance man during the time of the Washingtonians. He would go afoot five or ten miles to talk. One of his speeches was printed in the *Journal*. He was a good temperance man, he scarcely ever drank. I got Lincoln to join the Sons of Temperance about 1854. He joined and never appeared in it again. If Lincoln ever drank, it was as a medicine, I think. He took no part in the first temperance moves in 18—, when an act of the Legislature was passed and submitted to the people.

In 1840 he spoke frequently to Harrison Club; he advocated the tariff, bank, internal improvements by the general government, and the distribution of the proceeds of the sale of the public land, and particularly and generally all Whig measures. Lincoln was for Clay up to the time of General Taylor's race in 1848. He was for Clay on the Harrison, Van Buren, White, Webster & Co. He and I once went to Petersburg, he to make a speech against Peter Cartwright in his Congressional race, 1846. He skinned Peter and Erastus Wright, the abolition[ist]. (Note this, remember the Wright law suit. [Herndon]).

One day Lincoln was gone to Chicago to attend to the Rock Island Bridges case. While he was gone, say in 1857, Mrs. Lincoln and myself formed a conspiracy to take off the roof and raise the house. Lincoln came home, saw his house, and said: "Stranger, do you know where Lincoln lives? He used to live here." He scolded his wife for running him in debt. Again, when Lincoln was gone once I chose her, Mrs. L., a carriage, a fine one. Lincoln complained, but all to no purpose. Again when Lincoln was away from home, Mrs. Lincoln had a bad girl living with her; the boys and men used to come to her house in L.'s absence and scare her; she was crying and wailing one night, called me, and said: "Mr. Greeley, come, do come and stay with me all night, you can sleep in the bed with Bob and I. I don't want boys, they go to sleep too soon and won't and can't watch. Come, do, sleep with Robert and myself."

I lived next-door neighbor to Lincoln nineteen years; knew him and his family relations well; he used to come to our house with slippers on, one suspender and old pair of pants, came for milk; our room was low and he said: "Jim, you have to lift your loft a little higher. I can't stand in it well." He used to say to my wife that little people had some advantages; it did not take quite so much wood and wool to make their house and clothes.

Lincoln never planted any trees; he did plant some rose bushes once in front of his house; he planted no apple trees, cherry trees, pear trees, grapevines, shade trees, and suchlike things; he did not, it seems, care for such things.

He once, for a year or so, had a garden and worked in it; he kept his own horse, fed and curried it, fed and milked his own cow; he sawed his own wood generally when at home. He loved his horse well.

Lincoln and his wife got along literally well, unless Mrs. L. got the devil in her; Lincoln paid no attention, would pick up one of his children and walk off, would laugh at her, pay no earthly attention to her when in that wild furious condition. I don't think that Mrs. Lincoln was as bad a woman as she is represented; she was a good friend of mine. She always said that if her husband had stayed at home as he ought to that she could love him better; she is no prostitute, a good woman. She dared me once or twice to kiss her, as I thought, refused, wouldn't now.

Lincoln would take his children and would walk out on the railway out in the country, would talk to them, explain things carefully, particularly. He was kind, tender, and affectionate to his children, very, very. Lincoln, I think, had no dog, had cats. Bob used to harness cats. Bob and my boy used to harness up my dog and they would take him and go out into the woods and get roots.

Mrs. and Mr. Lincoln were good neighbors. Lincoln was the best man I ever knew; he gave my boy a position in the navy. Lincoln was a great reader, he read the Bible.

As to Mr. Lincoln I do not think he ever had a change of heart, belonged to no religious sects, was religious in his way, not as others generally. Had he ever had a change of heart, religiously speaking, he would have told me about it; he could not have neglected; he couldn't have avoided it.

In 1844 I used to play ball with Abe Lincoln, E. D. Baker, etc., others. The game was called fives, striking a ball with our hands against a wall that served as alley. In 1860 Lincoln and myself played ball, the game.

Lincoln went home from the *Journal* office directly after his nomination for President. He was agitated, turned pale, trembled. We, a good many, soon went up to see him at his house. Lincoln played ball the day before his nomination, probably he played some in the morning early.

HONORABLE H. E. DUMMER'S STATEMENT

Lincoln used to come to our office in Springfield and borrow books; don't know whether he walked or rode; he was an uncouth-looking lad; did not say much; what he did say he said it abruptly, sharply.

In 1859 I was in the Supreme Court room in the State House. Lincoln was or had been telling his yarns. A man, a kind of lickspittle, a fawner, said: "Lincoln, why do you not write out your stories and put them in a book?" Lincoln drew himself up, fixed his face, as if a thousand dead carcasses and a million of privies were shooting all their stench into his nostrils, and said: "Such a book would stink like a thousand privies." Lincoln had two characteristics: one of purity, and the other, as it were, an insane love in telling dirty and smutty stories. A good story of that kind has a point with a sting to it.

I will give you remembrances of Mr. L. in broken doses.

N. B. JUDD'S STATEMENT

I got on the cars with Lincoln at Springfield and went the trip through; never heard, don't think, that there is any truth in the Indiana or Ohio story about throwing train off the track or in killing Lincoln. Got Pinkerton's letter at Cincinnati, sent special messenger with letter there to me. One of Mr. Pinkerton's female detectives met me at N.G., spy, laid all the facts before me; I then arranged that on my arrival at Philadelphia I get a room and arrange to meet Pinkerton, went to the Continental, quit it, went down to —— Hotel. Met Pinkerton and Felton, President of Baltimore & Wilmington R.R. There the evidence was laid before me. Pinkerton laid all the evidence before me, was discussed. Pinkerton was exceedingly anxious that Lincoln should go on to Washington that night (eleven o'clock) train. Felton and I agreed to it. The conclusion was that Pinkerton should go to the Continental, see Lincoln, and lay the whole facts before him, which was done; went to my room; Lincoln was surrounded by the usual crowd. Lincoln was taken to a room. Probably Nicolay was there. Lincoln liked Pinkerton, had the utmost confidence in him as a gentleman and a man of sagacity. All the facts in debate were there given to Mr. Lincoln in detail. "Go you must, the world will laugh at you, I know, prepare to meet the charge of cowardice and [be] laughed at even by friends, and you must prepare yourself to be laughed at. So will your friends, I am convinced that there is danger, President Felton says there is danger, Pinkerton too says there is danger, there is danger, but you must prepare to be laughed at by friends and foe." Lincoln said: "I can't go tonight." I impressed this idea on Mr. Lincoln, and you must enlarge on it. The evidence was such as to convince all honest minds, yet the evidence could not be laid before the public because it would endanger the very agents of the government, Pinkerton's men, and all who were at that moment playing their wise game among the Secessionists, in the military companies—one was hung. I told Mr. Lincoln all and tried to impress the danger on him, told him that friend and foe would laugh at him, yet he must stand it, bear the sneers and scoffs and scorn of men, friend and foe alike. Evidence couldn't be got before the world. Mr. Lincoln said: "I have engaged to raise the flag on tomorrow morning over Independence Hall. I have engaged to go to Harrisburg. Beyond these I have no engagements; after these engagements are fulfilled, you are at liberty to take such course as you please." I then said to Mr. Lincoln: "We don't [want] to take any course that will endanger you or bring you into ridicule, because you are to bear the burden of the thing." Lincoln then said: "Well, I've known Pinkerton for years and have known and tested his truthfulness and sagacity and my judgment coincides with yours." I then said to Lincoln: "We will then complete the arrangements and I will tell you in detail on tomorrow in the cars between Philadelphia and Harrisburg." Mr. Nicolay knew of the interview, so did Lamon; neither knew of what was doing or said, or being said, yet they knew of the interview. Mr. Lincoln then returned to the parlors in the Continental, and Mr. Felton, Mr. Scott of Pennsylvania Central, and Mr. Sanford, general telegraph agent of the United States, were sent for and came to the room—the one [where] we had the interview with Mr. Lincoln, and there we made the arrangements, engaged all, nearly all, night in arranging and completing the program of next day. It was arranged that special car should leave Harrisburg at 6 p.m. and reach Philadelphia on the eleven o'clock train, in season for the train for Baltimore and Washington. (But one person of the party should accompany Mr. Lincoln; that was talked over at the time.) That every train on the Pennsylvania Central should be off the track from six till that Lincoln car had passed—Harrisburg to Philadelphia—come back, had passed, and going on reached Philadelphia. That Pinkerton should meet Mr. Lincoln with a carriage at or on the outside of the city, and carry him, L., to the depot of Baltimore & Wilmington R.R., so as not to go through the heart of the city. Pinkerton did so, did his part well, artistically so, keenly, shrewdly, and well. Pinkerton was and is a good friend to Lincoln. It was agreed that Felton should detain the eleven o'clock Baltimore train . . . until Mr. L.'s arrival. That Mr. Sanford should see to it, the telegraph, and take the proper measures for the execution of the plan, that no telegraphic message went over any of the wires until all this that evening was accomplished; his knowledge and skill being equal to that task, i.e., Sanford's. Raised, L. did, the flag, according to program, left for Harrisburg. In the morning just before the train was ready to start for Harrisburg, Mr. Lincoln sent for me to come to his room, and there I saw and met Fred Seward. Mr. Lincoln said: "Mr. Seward has been sent by his father to inform me of the same conspiracy, that you and Pinkerton explained to me last night" (Saw him—Fred Seward—at Philadelphia) "and advises that I proceed immediately to Washington; you can explain to him so far as you think fit what has been done." I said to Mr. Seward that arrangements had been made to pass Mr. Lincoln safely in Washington, and you may so assure your father; that the mode, the manner in detail, it is not necessary to detail. We left for Harrisburg, and on the way I gave to Mr. Lincoln a full and precise detail of all the arrangements that had been made. I said to him that the step to him was so important that I felt that it should be communicated to the other gentlemen of the party. Lincoln said: "You can do as you like about that." As soon as the ceremonies are over at Harrisburg I will fix an interview between him and Colonel Sumner, Major Hunter, Judge Davis, Captain John Pope, and Lamon, they being part of the President's party. I changed my seat. Nicolay said to me: "Judd, there is something up; what is it, if it is proper that I should know?" I said: "George, there is no necessity for your knowing and one man can keep a matter better than two." Arrived at Harrisburg ceremonies, got into the parlor, explained to Sumner and the party the facts as well as I could, and the plan and program that should carry Lincoln to Washington. Mr. Sumner spoke the first word. "That proceeding," said Sumner, "will be a d——d piece of cowardice." I replied to this pointed hit by saying: "That view of the case had already been presented to Mr. Lincoln." A discussion of the matter, Pope favoring our arrangement; Sumner said: "I'll get a squad of cavalry, sir, to cut our way to Washington, sir." I said: "Probably before that day comes, the inauguration day will have passed; it is important that Mr. Lincoln should be in Washington that day." After considerable discussion Judge Davis, who had expressed no opinion, but had put various questions to test the truthfulness of the story, turned to Mr. Lincoln and said: "You personally heard Mr. Pinkerton's story, you heard this discussion. What is your judgment in the matter?" Mr. Lincoln said: "I have listened to this discussion with interest. I see no reason, no good reason, to change the program, and I am for carrying it out as arranged by Judd." This silenced all discussions and now the question was: Who should go with him (all this was at Harrisburg) to Washington? I stated that it had been deemed by those who had talked it over that but one man should accompany Mr. Lincoln, and Mr. Lamon's name had been mentioned as that person. Sumner demurred, saying: "I have undertaken to see Mr. Lincoln to Washington." Mr. Lincoln then went to his dinner. Lincoln heard all this conversation. A carriage to the door of the —— Hotel to take Mr. Lincoln back to the cars and thence to Philadelphia. Lincoln was at the dinner table when the carriage had arrived to take him to the track and thence to Philadelphia. Lincoln was called and went to his room, and changed his coat, came downstairs into the hall with his party. I said to Lamon: "Hurry with him." He and Mr. Lincoln quickly passed out of doors, followed by the others of the party. I put my hand on Colonel Sumner's shoulder, who was going to get into the carriage, and said: "One moment, Colonel." He turned to me, and while he turned to me, the carriage drove off, and a madder man you never saw. At 2 a.m. I received a dispatch from Mr. Scott stating that Mr. Lincoln passed through Philadelphia. Lincoln was in a dress coat, dinner coat, changed his coat, his shawl, a felt hat, etc., that he carried with him, called by the world Scottish plaid.

H. C. Whitney's Statement

About one week after the first Bull Run I made a call upon Mr. Lincoln, having no business except to give him some presents which the nuns at the "Osage" Mission School had sent to him. A Cabinet meeting had just adjourned; Stackpole told me to go right to his room. Lincoln was writing on a card; an old gentleman was with him; when he had concluded, he read the writing aloud, it was something like this: "Secretary Chase: The bearer, Mr. —— wants to be appointed —— of Baltimore. If you find his recommendations to be suitable, and I believe them to have been very good, the fact that he is a Methodist and is urged by them ought not to make against him as they complain of us some." Said I: "The rebels do that." "Yes," said he, "but not in that way, Whitney." The old gentleman retired with the card, and Secretary Seward came in. Says Lincoln (rather sportively) before he got seated: "Well, Governor, what now?" Seward stated his case, which related to New Mexico. Says Lincoln: "Oh! I see, they have not got either a Governor nor government; well, you see, Jim Lane, the Secretary, is his man and he must hunt him up." Seward then left, under the impression, as I thought, that Lincoln wanted to get rid of him and diplomacy. Several other parties were announced. Lincoln stated that he was busy and could not see them; he was as playful and sportive as a child, told me all sorts of anecdotes, dealt largely in anecdotes of Charles James Fox, asked all about several odd characters that we both knew in Illinois. General James was announced. "Well, as he is a feller what makes cannings (cannon)"—James sent word that he must leave town that p.m. and positively must see Lincoln before he went—"I must see him. Tell him when I get through with Whitney, I'll see him."

No more announcements were made, and James left about five o'clock, declaring that Lincoln was a fool and had got closeted with a damned old Hoosier from Illinois, and was telling dirty stories while the country was going to hell. Lincoln got his maps of the seat of war and gave me a full history of the preliminary talk and steps about the Battle of Bull Run. He, L., was opposed to the battle and explained to General Scott by those very maps how the enemy could by the aid of the railroads reinforce their armies at Manassas Gap until they had brought every man there, keeping us at bay meanwhile. L. showed to him our *paucity* of railroad advantages at that point and their plenitude; but Scott was obstinate and would not hear of the possibility of defeat, and now "you see I was right, and Scott now knows it, I reckon. My plan was, and still is, to make a strong feint against Richmond and distract their forces before attacking Manassas." Said I: "Are you going to do it yet?" Says he: "That is the problem that General McClellan is now trying to work out." He then told me of the plan he had recommended to McC. to send gunboats up one of the rivers (not the James) in the direction of Richmond and divert them there while the main attack was made at Manassas. Said I: "I expect McClellan will be your successor." Said he: "I am perfectly willing if he will only put an end to this war." He then gave me his theory of the rebellion by aid of the map: "We must drive them away from here (Manassas Gap) and clean them out of this part of the State so as they can't threaten us here and get into Maryland; then we must keep up as good a blockade as we can of their ports; then we must march an army into East Tennessee and liberate the Union sentiment there, and then let the thing work; we must then rely upon the people getting tired and saying to their leaders: 'We have had enough of this thing.' Of course we can't conquer them if they are determined to hold out against us." In reply to a question about the blockade, he said: "The coast is so long that I can't keep up a very good blockade"; then he said: "The great trouble about this whole thing is, that Union men at the South won't fight for their rights." He told me of his last interview with Douglas. "He came rushing in one day and said he had just got a telegraph dispatch from some friends in Illinois urging him to come out and help get things right in Egypt, and that he would go, or stay in Washington, just where I thought he could do the most good. I told him to do as he chooses, but that he could probably do best in Illinois; upon that he just shook hands with me and hurried away to catch the next train." I seized a good opportunity to say of Judge Davis: "I expect you'll appoint him Supreme Judge, anyway." He at once grew sad and said nothing until I changed the subject. I never saw Lincoln in so jolly a mood; he ought to have been busy too, as Congress was about to adjourn. He said to me: "My business just now is to make generals." At another time I wanted a line from him to the Paymaster General, asking a favor for me. I went to his house at breakfast time and found a crowd; hence I went into his room at once and found him just come in. I stated my business; he said: "Let us go right over and get it done." I said: "I don't want you to go." "But I can do it better by going," he said; he never was more radiant. I took advantage of it to say: "Mr. Lincoln, William Houston, a brother of Sam Houston, is here wanting that little clerkship." He frowned like a bear and said: "Don't bother me about Bill Houston; he has been here sitting on [his] a——s all summer, waiting for me to give him the best office I've got." "But," said I, "if he will select a small clerkship." "I hain't got it!" roared Lincoln, with more impatience and disgust than I ever saw manifested by him. Said I: "That ends it"; and he at once became cheerful and jolly and we started on. Lincoln and I were at Centralia Fair the day after the debate at Jonesboro; night came on and we were tired, having been on the fair ground all day; the train was due at midnight; everything was full; I managed to get a chair for Lincoln in the Illinois Central R.R. office, but small politicians would intrude so that he could scarcely get a moment's sleep. The train came and was filled instantly. I got a seat at the door for L. and myself; he was worn out and had to meet Douglas next day at Charleston; an empty car, called "saloon" car, was hitched onto the rear of the train and locked up. I asked the conductor, who knew Lincoln and myself well (we were both attorneys of the road), if Lincoln could not ride in that car, as he was exhausted, etc., and the conductor refused. I afterwards got in by stratagem. At this time McClellan was in person taking Douglas around in a special car and special train, and that was the indignant treatment that Lincoln got from the Illinois Central R.R.; every interest of that road and every employee was against Lincoln and for Douglas. During the sitting of the first Philadelphia Convention in '56, Lincoln was attending a special term of court in our county. [This is not true. H.] Davis, L., and myself roomed together. At noon I would get the Chicago paper; one day the telegraph showed that Dayton was nominated Vice-President, that "Lincoln" received [?] votes; Davis and I thought it was our Lincoln, but Lincoln said he thought it was the other great man of the same name from Massachusetts. Davis and I were impatient for next day's news, and it showed that it was our Lincoln; but the main subject of the news was not apparently at all moved by the prominence given him. The next day after that, when I came to our room with the mail, I looked guiltily foolish, and also amused; it transpired that in coming through the parlor where the gong was, to get to our room, L. had hid it in the central table, and the landlord was looking all around for it, and was then at the stable hunting it. L. and I went to the parlor together and, while I held the door shut, he replaced it, and then went up the stairs to the room three steps at a time. He once told me of you [1] that "he had taken you in as a partner, supposing that you had system and would keep things in order, but that you would not make much of a lawyer, but that he found that you had no more system than he had, but that [you] were a fine lawyer, so that he was doubly disappointed." As late as '57, he once said to me, while we were going together to a speech-making: "I wish it was over." Upon my expressing my surprise, he said: "When I have to make a speech, I always want it over."

Opinions of Men

Tuesday, September 6, 1887.

(Let all this be private as to names.)

I saw Governor Palmer at his office privately and talked to him freely about Mr. Lincoln, his mother, and Thomas Lincoln, and their ancestry, and origin. This was at 9 a.m. I asked him his advice, asked him to give me his opinion as how best to proceed, in writing the Life of Lincoln; whether to state all the facts or to state none or only so much as history and the reading world demanded. I carefully and cautiously related the facts, told him all I knew as well for Thomas, Nancy, and Abraham as against them. Governor Palmer thought one moment and said: "This is too delicate a question and I do not wish to give any advice on the matter, will think more about it and then, if I think proper, I will tell you my opinion, will see you again, however, nothing happening, etc." I left the office. Zimri A. Enos came into the room about the time the Governor's and my conversation ended. Don't think he heard a word.

I saw A. Orendorff, stated substantially what I said to Governor

---

[1] Herndon.

Palmer, and in reply he said: "the People wished and greatly wished to have the story of Lincoln's legitimacy well settled and forever fixed"; he thought that on the whole and for the best, to tell the whole story and clean up Lincoln's legitimacy. This was about 9–10 a.m. at or near the bank just below Orendorff's office.

I saw at Senator Cullom's office Senator Cullom and Doctor William Jayne, had a private conversation with both of these men, told them the whole story as I had it on my finger's end, and the same as I told to Governor Palmer and Orendorff, and to all other persons, told them the story of Lincoln's supposed illegitimacy, went over all the facts, stating to show that I wished to make it appear that Lincoln was the legitimate child of Thomas and Nancy, that that was my intention. Cullom seemed surprised and said: "The public believes that you want to make him, Lincoln, illegitimate." I said: "In this you are mistaken. I want, first, to tell the truth and, secondly, I want by that truth to make Lincoln appear, nay, to be, the lawful child and legitimate heir of Thomas Lincoln and Nancy Lincoln, once Nancy Hanks." Cullom thanked me for this declaration of intentions on my part. I further said to him that in so doing I should have to touch up old Thomas Lincoln, and immediately after this running conversation I asked these gentlemen for their opinion and advice, etc., as to the best way in which to write the Life of Lincoln. These gentlemen said that "If you say anything about the matter, you had better tell it out, giving all the facts so as to put Lincoln in his proper place or attitude in history. Glad that you expressed your opinion of intentions about Lincoln's legitimacy, it being favorable to him." This conversation was the longest which I had with any person or persons, knowing that Cullom misunderstood my purposes, etc. I got up the meeting on purpose to hear Cullom's and Jayne's opinion. This was about 9—10 a.m., conversations all private.

I saw Judge Matheny at his office 11:30 a.m. and had a private conversation with him, told him all the facts just as I did to all others, Palmer, Orendorff, Cullom, and Jayne, and when I had stated over all the facts, I then asked him to give me his opinion, give me his advice as to the best method of dealing with the matter, and to which question he said: "If you can clearly make Lincoln out to be a legitimate, a lawful child of Thomas and Nancy and make it out that Nancy Lincoln, Thomas Lincoln's wife, was chaste, etc., I would do it by all means, not thereby injuring others, etc. The whole story is new to me, but by all means clear Lincoln and his mother, if you touch the subject." I said this cannot be done without touching up Thomas Lincoln. The judge said: "That's bad, but put Lincoln and his mother in the proper place." All persons examined, advice and opinions asked for, seemed to talk honestly and fairly, though I kept my eyes wide open.

I had a long and a good conversation with Governor Oglesby, told him over and over all the facts of the case just as I did to all others, and said to him that I had the materials out of which, by a lawyer's argument, that I could make it appear that Lincoln was the lawful child of Thomas and Nancy, told him that Thomas was castrated but that no time was fixed by the witnesses of the said event. The Governor then said: "The very idea that old Thomas Lincoln would fool Mrs. Johnston was foolish." (Here he gave his reasons.) "That theory won't do, better go upon the theory, proposition, that Nancy Hanks was the illegitimate child of the Virginia planter and that the people had mixed things up. This is the best explanation, but it would be better for your book to say nothing about it at all. That the people's good sense had settled the whole matter long ago. That the people don't care about such things anyway. They go upon merit, the man and his own genius and character." This conversation with the Governor was private as in all other cases, and it took place in the Governor's room at 11:30 a.m., possibly 12.

W. H. HERNDON.

1st Proposition. Was Lincoln illegitimate?

2nd. Proof. Is that if Mrs. L. was bad why did she not breed before marriage?

3rd. But she had a child in eight months less two days.

4th. Is this an invariable rule that no eight months' child ever lived? Grant it.

5th. But the presumption of law is that all those who are born in lawful wedlock are legitimate.

6th. But you say that Thomas Lincoln went in swimming and that people saw that his manhood was taken out; grant it, and yet no witness fixes the date.

7th. The presumptions of virtue arising from the facts are weightier than the presumptions of law.

8th. That Thomas Lincoln was castrated I admit, but that was after Sarah, Abraham, and the infant child Thomas were born. The fact that Mrs. Lincoln did not breed any more was caused by the fixing of Thomas her husband. Again to show that Thomas was fixed, did he not marry Mrs. Johnston in the bloom of life and he had no children by her? If Mrs. Lincoln was a bad woman, why did she not breed after Thomas was fixed? His utter laziness and want of energy is due to the fact of fixing.

9th. The persons who make the charge do not identify Mrs. Lincoln from the other Nancy.

10th. Abraham Lincoln in a letter to Haycraft—"You are mistaken in my mother."

11th. Here I conclude that Abraham Lincoln was a lawful child and lawful heir of Thomas and Nancy Lincoln.

12th. The simple word of Enloe is not to destroy a woman's character and make illegitimate one of the great ones of the earth.

13th. Let us take a simple case. Suppose that A. L. inherited a piece of land from Thomas and a suit were brought by the land, thus testing Abraham's legitimacy, would you decide on this evidence that Abraham was illegitimate and your answer would be No? Then why not state the facts and say, however, that each man and woman can form his or her own opinion, but that your opinion is that Abraham was legitimate.

BIG ME

My parents came from Virginia about the year 1808 and settled in Green County, Kentucky; was born in Greensburg, Kentucky, on December 25, 1818, a few months after Illinois was admitted into the Union; moved to Illinois in 1821 and settled near Springfield, Illinois; moved to the town in 1823; father went to merchandising in '26; was clerk in my father's store for years except when going to school; went to the old-time schools where each parent paid for his children's tuition; reading, writing, ciphering, geography, grammar, and some of the higher branches were taught; went to a most excellent high school in the city for two or three years—say from '34 to '36—went to Illinois College in Jacksonville for one year, '37; clerked in a store from '37 to '41; was married in '40 to Miss Mary Maxey, daughter of Colonel Maxey; kept store, clerked from '41 to '43, when I commenced to study the law regularly with Logan & Lincoln; before this studied law of nights after business hours; was admitted to the bar in 1843; entered into partnership with Lincoln in '43 and was such partner till the death of Mr. Lincoln; was studious, too much so for my own health; studied from twelve to fourteen hours a day, had a wife to support, had to push and hustle along, was poor and had to act vigorously and energetically; loved literature in every line and kept abreast of the times, particularly studied political economy, psychology, the features of the human face, and human nature generally; carried on these studies with the law after office hours; delivered lectures frequently in agriculture, horticulture, on the beautiful, on Lincoln and other subjects, and so in different cities and counties in this State; traveled around the law circuit with Lincoln for some years; was City Clerk of this city of Springfield for two terms, or two years, being elected by the people; was elected Mayor of the city in 1850; was district elector in Illinois during the Frémont campaign in 1856; stumped the State for Frémont and Dayton; was appointed Bank Commissioner for Illinois by Governor Bissell in '56, continued in that office by Governor Yates and continued by Governor Oglesby, holding the office six or eight years; stumped part of the State in '60 and '64 for Lincoln; lost my first wife in '60, and married Miss Annie Miles in '61, daughter of Major Miles of Petersburg, Illinois; continued for profession of the law till '72, when I went to farming, which I now follow; always loved nature, the study of it, loved the wild sports of nature, the grand and beautiful everywhere, loved hunting and fishing; did not forget literature, nor my study of political economy, psychology, the science of the human mind, philosophy, and human nature generally; though I held some offices by election, I never was ambitious in that line; had no ambition for wealth, had rather an ambition to know men and nature; from '54 to '65 was continually on the stump speaking for the Negro, liberty, and the Union; wrote editorials for the papers; spent ten of the very best years of my life for the Negro, liberty, and the Union; spent my money freely and lavishly in that way—was poor when I commenced life and hold my own very well. Am a social creature, generous, love my fellow-man, am progressive, somewhat of a radical, am not too old to learn, being now in my seventy-second year; am liberal in religion, a Democrat, a free trader absolutely; am a contented and a happy man, believe in the universal progress of all things, especially of man's uprising and upgoing; believe in the force and onward march of the Eternal Right and in the *oneness* of the universe. . . .

W. H. H.

Lincoln's Boat

As Mr. Lincoln was returning from Congress, with his wife and child, and after passing through some of the States of New England, he entered Canada and was at Niagara Falls. From Niagara he passed westward, going through Detroit. It is quite likely that he took a boat at Detroit for Chicago. In going to Chicago the boat on which Mr. Lincoln, wife, and child were passengers stranded on some sand bar. The passengers got very tired of their stay on the waters. The hands of the boat, by order of the commander of the boat, collected all the loose planks, empty barrels, boxes, and the like which could be had. These planks, barrels, and boxes were used as a kind of buoy; they were shoved by force under the hull of the boat and they, being light and disposed to float by their own small gravity and lifting power, lifted the boat above the surface of the sand bank. The boat rode by the floating power of the things that had been thrust under her. Mr. Lincoln was very attentive in watching the movements of the hands and the effect of what they did; he occasionally made suggestions that profited the commander. The boat rose gradually higher and higher and finally she was in the deep waters, ready for the onward go. It was at this time that Mr. Lincoln formed his ideas of his floating vessel, rather the idea of the means to make the stranded boats float. The idea of Mr. Lincoln was to make a kind of bellows, a great sack that would run around the boat and which could be folded up at pleasure and opened at pleasure, probably by machinery. Wind probably was to be blown into it; swelled out by wind and pushed down with the water and thus it was in idea a means of lifting up the boat.

Mr. Lincoln returned to his old home and he now and here set to work to perfect his patent or to execute his idea and to take out a patent on his boat. Walter Davis, a mechanic, had a shop in Springfield in North Fifth Street, and Lincoln went to that shop, where I have often seen him at work on the model of the boat and Davis's tools, and made his little model and sent it in to Washington and had it patented. That model is now in Washington, where it can be seen at any time. This invention was a perfect failure; the apparatus has never been put on any boat so far as known.

W. H. HERNDON.

LOCOFOCOS—A LINCOLN STORY

In the Presidential race of 1840–44 the Democrats were called Locofocos. The Whigs declared that the good old Democracy was no more, was dead, and that a bastard generation of poor machine politicians had grown up like a mushroom. The Democracy contended that they were the simon-pure Democracy descending by divine right from Jefferson and Jackson. The Whigs were charged with being the true offspring of the blue-light Federalists of 1812–14 and before, followers of Hamilton, the father of Federalism. The Whigs declared, in answer to this charge, that they were followers of Washington and others who framed the Constitution. Lincoln used to call his opponents Locofocos, denied that they were the true and genuine article, not a particle of Democracy about them, that they were a fraud, only an assumption of genuineness, and to point his charge frequently told this story: "Once an old farmer in the country heard a devil of a racket in his hen house, heard it often before, so he thought to get up and see what was the matter and kill the thing if it was some wild animal. He got up, lit his candle, and went gun in hand to see and fight it out. On going into the hen house he looked around on the floor and on the roosts and at last found his enemy, a polecat, crouched in the corner with two or three dead chickens. The farmer seized the polecat and dragged him out, and all who know the nature of such a cat know what followed—a devil of a stink. The polecat demurred as well as he could in his own language, saying that he was no such brute as charged, but an innocent animal and a friend of the farmer just come to take care of his chickens. The farmer to this replied: 'You look like a polecat, just the size of a polecat, act like one'—and snuffing up his nose—'and smell like one, and you are one, by God, and I'll kill you, innocent and as friendly to me as you say you are.' These Locofocos," said Lincoln, "claim to be true Democrats, but they are only Locofocos—they look like Locofocos, just the size of Locofocos, act like Locofocos, and"— turning up his nose and backing away a little on the stand as if the smell was about to smother him—"are Locofocos, by God."

This story would, as a matter of course, down the Democrats for a while. However, they laughed as heartily as the Whigs did. The effect was electric, it could not be resisted. Men nearly bursted their sides laughing, etc. You could feel the story coming in, looking into Lincoln's eyes as he addressed the crowd.

Jesse, correct it, if needed. How do you like it?   H.

The Man of Audacity—a Lincoln Story

February 27, 1891.

Lincoln was a diffident man, rather shy and not self-possessed in society, especially in a promiscuous crowd of ladies and gentlemen at a party; he admired audacity, a quick-witted man, one self-possessed and not having much cheek. Well, there was a party once, not far from here, which was composed of ladies and gentlemen, a fine table was set, and the people were greatly enjoying themselves. Among the crowd was one of those men who had audacity, was quick-witted, cheeky, and self-possessed, never off his guard on any occasion. After the men and women had enjoyed themselves by dancing, promenading, flirting, etc., they were told that the supper was set. The man of audacity, quick-witted, self-possessed, and equal to all occasions, was put at the head of the table to carve the turkeys, chickens, and pigs. The men and women surrounded the table, and the audacious man, being chosen carver, whetted his great carving knife with the steel and got down to business and commenced carving the turkey, but he expanded too much force and let a f——t, a loud f——t, so that all the people heard it distinctly. As a matter of course it shocked all terribly. A deep silence reigned. However, the audacious man was cool and entirely self-possessed; he was curiously and keenly watched by those who knew him well, they suspecting that he would recover in the end and acquit himself with glory. The man, with a kind of sublime audacity, pulled off his coat, rolled up his sleeves, put his coat deliberately on a chair, spat on his hands, took his position at the head of the table, picked up the carving knife, and whetted it again, never cracking a smile nor moving a muscle of his face. It now became a wonder in the minds of all the men and women how the fellow was to get out of his dilemma; he squared himself and said loudly and distinctly: "Now, by God, I'll see if I can't cut up this turkey without f——ting."

Lincoln was at the party and said that, as quick as a bolt of lightning, all the men and women threw off all modesty and broke out instantly, unanimously, harmoniously, into a universal, long, continual, and boisterous laugh, cheering the fellow for his complete success, his cunning audacious victory, and became the lion of the evening, swung around the women as if nothing happened. "I worshiped the fellow," said Lincoln.

As a matter of course no such thing ever happened, and yet it is a good story to show the power of audacity, self-possession, quick-wittedness, etc., and as such it pleased Lincoln admirably. The nib of the thing was what Lincoln was after. I have heard him tell it often and often.

W. H. HERNDON.

He said he was riding *bass-ackwards* on a *jass-ack,* through a *potton-catch,* on a pair of *baddle-sags* stuffed full of *binger-gred* when the animal *steered* at a *scump* and the *lirrup-steather* broke, and throwed him in the *forner* of the *kence* and broke his *pishing-fole.* He said he would not have minded it, much, but he fell right in a great *tow-curd;* in fact he said it give him a right smart *sick of fitness*—he had the *molera-corbus* pretty bad—he said, about *bray dake* he come to himself, ran home, seized up a *stick of wood,* and split the ax to make a light, rushed into the house, and found the door sick abed and his wife standing open. But, thank goodness, she is getting right *hat* and *farty* again.

Copy of a "piece" which Lincoln wrote and gave to the bailiff of one of the Springfield courts. Copied by me from the original manuscript now owned by C. F. Gunther of Chicago.[1]

[WEIK.]

Mr. Lincoln's Fairness to His Political Opponents

When Mr. Lincoln first ran for Congress, the opposing candidate was a Methodist preacher. During the canvass, an aspiring Democrat said to Mr. Lincoln: "Such is my utter aversion to the meddling of preaching in politics, that I will vote for you even at the risk of losing caste with my party, if you think the contest doubtful." Mr. Lincoln replied: "I would like your vote, but I fully appreciate your position, and will give you my honest opinion on the morning of Election Day." On that morning he called on the Democrat and said: "I am now satisfied that I have got the preacher by the ——, and you had better keep out of the ring."

A "Fuss" in the Lincoln Home

Stephen Whitehurst, editor of the *Conservative* and brother-in-law to Judge Matheny, told me that one day in 1856 or '57 a man by the name of Barrett was passing by Lincoln's house and saw a woman chasing a man with a table knife or butcher knife in her hand; they ran down through the Lincoln garden going from the west to the

---

[1] This piece is at present in the possession of the estate of the late Dr. Otto L. Schmidt.

east and towards Whitehurst's house. Barrett did not pay much attention to the parties, thinking that what he saw was sport or fun. Just as the man and woman were running down the garden walk going east some men and women were in the street going from east to west, so that all were meeting face to face. Mr. Whitehurst's back yard and Lincoln's back yard looked into each other, i.e., one in Lincoln's back yard could see into Whitehurst's and vice versa. Whitehurst on that hour and moment saw what was going on between the man and woman. Lincoln, for it was he, saw the men and women in the street coming from east going west meeting Lincoln and wife nearly face to face, and he knew that he and wife had been, would be, discovered, turned suddenly around, caught his wife by the shoulder with one hand and with the other caught his wife at the heavy end, her hips, if you please, and quickly hustled her to the back door of his house and forced, pushed, her in, at the same time, as it were, spanking her heavy end, saying to her at the same moment: "There, d——n it, now stay in the house and don't disgrace us before the eyes of the world." Whitehurst saw and heard all this and, when the affair was quite over, Barrett told Whitehurst what he saw just a moment before and a part of what Whitehurst had seen. Whitehurst and Barrett are men of truth, if I have the right Barrett in my mind. Whitehurst is, at all events. This story was told to me in 1867.

W. H. H.

I recorded these facts the hour they were told me and put them in a little book which I loaned to Lamon. This is my recollection.　H.

LINCOLN AND STRANGERS

I have read with great curiosity, much interest, and with much astonishment a story written by the Reverend J. B. Gulliver relating to a conversation between Lincoln and himself. Mr. Lincoln delivered his great Cooper Institute speech in February 1860. That speech, searching, profound, eloquent, created quite an excitement in New York, in fact in the whole country; it astonished the East in its learning and especially in the sharp, keen way in which things were put by Mr. Lincoln. It appears that the Reverend J. B. Gulliver heard his speech at Norwich, Connecticut, and was deeply struck with it. Of this I have no doubt. It further appears that Mr. Gulliver pos-

sibly followed Mr. Lincoln in order to find out, to historically understand, the ways and methods, the peculiar manner and power, of his
hero. It further appears from Mr. Gulliver's statement that he and
Mr. Lincoln had some conversation at the railroad station. It further
appears from the reverend gentleman that he got in the cars with
Mr. Lincoln and went with Lincoln. I do not know where. It further
appears that Lincoln invited Mr. Gulliver to take a seat with him in
the cars, which Mr. Gulliver did.

On this well and finely told story I wish to say a few words by way
of criticism of fact in order that the reading world may be made
aware of the floating false stories that run around the world, thus
putting the people on their guard. The people, being well put on their
guard, will know how to appreciate these stories and to form a just
estimate of the man. Many of these stories, like old cord and drift-
wood, are floating down the stream of time to the gulf of oblivion,
where it is hoped that they will all go before many years. The story is
finely told and very well written and I willingly admit the above facts
but not what follows in the story as written. I admit the good motives
of Mr. Gulliver, and I admit that he is, if living, a gentleman. The
article first appeared in the New York *Independent* of September 1,
1864, four years after the conversation, and copied by artist Carpenter in his *Six Months in the White House* on pages 308–18. . . .

In the first place, materially so, Mr. Gulliver makes Lincoln say:
"I can remember of going to my little bedroom after hearing the
neighbors talk, etc." His little bedroom, why, it was only on a little
trundle bed under his mother's bed. The very idea that the old settlers in Kentucky, Indiana, and Illinois had separate rooms for
their children is ridiculous to one who knows better; they had but one
room, with puncheon floor, in which the people cooked, ate, slept, and
courted; first, in the courting, was covering up the fire so that no
eye could see; it was the custom then to take the girl on your lap.
Mr. Gulliver further makes Lincoln say "and spending no small part
of the night walking up and down" the room. Tom Lincoln let his
boy walk up and down the puncheon floor half the night, rattling
things up, disturbing him and the family by his keen desire to know
what he had heard! This is an odd idea to me. "Did you read law?"
says Mr. Gulliver to Mr. Lincoln, and to which Mr. Lincoln replied:
"Oh, yes, etc., I became a lawyer's clerk in Springfield and copied

tedious documents, etc." History will tell us, does tell us, that Messrs. Stuart and Lincoln formed a partnership in the law business as early as the fall of '36 or spring of '37. Mr. Lincoln was never clerk for any man in the law business in Springfield or elsewhere, and never copied tedious documents for anyone. Mr. Gulliver further makes Mr. Lincoln say: "In the course of my *law* reading I *constantly* came across the word *demonstrate*." The word demonstrate is not generally used in law books. The word that the law and the lawyer use is *prove*, and not demonstrate. That word belongs to the field of mathematics, logic. All that the lawyer wants, all he can get, as a general rule, is moral evidence, facts, principles, and logical inferences. "And," continues Mr. Lincoln in the piece, "I left my situation in Springfield, went home to my father's house, stayed there till I could give any proposition in the six books of Euclid, etc." Mr. Lincoln had, when he came to Springfield, no situation as clerk in a law office and could not have quit it; he never after '37 went back to his father's house excepting on short visits. Mr. Lincoln then was twenty-six years old; and Lincoln never began to study Euclid before 1849–50. He did study Euclid from 1849 to 1854, carried it around with him when on circuit as lawyer in his saddle bags, in his buggy.

Here are nine or ten mistakes that are known to me to be mistakes, mistakes in fact. The reader is aware of Mr. Lincoln's reticence, secretiveness, his somewhat unsocial nature, his somewhat retired disposition, his well-known silence of the history of himself and his origin, etc. What part of this conversation ever took place no one will ever know, excepting Mr. Gulliver, unless he will truthfully re-write the piece. Gulliver was a stranger to Lincoln and to such it was his habit to play shut-mouth. I am willing to admit that Mr. Lincoln and Mr. Gulliver had a conversation and I do not doubt that Mr. Gulliver is a gentleman and a good Christian. I can admit no more. The world is full of just such stories, and the reader must now judge for himself; he has the keys and cue of Lincoln's nature and these will enable him to form just opinions as to facts and Lincoln's nature.

At page 236–41, Mr. N. Bateman, Superintendent of Public Instruction for the State of Illinois, tells a long story about Mr. Lincoln's conversation with him in relation to some subjects then before them, and among them was the question of Mr. Lincoln's religion or his belief in it. In that conversation Mr. Lincoln is made to say: "I am not a Christian. . . . I know that I am right, because I know that liberty is right, for Christ teaches it and Christ is God." The first part of the story is correct—that is, that Mr. Lincoln was not a Christian, but the second part, that is, that Christ was God is false. This very point Mr. Lincoln denied once in a well-written argument and he never abandoned nor repudiated his original ideas. From what I know of Bateman and from what I know of Lincoln I give it on my opinion that the whole story about his religion is false and stands on about the same foundation as the story of Gulliver. I will admit that Mr. Bateman is a gentleman and a Christian. The story is told to Holland by Bateman in '65 or '66, five years after the conversation, and how correct it is no one will ever know till Mr. Bateman shall truthfully rewrite it. The idea of Lincoln's "sublime religious passion" is to me ridiculous, utterly ridiculous. Had Bateman or Holland said "his sublime political passion," it would have been correct. Again Mr. Bateman makes Mr. Lincoln say that he believes in the efficacy of prayer. Whether this efficacy of prayer meant that it did the prayer good or whether it meant that God would listen to human prayer and change his laws to satisfy the prayer, or not, I do not know, but if it means that God would alter his laws to suit a man's wishes, it is false, false to all of Lincoln's thinking and his life. Lincoln believed in a Providence that ruled matter and mind and all ultimate substances by law, general, universal, and eternal. By those laws things were fated and doomed and this is Lincoln's belief and his philosophy.

Again the Honorable Isaac N. Arnold, a very good but credulous-minded man, rather supersensitive too, tells a story in his lecture delivered in England in '81 about Lincoln's religion. It is a fact no doubt that the Negroes of Baltimore did present Mr. Lincoln with a fine, extra fine copy of the Bible and no doubt that Lincoln made a short reply thanking them for the gift. Mr. Lincoln is made to say: "This great book is the best gift God has given to man. All the good from the Saviour of the world is communicated in this book." Was Lincoln a fool, an ass, or a hypocrite, or is this statement a willful falsehood? It is false. This speech was made, rather said to be made, in '64 and never appeared in print till '65 or '66, as I am informed.

Still these stories go along and grow as they do go along. The

Right Reverend Bishop Simpson, in his eulogy on Lincoln on the day that Lincoln was placed in his tomb, makes a great blunder, makes a terrible mistake. In 1839 I heard Mr. Lincoln's speech made against Martin Van Buren, his administration and the Democracy generally. I shall not quote here what he said, but Bishop Simpson, a truthful, honest gentleman and a noble Christian, takes that speech of '39 and applies it somewhere in 1857–58, possibly a little before or a little later, as a speech against slavery. Holland follows Bishop Simpson, and the author of the *Lincoln Memorial Album* follows Holland, and so I suppose the mistake, an honest one, will run around the world. In the Bible story of Arnold the newspapers first had it, then McPherson tried it, as I am informed, in his history, and then Arnold followed, and I suppose it too will run around the world, growing as it goes.

Again Mr. Lincoln delivered to the citizens of Springfield his farewell address just before leaving the people for Washington. The sad remarks were written out and given to someone. A copy of that speech was copied in the *Illinois Journal* and reproduced in newspapers and copied in Lamon's Life of Lincoln and thence with Arnold's *Lincoln and Slavery*, and none of the copies of this farewell address is exactly alike, and yet I suppose all will travel around the world as true and genuine, growing as they go around.

Not only do these falsehoods and mistakes pass along the line unchallenged as truthful, genuine, and correct, but supersensitive gentlemen take the liberty—a mean and despicable liberty—of changing, altering, and gutting Mr. Lincoln's letters and speeches. For instance, Mr. Lincoln used in one of his letters to Speed the word "gal." Mr. Arnold takes the liberty of changing the word "gal" and substitutes the more refined word "girl," and this is done in Arnold's Life of Lincoln. Holland changed Lincoln's expression in reference to his mother, "God bless her," to the more euphonious expression of "Blessings on her memory."

Again Mr. Lincoln made a speech in Sangamon County about the year '44, and in that speech Lincoln said, in reference to the speech which he was just going to make, this: "My politics are short and sweet like an old woman's dance." The author of the *Lincoln Memorial Album*, a refined and over-supersensitive man, takes the liberty of cutting out of that speech the above expression, because it sounded vulgar to his refined ears, and thus the thing goes on, and I suppose will ever go on unless the people are made aware of them. If the author of the *Album* did not get it, someone did before him. If it is so difficult now, close to Lincoln and his times, to get at the truth and the genuineness of things, how will it be in a hundred or more years hence? No wonder that Lincoln disliked to read biographies and histories. He had no faith in them and did not much read them.

Lincoln possibly will be a mystery and a myth during all the coming ages. The people love the incredible, the marvelous, the wonderful, the mysterious things never to be known, impossible things, things that thinking men laugh at, and historians, knowing this quality of nature in many men, pander to it. This I shall never do, but on the contrary I will tell the story of Lincoln's life as I saw him, hoping that when wrong I shall be corrected. I am desirous that the world shall know Mr. Lincoln thoroughly and the more that the world does know him to that world he will grow greater and greater.

LINCOLN'S PHILOSOPHY AND RELIGION

August 21, 1887.

. . . Mrs. Lincoln told me in 1866 in Springfield, on her examination by me at the St. Nicholas Hotel, that Mr. Lincoln's philosophy was "what is to be will be, and no cares (prayers) of ours can arrest nor reverse the decree." I have heard him say the same thing substantially and so have many others in and around Springfield, Illinois, his home, and where he lies buried, entombed. About the year 1846–47 Mr. Lincoln borrowed of James W. Keys and read, thoroughly read and studied, *The Vestiges of Creation*, written, as supposed, if not now known, by one of the Chamberses of Edinburgh, Scotland. The book was in the fifth or sixth edition as I recollect it. Mr. Lincoln on reading and studying the book became, and was for years, a firm believer in the theory of development [evolution] as presented in *The Vestiges of Creation*. Mr. Lincoln's speeches will show his unbounded faith in the theory of development. In after years, there was taken by me the *Westminster Review*, as well as some other reviews. I was a subscriber for the *Westminster Review* and read it. I purchased copies of the *North British* and read them. I had up to sixty all the works of Spencer, Darwin, Feuerbach's *Christianity*, and the like, many of the like. Lincoln read some parts of these books and reviews. I admit that he read none of them thoroughly at a sitting; he would read by snatches, a little here and there now and then. He soon grew into the belief of a universal law, evolution, and from this he has never deviated. Mr. Lincoln became a firm believer in evolution and of law. Of the truth of this there is no doubt and can be none. Mr. Lincoln believed in laws that imperiously ruled both matter and mind. With him there could be no miracles outside of law; he held that the universe was a grand mystery and a miracle. Nothing to him was lawless, everything being governed by law. There were no accidents in his philosophy. Every event had its cause. The past to him was the cause of the present and the present including the past will be the cause of the grand future and all are one, links in the endless chain, stretching from the infinite to the finite. Everything to him was the result of the forces of Nature, playing on matter and mind from the beginning of time and will to the end of it, play on matter and mind giving the world other, further, and grander results. What gave Mr. Lincoln such profound conviction of the progress of man and the power of truth? He said in his Cooper Institute speech this: "Let us have faith that right makes might and in that faith let us to the end dare to do our duty as we understand it."

Again he said and said often and often that, though the Declaration of Independence at that time, 1858, was not just yet a practiced fact here under all circumstances, and yet that it was a grand truth set up as a standard, an ideal standard, it may be, but to be ever worked for, struggled for, and approached . . . and again he said: "We (those who were against slavery) shall not fail; if we stand firm we shall not fail. Wise counsels may accelerate or mistakes delay it, but sooner or later the victory is sure to come." . . . Here and now Mr. Lincoln is advocating liberty and what a faith he has in the progress of man, in the right, in the final triumph and victory of freedom; he knows that all this will come about in God's own good time by His will worked out through evolution and through laws.

Mr. Lincoln firmly believed that conditions, circumstances, make the man and that man does not make the conditions. On this point he says this: "I attempt no compliment to my own sagacity. I claim not to have controlled events, but confess plainly that events have controlled me. Now at the end of three years' struggle the nation's condition is not what either party or any man desired or expected." Our prayers could not arrest nor reverse the decree, though we tried prayers. Again he says, in a speech in 1860 at Cincinnati: "I deem it due to myself and the whole country, in the present extraordinary condition of the country and of public opinion, that I should wait and see the last development of public opinion before I give my views of public opinion, or express myself at the time of the inauguration." Here is the theory of development, of evolution clearly stated. . . . Wise man—sagacious man. It follows logically that Mr. Lincoln did not believe, only in a limited sense if any, in the freedom of the human will. He has argued this question with me; he changed the expression and called it the freedom of the mind, instead of the freedom of the will. Mr. Lincoln said to me that motives ruled the man always and everywhere under the sun. I once contended that man could act without a motive; he smiled at my philosophy and it was not soon before I saw as he saw. . . .

Mr. Lincoln was a purely practical-minded man, having great practical sagacities and did not as a general rule ever speculate on unknowable things; he never read anything on such subjects as first and final causes. Time and space, noumena or phenomena, experienced ideas or universal inherent and necessary ideas, the attributes of being, psychology or metaphysics—these were to him trash. He discovered through experience that his mind, the mind of all men, had limitations attached or placed on it and hence he economized his forces and his time by applying his powers and his time in the field of the practical. In this field he thought, wrought, and acted. . . .

The question of Mr. Lincoln's Christianity can now be settled— easily settled to the minds of all reasonable men, and to such and only to such I address myself as best I can. If it is true that Lincoln believed that laws existed and ruled matter and mind, then there could be no such thing as a miraculous conception and it follows that Lincoln did not believe that Jesus was God, nor a special child of Him. If it is true that Lincoln believed in law, then there could be no special inspiration, no special revelations, no miracles in his mind; he demanded facts, well-authenticated facts, as foundations of his belief; he had no faith in "say soes," no respect for that kind of authority in the religious world. . . .

It would be expected by men that Lincoln would at some time in his life give utterance to his ideas, because the people knew that Mr. Lincoln had the courage of his convictions. Now for facts. In the years of 1835–36 Mr. Lincoln wrote out, fully wrote out, his ideas and intended to publish them in pamphlet or book form; he read his manuscript to Samuel Hill, his employer, before or soon after. Hill was the personal friend of Lincoln at that time and said to Lincoln: "Lincoln, let me see your manuscript." Lincoln handed it to him. Hill ran it in a tin plate stove, and so the book went up in flames. Lincoln in that production attempted to show that the Bible was false: first, on the grounds of reason, and, second, because it was self-contradictory, that Jesus was not the son of God any more than any man. Mr. Lincoln moved to Springfield in '36 or '37 and here he told his faith to his friends. His candid and courageous ideas thus uttered shocked his friends. These men have told me so. Finally it may be said that he was an infidel, one who did not believe that the Bible was the special divine revelation of God as the Christian world contends. He firmly believed in an overruling Providence, Maker, God, and the great moral of Him written in the human soul. His—late in life— conventional use of the word God must not by any means be interpreted that he believed in a personal God. I know that it is said that Mr. Lincoln changed his views. There is no evidence of this, especially as to the extent of the change, nor which way. Did he go toward the force and matter theory of the universe, toward Spencer and Darwin? Mr. Lincoln was a thoroughly religious man, not a Christian, a broad, liberal-minded man, was a liberal, a free religionist, an infidel, and so died. . . .

LINCOLN'S SUPERSTITION

That Mr. Lincoln was somewhat superstitious there can be no doubt, and to illustrate that side of his nature, that characteristic of his, I shall give you some examples manifesting his superstition. When Lincoln went down to New Orleans in '31 he consulted a Negress fortune teller, asking her to give him his history, his end and his fate; she told him what it was, according to her insight, which was no insight at all but simply a fraud to make money. It may be true that the Negress did believe that she was inspired or empowered to see the visions and end of all mortals. This story is said to be true. I cannot vouch for it, and yet it is told me and it is quite likely the case. . . .

Again, Robert Lincoln, when a mere boy, was bitten by a dog, one supposed to be mad. Lincoln took him to Terre Haute, Indiana, where there was a supposed mad stone with the purpose and most earnest intention of having it applied to Robert's bite and did so as well supposed. . . .

Mr. Lincoln held to a firm belief that he was doomed to a sad fate; he held firmly to the philosophy of fatalism all of his life; he said to me more than once: "Billy, I fear that I shall meet with some terrible end." He had, like all men, had his dreams, and he more or less through his life believed in dreams and acted on them. Mrs. Lincoln gives me this fine illustration of the fact of his superstition and his belief in dreams. She says: "Mr. Lincoln had a dream when down the river at City Point, after Richmond was taken; he dreamed that *The White House* was burned up, sent me up the river, went, met Stanton." Mr. Lincoln had fearful dreams and tried to unriddle them; he somewhat believing in them as facts or shadows of them foretelling the future; he had frequent apparitions and hallucinations. These were caused by the long, continuous, and hard study, thought, want of rest, and want of food; he sometimes forgot to eat. This so acted on his nervous system that he was prostrated, utterly prostrated; he was twice in his life partially deranged. Any good physician would from the facts say—deranged. Lincoln was most emphatically a superstitious man. That ran through his being like a bluish red vein runs through the whitest marble, giving the eye rest from the weariness of sameness. The sharp contrast gave beauty to both white surface and bluish red veins.

NANCY HANKS

Greencastle, Ind., August 20, 1887.

Dennis Hanks and all the others Hankses, their cousins and relatives call Nancy Hanks, Nancy Sparrow. Why is she thus called Nancy Sparrow? Lucy Hanks was her mother; Lucy, the mother of Nancy, married Henry Sparrow. Nancy Hanks was taken and raised by Thomas and Betsey Sparrow. Why did not her mother,

Lucy Sparrow, keep and raise her own daughter? Did Henry Sparrow object to the mother, his wife, keeping and raising her own daughter? Dennis Hanks says to me this substantially (to be quoted word for word) in a letter written by him to me, dated February, 1866: "Don't call her Nancy Hanks because that would make her *base-born*." Very well, Dennis, shrewd, sly Dennis. It is a universal custom, habit, and a practical rule of all English-speaking people, including the American, as a matter of course, to call all illegitimate children after and from the mother's name, and not the father's name, because of the cruel fiction of the law that such children are supposed to be the children of no one, rather a vast presumption, I willingly admit. If Henry Sparrow had been the father of Nancy Hanks, then she ought by law and justice to be called Nancy Sparrow, but unfortunately, Henry Sparrow, the husband of her mother, was not her father.

Nancy Hanks was born before her mother was married to Henry Sparrow. How is this, Dennis? Abraham Lincoln, always honest and truthful, says, substantially, under his own hand in a short Life of himself written at Springfield, Illinois, for Jesse W. Fell of Bloomington, Illinois, to be a kind of campaign biography of '60, this: "My mother's name is Nancy Hanks," or to put it exactly, Lincoln says in that short biography of himself written to Fell: "My mother, who died in my infancy, was of a family of the name of Hanks." Why did he not say, if such was the truth, that she was of the family of the Sparrows? Simply because she was not of the Sparrow family. Lincoln knew her origin but kept it to himself. In that Fell biography I guess I can state what Lincoln himself states in the matter; and if to call her Hanks is to make her base-born, charge her son with the offense, not me. Dennis, sly, shrewd Dennis, wishes to cover up the truth, smother up the sad fact, if it is such. Lincoln boldly and truthfully speaks out, and now the question comes: Who was the father of Nancy Hanks, Lincoln's mother? Lucy Hanks, her mother, was never married to any Hanks so far as we can find out, nor to any other person before or after she married Henry Sparrow, or before she had Nancy. When Nancy Hanks was born, who was Lucy Hanks's husband? This is quite a pertinent question. What did Lincoln say to Scripps, his campaign biographer? No one need for this matter rely on what I say or have said, that Lincoln told me that his mother was illegitimate—he told me that his mother was an illegitimate child of a Virginian planter or large farmer. However, the record tells its own story and speaks for itself and, had not the record spoken out, it is more than probable that I should have kept the secret forever, though I was not forbidden to reveal the fact after Lincoln's death. I never uttered this to mortal man, directly or indirectly, till after the death of Lincoln. And now again, who was the father of Nancy Hanks, the mother of the President of the United States? Will some gentleman, some lady tell me? The father of Nancy Hanks is no other than a Virginian planter, large farmer of the highest and best blood of Virginia, and it is just here that Nancy got her good rich blood, tinged with genius. Mr. Lincoln told me that she was a genius and that he got his mind from her. Nancy Hanks Lincoln was a woman of a very fine cast of mind, an excellent heart, quick in sympathy, a natural lady, a good neighbor, a firm friend; good cheer and hilarity generally accompanied her, and had she been raised at all, she must have flourished anywhere, but as it was, she was rude, tough, breaking and having difficulty through all forms, conditions, customs, habits, etiquette of society. She could not be held to forms and methods of things, and yet she was a fine woman naturally. It is quite probable that a knowledge of her origin made her defiant and desperate; she was very sensitive, sad, sometimes gloomy; who will tell me the amount and influence of her feelings, in this matter, caused by the consciousness of her origin? Let the world forgive her and bless her, is my constant prayer.

Lincoln often thought of committing suicide. Why? Did the knowledge of his mother's origin, or his own, press the thought of suicide upon him? Who will weigh the force of such an idea as illegitimacy on man and woman, especially when that man or woman is very sensitive, such as Lincoln was? God keep such people.

LINCOLN THE INDIVIDUAL

. . . It is now the time to describe the person of Mr. Lincoln: he was about six feet four inches high, and when he left the city, was fifty-one years old, having good health and no gray hairs or but few on his head; he was thin, wiry, sinewy, raw and big heavy-boned, thin through the breast to the back and narrow across the shoulders, standing he leaned forward; was what may be called stoop-shouldered, inclining to the consumptively built, his usual weight being about one hundred and sixty or eighty pounds. His organization, rather his structure and functions, worked slowly; his blood had to run a long distance from his heart to the extremities of his frame, and his nerve force had to travel through dry ground a long distance before his muscles were obedient to his will. His organism and structure were loose and leathery; his body was well shrunk, cadaverous and shriveled, having very dark skin, dry and tough, wrinkled and lying somewhat in flabby folds; dark hair, the man looking woe-struck. The whole man, body and mind, worked slowly, creakingly, as if it needed oiling. Physically he was a very powerful man, lifting, as said, with ease four or six hundred pounds. His mind was like his [body?] and blood, worked slowly, but his body and mind functioned strongly, though his blood moved slowly. . . . When this man moved and walked along, he moved and walked cautiously, but firmly, his long and big bony arms and hands on them, hanging like giant hands on them, swung by his side; he walked with even tread, the inner sides of his feet being parallel; he put his whole foot down flat at once, not landing on his heel; he likewise lifted his foot all at once, not rising from the toe, and hence he had no spring to his walk; he had the economy of full lift of foot though he had no spring to his walk or apparent ease of motion in his tread; he walked undulatory, up and down in motion, catching and pocketing time, weariness all up and down his person preventing them from locating. The very first opinion that a stranger or one who did not observe closely would form of Lincoln's walk and motion was that he was a tricky man, a man of cunning, a dangerous shrewd man, one to watch closely and not to be trusted, but his walk was the manifested walk of caution and firmness. In sitting down on a common chair or bench or ground, he was from the top of his head down to his seat no better than the average man; his legs and arms were, as compared with the average man, abnormally, unnaturally long, though when compared to his own organism, the whole physical man, these organs may have been in harmony with the man. His arms and hands, feet and legs, seemed to me, as compared with the average man, in undue proportion to the balance of his body. It was only when Lincoln rose on his feet that he loomed up above the mass of men. He looked the giant then.

Lincoln's head was long and tall from the base of the brain to and from the eyebrows. His head ran backward, his forehead rising as it ran back at a low angle, like Clay's and unlike Webster's, almost perpendicular. The size of his hat, measured on the hatter's hat block was $7\frac{1}{8}$, his head being from ear to ear six and a half inches. Thus measured it was not below the medium or average size. His forehead was narrow but high; his hair was dark, almost black, and lay floating where his fingers put it or the winds left it, piled up and tossed about at random; his cheekbones were high, sharp, and prominent; his eyebrows heavy and prominent; his jaws were long, upcurved, and massive, looked solid, heavy, and strong; his nose was large, long, and blunt, a little awry toward the right eye; his chin was long, sharp, and uncurved; his eyebrows cropped out like a huge jutting rock out of the brow of a hill; his face was long, narrow, sallow, and cadaverous, flesh shrunk, shriveled, wrinkled, and dry, having on his face a few hairs here and there; his cheeks were leathery and saffron-colored; his ears were large and ran out nearly at right angles from the sides of his head, caused by heavy hats in which he carried his big cotton or other handkerchief, his bank book, his letters, and his memoranda generally, and partly by nature; his lower lip was thick and on the top very red, hanging undercurved or downcurved, the red of his lips being a good sign of a tendency to consumption, if it was not on him, biting the life out of him; his neck was neat and trim and did not show much of the animal, though consumptives are quite passionate, goaty; his head was well balanced on his shoulders, his little gray eyes in the right place. There was the lone mole on his right cheek just a little above the right corner of his mouth and Adam's apple on his throat. Beneath this rough and uncouth exterior was a very fine, an exceedingly fine, physical organization, a fine and delicate network of nerves being woven through it along which feelings and thoughts traveled and flashed quicker than lightning. . . .

Mr. Lincoln sometimes walked our street cheerily, good-humoredly, perhaps joyously, and then it was, on meeting a friend, he cried: "Howdy!" clasping one of his friends in both of his wide long big bony hands, giving his friend a good hearty soul welcome. On a winter's morning he might be seen stalking and stilting it toward the market house, basket on his arm, his old gray shawl wrapped around his neck, his little Willie or Tad running along at his heels, asking a thousand little quick questions, which his father heard not, not even then knowing that little Willie or Tad was there fast running after him, so abstracted was he. When he thus met a friend on the road, he said that something that he had just seen, heard, or left put him in mind of a story which he heard in Indiana or Egypt or elsewhere, and tell it he would and there was no alternative in his friend but to patiently stand and hear it.

Thus I say stood, walked, looked, felt, thought, willed, and acted this peculiar and singular man; he was odd, angular, homely, but when those little gray eyes and face were lighted up by the inward soul on fires of emotion, defending the liberty of man or proclaiming the truths of the Declaration of Independence, or defending justice and the eternal right, then it was that all those apparently ugly or homely features sprang into organs of beauty, or sank themselves into the sea of his inspiration that on such occasions flooded up his manly face. Sometimes it did appear to me that Lincoln was just fresh from the presence and hands of his Creator. . . .

Mr. Lincoln's perceptions were slow, cold, precise, and exact. Everything came to Lincoln, whether a sensation or an idea, clean and clean-cut, stripped of all extraneous matter whatsoever. Everything came to him in its precise shape, rarity, and color. To some men the world of matter and of man comes ornamented with beauty, life, and action, and hence such men are more or less cheated in their perceptions, their perceptions being more or less false and inexact. No lurking illusion, delusion, error, false in itself and clad for the moment in robes of splendor, worn by the imagination, ever passed unchallenged or undetected over the threshold of his mind, that divides vision from the realm and home of thought. Names to him were nothing and titles naught, assumptions always standing back abashed at his cold intellectual glare. Neither his perceptions nor his intellectual vision were perverted, distorted, nor diseased; he saw all things through a perfect mental lens. There was no diffraction or refraction there, in this man's brains; he was not impulsive, fanciful, or imaginative, but cold, calm, precise, and exact; he threw his whole mental light around the object seen or felt and in time, quality, substance, person, thing, stood apart; form and color and size took their appropriate places and all was keenly, clearly, and cleanly seen in perfect exactness in his mind. Lincoln's fault if any was that he saw

things or persons less than they really were; he stripped off all extraneous clothing from around them, made them less beautiful and more
frigid. In his mental view he crushed the unreal, the inexact, the hollow and the sham; he rather saw persons and things in rigidity than
in beauty and in vital action; he saw what no man could well dispute, but he failed to see what might be seen and was seen by other
men. To some minds this great world, this vast universe, is all life
and beauty, a living soul beneath or behind the material, but to Lincoln no life was beautiful nor individual or universal that did not
manifest itself to him. Comparatively Mr. Lincoln had no fancy and
no imagination, the painting and creative faculties. Mr. Lincoln had
no sense of the beautiful except in the moral world. His own mind
was his own and exclusive standard; he was self-reliant, self-helpful,
self-supporting, never asking any man any questions, if he possibly
could avoid it. His perceptions were cool, persistent, pitiless in pursuit of an idea, a thing, a fact, a person. No error went undetected
and no falsehood unexposed if he was once aroused to search things,
ideas, facts, truths, persons. . . .

Mr. Lincoln had keen susceptibilities to the hints, insinuations,
and suggestions of nature and of man which put him in mind of something known or unknown; hence his power and tenacity of what is
called the association of ideas must have been great; his memory was
exceedingly retentive, tenacious, and strong; he could write out a
speech, as in the Cooper Institute speech, and then repeat it word
for word, without any effort on his part. This I know about the
"house divided against itself" speech; he wrote that fine effort, an argumentative one, in slips, put those slips in his hat, numbering them,
and when he was done with the ideas, he gathered up the scraps, put
them in the right order, and wrote out his speech, read it to me before it was delivered, and in the evening delivered it just as written
without notes or finished speech; his susceptibilities to all suggestions
and hints enabled him through his retentive memory at will to call
up readily, quickly, and accurately the associated and classified fact,
person, or idea.

As an evidence of this especially peculiar nature of Mr. Lincoln
let me ask one question: Were not his expressions and language odd
and original, standing out peculiar from those of all other men? . . .
Mr. Lincoln was often perplexed to give expression to his exact,

clean-cut ideas: first, because he was not master of the English language, not knowing its flexibility and its grandeur, and, secondly, there to him were no words in it containing the coloring, shape, and weight of his ideas; he was frequently at a loss for a word and hence in the beginning of his life was compelled to resort to stories, jokes, maxims, to embody and express his ideas, that they might be comprehended. . . . Lincoln's mind, commencing in his boyish-youthful days, to his greatness, underwent four changes as to the method of conveying his ideas: first, he used Æsop's Fables as a means to that end; secondly, he used the common maxims of the common people to give expressions to his thoughts; finding out that these would not always convey his ideas, he used, thirdly, stories, jokes, to that end; and, fourthly, as he became more and better acquainted with his mother tongue, he resorted to words and words alone to convey his ideas, though he never ceased to tell his stories and his jokes to those who he knew loved and could appreciate them. . . .

The truth about this whole matter is that Mr. Lincoln read less and thought more than any man in his sphere in America. No man can put his finger on any great book written in the last or present century that Lincoln ever read. When he was young he read the Bible and when of age he read Shakespeare. This latter book was scarcely ever out of his mind and his hands. Mr. Lincoln is acknowledged to be a great, very great man, but the question is: What made him great? I repeat that he read less and thought more than any man, of his standing and in his own sphere, in America or probably in the world; he possessed originality and power of thought in an eminent degree; he was cautious, skeptical, cool, concentrated with continuity of reflection, was patient, persistent, and enduring. These are some of the grounds of his wonderful power and success. . . .

Mr. Lincoln was a poor judge of the appropriateness of things or the fine propriety of condition; he would stalk into a ballroom and say, where all could, did, hear him: "Oh, how clean these girls look!" The reason of all of Lincoln's mistakes of this kind is that he had been high up in the world of thought and had by the laws of nature to let himself down easily somehow to balance things, to get his line again. . . .

The great predominating elements of Mr. Lincoln's peculiar nature, were: first, his great capacity and power of reason; secondly, his excellent understanding; thirdly, an exalted idea of the sense of right and equity; and, fourthly, his intense veneration of what was good and true. His reason ruled despotically all other faculties and qualities of his mind; his conscience and his heart were ruled by it; his great conscience was ruled by one faculty, his reason; his heart was ruled by two faculties, his great reason and his conscience. I know that it is generally believed that Mr. Lincoln's heart, his love and kindness, his tenderness, his mercy and his benevolence, were his ruling qualities, but this opinion [is] entirely erroneous in every particular. . . .

He made this remark to me one day, I think at Washington: "If ever this free people, if this government is ever overthrown, utterly demoralized, it will come from this struggle and wriggle for office, a way to live without work; from which nature I am not free myself." It puzzled him a great deal at Washington to know [how] to get at the root of this great and dread desire, this contagious disease of office holding, this contagious disease of national robbery in the nation's death struggle. . . .

Be it remembered that Mr. Lincoln cared nothing for simple unrelated facts, manners, modes, ways, and suchlike things. Be it remembered that he did care for truth, the right, the true, the good, and principles. In relation to simple facts, unrelated facts, unrelated to the substance of things, forms, rules, methods, ways, red tape, he cared nothing and, if he could be aroused, he would do anything for anybody at any time and at all places, and under all conditions, as well [for] foe or friend. As a politician, as a lawyer, and as an individual he would courteously grant all unimportant facts and forms, all non-essential things, to his friends, foe, or opponent; he did so because he did not care for those little things. Here he had no will. However, in truths, what was true, good, and right, and just, he would never surrender; he would die before he would surrender his ideas of these; he has said so and I believe him. . . .

This man, this long, tall, bony, homely, wiry, sad, gloomy man floated into our county in 1831, in a frail canoe down the north fork of the Sangamon River, friendless, penniless, powerless, and alone, begging for work in this city, ragged, struggling for the common necessaries of life. This man, this peculiar man, left us here in 1861 the President of the United States, backed by friends and power,

by fame and all individual and national forces, and it is well to inquire into the how.

To sum up, let us say that here is a very sensitive, diffident, unob-
trusive, natural-made gentleman ; his mind was strong and deep, sincere and honest, patient and enduring, with a good heart filled with
the love of mercy and with a conscience that loved justice, having
no vices, only negative defects with many positive virtues; he is
strong, self-reliant, honest, full of practical sagacities, manly, noble ;
he stands high in the foremost [ranks] of man in all ages, their equal,
if not their superior, one of the very best types of free institutions
and this Christian civilization ; and if I were to deliver a eulogy freed
from all rhetoric of extravagant eulogy, I say here was a man in his
general life [who?] thought strongly, willed firmly, and acted nobly,
and in whose life and death the world is lifted to a higher plane of
existence.

Lincoln's "Ingratitude"

The American world seems to be excited very much over the question of whether Lincoln gave or offered to give me an office while he
was President. This great question I can settle quickly. I suppose
that question has been asked me, it may be, a hundred or more times ;
it has been asked by three classes of people : first, those who hated
Lincoln, those who wished to talk and to write him down as very ungrateful because he did not give me an office ; secondly, those who hated
me, taking it for granted that, as Lincoln did not give me an office,
he would not, [who] argued too that Lincoln held me unfit for office ;
and the third class, those who wished truthfully to know the facts
of the case. I have eyed and closely watched the motives of these
men. The first class would disgustingly flatter me, tell me my great
services to Lincoln, tell me how I wrote, worked, and spent money
for Lincoln, how I made out his best briefs in the largest law cases,
and that Lincoln would argue his case from those briefs and get the
credit for them while I was the power behind them, and sometimes I
began to think that I was a very great man and a badly neglected
one. But I soon would recover and look at myself as I was. The second class would hint around and in fact tell it that Lincoln is sharp
in not giving me office because I was unfit to hold one. The third class

wished to know the facts for truth's sake. This class I always respected and explained to them the facts as they existed. The first and second class got no satisfaction from me, because I know what their motive was.

Mr. Lincoln, a short time before he had started for Washington, distinctly asked me if I wanted to hold any office under his administration. I told Mr. Lincoln that I did not, because at that time I had a good and a leading practice at the bar of Springfield and other places, and was making a good living. At that time I had some money. Mr. Lincoln then said to me: "Do you want to hold the office which you now hold?" and in reply I said: "Mr. Lincoln, I thank you, I do." I at that time held the office of Bank Commissioner of Illinois, which Mr. Lincoln got for me through his influence with Governor Bissell. Governor Yates was at the time of this conversation Governor of Illinois. Said Lincoln: "Let's go down and see Governor Yates." Lincoln and I were instantly admitted into the Governor's room. Mr. Lincoln repeated to the Governor his conversation with me and as stated above. Mr. Lincoln said to the Governor substantially this: "Governor, I want you to retain my friend in office, the office of Bank Commissioner, which he now holds—one which he received from Governor Bissell." "Oh," said Governor Yates to Mr. Lincoln, "I did not intend to remove Mr. Herndon by any means; he has always been my warm personal and political friend. I shall keep him"; and so things rested for a while. At last Governor Yates spoke to Mr. Lincoln and said: "See here, Lincoln, I have a friend of mine and a relative, A. Y. Ellis, who wishes to be Post Master of this city," meaning Springfield. "Will you, Lincoln," continued Governor Yates, "see to his application, which will be highly recommended in due time?" Mr. Lincoln replied to the Governor: "Certainly I will." A. Y. Ellis, the person spoken of by the Governor, got up his recommendation and made his application in due form and time. A. Y. Ellis did not get the office, which can be accounted for alone upon the hypothesis that Lincoln forgot his implied promise in the hurry and flurry of the war times. Lincoln was overwhelmed with business, drowned in cases, heavy, weighty cases. Or it may have gone—Ellis's application—to the Post Office department and the nomination sent to the Senate by a list without Lincoln's special notice. War swallowed up everything.

While Senator Cullom of this State was Congressman from the district of Sangamon County, say in 1861, '62, or '63, etc., I frequently wrote to our Congressman letters on business and some on politics, etc., in which we would say a thousand and one things. I distinctly remember among those letters written to now Senator Cullom this in substance: "Cullom, if you see Lincoln, tell him for me that if he has any large, honorable, and fat office with a big salary to give away and cannot get any person on earth to take it that I'll take and run it on his account, but under no other consideration." This, as a matter of course, was jocularly said. Cullom so understood it, so did Lincoln, and so will all persons who read this account. Lincoln was told and that too by Congressman Cullom what I requested him to say. Lincoln said to Cullom this: "If all persons did not bother me more than Herndon I should be a happier man." I know that it is dangerous to appeal to men's memories, but I will risk it.

In 1861 or '62 I went to Washington in order to get an office for my friend Charles W. Chatterton, did so at his urgent solicitation. I sent up my card to Mr. Lincoln, and as a matter of course I was instantly admitted. Lincoln and I chatted a moment only and, knowing well that Lincoln was hurried to the death, I at once told Lincoln what I wanted and for whom. Lincoln instantly gave me a card to Mr. Smith, Secretary of the Interior. I took the card, gave it, handed it, to his clerk, doorkeeper, or what not and was quickly admitted into Mr. Smith's room; had a running conversation with Mr. Smith about politics. Smith was conservative and I radical. I shut off the conversation as quickly and as decently as I could. I said to Mr. Smith that I wanted a clerkship for my friend. Mr. Smith took the trouble to go through all the clerks' offices and ask if any place was vacant and the universal answer of all the clerks was: "No, not any." The next morning I went and saw Mr. Lincoln and told him of my failure; he instantly got up off his chair and said: "Let's go down to the Indian Department and see Dole," and down we went. Lincoln spoke to Dole about an office. Dole said that I should have one and so Charles W. Chatterton was appointed Indian agent somewhere down in the Southwest. I have forgotten the name of the office and the name of the Indians. I got this office "speedily without delay, freely without purchase, and fully without denial."

Sometime after this the money world changed. The crash point had come and I went, like a thousand others, under pecuniarily. I asked Mr. Lincoln for an office and he quickly offered me one which had good pay, etc., but I could not accept it because it required my absence constantly from home. I offered the chance of the office to Judge Zane, who did not wish it for the same reasons for which I refused it. The very dispatch sent to me by Mr. Lincoln himself is now in the Lincoln Memorial Collection in Chicago. Mr. Lincoln's card to Mr. Smith will turn up sometime. This I have written from my memory and have not given dates. In conclusion let me say that, in my opinion, Lincoln would have given me any office which I asked him to give me, if he thought that I was capable of executing my duty. Not otherwise. Mr. Lincoln had no friend and no enemy in this matter: he looked to the good, the highest interest of the government, and I think this is as it should be.

Honest Abe—a Story of Lincoln's Youth

Mrs. Moore, Abraham's stepsister, told the writer of this, the following story, facts which explain Mr. Lincoln's love of truth from childhood to the day of his assassination better than a long and eloquent eulogy of the man could do. Mrs. Moore's maiden name was Matilda. Thomas Lincoln had two children by his first wife, Nancy Hanks; and Mrs. Johnston, Thomas Lincoln's second wife, had two children by her first husband. . . . The four children were raised up lovingly together from 1818 to 1831. Abraham and 'Tilda grew up together loving one another as brother and sister. Abraham was in the habit of going into the deep forest to fell trees, cut and maul rails, and 'Tilda, when young, it was her duty to carry a good warm dinner to Abraham in the woods. Abraham grew up to be about eighteen years of age and the girl about sixteen years of age. Mrs. Lincoln, a good old lady, and mother of 'Tilda, began to think that the two young ones should not run so wild in the forests together and alone; and therefore, to stop all possible tattle in the neighborhood, she told 'Tilda that she must not any more go into the forests to carry Abraham his usual dinner, that she must cook his dinner before she went into the woods and hand it to him when he started out for his day's work. 'Tilda did in part do what her mother told her. Abraham took his dinner and put it in his work basket and went to work. This was repeated from day to day. However, 'Tilda soon grew tired of her restraint. Abraham one morning ground his ax sharp and keen, put the maul and ax on his shoulder, and taking his dinner in the basket on his arm and so marched on into the forests with the maul, ax, and wedges, full of life and fun, not dreaming of 'Tilda's intentions. He wended his way southward down the cattle, hog, and deer paths to his place of cutting and felling trees preparatory to the making of the rails. 'Tilda that morning was determined to go into the woods and have a good long chat and a wild romp with Abraham. When Lincoln had traveled some three or four hundred yards from the house, 'Tilda ran quickly along the path in a silent and somewhat stealthy manner, and, all at once and unexpectedly to Abraham, she bounced on his back like a panther, putting her knees in the small of Abraham's back and locking her hands around his neck, and then threw Abraham down on his back, his face to the sun and his spine in the ground. In the fall of Abraham the pole of the ax fell on the ground and the sharp keen edge upward. In pulling Abraham backward, 'Tilda fell on the sharp keen edge of the ax and cut herself badly and quite severely; he was astonished at the bound and trick of the girl but he quickly saw that his sister had cut herself severely and seriously, if not fatally. Abraham and 'Tilda were both frightened. Abraham tore off the tail of his undergarment, for it was all he had to tear or use on that occasion. By Abraham's good sense, care, and attention, and a little skill, he closed the wound and stanched the blood. The wound was a deep wide gaping wound in the thigh near an artery. When all danger was over and passed and the blood stopped, Abraham said to 'Tilda: "Now, what are you going to tell your good mother, 'Tilda?" "Why, Abe," said his sister, "I'll tell my mother that I cut myself badly on the ax and that will be the truth about it." "Yes, that will be the truth," said Abraham, "but it won't be the whole truth, 'Tilda. 'Tilda, the very best thing that you can possibly do is to tell your mother the whole truth and nothing but the truth and risk your mother. This I advise you to do," and so she did but got a good-natured scolding. Abraham told his mother that 'Tilda had told her the full truth and nothing but the truth. The old lady put implicit confidence in Abraham's word. She said to the writer of this: "I never knew Mr. Lincoln to lie to me about anything." This is characteristic of Abraham; he manifested this love for the whole truth during his whole life.

LINCOLN IN SPRINGFIELD

Springfield, Ill., April 14, 1886.

I became acquainted with Mr. Lincoln in 1834, and from that time to the day of his death, I knew the man well, I may say intimately.

He moved to the city of Springfield in 1837, then but a small town or village, now quite a city. I studied law with Logan and Lincoln, two great lawyers in 1842–43. In 1843–44, Mr. Lincoln and I became partners in the law business in Springfield but did business in all the surrounding counties. Our partnership was never legally dissolved till the night of his assassination. The good man, the noble man, would take none of my fees made in the law business after his election to the Presidency. Mr. Lincoln was a safe counselor, a good lawyer, and an honest man in all the walks of life.

Mr. Lincoln was not appreciated in this city, nor was he at all times the most popular man among us. The cause of his unpopularity, or rather want of popularity here, arose out of two grounds: first, he did his own thinking, and, second, he had the courage of his convictions, and boldly and fearlessly expressed them.

I speak generally and especially of his political life. Mr. Lincoln was a cool, cautious, conservative, and long-headed man. Mr. Lincoln could be trusted by the people. They did trust him and they were never deceived. He was a pure man, a great man, and a patriot. In the practice of law he was simple, honest, fair, and broad-minded. He was courteous to the bar and to the court. He was open, candid, and square in his profession, never practicing on the sharp or low. Mr. Lincoln met all questions fairly, squarely, and open, making no concealments of his ideas or intentions in any case. He took no snap judgments, nor used any tricks in his business. Every man knew exactly where Mr. Lincoln stood and how he would act in a law case.

Mr. Lincoln never deceived his brother in a law case. What he told you was the exact truth. Mr. Lincoln was a sad man, a gloomy man, and an abstractive one, and hence he was not very sociable in his nature. He seemed to me to be an unhappy man at times, he dearly loved his children, but he was not the happiest man in the world domestically. As a friend, Mr. Lincoln was true, true as steel; he thought in his life and lived in his thoughts. In many things, Mr. Lincoln was peculiar, he did not trust any man with the secret of his ambitious soul.

I knew the man so well that I think I could read his secrets and his ambitions.

He was a wonderful man and his fame will grow on the ages.

WILLIAM H. HERNDON.

LINCOLN THE LAWYER

Mr. Lincoln was an extremely ambitious man and that ambition found its gratification only in the political field. Politics were his life and newspapers his food, merely using the law as a stepping stone to a political life and it was in this field that he seemed to be happy. There is no point in Lincoln's life that has been discussed more than the one of his great ability as a lawyer. Mr. Lincoln was at the same time a very great lawyer and a very little one. Judge Davis says, in his remarks, his eulogy on Lincoln as lawyer in the United States Circuit Court, held at Indianapolis in May '65, this: "In all the elements that constitute a lawyer he had few equals; he was great both at *nisi prius* and before the appellate tribunals; he seized the strong points of a cause and presented them with clearness and great compactness. His mind was logical and direct, and he did not indulge in extraneous discussion. Generalities and platitudes had no charms for him. An unfailing vein of humor never deserted him and he was always able to claim the attention of court and jury, when the cause was the most uninteresting, by the appropriateness of his anecdotes. His power of comparison was large and he rarely failed in a legal discussion to use that mode of reasoning. The framework of his mental and moral being was honesty, and a wrong cause was poorly defended by him. The ability which some lawyers possess of explaining any bad point of a cause by ingenious sophistry was denied him. In order to bring into full activity his great powers it was necessary that he should be convinced of the right and justice of the matter which he advocated, etc."

This statement by Judge Davis is correct in the general, but it is not true in the particular, for these remarks were eulogistic, which would not admit of any limitations or modification. Judge Davis said on his examination by me in '66 at Bloomington this: "Mr. Lincoln had no faculty or organizing power; hence a child could conduct the simple and technical rules, means and the modes of getting at justice, better than Lincoln. The law has its own rules and a student could get at them better than Lincoln. Sometimes Lincoln studied these, if he would not get the rubbish of a case removed, etc. He had no inventive or organizing ability, no administrative ability, etc." Here too is a good statement of Lincoln as lawyer and they—Davis's apparent contradictions—must and can be reconciled. The very idea that Mr. Lincoln was a great lawyer at the higher courts and a good *nisi prius* lawyer, and yet that a child, a student, could manage a case at *nisi prius* better than Mr. Lincoln could, seems contradictory. The facts of Mr. Lincoln's life as a lawyer will reconcile these apparent contradictions. Judge Davis knew Mr. Lincoln well and says and says truly to me in his examination that "Lincoln was not a well-read man, read no histories, novels, biographies, etc., studied Euclid, the exact sciences. His mind struggled to arrive at moral and physical, mathematical demonstration. He studied the Latin grammar on the circuit. He had a good mechanical mind and knowledge." How a man could be a great lawyer under these conditions seems impossible and yet Mr. Lincoln in a certain sense was a great lawyer, and in another sense an exceedingly little one. While passing I wish to say that I examined Judge Davis in '66 at Bloomington and he dictated while I wrote. That writing is in my hand now. One more word, much has been said about the Judge and yet I may say that the Judge had quick perceptions of human nature and was a man of veracity and integrity and, like all men, had his faults. This is admitted. I shall try and explain, and the reason why I quote Judge Davis so often is that Davis was himself quite a great man, knowing Mr. Lincoln very well, quite thoroughly. Davis had a good knowledge of human nature and looked into it quickly, saw through a man. . . . Mr. Lincoln traveled around the circuit with Judge Davis from 1847 to '58. . . . On this circuit Mr. Lincoln met with some fine lawyers, and good people. It was here that he seemed happy, *seemed* to be happy. Judge Davis says: "In my opinion I think Mr. Lincoln was happy as he could be when on the circuit, and happy in no other place. This was his place of enjoyment. As a general rule when all the lawyers, on a Saturday evening, would go home to see their families and friends, Lincoln *would refuse to go home.*" It seemed to me that Lincoln was "not domestically happy." I was frequently on part of the circuit with Mr. Lincoln and found out there and especially in Sangamon County, that Mr. Lincoln was very deficient in the technical rules of the law. Mr. Lincoln, to my knowledge, never thoroughly read any elementary law book. In fact I may truthfully say that I never knew him to read through and through any law book of any kind; he knew nothing of the laws of evidence, of pleading, or of practice, and did not care about them; he had a keen sense of justice and struck for that, throwing aside forms, methods, and rules of all law. Lincoln looked for justice through forms, pure as a ray of light flashes through a fog bank. Mr. Lincoln was not a general reader in any field of knowledge; he was purely a practical man, and when he wished to know a fact, he trailed it up and dug it out, root and branch, and then he thoroughly analyzed it, root and top, fiber and cell, and when all this was done, he used his information for practical ends. Mr. Lincoln was purely and entirely a case lawyer, nothing more; he thought slowly and acted slowly; he must have his time to think, analyze the facts, and then wind them into a whole story. If anyone can make a good circuit court lawyer, a good *nisi prius* lawyer out of these facts, let him. I have seen him lose cases which anyone could have gained, just ones. Even on the circuit, at *nisi prius*, if Mr. Lincoln had his time and thought that he was right, and could get the case swung to the jury, freed from technicalities, he was a good lawyer, but if he did not have his time, did not think that he was right, and could not get his case swung to the jury, freed from technicalities, then he was a very weak brother. In the circuit courts of the United States he was a good lawyer, because the practice of the courts was liberal, moved slowly, freed from technicalities, and gave Lincoln his own time to arrange his ideas and his plans for attack or defense. Here he was a good lawyer and it was from this point that Judge Drummond spoke. But it was in the Supreme Court of the State of Illinois that he was truly a great lawyer, and nowhere else. The Supreme Court has its rules and gives time, ample time, to read the record and gather up the facts of the case, the issues and the law arising thereon, abstracts of the case and the lawyers' briefs, stating the facts in a condensed form and the issues made thereby. No man can be caught by surprise here and thrown out of court. In this court there is, except on special occasions, no oral evidence admitted. The written record as made up alone goes to the court. The lawyers see each other's briefs, arguments, and the quoted law; they have ample time to hunt up the law and to argue the case, and in this court alone Lincoln was great truly and indeed. I have thus tried to reconcile these seeming contradictions of Judge Davis. I heard him once argue a case and it was argued extremely well, it was logical, eloquent. In making his argument he referred to the history of the law, a useless part as I then thought. I know better now. After the speech was through and Lincoln had come into the law library room where the lawyers tell stories and prepare their cases, I said: "Lincoln, why did you go so far back in the history of the law as applicable to this case?" and to which he instantly replied: "I dare not trust this case on presumptions that this court knows all things. I argued the case on the presumption that the court did not know anything," and in this he was right for our Supreme Court at that time did not know anything. Lincoln gained this very case by that very history which he was so careful to state fully.

A gentleman by the name of Colonel King who lived about eight miles east of Springfield, Illinois, was elected a justice of the peace for Sangamon County, and, having great confidence in Mr. Lincoln's judgment as to well-settled law practice, came into the office one day, soon after he was elected justice, and asked Lincoln how he should act in that capacity and how best to form his own judgments. In answer to this question of calling Mr. Lincoln said: "There is no mystery in this matter, King; when you have a case between neighbors before you, listen well to all the evidence, stripping yourself of all prejudice, if any you have, and throwing away if you can all technical law knowledge, hear the lawyers make their arguments as patiently as you can, and after the evidence and the lawyers' arguments are through, then stop one moment and ask yourself: What is justice in this case? and let that sense of justice be your decision. Law is nothing else but the best reason of wise men applied for ages to the transactions and business of mankind." This gives us an idea

as to the methods of Lincoln in forming his own opinions. It threw
light on the reason why the law was so. . . .

Mr. Lincoln was a cautious and an honest man, thoroughly honest morally and intellectually, if such a division can be made of the
mind of a man. When a client came into our office and wanted advice,
Mr. Lincoln listened to his story well, patiently, occasionally now
and then breaking in as the story progressed by asking a question;
the man would answer it, and then he would proceed and end his
story. Lincoln, after the man had finished his story, would ask more
questions, and they would suggest more. After the man was done telling his story fully and after Lincoln was done asking questions, he
would generally think awhile before answering. When he answered,
it was: "You are in the right," or: "You are in the wrong." If Mr.
Lincoln was not satisfied of the law as applicable to the man's case,
he would say: "I am not exactly satisfied about some point; come
into the office in an hour or so, and I will give you my opinion, a
positive one." The man would call again and then Lincoln would
say: "You are in the right," or: "You are in the wrong of the case
and I would advise you to compromise, or if you cannot do that, do
not bring a suit on the facts of your case because you are in the
wrong and [will] surely get defeated and have to pay a big bill of
costs." This was Lincoln's general way of doing business. If the man
was in a doubtful case, Lincoln would say so, but say at the same
time: if you must fight it out, I will help you to do so the best I
can. The man generally took Lincoln's advice.

It has been asked me repeatedly: "By what power, by what means,
was it that Mr. Lincoln got such a firm hold on courts, juries, and
lawyers?" When Mr. Lincoln entered court he spoke to all persons
in a polite way, calling them by some very familiar name, addressing
the Court in his best and kindest manner. When Mr. Lincoln was
addressing the Court on a law question only or on facts, he made
the instantaneous impression on the Court that he was fair, honest,
and would present the case fairly and honestly. The Court felt that
there was no falsehood nor trick in his argument. The Court believed
him to be a true gentleman, never suspecting that he would deceive
or try to gain his point by any evasion or suppression of law or
fact, but would meet each fairly and squarely. Mr. Lincoln did not

glory in winning a case through a false argument, but rather had an ambition of gaining it on a substantial ground of justice. This seemed to be his pride. The jury, good common sense men of the country or the city, patiently listened to Mr. Lincoln's argument before them, and he was just as fair before them and to them as he was to the Court. Lincoln's statement of the case, both of law and of fact, was an argument, a plain, short, condensed argument. This impression was stamped on the jury, nor did Lincoln ever seek to take advantage of it; he met all questions fairly and squarely, admitting what he could not deny and making the case plain to be seen by the jury. All rubbish and trash was removed away and from around the issues that now arose clear to the minds. If the case was a long, dry, tedious one and the jury got tired and showed signs of weariness, or of sleepiness, Lincoln would tell one of his fine stories and arouse them up to renewed attention, and then he would take up the thread of his argument and proceed on to the end of it.

From 1836 to 1861 Mr. Lincoln met at the bar such men as Judge Logan, the very type and style of a circuit court, a *nisi prius* lawyer, a little shriveled-up man, a thoroughly read man in all the departments of the law, quick as lightning and as technical as technicality itself; he was the best circuit court *nisi prius* lawyer on the circuit; he could gain a case where no other man could, unaccommodating in his practice, cold, ungenerous, snappy, irritable, fighting like a game fowl every point of his case and, when whipped at this point, he would grumblingly fall back on his next point, unlike Lincoln who only made one point and that was the turning point of the case. Logan fought a five-cent case just as energetically and as well as he fought one for ten thousand dollars, rather better because such a big pile of money broke him down through fear of losing the case. Judge McLean, one of the judges of the Supreme Court of the United States, said: "Judge Logan is the very best *nisi prius* lawyer whom I ever saw"; he is the best one that I ever saw. When you got into a case on one side and Logan was on the other side, you knew that you would be defeated, if there was any defeat in your case, and possibly, very possibly, you would be defeated right or wrong. This little dried and shriveled-up man was a terror to the profession, and it is my opinion that he lived and died, died rich too, without a warm friend in the world outside of his own family. Such was the Honorable Stephen T. Logan. On the other hand, if you met Mr. Lincoln on a case and you on one side and Mr. Lincoln on the other, you knew that you met a broad-minded and liberal gentleman, honest, fair, and that you would be defeated if you ought to be; such was Abraham Lincoln in this sphere of his activities.

There were Douglas, Lamborn, Bledsoe, Colonel Baker, Stuart, and Edwards, Honorable Milton Hay, Jesse B. Thomas, subsequently judge of the Supreme Court, Senator McDougal, and others from all parts of the State. These men were good, excellent lawyers and men of more or less renown throughout the State. The very best minds in the State, if not in the great West, met here, the capital of the State, and energetically struggled for wealth or fame. Many of them died rich and some died with a worldwide fame. These men were, take them as a whole, great men, full of energy and of great natural capacities, and were very ambitious and struggled to rise in the world; they were giants and fought like giants. The fire that moved these men seems dying out in this new generation. . . .

I wish to give an opinion of the men of Springfield, Illinois, from 1833 to 1850. These men were great men in any sense and would have been great anywhere and under any circumstances because they were large and great by nature; they were not, as a general rule, highly cultured, but they had what was better and had it in a large measure —a rude unpolished naturalness; they had great ambition and over-flowed with manly spirit, health, and strength; they came here to fight their way upward and they did so fight it; they met each other at the bar and on the stump and fought it out like strong brave men do fight it out. These men were at all times personal friends, bearing no ill will toward each other. I may say, I think, truthfully, that no city in the land of Greece, the grand old land of culture and philosophy, had in any seventeen years of its existence at one and the same time contemporaries, as many great men as the village of Springfield had from 1833 to 1850. There were Lincoln, Douglas, Baker, Logan, McDougal, Lamborn, Bledsoe, Calhoun, ——, and others, all men of great minds. The influence of one of these men will be practically felt the world around when the very name of Socrates and such men possibly shall have been forgotten or only to be remembered by the very learned in colleges alone.

Lincoln's First Appearance in the Supreme Court of Illinois

A case being called for hearing in that court, Mr. Lincoln noted that he appeared for the appellant, and was ready to proceed with the argument. He then said: "This is the first case I have ever had in this court, and I have, therefore, examined it with great care. As the Court will perceive by looking at the abstract of the record, the only question in the case is one of authority. I have not been able to find any authority sustaining my side of the case, but I *have found* several cases directly in point on the other side. I will now give *these cases* to the Court, and then submit the case."

The Stolen Hogs—a Lincoln Story

About the year 1850 a man was indicted in Coles County in this State for hog stealing. The man was poor and was unable to employ a lawyer. The tide of public feeling was against the man. The Court asked the man when brought to the bar to plead: "Are you guilty or not guilty?" "Not guilty," spoke the man quickly. "Who is your attorney?" said the Court. The man said: "I have none and too poor to employ one." "In that case," responded the Court, "I will appoint you one. Have you any preferences among the members of the bar?" "I have," replied the man promptly, "I'll take that long tall man sitting there," pointing to Lincoln. The Court promptly appointed Lincoln to defend the hog thief. Lincoln, whose sympathies were always for the underdog, willingly undertook to defend the man. In order to defend the case well, Lincoln got leave of the Court to take his client in the back room, in order to see what the man's defense really was. Mr. Lincoln and his client sat down, and Mr. L. said to the thief: "What is your defense, that is, what are the facts of the case?" The thief said: "I have no facts to tell you, Mr. Lincoln. The truth is, we'll jump in and fight 'em on general principles and clear me as I know you can." "This is curious. What, have you no facts to tell me! Here are a half-dozen witnesses on the back of this indictment who will swear against you and state that you stole the hogs," said the attorney. "Well, I can't help that," said the criminal. "But," said Lincoln, "this is curious, mysterious; how is it that you will tell me nothing and will not say guilty nor not guilty? It's curious indeed." The thief said: "It may be curious, mysterious, to you, but it is not to me; it's all right to me, so it is, it's clear, clear as gunshot." The man was very calm and yet he had a peculiar quiz on his face, something that spoke more than words, something that meant certainty, confidence in his acquittal. Lincoln moved awhile and scratched his head; he saw something funny in the case, but did not know where it came in. Lincoln was determined to find out the point and run the case through to the end. The man and his attorney returned into court and pleaded: "Not guilty." A jury was called and the trial proceeded. All the witnesses swore on the witness stand that the defendant stole the hogs and sold them to various persons. Here some of the jury was a little uneasy, looking here and looking there. The prosecuting attorney opened the case; it was a plain case of hog stealing and no doubt to all reasonable minds. About the time that the prosecuting attorney was to end his opening speech, the criminal leaned over to Lincoln and said: "Pitch in, go it on general principles with a whoop and a yell. I'll be cleared, *you bet*." Lincoln was amused very much and yet he kept his own secrets; he was determined to understand the man's calmness and certainty of acquittal. Lincoln arose and ran over the evidence quickly; he saw that all the jury were intent on every word he said; he likewise noticed that the jury paid no attention to the prosecuting speech, and those facts puzzled Lincoln more and more, and yet he was determined to see the end and where the pin came in. The prosecuting attorney, after Lincoln had ended his sympathetic and eloquent speech, made a short reply in conclusion. Mr. Lincoln then asked the Court to give this instruction: "If the jury on all the evidence in this case have any reasonable doubts of the defendant's guilt, they will find the defendant not guilty." The Court gave the instruction as asked. The case was plain, at least plain enough for reasonable people. The jury retired and was gone out to *deliberate* on their verdict for an hour or so. All was suspense and anxiety in the courtroom. At last the jury told the sheriff that they were ready to give in their verdict. The sheriff led the jury to the jury bench; they took their seats, were called, and each answered to his name. All twelve answered. "You found your verdict?" The jury all answered: "We have." The verdict was handed up to the clerk to read aloud. All was suspense and anxiety when the clerk read out aloud: "We the jury find the defendant not guilty." The prosecuting attorney quickly sprang to his feet and said to the jury: "Is this your verdict, gentlemen?" and all said: "It is our verdict, one and all." The prosecuting attorney made a motion for a new trial, which was denied as a matter of course on many grounds. This case, the conduct of the prisoner, his manner, his speech and certainty of acquittal, together with the verdict of the jury, puzzled and bothered Lincoln terribly; he could not understand it at all and no one in the court house did, except the criminal and the jury. Lincoln was so anxious to know the inner secrets, the whole inside of the case, the facts, that he took the man out of the court house and walked away from the hearing of every person. When they were seated Lincoln said: "Mr. ———, I do not understand this case at all but would like to know the inside of it, the whole facts of it, inside and outside from top to bottom." "Why, Lincoln, you did understand it, you went in on general principles and cleared me; is not that good evidence that you understood the case well and truly and did your duty?" Mr. Lincoln still insisted on knowing the facts and said: "Come, let me have no fooling now." . . . The man at last said: "Well, Lincoln, my good fellow, I'll tell you. I did steal the hogs and more of 'em than I was indicted for, many more, and sold 'em to my neighbors, the jury; they knew that if I was convicted that they would have to pay for the hogs that I sold 'em, as they belonged to Mr. ——— and Mr. ———, and the jury knew it from the evidence. Now, Lincoln, do you see where the joke comes in? I knew that I would be cleared; didn't I tell you so?" Lincoln was astonished at the fellow and his story; he, L., used to tell the story on circuit with great gusto and to the delight of his brother attorneys of the bar. Lincoln would laugh over the story most heartily, saying: "That case beat me, badly, more than any I ever had."

W. H. HERNDON.

LINCOLN AND DOUGLAS—THE JOINT DEBATES IN 1840

During the Presidential race between Harrison and Van Buren in '40, Lincoln and Douglas frequently discussed the political questions of the day on the stump. Some few years before this race a man by the name of Holland had issued the political or campaign life of Van Buren. In that Life, Holland stated that Van Buren had been in the Constitutional Convention which had formed the new Constitution of

New York and that Van Buren had voted in the convention for a clause in the Constitution giving the right of suffrage to free blacks and whites alike, provided they had the necessary property qualifications, which Van Buren advocated in the convention, of $———. This, as a matter of course, allowed the free Negroes to vote, if they were worth so much, and cut off all white men, it made no difference how great or what services they had rendered their country, unless they had the necessary qualification. This clause, this property qualification clause, cut off the Revolutionary soldier of '76 and the soldier of '12, great men, if they had not the qualification, but gave it to the Negro who had the qualification. This Democratic Life freely came out to Illinois and was distributed among our people. I purchased a copy and used it in all the ways I could. Mr. Lincoln read the Life and scored the Democracy on the free Negro franchise vote of Van Buren, in the New York Constitutional Convention. Lincoln used to read the facts out of the Life of Van Buren by Holland in his joint debates with Douglas—or in his presence. Lincoln made it too hot for the Democracy and drove them to the necessity of asserting boldly that Holland's Life of Van Buren was a Whig forgery. This broad and bold charge somewhat took the wind out of the Whigs. In order to settle the matter, one George May sent a copy of Holland's book to Van Buren, asking him if it was a true Life. Mr. Van Buren answered that it was correct, so far as it went into his Life. Douglas used to swell out hugely declaring the book to be a forgery. Lincoln and the Whigs kept their own secrets till a good opportunity showed itself to use the book and the Van Buren letter. In a joint debate between Douglas and Lincoln after the Van Buren letter had arrived, Douglas was swelling out in one of his grand eloquent ways, charging the Whigs with using a fraudulent and forged Life of Van Buren in order to swindle the democracy.

Lincoln watched his opportunity and said: "I understand that Mr. Douglas asserts, more or less directly, that Holland's Life of Van Buren is a swindle and a forgery. I would ask the Democracy if this is not so," and "Yes" rolled out of a thousand throats; Douglas implied by asserting to the truthfulness of the charge. Lincoln then referred to and quoted from Holland's Life the facts of the case, and here the Democracy cried out: "Fraud, swindling, forgery!" "You say, gentlemen," said Lincoln, "that this book is a fraud, a swindle, and a forgery?" "Yes, yes!" howled the Democracy. "Well," said Lincoln, "I have a letter in my hands which will settle that little matter forever." "Read it, read it!" cried the crowd. Lincoln then read out slowly Van Buren's letter in which Van Buren said that it was a correct Life as far as it went in his history. This ruse of Lincoln completely squelched in all after time the charge of Whig fraud, swindle, and forgery. Douglas, in the debate that day with Lincoln, had the conclusion, and in reference to that Van Buren Life said: "Any man who would write such a Life and send it out to the great West expecting that it would advance his hero's interest was a d——d fool," at the same time slinging the book as far into the crowd as he could. The Life of Van Buren by Holland did him great harm out West, but the charge of Whig fraud, Whig swindle, and Whig forgery was never heard of any more.

This is a true story and published at the time in the *Journal* and Ohio papers; have talked to men who heard this debate.

W. H. HERNDON.

Jesse, write it out better, these are simply notes but true ones. Carefully keep, are good for next edition of our book. How do you like it?   H.

HERNDON'S STATEMENT——MEMORANDA

January 8, 1886.

I have lectured four or five times in this city on Mr. Lincoln, never published but one, and that was on Ann Rutledge, loaned the others to Lamon, who never gave them back to me, lost them, or claims that I sold them to him——not so. One of my friends stenographed one or two of my lectures, which abstract will be found in Carpenter's *Six Months in the White House* . . . and likewise in the *Lincoln Memorial Album* written, got up, by Captain Oldroyd of this city. . . . These will be found in the *Truth Seeker* of New York. Three letters of mine in the February 24 and March 10, 1883, and at other places since in the same paper, and some things before in the last years of Bennett. Much of what I have written about Lincoln and probably Mrs. Lincoln will be found in the *Illinois Journal* of this city, and some in the Chicago *Tribune*——all of which will be found since 1866, probably in 1865, probably some things are in the drawer at my house. I kept nothing——none of my writings——friends wanted 'em and I gave 'em away, kept nothing except by accident, am sorry now that I did not keep a copy of all things, regret it much. . . . When men, writers, biographers, correspondents, asked information about Lincoln, I freely gave it, did so to all interviewers, all men in short. Never sold a letter of Lincoln, gave them away; never received a dollar from man nor woman for what I wrote, except for a lecture which I delivered in Petersburg in 1882 and except for a lecture delivered in Pekin in this State in 1882–83. I have helped all people to facts, characteristics, qualities, etc., of Lincoln and never charged a cent, except as above.

I have helped Doctor Holland to some of the facts of Lincoln's life, many in fact. I have helped Arnold to facts for both of his works on Lincoln, gave him a list of Lincoln's speeches, when and where to find them, saved him a month's solid toil; Arnold said to me in presence of Robert Hazlitt, now in the Southwest, probably in Kansas, and who copied the speeches for Arnold, that he would give me the credit; he probably never could have found them, didn't know where to begin nor end. I have helped Lamon in his Life of Lincoln; he wrote—rather, Chauncey F. Black of York, Pennsylvania, wrote—the Life as part of it from my manuscript, notes, memoranda.

I have corresponded much with Isaac N. Arnold about Lincoln, have sent him printed letters of mine and speeches of Lincoln which Lincoln sent me from Washington. Arnold has many of my letters which I wrote him, as mere notes, didn't try to be artistic, etc.—write rapidly—and gave them to him as notes.

I have corresponded much with Jesse W. Weik of Greencastle, Indiana; probably have written to him fifty letters and will write more to him hereafter much if I live and have time, etc. I have corresponded a good deal with Geo. E. Remsberg of Atchison, Kansas; gave him some ideas of Lincoln, sent him lectures, slips, speeches, notices, etc. I have corresponded some with I. W. Wartman of Evansville, Indiana; sent him letters, speeches, notes, slips, etc., I have corresponded some with C. O. Poole, Esq., of New York—106 West 29th Street—have sent him letters—one important one I think—notes, slips, speeches, etc. I have corresponded with many other people—don't now recollect their names. The above gentlemen, if they have saved anything that I have written, will give copies or loan originals to be copied. I have tried to accommodate all persons when they have asked for facts, opinions, etc.; have talked freely to all persons, and it is quite likely have been misunderstood and misrepresented, but I stand on the record and am willing to be tried in the sharp keen court of harsh criticism now or in the future if I shall travel that far. I have tried in all that I have said or written to be truthful and impartial. I felt it my religious duty to tell all that I knew about Lincoln—facts, opinions, attributes, characteristics, qualities, etc. I did this to benefit my fellow-man; and more will forever be known of this great man in the future than any man in the world; he will be known inside and outside, topside and bottom side; and the more that he is known, the better the world will like him.

It is my intention to give my records at home in my drawer in reference to Lincoln and others to the Historical Society of Chicago, hoping that it will give my wife something for them. There will be many facts, new ones, not used by biographers, interviewers, or others. I think this is so—I hope that said records shall be kept free from alteration or erasure. If I have made some mistakes, the world will find it out. All that I ask is this—I tried to be correct, exactly so, and if I have failed in this it has been an error of my judgment. I ask not mercy, but justice—that's all. I loved Lincoln and, if I have erred, I think it will be found on Lincoln's side. I did much for Lincoln that the world will never know, don't intend to blow my own horn. What Lincoln has said I shall abide by and what I have said I surely stand by to the end of time, unless I shall be convinced that I have erred and then I shall correct and publish it to the world, if I can get its ear.

Some of my records have been lost. The rats and mice have chewed up some and nibbled others. In lecturing in this city and elsewhere I carried some of my important and original notes with me to the lecture room in order to show the people, if contradicted, the truth of the case. In other words I intended to use them as evidence then and there, and it is quite probable that I lost some of my original memoranda at that time or times. I have missed some and think that I loaned Lamon some.

I lived in Springfield from 1820 to 1871, moved into the country in 1871, and lost some of my papers in the hurry, bustle, and act of moving, and yet the papers are nearly complete, full, and exact as I wrote and gathered them at the time or times. It is now twenty-one years since I began to gather up the evidence of Mr. Lincoln's life and am at it today and will continue to do so for the next ten years if I live. There is one little book which I loaned to Mr. Lamon that I never intended any other mortal man or woman to see, if anything in it was to be made public. I think that Mrs. Dale had a peep in it.

In delivering my lectures I did not always follow the written words, but as ideas would come up I would orally state the ideas in unwritten words. In some cases I modified verbally what I had written, though I did not vary materially the written words as I now remember. Probably the most of the renditions were modifications and additions, etc.

When Mr. Arnold came to my house in the country, six miles northwest of this city, he brought with him Robert Hazlitt, who was to a certain extent Mr. Arnold's amanuensis, and Mr. Arnold begged of me a note, memoranda, which would tell him where all of Lincoln's speeches could be found. I willingly gave Mr. Arnold the data of the places and times and numbers of the papers, etc., where they could be found. I fear that Mr. Arnold only took such speeches as suited him. In my papers will be found an index of the places, papers, data, etc., where to be found. Arnold with Hazlitt came to my house in the country about the year 1879–1880, probably a year or so before. I recommended Hazlitt to Arnold. Hazlitt did as Arnold and Hazlitt told me, but how many I cannot say, nor what ones.

Lamon now has my three lectures in writing or has lost them; he gave me two (2) thousand dollars for the manuscripts, bound notes of memoranda, three, I think; he got from me some unbound memoranda, some of which I only loaned him. Chauncey F. Black of York, Pennsylvania, wrote the Life of Lincoln and not Lamon. Black and I have considerably corresponded. If I could get hold of a little memorandum book now in the possession of Lamon, I would burn it to ashes; it should quickly go; I loaned it to him foolishly, not thinking what use *could* be made of it, regret taking the notes, was a fool for it, I suppose.

When I met a man or woman who knew anything good or bad and was willing to tell it, I generally took notes then and there of what was said about Lincoln. I think I knew Lincoln well. Thousands of stories about the man I rejected, because [they] were inconsistent with the nature of the man—foolish, idiotic, nonsensical, childish, or bad, evil, brutish, etc. I think I have a good memory and depended much on it. Thousands of things I remember distinctly, at least I think I do, which I never reduced at the time to writing; hold them still in my mind. I have written many letters relating to these things. Sometimes I met women at parties or other places; they and I would chat about Lincoln, had no paper, no pencil nor paper, stored such chats away in my memory and hold them as well as I can. Lincoln tramped over the toes of a great many people in this city and they are shy to talk about him; in secret give him the devil, on the pavements glory. I know of just such men. *Jealousy is the cause of this secret hate as I think.*

It was said by some critics of Lamon's Life of Lincoln that they discovered three fingers, three styles of composition, in the book, and some said that I had a finger in it. This is not so; I never wrote a chapter, paragraph, sentence, nor word in the book directly or indirectly, except where I am correctly quoted. I never suggested how the book should be written nor when nor where nor otherwise. I do not agree to all that is said in the book, and never did, nor never will, and yet it is the truest life that was ever written of a man *taken as a whole.*

In my records of Lincoln, manuscripts of Lincoln sold to Lamon, there is copied some of the early speeches of Lincoln; they are material, law, and [undeciphered]. Why did I have them copied? I did so because I wanted to show, had I written Lincoln's Life, that Lincoln was a growing man, progressive, got more mental and more spiritual, etc. I wanted to contrast these early efforts with the Gettysburg speech, an oration that will never die. It was my opinion in 1865 when Lincoln was assassinated that he was then an undeveloped man, that he had not arrived at the maximum of his mental power. He was of slow development and was in the mental world just budding to bloom. He died at the age of fifty-six years a sinewy tough iron-framed man; he had no extra flesh on him, but was all nerve and sinew; he was not what is generally termed a muscular man, but a sinewy one and a very strong and glorious one.

I made these notes at different times and this day copied them and burnt up the pieces, dirty, worn and torn. If I think of anything of importance will add.

W. H. HERNDON.

"Truth needs no color, beauty no pencil, in dealing with the history of a man's life." If the man who is written about is truly great the public will inevitably become interested in him and his history; and will in the end know the truth and no man need hope to evade it. The biography of a man, like the history of a nation, if truthfully written, will be a real history. If, on the other hand, important, leading, and essential facts are evaded, or suppressed, or falsehood suggested, the biography is an ideal life—the history of no man. If the story of the life is truthfully and courageously told, nothing evaded, nothing suppressed, and no falsehood suggested, the reader sees and feels the presence of a real man. The reader sees the man, lives with him, and is moved to think and act with him. If the story is colored or the facts distorted, the reader is imposed upon, as people are whose goods and monies are obtained from them by the rogue under false pretenses. There is but little difference so far as crime is concerned between the two. One steals goods and one steals the wish to know the truth out of the mind of another, which theft may mislead the man during life. Mr. Lincoln placed the very highest regard on the primary importance of truth, a greater and higher regard than most men in public or other life; he wished to be known as honest and brave in the world of truth; and in writing what I do of his history that attribute, quality, or characteristic of his shall be kept steadily in view. I want to tell the truth about Lincoln and nothing but the truth and the whole truth. If he was alive, I am sure that he would most heartily approve of my course, though, dead, I am equally confident that his memory deserves it. I know that the people need the truth, but the question is: Will the people who so much need the truth and the whole truth meet and stand by it? Do the people "love God's naked truth," as Carlyle puts it? Or do they wish to show around it?

Doubtless there are some persons of a peculiar cast of mind who will object to having dug up old facts out of the tomb where they have long been buried. These people do say to me: "Why unearth these things, these sad facts long since buried out of sight, where they should be, and hold them up anew to the public gaze again? How would Mr. Lincoln *feel*, how would Mrs. Lincoln *feel*, to see them exhibited, openly exhibited to the world again?" I answer this question, firstly, by saying that these facts are indispensable to a full knowledge of Mr. Lincoln in all the walks of his life in every direction; secondly, that is not a question of *feeling in the living nor in the dead*, but the real question is: What do the people need, absolutely need, in order to understand Mr. Lincoln and the history of the stirring, exciting bloody times in which he lived and of which he was an important part? Another question is: Shall I tell these facts or shall I tell a lie? I do propose to courageously tell those facts and do not intend to tell a lie. The facts have never been buried nor ever will be; they are floating around in the minds of brave men and women, who are determined that they shall never die, because they believe by unearthing, as it were, these very facts that Mr. Lincoln can be and will be thoroughly known; they are necessary facts, indispensable truths, and ought to be told, and shall, for these reasons, be told. Those who do not love the truth and cannot endure it, cannot look it square in the face, had better dash this book down, dash it down instantly and at once, and be done with [it] and the disturbing and irritating truths in it.

We can somewhat know a man by contrasts, by comparison with other men and looking at the times in which we live. How does any man know that Lincoln was a great man, except by comparison with other men, and keeping steadily in view the age in which he lived? It is said that the most of our great statesmen were self-made men, and this is as a general rule true, rising from the bottom round of the ladder and climbing to the topmost round, gradually through struggle; Lincoln rose from a lower depth, from a stagnant, filthy, putrid pool, like the gases of it set on fire by its own energy and self-combustible power in jets rising, blue, on fire, bright, blazing, pure up toward the sky far, far above the topmost round. Lincoln too had his terrible struggles, but he rose above them all and is still rising and will be the great ideal man of the English-speaking people, soon to be a thousand million, the rulers of the world. I think I should commit a crime if I did not tell the facts of his life, deep down, as to his family and himself, where great contrasts can be seen, such contrasts as the world never saw. Lincoln will grow and gradually loom up out of all this as I distinctly see.

My memories, my memory of Mr. Lincoln is compounded mostly

of my own observations, experience, and I may say my own reason, and what truthful men and women, sagacious, far- and deep-seeing ones, have in person told me and which through my observation, my experience, and my reason I earnestly and sincerely believe. The usual memories—a broad word—my memory, my recollection of the man, opens a broad wide field in which to relate what I know and believe, and I shall gladly avail myself of its privileges and advantages. I shall use the word I, not wishing to pretend not to know that there is such a word. I have no time and not much inclination to shy around it. Much of what I shall say, much of what I shall relate, would be rejected by sober grave history and, as I am well aware, in time will be thrown away as trash. But it is believed, at least it is hoped that there are some grains of gold in it, which will be saved from wreck and stamped with the public approbation and made current among men.

The chapters are so arranged that those who wish to look immediately into Mr. Lincoln's attributes, qualities, and characteristics, not caring much to know his further history, because so well and thoroughly known to the reading world, may turn to chapter —— and read every other one and including chapter —— where he will find what he wants and in these chapters he will find all that I know of this great man's nature and its manifestations. In these chapters, kept separate and apart to suit and especially to accommodate the reader, the idea of the man is kept distinct and thoroughly developed. This is done purposely, but it causes much repetition on that account, for which I shall be severely criticized, I know. This could not be avoided if I kept my place. However, this course is determined upon. One of my principal reasons, one of my principal objects in writing these memoirs, is to specially show the qualities and characteristics of Lincoln, and this I have done radically.

That there will be, in the hurry of my task, mistakes made, I have not much doubt. I hope that they will be flailed out quickly and the truths kept. Records gathered up for more than twenty years by me had to be read, searched, facts chosen and collected. This was a great trouble and in many cases a severe and unpleasant task. Men would vary in the facts and their ideas, and I had to choose between friends which statement to take. This was trying and unpleasant indeed. I shall, nothing happening, leave the records pure, untouched, clean, behind me and out of which a breezy biography of Lincoln can be written hereafter.

The purpose and intention—at least among them—are to present Mr. Lincoln to the reader individually, domestically, as lawyer and politician and statesman, as citizen and President. A mere thread of Lincoln's history will run through the book, except chapters ——, which will give a full, a very full and complete history of the youth and young manhood of Lincoln, fuller than ever before published, and this fact will justify me in some repetition. This much is stated in advance, so that no man shall be disappointed as to the purposes and extent of the work. There will be found too much iteration, I fear, but I cannot well avoid it. I am driven to this field, am driven by necessity to this limited field and scope of Lincoln's life, by the fact that when Lamon shall have finished his book and Nicolay and Hay shall have finished theirs, as Arnold has completed his work, the historic facts of Lincoln's life will have been completely exhausted and nothing left to write about. I wish to get out of all beaten tracks as well as I can and hence the reader has what he has, good or bad, wise or unwise.

I take this my first general and large opportunity to acknowledge my obligations and to give my thanks to the hundreds of friends in Kentucky, Indiana, Illinois, and other States who have furnished me with facts and have given me their ideas and opinions, evidence and proofs, which have enabled me to do what I have done. I am especially indebted and very thankful to my friend, Jesse W. Weik, of Greencastle, Indiana, who was kind and generous enough to advance me money with which to support my family and myself while I wrote, and not only is this so but I am additionally indebted and thankful to him for his industry and literary assistance in aiding me to write these memoirs and in encouraging me to write this Life, which I never could have done without such pecuniary aid, industry, and literary ability.

APPENDIX

A Poem by Lincoln

This poem by Lincoln, never before completely or accurately reprinted, was in the possession of Mr. and Mrs. Robert Lincoln and was presented by their daughter, Mrs. Charles Isham, to the Library of Congress. Lincoln refers to it in a letter to Andrew Johnston on February 24, 1846, as follows:

"In the fall of 1844, thinking I might aid some to carry the State of Indiana for Mr. Clay, I went into the neighborhood in that State in which I was raised, where my mother and only sister were buried; part of the country is, within itself, as unpoetical as any spot of the earth, but still, seeing it and its objects and inhabitants aroused feelings in me which were certainly poetry; though whether my expression of those feelings is poetry is quite another question. When I got to writing, the change of subject divided the thing into four little divisions or cantos, the first only of which I send you now, and may send the others hereafter."

My childhood home I see again,
    And gladden with the view;
And still as mem'ries crowd my brain,
    There's sadness in it too—

O memory! thou mid-way world
    'Twixt Earth and Paradise;
Where things decayed, and loved ones lost
    In dreamy shadows rise—

And freed from all that's gross or vile,
    Seem hallowed, pure, and bright,
Like scenes in some enchanted isle,
    All bathed in liquid light—

As distant mountains please the eye,
    When twilight chases day—
As bugle-tones, that, passing by,
    In distance die away—

As leaving some grand water-fall
    We ling'ring list its roar,
So memory will hallow all
    We've known, but know no more—

Now twenty years have passed away,
  Since here I bid farewell
To woods, and fields, and scenes of play
  And school-mates loved so well—

Where many were, how few remain
  Of old familiar things!
But seeing these to mind again
  The lost and absent brings—

The friends I left that parting day—
  How changed, as time has sped!
Young childhood grown, strong manhood gray,
  And half of all are dead—

I hear the lone survivors tell
  How naught from death could save,
Till every sound appears a knell
  And every spot a grave—

I range the fields with pensive tread,
  I pace the hollow rooms;
And feel (companion of the dead)
  I'm living in the tombs—

And here's an object more of dread,
  Than aught the grave contains—
A human-form, with reason fled,
  While wretched life remains—

Poor Matthew! once of genius bright,—
  A fortune-favored child—
Now locked for aye, in mental night,
  A haggard mad-man wild—

Poor Matthew! I have ne'er forgot
  When first with maddened will
Yourself you maimed, your father fought,
  And mother strove to kill;

And terror spread, and neighbors ran,
  Your dang'rous strength to bind;
And soon a howling crazy man,
  Your limbs were fast confined—

How then you writhed and shrieked aloud,
  Your bones and sinews bared;
And fiendish on the gaping crowd,
  With burning eye-balls glared—

And begged, and swore, and wept, and prayed,
  ˙With maniac laughter joined—
How fearful are the signs displayed,
  By pangs that kill the mind!

And when at length, tho' drear and long,
  Time soothed your fiercer woes—
How plaintively your mournful song,
  Upon the still night rose—

I've heard it oft, as if I dreamed,
  Far-distant, sweet, and lone;
The funeral dirge it ever seemed
  Of reason dead and gone—

To drink its strains I've stole away,
  All silently and still,
Ere yet the rising god of day
  Had streaked the Eastern hill—

Air held his breath; the trees all still
  Seemed sorr'wing angels round;
Their swelling tears in dew-drops fell
  Upon the list'ning ground—

But this is past, and naught remains
  That raised you o'er the brute—
Your mad'ning shrieks and soothing strains
  Are like forever mute—

Now fare thee well: more thou the cause
  Than subject now of woe.
All mental pangs, by time's kind laws,
  Hast lost the power to know—

And now away to seek some scene
  Less painful than the last—
With less of horror mingled in
  The present and the past—

The very spot where grew the bread
  That formed my bones, I see.
How strange, old field, on thee to tread,
  And feel I'm part of thee!

[*Facsimile of the poem follows.*]

My childhood home I see again,
  And gladden with the view;
And still as mem'ries crowd my brain,
  There's sadness in it too—

O memory! thou mid-way world
  'Twixt Earth and Paradise,
Where things decayed, and loved ones lost
  In dreamy shadows rise—

And, freed from all that's gross or vile,
  Seem hallowed, pure, and bright,
Like scenes in some enchanted isle,
  All bathed in liquid light—

As distant mountains please the eye,
  When twilight chases day—
As bugle-tones, that, passing by,
  In distance die away—

As leaving some grand water-fall
  We ling'ring list its roar,
So memory will hallow all
  We've known, but know no more—

Now twenty years have passed away,
  Since here I bid farewell
To woods, and fields, and scenes of play
  And school-mates loved so well—

Where many were, how few remain
  Of old familiar things!
But seeing these to mind again.
  The lost and absent brings—

The friends I left that parting day—
  How changed, as time has sped!
Young childhood grown, strong manhood grey,
  And half of all are dead—

I hear the lone survivors tell
  How nought from death could save,
Till every sound appears a knell
  And every spot a grave—

I range the fields with pensive tread,
  I pace the hollow rooms,
And feel (companion of the dead)
  I'm living in the tombs—

A   here's an object more of dread,
  Than aught the grave contains—
A human-form, with reason fled,
  While wretched life remains—,

Poor Matthew! once of genius bright,—
  A fortune-favored child—
Now locked for aye, in mental night,
  A haggard madman wild—

Poor Matthew! I have ne'er forgot
 When first with maddened will,
Yourself you maimed, your father fought,
 And mother strove to kill;

And terror spread, and neighbours ran,
 Your dang'rous strength to bind;
And soon a howling crazy man,
 Your limbs were fast confined—

How then you writhed and shrieked aloud,
 Your bones and sinews bared,
And fiendish on the gaping crowd,
 With burning eye-balls glared—

And begged, and swore, and wept, and prayed,
 With maniac laughter joined—
How fearful are the signs displayed,
 By pangs that kill the mind!

And when at length, tho' drear and long,
 Time soothed your fiercer woes,
How plaintively your mournful song,
 Upon the still night rose—

I've heard it oft, as if I dreamed,
 Far-distant, sweet, and lone;
The funeral dirge it ever seemed
 Of reason dead and gone—

To drink its strains I've stole away,
All silently and still,—
Ere yet the rising god of day
    Had streaked the Eastern hill—

Air held his breath, the trees all still
    Seemed sorr'wing angels round,
Their swelling tears in dew-drops fell
    Upon the list'ning ground—

But this is past, and nought remains
    That raised you o'er the brute.
Your madd'ning shrieks and soothing strains
    Are like forever mute—

Now fare thee well, more thou the cause
    Than subject now of woe.
All mental pangs, by time's kind laws,
    Hast lost the power to know—

And now away to seek some scene
    Less painful than the last—
With less of horror mingled in
    The present and the past—

The very spot where grew the bread
    That formed my bones, I see.
How strange, old field, on thee to tread
    And feel I'm part of thee!

Index

455